SOCIAL JUSTICE
IN ENGLISH
LANGUAGE TEACHING

Christopher Hastings and Laura Jacob, Editors

Foreword by Bonny Norton

www.tesol.org/bookstore

TESOL International Association
1925 Ballenger Avenue
Alexandria, Virginia 22314 USA
Tel 703-836-0774 • Fax 703-836-7864
www.tesol.org

Senior Manager, Publications: Myrna Jacobs
Cover Design: Kathleen Dyson
Copy Editor: Tomiko Breland
Layout and and Design: Capitol Communications, LLC
Printer: Gasch Printing, LLC

ISBN 9781942799429
Library of Congress Control Number 2016930003

Publisher's Note: The opinions expressed in this book reflect those of the individual authors, and may or may not reflect the opinions or official positions of TESOL International Association. We respect the rights of these authors to state their personal opinions and we are providing this forum in the spirit of academic freedom.

CONTENTS

PART I: SOCIAL JUSTICE AND ENGLISH LANGUAGE TEACHING: SETTING THE STAGE

PART II: PEACEBUILDING AND ENGLISH LANGUAGE TEACHING

PART III: POSITIONING FOR ADVOCACY

PART VII: CLASSROOM PRACTICES

Foreword

As the field of TESOL navigates the complex terrain of social justice in English language teaching, contributors to this collection bear witness to the range of struggles, both overt and covert, experienced by English language learners and their teachers in diverse regions of the world. Such challenges range from those of undocumented migrant youth in Texas, USA, to those of migrant workers in Qatar. The contributors note that both experienced and pre-service English teachers need to better understand the conditions under which our learners speak, read, or write the language we teach, and to respond professionally to the needs of students who have been marginalized and silenced in their communities. Struggles for social justice are not limited to students, however, as contributors document the challenges of minority, NNEST, or LGBTQ teachers. It is clear that TESOL as a profession needs to advocate for teachers who seek greater legitimacy in our profession.

Implicit in many of the contributions is the question of how we theorize "language" with reference to a social justice agenda in the teaching of English. This is a question I have grappled with in my own teaching and research, and can be illustrated by a disturbing incident described by Alysha Janus (2015) in her e-book "Juche" on the teaching of English in North Korea:

> Beyond a doubt, the stars of the teachers' class are two young women: Kim Hui and Kim Ok. They are head and shoulders above the others in terms of knowledge and also communicative competence. In a conservative society like North Korea, however, their obvious superiority presents problems on two fronts: their gender and their age, since older men, who wield most of the power, are likely to lose face. One day during class, Kim Ok is particularly on the ball, volunteering correct answers to many of the questions I ask and contributing fluently to activities. I notice one of the older men write something on a slip of paper and pass it forward until it gets to Kim Ok, who suddenly goes bright red and says nothing for the rest of the lesson. As they are leaving the room, I hear Kim Hui say to Kim Ok: "You will be criticized for that."

This incident, which finds echoes in some of the reflections in *Social Justice in English Language Teaching*, provides convincing evidence that "language" references not only linguistic features such as vocabulary and grammar, but also the social meaning of words and sentences in a given social context. While Kim Ok was communicatively competent and could provide a range of "correct" responses with reference to the linguistic features of standard English, the social meaning of her utterances was considered inappropriate by more powerful members of her community. As social theorists such as Pierre Bourdieu would argue, Kim Ok did not have the "right to speech" or the "power to impose reception," given the unequal relations of power in her classroom, and North Korean society more broadly. In this view, language is theorized not as a neutral medium of communication, but as a social practice in which identities are negotiated, often within the context of unequal relations of power. By extension, when language learners or teachers speak, they are not only exchanging information, but are also navigating their relationship to a frequently inequitable social world. As documented by the contributors to this collection, the "criticism" that some English language learners and teachers experience may not be as overt as that experienced by Kim Ok in North Korea, but may often be as devastating.

What then does this mean for both practice and policy, in a terrain that contributors acknowledge is itself a site of struggle? As noted in this collection, teaching, like language, is not a neutral act, but references a social vision, implicitly or explicitly, which may either constrain or enable human possibility. While recognizing that there are no easy answers to the question of what to do to promote greater social justice in our classrooms and communities, contributors nevertheless make a compelling case for the human agency of teachers, and the possibility of harnessing talent, creativity, and passion in the interests of social change. This collection, in and of itself, represents precisely the kind of initiative that can serve as a roadmap for other teachers of English who are committed to a vision of social justice. Indeed, while co-editors Laura Jacob and Christopher Hastings suggest that this project was born out of a community rather than a set of ideas, it will be clear to readers that there is a powerful set of ideas that help to frame this inspiring collection. The Social Responsibility Interest Section (SRIS) of TESOL International has talked the talk and walked the walk.

Bonny Norton
Professor and Distinguished University Scholar,
Department of Language and Literacy
University of British Columbia

Introduction

Chris Hastings and Laura Jacob

S ome projects are born out of ideas; this one was born out of a community. The Social Responsibility Interest Section (SRIS) of TESOL International Association. SRIS is made up of English language teachers who are committed to the ideal that language, culture, and context are inseparable. Consequently, we share the belief that language teaching should not be separated from its context; that issues of human rights, peace, global citizenship, and the environment deserve a significant place in the classroom. It is with this understanding that SRIS "aims to promote social responsibility within the TESOL profession and to advance social equity, respect for differences, and multicultural understanding through education." The people of SRIS brought a wealth of experiences, expertise, and resources to this work.

This project came about organically. No formal call for proposals was sent out; instead it was a project that was born of the relationships between TESOL educators. It arose out of conversations and emails that Laura originally sent around the group's listserv, expressing a desire to share the work that SRIS members are doing to promote justice in their communities of practice around the world. As teachers expressed an interest in contributing, Laura and Chris volunteered to organize and edit the chapters. This compilation represents the power of ELT to work for peace and social change, and it is intended to be a small sample of work currently being done in the field.

The contributing authors considered this to be a valuable contribution to the field because there are only a limited number of books that address the importance of social justice in the profession. TESOL is a field frequently affected by the world's sociopolitical climate. English language learners are often pushed to the periphery of society and are subject to inequitable power structures. Those actively engaged in the profession work with students marginalized by global and local trends, helping them to realize their full potential and contribute to their communities.

One limitation of compiling such a collection is that important areas of the field will inevitably be missed. We acknowledge that several areas of social justice in ELT are lacking in this volume, as it was a product of the authors who volunteered to contribute. It is intended to be, not a complete survey or introduction to the field, but rather a sampling.

This book addresses social justice concerns across the globe as they relate to the TESOL profession. Linguistic and nonlinguistic issues are considered, such as gender, race, and socioeconomic status within the context of English language teaching, while addressing the critically important themes of social justice and equity. This anthology of articles gives current teachers and teachers-in-training as well as undergraduate and graduate students in TESOL an idea of the needs for advocacy in the TESOL profession, provides a vision for addressing global injustices in the classroom, and offers concrete classroom activities through personal and professional examples.

It is intended to be used by teacher educators, university-level ESL instructors, graduate students interested in social justice issues, and undergraduate level students enrolled in TESOL teacher preparation programs. It provides a taste of different aspects of the literature while painting a holistic picture and simultaneously giving it a personal voice to the work of social justice in ELT.

SRIS represents the beauty and potential of an Interest Section in TESOL. It is represented throughout the year as a supportive listserv and gathers during TESOL's annual convention for fruitful discussion, inspiration, and collaboration. The members that make up SRIS are passionate, devoted individuals (as you will see as you read their chapters in the following pages!) who reach out to each other throughout the year to support one another in their fields of work and to encourage one another to promote true social change in each of their contexts.

This diverse collection of voices from the field in ESL and EFL contexts both personalizes the issues TESOL educators face and serves as a resource for those wanting to address social injustices in their individual TESOL contexts.

Generally speaking, each chapter in this compilation represents one of two realities: that English language learners are often on the margins of society and that those of us who teach them must work to advocate for their needs. We hope that the chapters will help educators identify the needs of other students or the areas of privilege represented in the ELT world, where more advocacy work is needed.

———

The first part, Social Justice and ELT: Setting the Stage, introduces the topic and the need for a volume that focuses on social justice in the English Language Teaching profession. In the first chapter, "A Short Introduction to Social Justice and ELT," Charles Hall provides some perspective on the history of social justice in language teaching, discussing how justice is determined by its context and encouraging readers to consider social injustices they have encountered. In the second chapter, "The First Step Toward Social Justice: Teacher Reflection," Lavette Coney invites teachers to reflect on their own background, to peer at the state of the profession and be honest about the prevalent racism within. In Chapter 3, "Critical Pedagogy's Power in English Language Teaching," Mayra Daniel argues for the importance of having a critical pedagogical lens in the ELT field.

The second part, Peacebuilding and English Language Teaching, focuses our attention on the role English can play in working for peace across hostile borders. In "Bringing Peacebuilding into the English Language Classroom," Valerie Jakar and Alison Milofsky discuss the connection between peacebuilding and English language teaching by sharing their personal paths to peacebuilding and providing guidelines for bringing peacebuilding into the classroom. In Chapter 5, "Tension and Harmony:

Language Teaching as a Peacebuilding Endeavor," Michael Medley discusses the integration of peace and language education by reflecting on his own identity as a peaceable language teacher. In "Healing Colonial Pain: English as a Bridge Between Japan and Korea," Kip Cates explores the part that ELT can play in promoting better relations and mutual understanding between Koreans and Japanese students, and the responsibility that educators have to teach English for peace and facilitate opportunities for international exchange.

In the third part, Positioning for Advocacy, special attention is given to the power dynamics behind the English language. Ali Fuad Selvi, Nathanael Rudolph, and Baburhan Uzum argue for "the adoption of a glocal perspective that maintains, creates, and promotes spaces, discourses, and practices for innovation, incorporation, collaboration, and inclusivity for all" in Chapter 7, "Equity and Professionalism in English Language Teaching: A Glocal Perspective." In "Ideological English: A Theme for College Composition," Jennifer Mott-Smith discusses the social inequity and discrimination present as different social groups' language forms are judged, and how educators might address that by encouraging students' ownership of English. In Chapter 9, "Provincializing English: Race, Empire, and Social Justice," Suhanthie Motha argues for provincializing English, "or seeking to support in learners and teachers a critical analysis of the ways in which the language is racialized and colonized, of how learning English changes us, and of how participating in the teaching of English changes the world" (S. Motha [2014], *Race, Empire, and English Language Teaching: Creating Responsible and Ethical Anti-racist Practice*; quoted in Chapter 9 herein).

The fourth part, Language Rights, Privilege, and Race, asks us to look at the injustice, privilege, and systemic racism prevalent in society that also play into the ELT profession. In his chapter, "Language Rights and Indigenous Education in Australia," Adriano Truscott informs us about Indigenous education in Australia, the context of language policy and rights, the role of TESOL in the protection of such rights, and classroom practices that enhance self-esteem, develop biculturalism, and encourage the Indigenous cultures of the classroom to thrive. In Chapter 11, "Student Voices Inform Practice: Perceptions of Linguistic and Cultural Discrimination," Elisabeth L. Chan shares how she became involved in social justice issues within TESOL and discusses how her own perceptions of race, language, and culture were formed. She also discusses her research on international students' perceptions of race, language, and culture, gives the implications of her findings, and closes by sharing social justice activities for the language classroom. In "Understanding Privilege: Considerations for Teaching and Teacher Training Toward Social Justice," Heidi Faust examines the role that privilege plays in creating opportunities and barriers in different contexts through personal reflections and invites readers to reflect on their own experiences through a series of activities modeled for personal awareness, teacher training, and for use with students in the classroom. In "Racializing Justice in TESOL: Embracing the Burden of Double Consciousness," Shelley Wong and Rachel Grant share tools for countering racism in places where it is entwined with culture.

In the fifth part, Gender and Sexual Orientation Justice, we turn our focus to gender discrimination and identity development for the LGBT community. In Chapter 14,

"Gender Sensitization as a Learning Outcome," Kirti Kapur helps teachers empower their students by examining the origins of gender relations in their everyday lives. She discusses how gender sensitization can be both a direct and an indirect result of language instruction and critical pedagogy. In "Exploring Perceptions of Gender Roles in English Language Teaching," Mayra Daniel and Melanie Koss consider the impact of "cultural norms in ELT and of the links between gender, social identity, and English language acquisition." In "Walking in the Words of 'the Other' Through Ethnodra-matic Readers Theatre," Carter Winkle shares an enthnodrama that can be used to help teachers engage their students around issues of gender and sexual identity in ELT. The drama seeks, not to provide answers for students and teachers, but to provoke much needed dialogue.

The sixth part, Working Across Borders/Advocating for Students, peers deeply into the lives of English language learners in the state of Texas and provides vision for justice for those students who are undocumented immigrants in the United States. In their chapter, "When Nobody Seems to Care: Preparing Preservice Teachers for English Language Learners in Texas Classrooms," Baburham Uzum and Mary Petron discuss the issues facing ELL students in Texas and encourage the use of service learning projects as an opportunity to empower teachers and students to address these issues. Christine Poteau, in "Pedagogies, Experiences, Access, Collaboration, and Equality (PEACE): Reforming Language Pedagogies to Promote Social Justice for Undocumented Immigrants," discusses the challenges that both documented and undocumented immigrants face when going to a new country, shares research on the role that intercultural competence skill development can play in social justice education, and highlights challenges and benefits of different pedagogies. In Chapter 19, "Teaching Undocumented Immigrants in the United States: A Seditious Secret and a Call to Action," Michael Conners discusses his background as a veteran who has become engaged in social justice issues in the TESOL community, examines the complexities of working with undocumented students, and shares the results of an action research project to empower students to be agents of change.

The final part, Classroom Practices, provides relevant program objectives, activities, and classroom lesson plans that provide pathways to promote justice in relevant ways. In "Using Drama to Combat Prejudice," Alexis Finger shows how drama can be used by teachers and students to fight prejudice. In Chapter 21, "We Are All Environmental Educators (Whether We Know It or Not)," David Royal discusses the many roles that English language teachers play as cultural ambassadors, advisers, entertainers, and even environmental educators. In the final chapter, "A Community Adult English Literacy Program for Migrant Workers in Qatar: Context-Specific Critical Pedagogy and Communicative Language Teaching at Work," Silvia Pessoa, Nada Soudy, Natalia Gatti, and M. Bernardine Dias report on the motivations, challenges, and curriculum design of a community English literacy program for migrant workers in Qatar. The authors describe the program and its curriculum and argue for the effectiveness of adult literacy programs that use a context-specific critical pedagogy and communicative language teaching approach to ensure the literacy and communicative competence development of the adult learners for empowerment and personal advancement.

PART I:
SOCIAL JUSTICE AND ENGLISH LANGUAGE TEACHING: SETTING THE STAGE

CHAPTER 1

A Short Introduction to
Social Justice and ELT

Charles Hall

Alfaisal University

> I believe that education is the civil rights issue of our generation. And if you
> care about promoting opportunity and reducing inequality, the classroom is
> the place to start. Great teaching is about so much more than education; it
> is a daily fight for social justice.
>
> —*U.S. Secretary of Education Arne Duncan, October 9, 2009*

If you are reading this book, there is a high probability that you agree with the quote above, though you may not share Duncan's approach to educational reform. You might have become an educator to help bring about social justice and to reduce inequality. Oddly, the fact that the 2014 Nobel Peace Prize was awarded to two champions of education reveals how far we have yet to go just to achieve basic universal education for all humans, whether boys or girls, men or women, rich or poor, Buddhist or Muslim.

As is often the case in our hyperliterate world, many might believe that the link between education and social justice is a modern development. However, in this chapter we will see that the tension, sometimes overt but more often insidious, between views that education should maintain the status quo and that it should challenge the status quo are almost as old as formal education itself. Nonetheless, we might ask why a volume on social justice and English Language Teaching (ELT) is needed at this time. The answer is simple: Using English in some manner is no longer a luxury; it must be part of that basic universal education we wish for all. Keeping English from anyone, whether actively or indirectly, must now be seen as a social injustice.

As English has become the first truly global lingua franca, appropriate knowledge of English is as essential a tool as basic literacy and numeracy (Hall, 2015; Hall, Arrol, & Diaz, 2013). ELT is just as important as reading, math, and history, and ELT is just as open as the other essential subjects are to uses and abuses in any educational system or even lack of one. The urgency of social justice for all education is clear in the justification by the Nobel Peace Prize Committee for jointly awarding Kailash

Satyarthi from India and Malala Yousafzai from Pakistan the prize: *"for their struggle against the suppression of children and young people and for the right of all children to education"* ("The Nobel Peace Prize 2014," para. 1).

As we briefly explore the history of social justice and English Language Teaching, it is important to remember that many people disagree with the social justice education movement. For some, so-called modern education should teach only narrowly defined "basics." Indeed, there are those who would dismiss social justice as a code word for progressive politics (Leo, 2010) that they see as undesirable, while others see the concept as nebulous (Sowell, 2012). Others sincerely believe that social justice in education amounts to partisan indoctrination. For example, the Texas Republican Party made an explicit attack on "critical thinking," a (fortunately) controversial part of their election platform in 2012:

> Knowledge-Based Education—We oppose the teaching of Higher Order Thinking Skills (HOTS) (values clarification), critical thinking skills . . . which focus on behavior modification and have the purpose of challenging the student's fixed beliefs and undermining parental authority. (Whittaker, 2012, para. 3)

For our part, we do understand that it is indeed possible to entertain the notion that education and social justice should be separated. We also assume that most readers of this chapter would assume that social change is a positive, democratizing term, but it is possible for education to bring about social change that entrenches social/ethnic/racial/gender/economic differences even further, sometimes in the name of social justice. We need only remember Kipling's famous 19th-century phrase "the White Man's Burden," which described what was seen (and by some still is) as the need for white Europeans and Americans to bring civilization (i.e., social justice?) to the "savages" through, among other vehicles, education (Cody, n.d., para. 2). Since the author of this chapter is from the United States, let's look at two examples from that country's history that show us how misguided the term *social justice* can be.

As an extension of U.S. efforts to assimilate First Americans (Amerindians) to European-American culture in the 19th century, "Indian boarding schools were founded to eliminate traditional American Indian ways of life and replace them with mainstream American culture" (Smithsonian National Museum of the American Indian, 2007). Students in these schools were prohibited from speaking their native languages, in alignment with educational policies that endeavored to decrease the use of indigenous American languages (Spring, 2007). While these policies were part of a larger "civilizing movement" (what some might call a land grab) by white, brown, and later black Americans, the goal of these schools was what then was perceived as social justice and social change. The founders and administrators of these schools firmly believed they were helping the Indian children by giving them access to mainstream (dominant) U.S. culture, since many believed that "Indians would ultimately confront a fateful choice: civilization or extinction" (Adams, 1995, p. 6). Of course, today most of us believe that this approach was misguided and hurtful. However, we must remember that for many missionary teachers at the time, the goal was "social justice."

On the other hand, the efforts of early 20th-century white Hawaiians to exclude non-white Hawaiians from the patently superior white schools (there was no attempt at "separate but equal" here) were clearly and overtly racist, yet also done in a very different spirit of "social justice." To meet the "needs" of the influx of middle-class white immigrants from the mainland, Hawaii established "English Standard" schools in 1924. Admission to these public schools was based on an oral exam in English. If the Filipino, Portuguese, Japanese, or Chinese child used any creole forms, s/he failed the test and was sent to the inferior schools (Okihiro, 1992). This action is clearly not part of our definition of social justice, yet we can imagine that the white immigrants thought their actions completely socially "just" at the time as they attempted to protect their white children from the influence of the inferior "others."

Keeping in mind that not everyone believes the role of education is social change or justice or shares our definition of that term, we begin our discussion with a brief mention of Paulo Freire. Freire is actively cited by researchers in social justice and critical education as the inspiration and parent of the modern movement, although the priest Luigi Taparelli is credited with first using the term *social justice* in 1840, shortly before the crucial revolutions of 1848 (Zajda, Majhanovich, Rust, & Sabina, 2006, p. 1). Before further discussion of Freire, however, we would like to go back a little further, to consider the traditionally Western use of education. Let us look back at Socrates, whose life and death highlights the rewards and dangers of social empowerment. He was executed, not for being a radical, but for helping students to reflect on their own beliefs. The destruction of one of the most brilliant minds ever shows us in a dramatic fashion that education can be dangerous to the status quo. Millennia later, the Texas Republican Party echoes the beliefs of Socrates's executioners that the goal of those who promote critical thinking is "challenging the student's fixed beliefs and undermining parental authority" (Whittaker, 2012, para. 3). Socrates must die for Texas to live.

Although there were moments of educational brilliance in the next two millennia, we choose to turn now to John Amos Comenius (1592–1670 CE), a Czech academic who is now largely unknown outside Europe. Why has this man, who was asked to be president of Harvard University in 1654 (John Amos Comenius, 1892, para. 2), disappeared from our literature? When we read what was said about him on the 300th anniversary of his birth in an 1892 article in the *Harvard Crimson*, it almost seems as though we were reading a synopsis of the most advanced ESP (English for Specific Purpose) methodology from 2015:

> The principles which Comenius represented are embodied in his various writings, the most important of which are the "Great Didactic," the "Gate of Languages" and the "World Illustrated." The object of the first of these was, as expressed in the subtitle, "to teach everybody everything" and "to search out a rule in accordance with which the teachers teach less and the learners learn more". . . . To educate humanity so as to give it an adequate consciousness of itself and to make it useful and happy are the aims which Comenius had always in view. The system of teaching he recommended was by a proper consideration of the learner and the

subject-matter. This method will always be successful since it is in sympathy with nature. Individual tastes and capacities were to be kept in mind and correlation and coordination were indispensable. (John Amos Comenius, 1892, para. 2)

A brief introduction to his body of work presents some common underlying principals, which include

- learning foreign languages through the vernacular;

- obtaining ideas through objects rather than words;

- starting with objects most familiar to the child to introduce him to both the new language and the more remote world of objects;

- giving the child a comprehensive knowledge of his environment, physical and social, as well as instruction in religious, moral, and classical subjects;

- making this acquisition of a compendium of knowledge a pleasure rather than a task; and

- making instruction universal (Johann Amos Comenius, n.d.).

Looking at that list, we must ask ourselves why we don't know more about him today. Indeed, much of his work could be compared to the movement toward student-centered, or the more appropriately labeled "learning-centered," classroom we strive for today:

Craftsmen do not hold their apprentices down to theories; they put them, to work without delay so that they may learn to forge metal by forging, to carve by carving, to paint by painting, to leap by leaping. Therefore in schools let the pupils learn to write by writing, to speak by speaking, to sing by singing, to reason by reasoning, etc., so that schools may simply be workshops in which work is done eagerly. Thus, by good practice, all will feel at last the truth of the proverb: Fabricando fabricamur. (as quoted in Piaget, 1993, p. 177)

Nonetheless, few ELT professionals have ever heard of Comenius or of his ideas, nor is he cited in the literature. We purposefully highlight Comenius to disprove the assertion that ELT, social justice, and social change are somehow new trends or that developments in language instruction are all modern. To quote an even older text, "There is nothing new under the sun."

Likewise, we are hardly vanguards in the belief that education should be used as an agent of social change. From John Dewey, whose work in the first half of the 20th century highlighted the role of education in democracy, to Jane Addams, who founded Chicago's Hull House in the 19th century to help immigrants and the poor, we easily find major figures who believed that education can and indeed should be an agent of social change and justice as we understand it today.

Now with a bit of historical awareness, we can return to the late 20th century, to Brazilian educator Paulo Freire. Although he did not explicitly work with language instruction, we can see that his work empowering communities to challenge systems of oppression by encouraging students to co-create knowledge easily relates to the push toward learning-centered and learner-centered classrooms and education that language educators will readily identify. This drive to use education to challenge systems of oppression is intrinsically and explicitly political and ideological. Yet, as we have seen, these notions are not new to education, nor are they limited to social justice contexts.

Given what we have just written, we can hardly disagree with Pennycook (1989) who said all education is political. Understanding that this statement is now almost a truism, language teachers can recognize the importance of the assertion that "differential power relations and political interests are crucial in understanding the global spread of English teaching" (Pennycook, 1994; Phillipson, 1992; Tollefson, 1995, cited in Johnston, 1999). The result of this is that language (or any) teachers, whether they care to be or not, are political entities. So, when we think of critical pedagogy, as Freire (1970) and Giroux (1988) would refer to it, we are considering a critical view of educational practices that will transform both the classroom and society. Although methods and approaches are political in nature and critical pedagogy has a stated political goal of transforming society, the means to this end are not prescribed, as each individual context determines its path. Myles Horton (1990) and Paulo Freire's conversations on critical pedagogy capture this with the title of their book *We Make the Road by Walking*. In our context of language teaching, language is "a practice that constructs, and is constructed by, the ways learners understand themselves, their social surroundings, their histories, and their possibilities for the future" (Norton & Toohey, 2004, p. 1). As language teachers, we continue to expand our understanding of our learners' needs and contexts; however, to achieve that understanding, we, in turn, find it essential to examine our own roles in the equation.

Perhaps it is no accident that the goals of social justice and critical pedagogy seem to have evolved along a path similar to that of language education perspectives. We can see this development in Long and Robinson (1998), who emphasize the importance of the learner-centered classroom, where the teacher's first focus and concern is with understanding their student population, rather than simply focusing on the skills to be covered, an approach that they note the majority of the world's schools put first in curriculum design (as quoted in Celce-Murcia, 2001, p. 235). Nonetheless, Freire might correlate this criticism of the standard model of the curriculum to his analysis of traditional teaching as the Banking Concept, which sees the teacher's role as a dispenser of knowledge to be received and repeated back at a later date. In *Pedagogy of the Oppressed* (1970), Freire asks us instead to look to dialogue and problem solving in the classroom as an emancipatory practice. His goal of liberation for students is not intended to be accomplished in a teacher-centric model, where teachers "free" students; rather it is to organically arise from the population,

> a pedagogy which must be forged *with*, not *for*, the oppressed (whether individuals or peoples) in the incessant struggle to regain their humanity. This pedagogy makes oppression and its causes objects of reflection by the oppressed, and from that

reflection will come their necessary engagement in the struggle for their liberation. And in the struggle this pedagogy will be made and remade. (as quoted in Piaget, 1993, p. 33)

By empowering students and communities, Freire's goal for teachers in education was that of a facilitator who helps learning to happen, rather than by dictating what knowledge will be shared. We maintain, however, that even Freire had not gone far enough toward embracing learning-centered education in which the teacher is just as much a learner as the students are (Hall, 2015).

There are relations to other major themes in TESOL. Gardner's (1983) call to respect the Multiple Intelligences (MI) of their students is an example of how teachers are advised to take a multifaceted approach to teaching. In spite of recent criticism of MI (Armstrong, 2009), it is easy to see how MI ties in to the position of critical pedagogy (CP) by helping teachers meet learners/communities at a level or in a fashion that allows them to use their specific strengths and needs. Similarly, in Second Language Pedagogy, this move toward learner-centered education has meant a shift from exclusive use of Grammar Translation and Audio-lingual Language teaching methods to incorporating communicative strategies as proposed by Brumfit and Johnson in *The Communicative Approach to Language Teaching* (1979). In seeing the learner's real use of the language as a goal, the Communicative Approach (CA) conforms to CP. Of course, we also must remember that for certain groups, the appropriate use of Grammar Translation and Audio-lingual Language methods are more desirable than the CA. For example, we want our air traffic controllers to be accurate rather than "fluent" (Hall, 2013). Yes, some proponents of CA can be ideologically inflexible and therefore completely anti-CP!

Likewise, the growth of ESP can be seen as an outgrowth of social justice, since it has, as one part of its approach, a focus on the needs and the wants of all stakeholders, not just the students. Indeed, we can see ESP projects throughout the world that try to work with the "poorest of the poor" to help them have access to English as a Lingua Franca (ELF) (Hall, Arrol, & Diaz, 2013). Without ELF, social progress is almost impossible today. In fact, the author of this chapter uses ESP to also mean "English for Social Progress" to reflect the explicit goals of projects in which he has personally been involved in countries such as Peru, Bolivia, Indonesia, and East Timor (Hall, 2015).

We are not going to try to define or delimit what social justice in education is. For example, many might think that mathematics would hardly be a nexus for social change, but many math educators work for social justice. Indeed, as an outgrowth of his interest in using applied linguistics to promote social justice, the author of this chapter co-authored a book chapter on using technology to reduce the racial gap in college math courses (Hu, Xu, Hall, Walker, & Okwumabua, 2013).

In education, social justice can be interpreted and applied countless ways. It is determined by each group, in each individual culture and context. Thus, there can be no explicit, definitive list of social justice topics to cover, because each culture creates its own injustices that must be addressed. In Nobel laureate Malala's Pakistan, girls must struggle to retain their right to education. On the other hand, girls in Canada, for example, are not subject to attacks by adult terrorists for wanting to learn, but there we find other types or degrees of social injustice that must be dismantled. There can be no end to possible social injustices because our "most egregious" social injustices are culturally defined and perceived through our experiences. As a result, this chapter is only illustrative, not comprehensive; likewise, we will be examining only a limited number of topics in this volume and we would ask you, the reader, to consider the social injustices or justices you have encountered, experienced, ignored, or worked against. Perhaps we can learn from your experiences and share with you from ours as we explore language teaching and social justice.

References

Adams, D. W. (1995). *Education for extinction: American Indians and the boarding school experience, 1875–1928*. Lawrence: University Press of Kansas.

Armstrong, T. (2009). *Multiple intelligences in the classroom* (3rd ed.). Alexandria, VA: ASCD. Retrieved from http://www.ascd.org/publications/books/109007/chapters/MI-Theory-and-Its-Critics.aspx

Brumfit, C. J., & Johnson, K. (1979). *The communicative approach to language teaching*. Oxford, England: Oxford University Press.

Celce-Murcia, M. (2001). *Teaching English as a second or foreign language* (3rd ed.). Boston, MA: Heinle ELT.

Cody, D. (n.d.). The British empire. *The Victorian Web*. Retrieved May 31, 2015, from http://www.victorianweb.org/history/empire/Empire.html

Duncan, A. (2009). A call to teaching: Secretary Arne Duncan's remarks at the rotunda at the University of Virginia. U.S. Department of Education Press Room: Speeches. http://www2.ed.gov/news/speeches/2009/10/10092009.html

Freire, P. (1970). *Pedagogy of the oppressed*. New York, NY: Herder and Herder.

Gardner, H. (1983). *Frames of mind: The theory of multiple intelligences*. New York, NY: Basic Books.

Giroux, H. A. (1988). *Teachers as intellectuals: Toward a critical pedagogy of learning*. Granby, MA: Praeger.

Hall, C. (2013, June). *To serve and to protect: International police English and tourism*. Paper presented at the First International Uniformed Forces Conference, Bogor, Indonesia.

Hall, C. (2015, May). *Killing off general English: Why everything is ESP*. Paper presented at the 8th Annual KSAALT Conference, Khobar, Saudi Arabia.

Hall, C., Arrol, D., & Diaz, A. (2013, March). *Helping the poorest of the poor in the tourist industry*. Paper presented at International TESOL, Dallas, TX.

Horton, M., & Freire, P. (1990). *We make the road by walking: Conversations on education and social change* (Reprint ed.). Philadelphia, PA: Temple University Press.

Hu, X., Xu, Y., Hall, C., Walker, K., & Okwumabua, T. (2013). A potential technological solution in reducing the achievement gap between white and black students. In D. Albert, C. Doble, D. Eppstein, J. Falmagne, & X. Hu (Eds.), *Knowledge spaces: Applications to education* (pp. 79–91). Berlin, Germany: Springer.

Johann Amos Comenius. (n.d.). In *The New International Encyclopædia*. Retrieved May 31, 2015, from https://en.wikisource.org/wiki/The_New_International_Encyclopædia/Comenius,_Johann_Amos

John Amos Comenius. (1892, March 4). *Harvard Crimson.* Retrieved May 31, 2015, from http://www.thecrimson.com/article/1892/3/4/john-amos-comenius-professor-hanus -delivered/

Johnston, B. (1999). Putting critical pedagogy in its place: A personal account. *TESOL Quarterly, 33*(3), 557–565. doi:10.2307/3587680

Leo, J. (2010, March 17). Code words: The apparently harmless lingo of the Left can't be taken at face value. *National Review Online.* Retrieved August 8, 2014, from http:// www.nationalreview.com/article/229335/code-words/john-leo

Long, M., & Robinson, P. (1998). Focus on form: Theory, research, and practice. In C. Doughty & J. Williams (Eds.), *Focus on form in classroom second language acquisi- tion* (pp. 15–63). New York, NY: Cambridge University Press.

The Nobel Peace Prize 2014. (n.d.). Retrieved May 31, 2015, from http://www.nobelprize .org/nobel_prizes/peace/laureates/2014/

Norton, B., & Toohey, K. (2004). *Critical pedagogies and language learning.* Cambridge, England: Cambridge University Press.

Okihiro, G. (1992). *Cane fires: The anti-Japanese movement in Hawai'i, 1865–1945.* Philadelphia, PA: Temple University Press.

Pennycook, A. (1989). The concept of method, interested knowledge, and the politics of language teaching. *TESOL Quarterly, 23*(4), 589–618. doi:10.2307/3587534

Pennycook, A. (1994). *The cultural politics of English as an international language.* London, England: Longman.

Phillipson, R. (1992). *Linguistic imperialism.* New York, NY: Oxford University Press.

Piaget, J. (1993). Jan Amos Comenius. *Prospects—The International Quarterly Review of Comparative Education, 23*(1/2), 173–196.

Smithsonian National Museum of the American Indian. (2007). Boarding schools: Strug- gling with cultural repression [chapter 3 of *Native Words, Native Warriors,* companion website to NMAI traveling exhibition]. Retrieved August 7, 2014, from nmai.si.edu /education/codetalkers/html/chapter3.html

Sowell, T. (2012, June 28). The mysticism of "social justice": There is little politicians can do to rectify cosmic injustice. *National Review Online.* Retrieved August 8, 2014, from http://www.nationalreview.com/article/304176/mysticism-social-justice-thomas -sowell

Spring, J. H. (2007). *Deculturalization and the struggle for equality: A brief history of the education of dominated cultures in the United States.* Boston: McGraw-Hill Higher Education.

Tollefson, J. W. (1995). *Power and inequality in language education.* New York, NY: Cambridge University Press.

Whittaker, R. (2012, June 27). GOP opposes critical thinking. *The Austin Chronicle.* Retrieved May 31, 2015, from http://www.austinchronicle.com/daily/news/2012-06-27 /gop-opposes-critical-thinking/

Zajda, J., Majhanovich, S., Rust, V., & Sabina, E. (Eds.). (2006). *Education and social justice.* New York, NY: Springer.

CHAPTER 2

The First Step Toward Social Justice: Teacher Reflection

Lavette Coney
The Fessenden School

Social Equity Work as a Lifestyle Choice

As a young African American girl, I knew that social justice didn't exist for everyone, but I didn't know how to fix it. In middle school, I realized that I wanted to solve the disease of racism. My sense of social responsibility was evident early on. As a person of color, I have had a long and varied history regarding social equity. The importance of social justice has not evolved over my lifetime, but the ways in which I access it have. Recognizing my part in social responsibility has occurred by default because of my economic, gender, and ethnic makeup. Growing up in Boston, I didn't have the luxury of ignoring issues of equity. As an adult, I feel even stronger about the commitment I made to my teenage self to fight for social justice. Therefore, using my position of limited power, I do my best to dismantle the main cause of the inequalities that exist in U.S. society, or what I have researched to be the underlying factor for a great many of them: racism. Pondering and agonizing over this moral and social dilemma of racism has been my life's work. It continues to be the biggest unresolved social issue in our society. There are those who say, "Why does everything have to be about race?" My reply is, "Because it is." Race is a social construct that affects everyone and everything we do, including the individuals in our field. Thus, the importance of social responsibility in the field of TESOL, the field in which I have been teaching for the past 20 years, weighs heavily upon me. Within the field of TESOL, internalized racism of individual teachers and racism with our institutions remains an issue and are at the root of what needs to be changed in our teaching practices (Larrivee, 2000). Our teaching practices are informed by our personal beliefs, perceptions, and life experiences, yet they are often overlooked when we train to teach English. Thus, providing teachers, instructors, and facilitators of English with the tools to critically reflect on race and power is paramount.

Importance of Teacher Reflection in Social Justice Work

Institutionalized and internalized racism in teacher pedagogy take a back seat to many other aspects of our profession that have been, or are being, researched. For decades, the field of English language teaching (ELT) has gone unquestioned about its lack of responsibility in educating teachers about why English is taught and has become the dominant language. The root causes and effects of colonialism have made English the powerhouse it is today, but this reality has come laden with unchecked perceptions that are a result of living in a racist society. One can not live in a racist society and be untouched by it. The connections between ELT around the world, colonization, and racism are undeniable (Phillipson, 1992). The English language cannot be separated nor be in isolation from the social and political conditions in which it operates (Hornberger, 2008). Therefore, it would stand to reason that a field such as TESOL, operating in the 21st century, would be investing heavily in teacher education and training to require teachers, instructors, or facilitators of English language learners to reflect personally on the topics of diversity, racism, and White privilege (Nieto, 2000) because student outcomes (educational, emotional, psychological and health) can be affected.

TERMINOLOGY DEFINED

This chapter uses various key terms repeatedly; thus, it is important to define them early. The terms *teachers, facilitators,* and *instructors* will be used interchangeably. In some cases, the following meanings will be ascribed: *teacher* will be used in the traditional sense, *instructor* where the primary goal is to inform, and *facilitator* where the person acts as a guide. As for the term *diversity,* Kubota and Lin (2006) have extensively defined the concepts of White privilege and institutionalized and internalized racism, and this chapter will use those definitions. *Race* is described as a non-biological term, which has to be treated as an evolving term. *Ethnicity,* unlike race, distinguishes people using various characteristics, such as ancestry and language. However, *culture* and its relationship with race and ethnicity is more complex, and is used as "a more benign and acceptable signifier than race" (Kubota & Lin, 2006, p. 476). As for *Whiteness,* the authors define that term as an invisible and unmarked norm. In addition, the term TESOL represents the field of study, unless contextually noted in particular sections of the paper as the organization.

Diversity is generally understood through Loden and Rosener's (1990) Diversity Wheel, which identifies characteristics (shown on an inner circle) that are core to our identities, and secondary dimensions (shown on an outer circle) that are important differences generally acquired later in life. The inner circle is divided into six sections: race, ethnicity, age, gender, physical abilities/qualities, and sexual/affectional orientation. The outer part of the wheel lists these dimensions: work experience, income, marital status, military experience, religious beliefs, geographic location, and education. The inner and outer circles help show how the characteristics are interrelated to affect individuals.

Racism in its simplest form can be explained in this way: race + power = racism. Critical race theory rejects the definition of racism found in standard dictionaries. Tatum (1997) even attributes this term exclusively to White people. It is systemic and institutionalized at its most damaging level. Institutionalized racism is vastly different from interpersonal racism.

The National Association of Independent Schools (NAIS) (2005) defines *diversity, multiculturalism, inclusivity,* and *equity and justice* in this way:

> Diversity is who we are. It is quantitative. It is defined by "otherness." Most obviously it is determined by race, gender, and culture. On a more subtle level, it includes class, sexual orientation, religion, ability, and appearance. In a democratic nation we define ourselves through diversity. We believe in equal opportunity and equal access. Diversity exists in spite of, and sometimes because of, the action we take.
>
> Multiculturalism is an evolving process. It is qualitative. It is the shift that occurs when we stop defining everyone by one cultural norm and move to an understanding of multiple norms. Critical to this process is the breaking down of systemic barriers to equity and justice. Chief among these are the various "isms," such as racism and sexism. Multiculturalism exists only when we make an informed commitment to change.
>
> Inclusivity is building and sustaining communities in policies, programs, and practices. Diversity (the numbers) is the foundation from which to establish and sustain inclusivity.
>
> Equity and Justice focuses on empowerment and co-ownership of the community in strategically building on and sustaining diversity, multiculturalism, and inclusivity. (NAIS, 2005)

White privilege is another term to consider when investigating teacher education and professional development. Here is how DiAngelo (2006) describes Whiteness: "Whiteness scholars define Whiteness as reference to a set of locations that are historically, socially, politically, and culturally produced, and intrinsically linked to relations of domination" (p. 1984).

The concept of teacher reflection referenced in this chapter branches off from Plato, who espoused that a teacher should facilitate the reflection necessary for intellectual autonomy; Dewey, who encouraged a state of questioning and a drive to find answers; and Schön who proposed continuous learning as a part of professional development, with reflection on and in action. Instead, this chapter proposes to deal more directly with the race and power dynamic with critical teacher reflection more along the lines of Tyrone Howard, who proposes "that the development of culturally relevant teaching strategies is contingent upon critical reflection about race and culture of teachers and their students" (195). Howard further proposes that reflecting on our practice in a deep and meaningful way that can create ripple effect of positive and equitable change. The teacher becomes the object of analysis in respect to our social responsibility to deal with it from within, so that we are aware when aversive racism takes over and we act upon it. She or he becomes the object of self-inquiry through his or her experiential lens. I view reflection as a crucial cognitive practice, which would have the teacher reflect on the various research topics like aversive racism (Gaertner and Dovidio), intergroup bias (Amodio), racial identity development theory (Tatum), whiteness (Jensen, Tochluk), white fragility (DiAngelo),visible and invisible race (Butler), and more.

As the reader can gather, there are a number of complex factors that play into this idea of "race" in the field of TESOL. These terms help guide the discussion necessary for teachers to have in order to be most effective in dispensing guidance and materials to students acquiring and learning language. Thus, critical reflection as a tool for ongoing personal and professional development will move us closer to a more humanistic and just way of providing instruction in the English language.

HISTORY EXAMINED

A number of complex factors play into this idea of "race" in the field of TESOL (Howatt, 2004). The current research on diversity, race, culture, and identity in second language should also drive professional development in the field. We must consider the impact of these topics in the TESOL field in order for us to be considered relevant. There has been a long tradition of focusing on methodology without much attention to the roots of the discipline and why it exists in the first place. How did our profession come to be? Must we always be mindful of reasons why English is being taught in the first place? How was it "decided" that English would be the global language? We live in a world that demands us to deal with the past that has plagued our present society in terms of social equity and justice. For decades, the field of TESOL has been known as the "nice" profession (Kubota, 2002) because we help prepare people throughout the world to communicate with one another using one language, English.

Our field of study is rare in its self-assessment: We as a group believe that we are predisposed to understand and empathize with the Other. Our population of students automatically is from countries, most likely previously colonized, where English is not spoken by the majority of people (Lin & Luke, 2006; Pennycook, 1998; Phillipson, 1992). In order to resist all forms of imperialism, including linguistic (Canagarapah, 1999), we have to be informed.

Since the literature is pointing in this direction of recognizing the reasons why English is the international language and how it is impacting us, we as TESOL educators should heed the call. I asked myself, "What is the TESOL International Association's position on how we got here? How are we as an organization owning and reflecting on our past, in terms of our mission and values?" I found that as an institution, it is closely aligned to diversity and inclusion in its noncritical sense. TESOL International Association is a professional association that includes people from diverse backgrounds, but much of the deeper, critical work of dissecting race, White privilege, and social justice throughout all the tenets of the organization is yet to be done. On the TESOL website, the mission, core values, and nondiscrimination policy are outlined as follows:

TESOL's Mission

TESOL is an international association of professionals advancing the quality of English language teaching through professional development, research, standards, and advocacy.

Core Values

- Professionalism demonstrated by excellence in standards, research, and practice that improve learning outcomes
- Respect for diversity, multilingualism, multiculturalism, and individuals' language rights
- Integrity guided by ethical and transparent action
- Commitment to life-long learning

Vision Statement

To become the trusted global authority for knowledge and expertise in English language teaching

Nondiscrimination Policy

In principle and in practice, TESOL values and seeks diverse and inclusive partici-pation within the field of English language teaching. TESOL promotes involvement and broad access to professional opportunities for all and works to eliminate any kind of discrimination including, but not limited to, language background, race, ethnicity, gender, religion, age, sexual orientation, nationality, disability, appear-ance, or geographic location (http://www.tesol.org/about-tesol /association-governance/mission-and-values).

TESOL International Association has made moves to address issues of race in the profession, as can be seen in multiple position statements favoring diversity and equity, a 2006 Special Topic Issue of TESOL Quarterly on Race and TESOL, and a nascent "diversity collaborative initiative," but there is a need to go beyond this. It is an issue when a professional association made up of a diverse group of professional educators who validate the merits of diversity and multiculturalism does not do enough to explicitly inform teachers in a meaningful way about the many facets of diversity, like systemic racism and privilege. Certain TESOL special interest groups, like the Social Responsibility Interest Section and the Nonnative English Speakers in TESOL Interest Section deal with issues of race and privilege as a part of their larger goals, but there is not a specific forum where their importance is emphasized. This begs the question: When these issues are not confronted, does this reflect deeper issues of institutional and structural racism? Our thinking must move into 21st century, because the deeper issues become apparent when various groups commingle within the organization. What does respect for diversity and multiculturalism mean in the context of profession developments for educators to collaborate with learners from various cultural and linguistic backgrounds when the professional educators are not given the needed space to specifically address race issues and to be a support and resource for those trying to address race issues in the field? The mission and values are too vague for the issue of equity at various levels of the profession to be addressed consistently throughout the organization.

A number of articles, written in the 1980s and late 1990s, were nominally about diversity, but under the classification of multiculturalism (Ladson-Billings, 1999a). However, the focus of this chapter is deeper and demands more work on the part of the policy makers and administrators who dictate what facilitators learn in order to be effective.

ANECDOTAL TO REALITY

In order to test my assumptions on which ethnic group makes up the majority of teachers, instructors, and facilitators, the data had to be checked. The profession is also strikingly "White" (Feistritzer, 2011, p. x). The anecdotal information matched the reality: A majority of the teachers in the field of education and TESOL throughout the world are White, even desired over others, and White females: "Teaching is still an overwhelmingly female occupation. It would stand to reason that many if not most have internalized racism, since we live in a racist society.

The combination of the curricula chosen by a White establishment, female teachers of European descent, unchecked White privilege, and a diverse student population does not lend itself to informed teaching. In this case, the teachers do not have to think about race, yet they are teaching those who do (McLaren & Muñoz, 2000). The situation seems like a recipe for disaster. Why would White privilege not be dealt with when many of the teachers who teach students of Color are in a role that inherently involves power differentials of teacher/student or gatekeeper/learner? Privilege is the basis for that relationship. Peggy McIntosh, in *The White Privilege Conference* (2015), wrote,

> Privilege exists when one group has something of value that is denied to others simply because of the groups they belong to, rather than because of anything they've done or failed to do. Access to privilege doesn't determine one's outcomes, but it is definitely an asset that makes it more likely that whatever talent, ability, and aspirations a person with privilege has will result in something positive for them. (n.p.)

Researching the literature, I wanted to know what various teaching programs offered in terms of diversity and White privilege. One of the most prestigious institutions for teacher education is Teachers College at Columbia University. Even though the program claims to provide a foundation in pedagogical questions, it does not have the issue of race as its primary study emphasis. It is unfortunate that the program emphasis is not in alignment with the topic of equity and social justice at its core, since "it is difficult to for a white person to get a good education in race and gender in our colleges and universities" (McIntosh, 2009, p. 5). More can and should be done.

TEACHING IS NOT A NEUTRAL ACT

There is no indication that what seems to be an essential issue in this field is going to take a pivotal role. Arguably, in the field of diversity work, everything is steeped in some form of racism. Therefore, how is it possible for institutions to ignore the obvious? Is it because of the political nature of racism? If it is true that race is linked to our existence, then researchers, teachers, facilitators, and instructors must move quickly to meet the demands that diversity requires in this type of work.

Instead of confronting racial issues as they pertain to the various subtopics and issues of TESOL's 40-year review, Canagarajah (2006) speaks broadly of issues of bias in a larger discussion of Critical Pedagogy (CP) and Critical Thinking (CT), stating that "CP . . . is more dialogical and reflexive in that it encourages students to interrogate thinking in relation to material life, one's own biases, and one's social and historical positioning" (15–16). While Canagarajah makes a good start with encouraging students to critically examine their relationships to the world and their own biases, his advice should also be expanded to English language teachers. Similarly, the discussion of identity focuses primarily on the role it plays in language learning, while the scope of the discussion should be expanded to the role identity plays in teaching language. Kincheloe (2004) asserts that a more critical approach is needed, as TESOL's focus has been directed at topics such as assessing language skills, meeting student population needs, and special content areas on the environment, without regard for the obvious. There has been much research and data collected on providing either multicultural content to learners or recognizing the diverse student populations in order to provide appropriate materials in the classroom. In addition, we have paid attention to teacher education, training, and observation, but rarely do we combine the two. The focal point has not been on the dispensers of the content and teaching.

Compared to other disciplines, such as anthropology, sociology, and education, the field of TESOL is lagging behind (Kubota & Lin, 2006) in catching up with an obvious issue that plagues the profession. Consideration and research is being devoted primarily to the issues of acquisition, technology, World Englishes, and pedagogy; but the fact that we live in a society fundamentally rooted in injustice, subconscious and conscious, leads us to the conclusion that such issues should be addressed primarily (Norton & Toohey, 2004). In reality, these issues matter (Leung, Harris, & Pumpton, 1997). However, my focus here will be on ethnic and cultural bias.

There are a number of articles focusing on bridging the cultural divide in the classroom between English language learners and textbooks that will reflect the diversity in the classroom. Rarely, however, does one find a mirror being placed in front of the teacher to reflect inward for professional development in the area of race. If student outcomes are related to teachers' professional development, then it stands to reason that teachers should be well versed in matters of diversity, "race," and ethnicity (Dee,

2005; Ladson-Billings, 1999b; Lippi-Green, 2002). This is especially true when it come to the "mirror image" identity awareness, internalized racism, and "affective filter" as it pertains to anxiety, stress, and motivation.

ETHOS, PEDAGOGY, AND TEACHER TRAINING

Teacher beliefs can and do include bias, such as nativism and perceptions of who English belongs to. The assumption is that English language instructors, teachers, and facilitators are equipped to work with learners from other countries. Perceptions can be especially damaging if an instructor both belongs to the dominant group and has not done the reflection necessary to always be mindful of one's approach when choosing content and materials and of how one interacts with the language learners (Delgado & Stefancic, 1997). Antiracist work has to be employed, because the research has informed us to put it into practice (Kailin, 2002). In many cases, racism is based on lack of knowledge and actual experience among various ethnic groups other than one's own. We do not know what kind of biases are being brought to the desk.

More likely than not, TESOL teachers have internalized biases, i.e. 'hidden biases' about the various cultural groups that they encounter in the classroom. In addition, if educators have not looked inwardly to decode or deconstruct both the institutionalized and the personalized racism that exists in this country and other countries, they will do a disservice to the students they teach.

The perspectives come out of living in a society that ignores race or misinterprets its power and also out of how we operate through our pedagogy and in our research. This is evident in Lin's account of commonly held blind preferences for the selection of a white teacher over a nonnative English-speaking teacher in the name of nativism (Kubota & Lin, 2006) and in Kubota's discourse with Atkinson (Kubota, 2002). Teaching also underscores the role that English as an international language plays for global communication (Warschauer, 2000). Even though teaching is moving into other technologies, such as computer-based learning and distance learning, people—with their biases and racism—will produce those programs. In addition, Bashir-Ali's (2006) research provides evidence for teachers' lack of empathy and understanding, which has both positive and negative implications for the future of the discipline. Such items would need to be addressed in order to meet the vital needs of the learner.

CULTURALLY RESPONSIVE PEDAGOGY/TEACHER OBLIGATION

Preparing teachers for a truly inclusive environment makes self-reflection on racism and White privilege mandatory. The discourse between Atkinson (2002) and Kubota (2002) demonstrates this clearly. When White researchers do not understand the concept of race and its various facets and levels, Atkinson's response to Kubota is inevitable. No one wants to be viewed as racist, but one needs to understand that being part of a racist society and benefiting from it makes a person racist. Being racist is not only at the individual level. Racism occurs at personal, interpersonal, institutional, and cultural levels. Castagno (2008) describes how a discussion on race can be silenced by a reaction of denial and dismissal. A White male, for example, has to comprehend how privilege works. Instead of being outraged at being called a racist, he should take responsibility for the privilege he receives as a White male.

It stands to reason that a teacher's views and perceptions can have an effect on the learner (Morgan, 2004), but rarely does the onus focus on the main instrument of change: teachers, facilitators, and instructors of TESOL. Other disciplines, such as psychology and sociology, recognize that teacher education has to include diversity work and White privilege study.

A teacher's cultural competency is of great importance within 21st-century learning paradigms. Cultural competency is essential for 21st-century learning for both students and teachers. A paradigm shift has to occur in order to view this as an asset, not a deficit.

The struggle for social justice must be employed in all disciplines in order to eradicate the negative impact of social injustices. The field of TESOL is no exception. Lifelong learning would include this essential piece that has many implications for education and for wider societal obligations (Ladson-Billings, 1999b).

If preservice teachers are to develop the knowledge, attitudes, beliefs, and peda-gogical skills to address their own ideas about social injustice, then they must be given education courses dealing with diversity and White privilege theory before they enter classrooms. These courses must include the work necessary to address issues of race, ethnicity, and social injustice in preservice and in-service education on an on-going basis throughout their training. One or two classes during the teacher educational program would not be sufficient. Social justice work can not be dealt with once in awhile. The nature of injustice is insidious, thus it should be treated as such.

IMPLICATIONS FOR INDEPENDENT SCHOOLS

The data point to public educational institutions, not private entities; thus there is room for much research in this area. With their push to diversify, private/independent schools have specific, unique challenges and responsibilities to meet these goals. However, their exclusive nature and the original intent for such schools has meant that progress is slow. Some schools are intentional in this pace and others are not.

National organizations, such as NAIS (National Association of Independent Schools), and regional organizations, such as AISNE (Association of Independent Schools of New England), are contributing to the issue of educating teachers and administrators on various aspects of diversity work. Some smaller organizations, such as DiversityWorks, VISIONS, and Ibis, provide consulting to educational institutions and professional training for the faculty and staff. In addition, NAIS has an equity and justice preamble and principles to guide the member schools. Unfortunately, the organization has no mandate over the schools and some schools choose to ignore these principles.

Conclusion

Although a clear need for English language educators to address issues of social injustice in education has been demonstrated in the literature, only limited progress has been made and the status quo remains in most institutions. The research can open up new avenues of inquiry. After reviewing the literature, there may also be implications to levels of self-esteem and lower anxiety issues associated with "comprehensible input" (Krashen, 1981). The affective filter hypothesis embodies Krashen's view that a number of "affective variables" play a facilitative, but non-causal, role in second language acquisition. These variables include motivation, self-confidence, and anxiety. Krashen claims that learners with high motivation, self-confidence, a good self-image, and a low level of anxiety are better equipped for success in second language acquisition. Low motivation, low self-esteem, and debilitating anxiety can combine to "raise" the affective filter and form a "mental block" that prevents comprehensible input from being used for acquisition. In other words, when the filter is "up" it impedes language acquisition. On the other hand, positive affect is necessary, but not sufficient on its own, for acquisition to take place. Greater understanding of who we are, what impact that will have, and about the world we all live in will all help us to become true facilitators of the English language, thus becoming more effective in our practice.

Are school culture, community, interpersonal relationships, curriculum, and institutional policy all operating under the guidelines of diversity in terms of equity and justice? The impact would be tremendous if teachers were trained in anti-racist theory and practice (Lawrence & Tatum, 1997). The research shows that teacher beliefs are integral to learner outcomes. There are benefits, not costs, in doing this work. Granted, it will be challenging for those who deny other people's realities, but once this diversity work is understood, the benefits outweigh the costs. This new understanding and approach would sustain the whole school in a vastly meaningful and transformative way. An atmosphere of cultural inquiry and lifelong learning is essential to greater understanding and empathy. How responsible does a teacher feel toward any given learners' outcomes? If a teacher wants to be responsible, she must be proactive in this endeavor by working her hardest to ensure that her underlying perceptions do not interfere with how her students are learning.

Isn't the mission of advancing excellence in English language teaching what the collective wants? As the discipline continues to move on within this complex society, providing adults who teach, facilitate, and instruct learners of English with continual self-reflection should remain a priority. We need to define high standards and guide ethical behavior around equity and justice. Starting with the "agents of change" is a logical beginning. Research that ignores or simplifies the issue of diversity, racism, and social justice will have very little impact on the quality of the language learner experience.

Professional Practices to Implement Teacher Reflection Work

How can a teacher teach students to be socially responsible when she has not done the work herself? The TESOL professional should do her research or be well read on the topic, push herself to have real-life experiences that will teach her about said issues, keep Teacher Reflection Journals, and have continual dialogues with other individuals working on dismantling White privilege and seeking equity in the lives of others and in their classrooms.

Self-Reflection and Deconstruction of Cultural Identity

Underlying all relationships, whether teacher to student or student to student, is the need to connect on various levels. Thus, professional development programs in the field of TESOL should require that student teachers take courses that look closely at issues on diversity and inclusion, such as stereotype threat, adverse racism, and White privilege. Such courses should be consistent throughout their academic career or teacher training. If students in teacher education programs are to teach diverse student populations, they must also reflect on and deconstruct their cultural norms and expectations, because all these factors will play out and have an impact on the students they teach in and outside of the classroom. This is especially relevant and imperative when the majority of teachers in public, private, and parochial schools are of European descent, that is, White. Therefore, the practitioner, the teacher, must reflect on the self (Irving, 2014; Jensen, 2005; Kubota & Lin, 2009). Teachers can gain access to many resources (Butler, 2012; Tochluk, 2010) that can initiate awareness of this social ill that affects us all.

Robert Jensen (2005) stated, "To accept whiteness, to truly believe in it, is to deform oneself. The privileges and material benefits that come from being white in a white-supremacist society come at a cost to us white people. Whiteness is based on lies not only about others but lies about ourselves, and we can't lay claim to our full humanity until we find our way out of the web of denial" (pp. xix–xx).

References

Amodio, David M. "The social neuroscience of intergroup relations." European review of social psychology 19.1 (2008): 1–54.

Atkinson, D. (2002). Comments on Ryuko Kubota's "Discursive Construction of the Images of U.S. Classroom": A reader reacts. *TESOL Quarterly, 36*(1), 79. doi:10.2307/3588362

Bashir-Ali, K. (2006). Language learning and the definition of one's social, cultural, and racial identity. *TESOL Quarterly, 40*, 628–639.

Butler, S. (Director). (2012). *Cracking the codes: The system of racial inequity* [Motion picture on DVD]. United States: World Trust Educational Services.

Butler, S., Butler, R., & Shwartz, P. (2006) *Mirrors of privilege: Making whiteness visible.* World Trust Educational Services, Incorporated, 2006.

Canagarajah, A. S. (1999). *Resisting linguistic imperialism in English teaching.* Oxford, England: Oxford University Press.

Canagarajah, A. S. (2006). TESOL at forty: What are the issues? *TESOL Quarterly, 40*, 9–32.

Castagno, A. (2008). "I don't want to hear that!": Legitimizing Whiteness through silence in schools. *Anthropology & Education Quarterly, 39*(3), 314–333.

Dee, T. S. (2005). A teacher like me: Does race, ethnicity, or gender matter? *American Economic Review, 95*(2), 158–165.

Delgado, R. & Stefancic, J. (Eds.). (1997). *Critical White studies: Looking beyond the mirror.* Philadelphia, PA: Temple University Press.

DiAngelo, R. J. (2006). The production of Whiteness in education: Asian international students in a college classroom. *Teachers College Record, 108*(10), 1983–2000.

Diversity Works, Inc. (2007). Comprehensive diversity education for business, education, and community. Retrieved from diversityworksinc.net/about.htm

Feistritzer, C. E. (2011). *Profile of teachers in the U. S. 2011.* Washington, DC: National Center for Education Information.

Gaertner, S. L., & Dovidio, J. F. (1986). The aversive form of racism. Academic Press. Chicago

Hornberger, N. (2008). *Encyclopedia of language and education* (2nd ed.). New York, NY: International Springer Science, Technology, Medicine.

Howard, T. C. (2003). Culturally relevant pedagogy: Ingredients for critical teacher reflection. Theory into practice, 42(3), 195–202. Chicago

Howatt, A. P. R., with Widdowson, H. G. (2004). *A history of English language teaching* (2nd. ed.). Oxford, England: Oxford University Press.

Ibis Consulting Group. (2015). Diversity e-learning. Retrieved from http://www.ibis consultinggroup.com/diversity-e-learning

Irving, D. (2014). *Waking up white, and finding myself in the story of race.* Cambridge, MA: Elephant Room Press.

Jensen, R. (2005). *The heart of whiteness: Confronting race, racism, and white privilege.* San Francisco, CA: City Lights Books.

Kailin, J. (2002). *Into racist education: From theory to practice.* Lanham, MD: Rowman & Littlefield.

Kincheloe, J. L. (2004). *Critical pedagogy.* New York, NY: Peter Lang.

Krashen, S. (1981). *Second language acquisition and second language learning.* Oxford, England: Pergamon Press.

Kubota, R. (2002). The author responds: (Un)Raveling racism in a nice field like TESOL. *TESOL Quarterly, 36*, 84–92.

Kubota, R., & Lin, A. (Eds.). (2006). Race and TESOL: Introduction to concepts and theories. *TESOL Quarterly, 40*(3), 471–493.

Ladson-Billings, G. J. (1999a). Just what is critical race theory, and what's it doing in a *nice* field like education? In L. Parker, D. Deyhle, & S. Villens (Eds.), *Race is—race isn't: Critical race theory and qualitative studies in education* (pp. 7–30). Boulder, CO: Westview.

Ladson-Billings, G. J. (1999b). Preparing teachers for diverse student populations: A critical race theory perspective. *Review of Research in Education, 24*, 211–247.

Lawrence, S. M., & Tatum, B. D. (1997). Teachers in transition: The impact of anti-racist professional development on classroom practice. *Teacher Record, 99*(1), 162–178.

Larrivee, B. (2000). Transforming teaching practice: Becoming the critically reflective teacher. *Reflective Practice, 1*(3), 293–307. doi:10.1080/713693162

Leung, C., Harris, R., & Rampton, B. (1997). The idealized native speaker, reified ethnicities, and classroom realities. *TESOL Quarterly, 31*, 543–560.

Lin, A. M. Y., & Luke, A. (2006). Coloniality, postcoloniality, and TESOL: Can a spider weave its way out of the web that it is being woven into just as it weaves? *Control Inquiry in Language Studies 3*(2–3). doi: 10.1207/s15427587clis032&3_1

Lippi-Green, R. (2002). Language ideology and language prejudice. In E. Finegan & J. R. Rickford (Eds.), *Language in the USA: Perspectives for the twenty-first century* (pp. 289–304). Cambridge, England: Cambridge University Press.

Loden, M., & Rosener, J. (1990). *Workforce America!: Managing employee diversity as a vital resource*. New York, NY: McGraw-Hill.

McIntosh, P. (2009). *White people facing race: Uncovering the myths that keep racism in place*. Saint Paul, MN: The Saint Paul Foundation.

McLaren, P., & Muñoz, J. (2000). Contesting Whiteness: Critical perspectives on the struggles for social justice. In C. J. Ovando & P. McLaren (Eds.), *Multiculturalism and bilingual education: Students and teachers caught in the crossfire* (pp. 22–29). Boston, MA: McGraw Hill.

Morgan, B. (2004). Teacher identity as pedagogy: Towards a field-internal conceptualisation in bilingual and second language education. *International Journal of Bilingual Education and Bilingualism, 7*, 172–173.

NAIS. (2005, October 20). Diversity and multiculturalism. Retrieved October 14, 2015, from http://www.nais.org/Articles/Pages/Diversity-and-Multiculturalism-147595.aspx

Nieto, S. (2000). Placing equity front and center: Some thought on transforming teacher education for a new century. *Education and Education Research, 51*(3), 180–187.

Norton, B., & Toohey, R. (Eds.). (2004). *Critical pedagogies and language learning*. Cambridge, England: Cambridge University Press.

Pennycook, A. (1998). *English and the discourse of colonialism*. New York, NY: Routledge.

Phillipson, R. (1992). *Linguistic imperialism*. Oxford, England: Oxford University Press.

Tatum, B. D. (1997). *Why are all the Black kids sitting together in the cafeteria? and other conversations about race*. New York, NY: Basic Books.

Tochluk, S. (2010). *Witnessing whiteness: The need to talk about race and how to do it*. Lanham, MD: Rowman & Littlefield Education.

Visions, Inc. (2012). http://visions-inc.org/

Warschauer, M. (2000). The changing global economy and the future of English teaching. *TESOL Quarterly, 34*(3), 511–535.

The White Privilege Conference. (2015). What is white privilege? Retrieved October 14, 2015, from http://www.whiteprivilegeconference.com/white_privilege.html

Resources

Bonilla-Silva, E. (2003). *Racism without racists: Color-blind racism and the persistence of racial inequality in the United States*. Lanham, MD: Rowman & Littlefield.

Castex, G. M. (1990). *An analysis and synthesis of current theories of ethnicity and ethnic group processes using the creation of the Hispanic group as a case example* (Unpublished doctoral dissertation). Teachers College, Columbia University, New York, NY.

Cummins, J. (2000). *Language, power and pedagogy: Bilingual children in the crossfire*. Tonawanda, NY: Multilingual Matters.

Curtis, A., & Romney, M. (Eds.) (2006). *Color, race, and English language teaching: Shades of meaning*. Mahwah, NJ: Lawrence Erlbaum.

Frankenberg, R. (1993). *White women, race matters: The social construction of whiteness*. Minneapolis: University of Minnesota Press.

CHAPTER 3

Critical Pedagogy's Power in English Language Teaching

Mayra C. Daniel

Northern Illinois University

De Kalb, IL

Teachers always deserve to be part of the conversation about standards and educational reform, not deskilled functionaries who mechanically do what they are told by external inquisitors.

—*J. L. Kincheloe*, Critical Pedagogy Primer

English language educators' philosophies of instruction and views of how to promote equity and social justice shape the school environment for learners around the world. There is little doubt that consideration of the goals of critical pedagogy leads teachers to legitimize the identities of English language learners (Igoa, 1995). Students engaged in informed questioning of what they see, hear, and read will develop the critical consciousness they need to advocate for themselves and others (Atkinson, 1997). Thus it is crucial that teachers investigate their cultural stances and examine how engaging students in dialogue empowers or disempowers them.

This chapter addresses how critical pedagogy (CP) is evidenced in classroom settings when educators select curricular materials that engage learners in critical thinking. Freire (2002) encourages exploration of what he terms the *"essence of dialogue"* or *"the word."* He tells us:

> Within the word there are two dimensions, reflection and action, in such radical interaction that if one is sacrificed, even in part, the other immediately suffers. There is no true word that is not at the same time a praxis. Thus, to speak a true word is to transform the world. (p. 87)

CP encourages avenues to dialogue as a path to explore and understand the cultural norms of English speakers. It rejects denial of an individual's first language and culture, and regardless of the reasons for learning English, it encourages the person to compare and contrast their worlds.

In this chapter I encourage you to consider how critical literacy (CL) in English language teaching (ELT) promotes CP's ideals of equity and social justice. Specifically, I discuss how CL ideologies used in preparing teachers of English result in transformed classrooms.

Critical Pedagogy

Kincheloe (2008) considers educational models political agendas that privilege students from "*dominant cultural backgrounds*" (p. 8). He challenges educators to accept that "many times, those who develop pedagogies are unconscious of the political inscriptions embedded within them" (p. 9). English teachers who are critical pedagogues understand the power of home-to-school connections. They value learners' cultural capital and incorporate what they know about their learners' individual circumstances in instructional planning. For the purpose of this chapter, CP is defined in the English language classroom as a pedagogy of validation firmly entrenched in the belief that all English language learners can acquire English and reach their goals as they each define the level of maximum potential and achievement for their individual circumstances.

English educators have the responsibility to help learners challenge the social order (Kachru, Kachru, & Nelson, 2006) and introduce them to the possibility that critical thinking can become a cultural practice (Atkinson, 1997). Learners' sociocultural identity is a key factor in academic success. Culturally sensitive pedagogy leads students to become active participants in their schooling and in their communities. "Quality education encourages students to become aware of, if not actively work against, social injustice" (Leonardo, 2004, p. 13).

Critical Literacy

CP provides the philosophical underpinnings to CL. In his introduction to the 30th anniversary edition of Paulo Freire's seminal work *Pedagogy of the Oppressed*, Macedo (2002) cautions us to be wary of educators who "mistakenly transform Freire's notion of dialogue into a method, thus losing sight of the fact that the fundamental goal of dialogic teaching is to create a process of learning and knowing" (p. 17). Please work with me now to define CL as Freire does: as a powerful vehicle that helps teachers and students dialogue in transformed classrooms. I propose to you that CL is a way of interacting in the English language classroom to offer students safe spaces to think and challenge each other (Daniel, 2008; Kincheloe, 2008), to stop marginalization (Breunig, 2009), and to acknowledge the privileging of English and dominant ways of being in the world (Collins & Blot, 2003; González, Moll, & Amanti, 2005). Inherent in CL are students' rights to question societal norms and engage in literacy experiences that place them in the position of decision-maker (Cadiero-Kaplan, 2004).

CL allows individuals to promote and support the social transformation of their society and social institutions that place power in the hands of the dominant society.

One of its major goals is the preparation and equipping of learners to problematize their world, to deconstruct, critique, reform, and reconstruct the ideological foundations of knowledge, culture, and schooling practices. It recognizes that all ideologies are political and thus reflect individual agendas (Canagarajah, 1999). Proponents of CL seek to empower and encourage English learners to become citizens who proactively uncover hegemonic structures and work to institute more democratic, egalitarian, and inclusive policies at all levels of schooling. CL is holistic in scope and inclusive in its adoption and use of the tools and methods from other ideologies that are not subversive to its main goal of promoting critical thinking.

Critical Pedagogy and Critical Literacy in My World

First, I want to discuss how I experienced the power of CP during visit to a U.S. middle school classroom in 2010; then, I will share details of a definitive time in my life. On a visit to a multilingual mathematics classroom I noted what I would see as a daily occurrence! I saw students take action to help an English learner who was struggling to understand. Three students rallied around to reassure their classmate that with their help she could understand the lesson. The teacher in this classroom provided safe spaces for students to freely move around the classroom and speak in different languages. In this same school, I saw a teacher's aide responding to learners' needs and promoting social justice. She organized an after-school club that provided a forum to discuss social justices issues. The meetings gave the students a place to voice their objections to the politics and negative biases they were subject to in their school.

My immigrant experience as a Cuban American contributed to my ideologies of literacy. My experiences both before and after arrival to the United States led to my philosophical stance of social justice in action. I felt disempowered as a second language teacher when I found that my students' American history book covered the 1961 Bay of Pigs invasion in Cuba in one paragraph. I remember being a very frightened child listening to her family's conversations about the failed coup of Castro's regime. In my opinion, the textbook had a glaring bias that presented a singular perspective of the failed disembarking of troops backed by the U.S. Central Intelligence Agency.

Although my family escaped a communist regime, I recognize that I perhaps harbor some socialist views about the ways schooling perpetuates what Cummins (2000) refers to as coercive relations of power. I have yet to see a widespread social justice effort implemented in ways that benefit English language learners in U.S. schools.

My Privilege

I was a member of a lucky group of immigrants because the U.S. welcomed Cuban immigrants through well-oiled doors. In retrospect, I recognize that I created new sociocultural meanings because the juncture of the home culture with what went on at school combined to affirm that I had the right to question what I did not understand.

I arrived in the United States with unearned privilege (McIntosh, 1993). My home environment formed a cocoon that validated my bilingual bicultural identity and empowered me to survive. My teachers encouraged dialogue as well. Nevertheless, unlike other children, I was an English language learner who lived a golden experience because my teachers defined me from a positive perspective because of my parents' education and economic circumstances.

When I read *Tom Sawyer, Farenheit 451, The Chosen, Jane Eyre,* and works by Socrates and Plato in high school, I was enthralled both by characters who were nothing like the people who formed my inner circle and by the Utopian ideals of social justice and equity in the narratives. The novels provided a context of cultural norms and situations for investigation. They allowed me to consider what is immanent in thinking and perceiving and what our reality could be if we allowed ourselves to react to injustice and bring about social reform (Kincheloe, 2008). They widened the scope of what I was learning from the school to the community. They placed me on the path to better understanding and interpreting, to reading the word and the world (Freire & Macedo, 2005), to conscientization (Freire, 1974a). I did not fully understand the behaviors of the characters in the books nor grasp the value of critiquing, reflecting, and, ultimately, widening my perspectives. The novels introduced me to English speakers, their life challenges, and their commitment to advocacy. Some of the characters became role models who energized me as they provided topics for discussion that required I dialogue with classmates and justify my interpretations.

Critical Literacy's Contribution to ELT

TESOL (2010) challenges English language educators to explore and implement culturally responsive pedagogy. Meeting the TESOL challenge involves teaching English and actively advocating for the rights of English learners and their families. Using CL paradigms, teachers adjust their pedagogy to the local realities of communities and acknowledge learners' cultural capital (Aliakbari & Faraji, 2011; Bartolomé, 1996; Collins & Blot, 2003; Daniel, 2008; Freire, 1985; González, Moll, & Amanti, 2005). Because language acquires meaning through its users, effective ELT takes learners to examine and question the cultural norms of English speakers. Students can be encouraged to give voice to their ideas and grow in their understanding of their identity, their cultural histories, and their rights as plurilingual citizens (Canagarajah, 2005; Pennycock, 2007).

This author rejects the notion that English is devoid of power when used as a lingua franca by speakers of different mother tongues. My personal philosophy is that English still holds power in these interpersonal interactions.

The Politics of Transformative Literacy

Let's keep in mind that in countries where education has followed transmission models, it is revolutionary to consider the possibility that a learner's interpretation of a text could differ from the teacher's. Freire's work supports constructivist practices that extend beyond banking models of education. He tells us that "liberating education consists of acts of cognition, not transferals of information" (Freire, 2002, p. 79). Regardless of the economic issues that limit who has access to English in many nations, effective educators will teach English using their contexts, which are situated in local realities. There is no global "equal access" to English language education. In these settings education needs to become "the practice of freedom—as opposed to education as the practice of domination" (p. 81). In the developing world, access to ELT is often a social marker that is perceived to lead to greater financial stability and is understood as being within the birthright of the elite or of those who manage to open privileged doors (Daniel, Mondschein, & Palomo, 2014).

Nevertheless, teachers must often deliver curricula that have been selected by educators who are far removed from the local context and thus lack an understanding of local socio-cultural issues (Truscott, Daniel, & Rasmussen, 2015). Teachers need to feel safe to question the appropriateness of the English language curriculum used in their schools be they in Australia, Guatemala, or Saudi Arabia. Freire (1974b) encouraged educators to see the world as always being in the process of transformation.

Culturally responsive teachers transform practice into a series of meaning-making events. Their lessons evidence their understanding that literacy is inherently a political enterprise that often treats learners differently. They lead students to become aware that social injustice can be remedied if the reproductive processes used in schooling that maintain the status quo are challenged (Canagarajah, 1999; Giroux, 2006). Situated practice positions English language learners as readers and writers in the midst of developing new understandings of who they are and of the people whose language they are studying. Clearly, teachers need the freedom to implement a transactional model of reading instruction in the English language classroom (Rosenblatt, 1978).

Authentic materials such as newspapers, newscasts, and advertisements empower learners to reach higher levels of understanding about the English-speaking world. It is important that learners know it is safe to question the veracity of the English-speaking media. This is the case whether learners are reading for efferent or aesthetic purposes, to complete a required task, or to satisfy their curiosity (Edelsky, 1996, 1999; Freire, 1985; Gee, 1996; Greene, 1996). English learners enter a new world when they read texts written by English speakers because authors transmit cultural messages and prejudices that shape readers' self-perceptions as they interact with texts written in English. These learners develop intercultural understandings when provided opportunities to examine behaviors that are not universal. "The environment is a social construct. It does not consist of things, or even of processes and relations; it does consist of human interactions, from which things derive their meaning" (Halliday, 1975, p. 141).

Promoting Advocacy and Social Action
Through CL Practices

The primary goals of CL are to encourage critical analyses of texts and questioning in learners, promote social justice, empower English language learners, and bring about a transformation of lives through dialogue. Freire (2002) challenged us to understand the limited and disempowering scope of the banking model of education, which considers that "knowledge is a gift bestowed by those who consider themselves knowledgeable upon those whom they consider to know nothing" (p. 72). Immigrants forced to leave their countries of origin for political reasons, economic issues, and/or war will study English in order to meet their family's basic needs. They need not be the underdogs in their adopted countries. When teachers engage learners in a CL dialogue, they help them see that they are at the helm of their own futures. Freire's work (1974a) supports educators who give English learners the keys to eliminate the uncertainties they are experiencing and help them understand how oppressive systems work (Shor, 1999). What better way is there to be part of the action than to know one is free to discuss behavior one does not understand and finds manipulative and/or accepted as the status quo within the dominant dialogue?

CP and CL in Programs of Teacher Preparation

In this next section, I focus on the responsibilities that tertiary educators face in preparing English language educators. In my work I identify topics for classroom discussions that help teachers see and acknowledge the need for schools to provide safe and productive third spaces for plurilingual learners (Bhabba, 1994). Philosophical conversations are the foundation of critical thinking and concrete actions. They lead teachers and students to know they have the power to be change agents. This validates English learners' identities and tells them that what schooling and society requires may not be justifiable (Janks, 2001). In its professional standards TESOL (2010) challenges tertiary institutions to prepare educators who are knowledgeable about issues in ELT related to language acquisition, culture, instructional methodologies, assessment, advocacy, and professionalism. In planning lessons to prepare teachers for ELT it is important to answer two questions: Do they understand unearned privilege? (McIntosh, 1993) and Am I making the rationale concrete enough for the classroom context so that teachers will be able to implement problem posing educational models in ELT that lead learners to critical consciousness?

CL considers how politics control education and perpetuate existing power relations (Canagarajah, 1999; Freire & Macedo, 2005). Shor (1993) references Freire when he states:

> This is a great discovery, education is politics! When a teacher discovers that he or she is a politician too, the teacher has to ask, What kinds of politics am I doing in the classroom? That is, in favor of whom am I being a teacher? (p. 27)

CL helps teachers provide a venue for all stakeholders to examine and interpret their perceptions (Kincheloe, 2008). Teachers need to understand and espouse CL as a valuable and equity promoting teaching philosophy before they begin to use it in practice (Leonardo, 2004). Breunig (2009) encourages academics to explore what she labels the *knowledge/action gap* "between students' knowledge about critical theory and direct social action" (p. 260). Advocacy requires that educators explore who they are and how they view society and schooling. Curricula should include tasks that situate teachers as ethnographers and reflective practitioners. I address Breunig's gap by creating assignments such as home visits that require teachers go into communities and apply theory to practice. This is key to gaining an understanding of how society empowers and disempowers and to deliver a humanistic curriculum (Bartolomé, 1996). When teachers visit an English learner's home with the purpose of exploring the family's funds of knowledge (González et al., 2005), they walk away with valuable information to subsequently plan lessons for this learner. Real communication only takes place once we realize that "the oppressed are not 'marginal,' are not people living 'outside' society." They have always been "inside"—inside the structure that made them "beings for others" (Freire, 2002, p. 74).

Planning Empowering Instruction

Culturally responsive teaching means the teacher understands the specificity of context in selecting curriculum (Gay, 2010). ELT across diverse international contexts must consider the historical, social, political, and situated nature of second language learning. Sabihah (a pseudonym), a teacher who works in a Chicago suburb where English learners represent 156 different languages, told me, "My role is to play devil's advocate and help my ELs [English learners] see an issue from more than one perspective." Natalia (a pseudonym) shared her vision of CL. She said, "I help students learn that one can disagree with another person's ideas without using words or actions that make someone feel belittled or devalued."

These examples illustrate how teachers help English language learners develop a voice that validates their rights as individuals with a past, a present, and a plurilingual future. These types of efforts will stop school systems from privileging only dominant discourses in ELT. CL practices expand students' cultural capital because it introduces them to the thoughts, attitudes, and communication modes of English speakers and validates their rights to bring their cultures into the schoolhouse. Teachers eliminate social injustices when they identify the seemingly innocuous yet malicious forms that disempowering schooling practices take in classrooms. Teachers begin by selecting curricular materials that provoke meaningful and provocative conversations. These materials increase learners' commitment to social justice as they examine and interpret authors' words and the world within them (Daniel, 2008). Students of all ages and grade levels can identify societal issues in dialogue that begins at their zone of proximal development (ZPD). Vygotsky (1987) explained the ZPD as the instructional level that is appropriate for a learner both academically and socioculturally. When teachers plan instruction at the ZPD, the students efficiently use the knowledge that they have to make sense of what they do not yet understand. At the same time the positive and collaborative sociocultural environment encourages the learners to work to gain knowledge. Meaningful conversations require learners to produce language that begins with questioning, promotes the development of persuasive English language skills, and fosters their ability to justify stances and the thinking processes that led to their conclusions.

CL prepares learners of all ages and their teachers to voice their questions and opinions. Kincheloe (2008) encourages educators to explore the complexities of trans-formative education. He tells us, "Critical pedagogues who take complexity seriously challenge reductionist, bipolar, true-false epistemologies" (p. 37). I encourage teachers to plan instruction through a CL lens that will reveal to all students the complexities of life in a plurilingual society where English is more and more being supplanted by other world languages. No student is a blank slate without opinions and prejudices. What you need is to make certain that you do not inflict your point of view on students, but instead teach them that language is never neutral (Hawkins & Norton, 2009). The goal is for the students to become collaborators in inquiry with you, develop a critical awareness, and become adept at analyzing how authors position readers. Teachers with a vision can begin the work with young English language learners who will continue the conversations at home with their parents. Older learners will similarly want to extend conversations beyond the classroom context if topics provoke them to advocacy.

In the next sections of this chapter we will explore ways to transform practice by selecting narrative texts and topics for classroom conversations that will empower English language learners to validate their pluricultural and plurilingual identities and move them to promote social justice.

Selection of curricular materials requires that teachers consider if

1. the English proficiency level of the learner aligns to scaffolding instruction using the selected text and topic;

2. the topic is relevant, culturally comprehensible, reflective of the learners' realities, and not offensive; and

3. the material will take the learners to critical consciousness and empowerment.

Classroom activities that provide English learners opportunities to use English as they examine cultural misunderstandings help create a good context for ELT. English speakers from countries with English as a lingua franca encounter communication challenges when interacting with English speakers from other nations. For example, students from India who are thrust into a U.S. school may find that their classmates are confused by their accents. Young English learners relish opportunities to compare differences between familial backgrounds, while adolescents who want to fit into a peer group question parental expectations across cultures. Adult learners want to understand the influences of behaviors and cultural norms on language use, because they need to communicate effectively within a new society both in business and within their communities.

Transforming ELT

Teachers should ask themselves questions that will help them select provocative materials for ELT (Daniel, 2006). The goal is to enroll English learners in tasks focused on themes of social injustice that will lead them to critical consciousness. Hawkins and Norton (2009) highlight that educators who support critical practices work with students to "deconstruct language, texts, and discourses in order to investigate whose interests they serve and what messages are both explicitly and implicitly conveyed" (p. 3). They also remind us that language is not neutral and "is shot through with meanings, inflections, intentions and assumptions" (p. 3).

Faundez (2001) cautions educators to remember that "in the final analysis, when people speak of ideology, they wrongly think only of ideas, and they don't realize that these ideas gain strength and are really a form of power only to the extent that they take concrete shape in the actions of our daily lives" (p. 213). Educators in ELT need to purposefully create tasks that encourage critical thinking. The following questions will help teachers achieve this goal as they plan lessons using literature or media produced materials.

- Why is this topic appropriate for my student population?
- How will my learners relate to this book?
- What do I know about my students' lives that I can bring to the conversation?
- How does this text give English learners a voice?
- What do I need to do to prepare my students to engage with this text?
- What questions should I ask?
- How will I provide a forum for reflective dialogue?
- What can I say to help students deconstruct the message within the text?
- Does this text privilege or exclude English learners?
- What biases does this text bring to the conversation?
- Will deconstructing this text validate all learners' uniqueness?
- Does the author assume stereotypical stances as the norm?
- Is there anything in this text that is culturally inappropriate?
- If students don't ask crucial questions, how can I facilitate the conversation?

Critical Literacy Practices in ELT

Learners engaged in a dialogue gain knowledge of the social framework of texts and become privy to cultural messages that facilitate their adaptation to and understandings of new environments (Daniel, 2008; Freire, 1985; Luke, O'Brien, & Comber, 2001). Teachers collaborate with English learners to help them problematize texts through questioning, examining, and reflecting. As the field of ELT has grown to require more of learners, changed expectations take us beyond the behaviorist approaches of some 50 years ago that required readers to access the explicit messages within texts and develop automaticity via drills and memorized dialogues. We now embrace theories of second language acquisition that empower students to create meaning while they are acquiring vocabulary, syntactic expertise, and functional notions (Norton, 2008; Hawkins & Norton, 2009). Today, we encourage learners to comprehend the implicit meaning of textual messages, and we also collaborate with them to examine, question, and judge the ideas authors present. In addition, educators ask students at all levels of English language proficiency to consider what is unvoiced and may contribute to the incomplete and biased presentation of an issue by an author (Shor, 1996).

Leading Students to Ask Daring Questions

Learning is enhanced when teachers prepare learners to critically analyze their world. Problem-solving pedagogy welcomes learners to codesign new ways of interacting in communities. Students who adopt a questioning stance will identify oppression in their everyday lives and be encouraged to take action. Once you read the questions that follow you will see that teaching English language learners to explore attitudes through these types of questions will focus them on creating new interpretations and understandings of the English-speaking worlds.

- What is my opinion of the way the characters in this book act, dress, and speak to each other?
- How do I react to this topic?
- Is the way I think about this topic different from the author's?
- How would people in my culture react to this text?
- Do I understand why the author wrote this?
- What does this text tell me about the author?
- Is the author qualified to write this text?
- Do I detect any biased statements?
- Is the author privileging what is familiar to his/her culture group?
- What is the author not saying that I consider important?
- Are all voices heard in this author's words? Which voices are silenced?
- Is there truth both in my interpretation and in the author's?

Taking Action to Change the Schoolhouse: Selecting Revolutionizing Texts

Selection of the appropriate curriculum is paramount in engaging English language learners. One of the books that I introduce to teachers is *The Conquerors* (McKee, 2004). At first glance, this book appears to be written for young children, but it can be used to engage older learners in a discussion about interpersonal relationships, war, and peace. English learners who live in war-torn countries or areas where individual rights go unacknowledged welcome conversations that allow them to express their ideas, fears, and political stances. McKee introduces readers to a general whose pride seems rooted in his ability to conquer many countries. The general faces the dilemma of repeatedly failing to conquer the people of one kingdom. Every time he sends new troops, his soldiers become friends with the citizens, collaborate on projects, and live in harmony with the people. Finally, when he goes to conquer the country himself the unthinkable happens: He realizes the value of tolerance across nations.

Consider using the books listed below and search for appropriate titles for your students. These books transcend learners' age limitations and their topics are of high interest to teachers and to students from many backgrounds. These are but a small example of what is available to teach English and raise awareness of social injustices:

- *Sadako and the Thousand Paper Cranes* (Coerr, 1987)
- *The Circuit* (Jiménez, 1997)
- *I Know Why the Caged Bird Sings* (Angelou, 2009)
- *Breaking Through* (Jiménez, 2001)
- *Crow Boy* (Yashima, 1955/1976)
- *An Island of English* (Fu, 2003)
- *Nory Ryan's Song* (Giff, 2000)
- *Learning and Not Learning English* (Valdés, 2001)
- *"change my life forever": Giving Voice to English Language Learners* (Barbieri, 2002)

Conclusion

In this chapter, my goal was to focus on the underlying rationale for effective ELT in theory and practice. I began with a definition of CP that led into exploring the ways CL paradigms use authentic materials to encourage English language learners to question the social order and find their voice. I looked at the reasons programs of teacher preparation must educate through culturally responsive instruction. Last, I propose that teachers who lead learners to question what they see, hear, and read will help them become citizens who influence their worlds and those of their future students. Without doubt, students who critically examine their world are afforded opportunities to discover hegemonic structures within societies. Although this process may be slow, dialogue is the only path for educators to address Freire's (1974a, b) theory of conscientization and whittle away at power structures that perpetuate assimilationist practices in ELT.

References

Aliakbari, M., & Faraji, E. (2011). Basic principles of Critical Pedagogy. *2nd International Conference on Humanities, Historical, and Social Sciences.* IPEDR 17. Singapore: IACSIT Press.

Angelou, M. (2009). *I know why the caged bird sings.* New York, NY: Ballantine Books.

Atkinson, D. (1997). A critical approach to critical thinking in TESOL. *TESOL Quarterly, 31*(1), 71–95.

Barbieri, M (2002). *"change my life forever": Giving voice to English language learners.* Portsmouth, NH: Reed Elsevier.

Bartolomé, L. (1996). Beyond the methods fetish: Toward a humanizing pedagogy. In P. Leistyna, A. Woodrum, & S. Sherblom (Eds.), *Breaking free: The transformative power of critical pedagogy* (pp. 229–252). Cambridge, MA: Harvard Educational Review.

Bhabba, H. K. (1994). *The location of culture.* New York, NY: Routledge.

Breunig, M. (2009). Teaching for and about critical pedagogy in the post-secondary classroom. *Studies in Social Justice, 3*(2), 247–262.

Cadiero-Kaplan, K. (2004). *The literacy curriculum and bilingual education: A critical examination.* New York, NY: Peter Lang.

Canagarajah, S. (1999). *Resisting linguistic imperialism in English teaching.* Oxford, England: Oxford University Press.

Canagarajah, S. (2005). Critical pedagogy in L2 learning and teaching. In Eli Hinkel (Ed.), *Handbook of research in second language teaching and learning* (pp. 931–949). Mahwah, NJ: Lawrence Erlbaum.

Coerr, E. (1987). *Sadako and the thousand paper cranes.* New York, NY: Puffin Books.

Collins, J., & Blot, R. (2003). *Literacy and literacies: Texts, power, and identity.* Cambridge, England: Cambridge University Press.

Cummins, J. (2000). *Language, power, and pedagogy: Bilingual children in the crossfire.* Clevedon, England: Multilingual Matters.

Daniel, M. (2006, January). *Taking all children to the head of the class: Bilingual learners explore cultural nuances in text.* Paper presented at the National Association of Bilingual Education Conference, Phoenix, AZ.

Daniel, M. (2008). Helping English learners: Preparing teachers to promote critical thinking and language acquisition. In M. Foote, F. Falk-Ross, S. Szabo, & M. B. Sampson (Eds.), *College Reading Association yearbook: Navigating the literacy waters: Research, praxis, and advocacy* (Vol. 29, pp. 123–132). Commerce: Texas A & M University–Commerce.

Daniel, M., Mondschein, M., & de Palomo, L. (2014). The Guatemalan literacy project: Collaboration among literacy educators. In C. B. Leung, J. C. Richards, & C. A. Lassonde (Eds.), *International collaborations in literacy research and practice* (pp. 89–116). Charlotte, NC: Information Age.

Edelsky, C. (1996). *With literacy and justice for all: Rethinking the social in language and education* (2nd ed.). London, England: Taylor & Francis.

Edelsky, C. (1999). Education for democracy. In J. B. Allen (Ed.), *Class actions: Teaching for social justice in elementary and middle school* (pp. 147–157). New York, NY: Teachers College Press.

Faundez, A. (2001). Learning to question: A pedagogy of liberation. In A. M. Araújo Freire & D. Macedo (Eds.), *The Paulo Freire reader* (pp. 186–230). New York, NY: Continuum International.

Freire, P. (1974a). *Education for critical consciousness.* London, England: Sheed and Ward.

Freire, P. (1974b). *Pedagogy of the oppressed.* New York, NY: Seabury Press.

Freire, P. (1985). *The politics of education: Culture, power, and liberation.* New York, NY: Bergin & Harvey.

Freire, P. (2002). *Pedagogy of the oppressed.* New York, NY: Continuum International.

Freire, P., & Macedo, D. (2005). *Literacy: Reading the word and the world.* London, England: Taylor and Francis.

Fu, D. (2003). *An island of English: Teaching ESL in Chinatown.* Portsmouth, NH: Heinemann.

Gay, G. (2010). *Culturally responsive teaching: Theory, research, and practice.* New York, NY: Teachers College Press.

Gee, J. (1996). *Social linguistics and literacy: Ideology on discourses.* London, England: Taylor & Francis.

Giff, P. Reilly. (2000). *Nory Ryan's song.* New York, NY: Delacorte Press.

Giroux, H. A. (2006). Theories of reproduction and resistance in the new sociology of education: Toward a critical theory of schooling and pedagogy for the opposition. In C. G. Robbins (Ed.), *The Giroux reader* (pp. 3–45). Boulder, CO: Paradigm.

González, N., Moll, L., & Amanti, C. (Eds.). (2005). *Funds of knowledge for teaching in Latino households.* Mahwah, NJ: Lawrence Erlbaum.

Greene, M. (1996). In search of critical pedagogy. In P. Leistyna, A. Woodrum, & S. Sherbloom (Eds.), *Breaking free: The transformative power of critical pedagogy* (pp. 13–30). Cambridge, MA: Harvard Educational Review [Reprint Series No. 27].

Halliday, M. (1975). *Learning how to mean.* New York, NY: Elsevier North Holland.

Hawkins, M., & Norton, B. (2009). Critical language teacher education. In A. Burns & J. Richards (Eds.), *Cambridge guide to second language teacher education* (pp. 30–39). Cambridge, England: Cambridge University Press.

Igoa, C. (1995). *The inner world of the immigrant child.* Mahwah, NJ: Lawrence Earlbaum.

Janks, H. (2010). *Literacy and power.* New York, NY: Routledge.

Jiménez, F. (1997). *The Circuit.* New York, NY: Houghton Mifflin.

Jiménez, F. (2001). *Breaking through.* New York, NY: Houghton Mifflin.

Kachru, B., Kachru, Y., & Nelson, C. L. (2006). *The handbook of world Englishes.* Oxford, England: Blackwell.

Kincheloe, J. L. (2008). *Critical pedagogy primer.* New York, NY: Peter Lang.

Leonardo, Z. (2004). Critical social theory and transformative knowledge: The functions of criticism in quality education. *Educational Researcher, 33,* 11–18.

Luke, A., O'Brien, J., & Comber, B. (2001). Making community texts objects of study. In H. Fehring & P. Green (Eds.), *Critical literacy* (pp. 112–113). Newark, DE: International Reading Association and Australian Literacy Educators' Association.

McIntosh, P. (1993). White privilege: Unpacking the invisible knapsack. In V. Cyrus (Ed.), *Experiencing race, class, and gender in the United States* (pp. 209–213). Mountain View, CA: Mayfield Publishing.

McKee, D. (2004). *The conquerors.* New York, NY: Handprint Books.

Norton, B. (2008). Identity, language learning, and critical pedagogies. In J. Cenoz, *Knowledge about language* (pp. 45–58). Vol. 6 of N. H. Hornberger (Ed.), *Encyclopedia of language and education* (2nd ed.). New York, NY: Springer.

Pennycock, A. (2007). *Global Englishes and transcultural flows.* London, England: Routledge.

Rosenblatt, L. M. (1978). *The reader, the text, the poem: The transactional theory of the literary work.* Carbondale: Southern Illinois University Press.

Shor, I. (1993). Education is politics. In P. Mc Laren & P. Leonard (Eds.), *Paulo Freire: A critical encounter.* New York, NY: Routledge.

Shor, I. (1996). *When students have power: Negotiating authority in a critical pedagogy.* Chicago, IL: University of Chicago Press.

Shor, I. (1999). What is critical literacy? In I. Shor & C. Pari (Eds.), *Critical literacy in action* (pp. 1–30). Portsmouth, NH: Heinemann.

TESOL/NCATE Teacher Standards Committee. (2010). *Standards for the recognition of initial TESOL programs in P–12 ESL teacher education.* (2010). Alexandria, VA: Teachers of English to Speakers of Other Languages.

Truscott, A., Daniel, M., & Rasmussen, M. (2015, March 28). *TESOL and Indigenous education in the U.S., Guatemala, and Australia.* Paper presented at the TESOL International Convention and English Language Expo, Toronto, Canada.

Valdés, G. (2001). *Learning and not learning English.* New York, NY: Teachers College Press.

Vygotsky, L. S. (1987). *Mind in society: The development of higher cognitive processes* (M. Cole, V. John-Steiner, S. Scribner, & E. Souberman, Eds.). Cambridge, MA: Harvard University Press.

Yashima, T. (1976). *Crow boy.* New York, NY: Puffin Books. (Original work published 1955)

PART II:
PEACEBUILDING AND ENGLISH LANGUAGE TEACHING

CHAPTER 4

Bringing Peacebuilding into the English Language Classroom

Valerie S. Jakar
Shaanan Academic College of Education

Alison Milofsky
United States Institute of Peace

n this chapter, we consider the intersection between peacebuilding and English language teaching. We begin by sharing our personal paths to peacebuilding and we then provide general guidelines for bringing peacebuilding into the classroom. We highlight examples of peacebuilding in practice to illustrate the implementation of these guidelines.

Introduction

What does it mean to teach peace? How do we engage language learners in difficult conversations around identity, conversations that encourage individual and group reflection and lead to social change? How do we privilege the stories of our students when those stories bring conflict front and center in our classrooms? As educators, we have to challenge ourselves to think through our assumptions, to open ourselves to multiple perspectives on tricky social and political topics in order to create a space that welcomes our students to do the same as we teach for peace.

Teaching peace is a commitment. It is hard and it is constant and at the same time it feeds the soul. Those who choose to bring peacebuilding into the classroom often have their own journey to share, as do the authors of this chapter. In order to understand the perspectives presented here, it is important for us, the authors, to share who we are and how we came to the work of social justice and peacebuilding (two overlapping concepts). Self-reflections are a critical step in engaging in social justice education. Knowing ourselves helps to create a mindfulness that encourages us to think about how we see and interact with our students and our peers around social issues. And this reflection can facilitate the creation of a space in which our students feel comfortable exploring who they are and how they fit in the world.

Alison Milofsky

Injustice anywhere is a threat to justice everywhere.

—*Martin Luther King Jr.*

My formal path to social justice and peacebuilding began when I served as a Peace Corps Volunteer in Slovakia from 1996 to 1998. While there, I developed a hyper-awareness of the discrimination the Roma face on a daily basis. For 2½ years I worked as a teacher trainer in the pedagogical faculty of a university, preparing my students to be English teachers. My own teacher education in a master's program in TESOL equipped me to teach these students the English language and to prepare them to teach others, but nothing in my past experience shaped my ability to address the discriminatory views of my students and my colleagues. My attempts at having rational conversations to address their othering of the Roma did nothing to shed light on the plight of the Roma or on my students' deep-seated prejudice. I needed a different knowledge base and a new set of skills to engage those around me in conversations about identity, othering, discrimination, and the conflicts that can arise when groups mistrust one another.

When I left the Peace Corps, I left the formal classroom as well and began working at a nonprofit organization that has, as part of its mission, prejudice awareness and reduction. My job included providing workshops for students and teachers on combating discrimination (Milofsky, 2014). What I learned from this work is that hate is not rational and, therefore, attempts at rational discussions to address hateful attitudes are ineffective. I also learned that empathy and understanding the lived experience of those different from ourselves is key in building relationships and breaking down barriers. Today, I try to incorporate this understanding as a facilitator of intergroup dialogues around race and gender for undergraduate students and conflict transformation trainings for emerging young civil society leaders in conflict zones.

Valerie Jakar

It is hard to imagine a more important task than the struggle for what Jewish tradition calls Tikkun Olam—the repair and healing of our world.

—*Shapiro, "Toward a Critical Pedagogy of Peace"*

More than 50 years ago, as a high school senior in London, England, I was introduced to the Council for Education in World Citizenship (CEWC), which was a United Nations–sponsored organization seeking to bring young people together in a learning situation. That early nurturing process, instilling into us an understanding that we, the privileged Westerners, should seek to reduce inequity in the world, has remained with me. Since that time, I have always been associated with UN entities and other social-responsibility oriented groups: as a student, as a teacher of ESOL, and as a member of a UNICEF educational development committee in Israel, where I have lived and worked for the last 35 years. Throughout my years in the teaching profession, inspired by colleagues such as teacher-educators Natalie Hess and Esther Lucas and folklorist Simon Lichman, I have sought to promote mutual understanding and appreciation among my peers, my students (and by association, their students), and my fellow teachers. The people who live in my region are known to be in an intractable conflict situation, with little movement toward political conciliation between Israel and the Palestinian Authority[1] over the last 20 years.

It was Amos Oz, a revered Israeli author, who asked, "What do you do when both sides are right?" (2002). In my role as teacher-educator and EFL specialist, I have striven to acknowledge that both "sides" may well be "right" and that it is my role to help them understand each others' "rights" and reasons. Within Israel there are conflicts of opinion on religious issues and practices among Jews, among the Christian sects, and among Islamic groups. In some sectors of our society, family conflicts have created horrible situations where lives are lost or bodies are mutilated. Within families and within schools, conflicts arise that cannot be resolved without help. In many of these situations it is the children who are harmed, either physically or emotionally (or both). I continue to try to create opportunities for encounters between individuals or groups of educators (mostly teachers of English) from different ethnic, national, or religious heritages, despite comments such as "That's ludicrous! Why bother when you are in an intractable situation?"

Over the years, despite the despondency and frustration felt by those who endeavored to create peacebuilding situations but failed, social justice–minded people, including many educators, continue to develop programs that aim to generate positive feelings, empathy, and an appreciation of "the other." As in our famous irrigation systems, the effect of small but regular input (the drip method) in a stable environment, with some boosts of positive influences (the fertilizer) such as learning about empathy, may be more effective than other, more erratic approaches. Thus, through a series of workshops or ongoing encounter programs, we have succeeded in establishing a sense of community among teachers of English who are driven, with passion, toward creating a community of understanding.

OUR CHARGE, OUR EXAMPLES

Our experiences provide you with a sense of the lenses through which we see the world. They also give you a sense of what informs our peacebuilding perspectives. Most important, by sharing pieces of our stories, we raise the notion that stories and personal experiences matter. We, as educators, must reflect on who we are and what stories we want to share with our colleagues and students. Sharing stories builds trust and contributes to understanding, allowing our students to see the humanity within us and inviting them, as well as ourselves, to see the humanity within others.

---

[1] Nomenclature is often tricky. Some refer to the two main opponents in the "Middle East struggle" as Jews and Arabs, some would note them as Israelis and Palestinians.

Peacebuilding as a Tool for Learning

Peacebuilding is a process of establishing peaceful relationships and building institutions that can manage conflict without resorting to violence. As such, peacebuilding occurs at multiple levels, ranging from intrapersonal and interpersonal to international. Peacebuilding is relevant in all contexts. It is not just the work of countries experiencing or emerging from violent conflict. Countries without violent conflict must work to secure structural peace, combating discrimination and seeking social justice and equality for all of its citizens.

Peace does not simply exist; rather, it is created through the work of individuals. The English language classroom can serve as a place of transformation, a space to engage youth in conversations around peace and conflict, to develop critical thinking skills as well as the skills that allow them to manage conflict, and to understand how they can participate in peacebuilding both individually and collectively.

The English language classroom can be a space for content-based curriculum rooted in social justice issues. Within such a curricular approach, conflict transformation and peacebuilding become the vehicle through which students learn English. The basic concepts and skills in conflict transformation and peacebuilding deal with reducing prejudice, building relationships, communicating effectively, and using negotiation to manage disagreements. With such closely aligned purposes, and since communication skills are a large part of language teaching, the English language classroom becomes a natural site for teaching peacebuilding.

What does it mean to have a peacebuilding lens in the classroom, to teach peacebuilding? And how do we teach peacebuilding? Teaching peacebuilding is not a step-by-step process but there are a few guidelines that can help you think about how to structure your classroom and frame your conversations with students in ways that contribute to peace. In essence, teaching peacebuilding is the application of good teaching practices (Milofsky et al., 2011).

Emphasize multiple perspectives. Conversations on difficult topics allow us to experience and learn different perspectives. It is, therefore, important for our students to develop the capacity to listen to one another and truly hear what each other has to say. In the process of conversation, disagreement may occur, but this provides students with an opportunity to clarify their own perspectives and consider how other people's views can inform opinions. Disagreement is natural and should be considered a healthy part of conversation. Learning to manage conflict is often about effectively dealing with disagreement before it escalates to violence.

Teach dialogue skills. Debate is a useful educational exercise and has a place in the classroom when discussing complex topics. However, the process of dialogue can contribute significantly to the classroom climate, encouraging an open mind and developing active listening skills. Unlike debate, which concludes with a winner and involves a process of listening for holes in the opponent's arguments, dialogue assumes there is no winner or loser. In the process of dialogue, listening is for the purpose of enhancing one's understanding of a topic and demonstrating that the listener hears the intended meaning.

Engage students in interactive lessons using creativity. The methods used to teach conflict management and peacebuilding focus on interaction between learners. These methods can include role play, small-group work, experiential activities, and large-group discussion. By using interactive strategies, educators are able move students from the abstract to the concrete, encouraging students to make decisions about how they will act when faced with conflict and what can be done to address conflicts beyond the interpersonal level.

Share real stories. It is important that students have the opportunity to share their stories and to hear the voices of other people whose lives have been affected by conflict. Stories can help clarify concepts that may otherwise seem elusive, making the abstract real. At a deeper level, real stories bring home the impact of conflict on individual lives by tapping into students' empathy.

Leave students feeling empowered. Difficult topics that involve human suffering can be overwhelming for any individual. It is important to alleviate any despair students might feel by helping them understand that they can take ownership of how they approach interpersonal conflicts. Teaching them these critical skills reveals to students that they have the possibility to empower themselves, that they can take action as an individual or as a community of young people, and that they can make a difference. These teaching practices can help English language teachers engage students in the conversations and skills development that will enhance their understanding of the "other." Peacebuilding is a process—an active process—that involves the work of individuals as well as of institutions. When educators provide the skills transfer that will allow their students to engage with the "other" and to communicate with one another to resolve differences, they are developing the capacity of their students to build peace while developing their own capacity as peacebuilders.

Peacebuilding in Practice: Social Justice Programs and Israeli Education

There is no one way to engage in education around peacebuilding. Below are a few examples drawn from the experiences of educators in Israel who have sought out opportunities to bridge the divide between students in schools and communities. In the examples below, Valerie shares some highlights of her work.

PROGRAMS FOR SCHOOLS

Currently, an online project, TEC (Technology, Education, and Cultural Diversity) is being developed that brings together schoolchildren, preservice educators (English teachers), schoolteachers and teachers' college faculty from Israel (for Hebrew and Arabic speakers), New Zealand, Holland, and Northern Ireland using English as

45

the language of communication (Shonfeld, Hoter, & Gayanim, 2012). The goals and the content of this project (meaningful topics of relevance to young people, including environment, individuals' communities, their places of worship, customs and rituals) are similar to a nondigital program that was used some 10 years ago in junior high schools where either Arabic or Hebrew (plus English) were the languages of instruction. The program of study was created for history or social studies classes. Two volumes of text were devoted to the major religions of the Holy City (Judaism, Christianity, and Islam). One volume was devoted to rites, rituals, customs, and festivals; the other was devoted to religious texts of the three faiths. The idea behind the project was that people would read about their own faith group as well as the two other faith groups.

A unit of study that became an ongoing program. We used the same (English) materials in an in-service education course for a multiethnic, multicultural group of teachers who worked toward creating a curriculum of mutual understanding—knowing the other and knowing oneself—on topics such as mourning, birth rituals, and rites of passage. While working collaboratively on the materials, the teachers became a cohesive group, sharing their stories, their songs, their fears, and their aspirations; several teachers instituted curricular changes in their EFL programs so that they could introduce materials and activities connected to multicultural education into their programs of teaching.

Two teachers took topics that were featured in their textbooks and expanded on them, bringing in global issues and, in one case, a comparative religion unit. The teachers were in regular *mamlachti* (secular national) schools, at the junior-high level, so they had to exercise some behavior management before they could engage in talking about the content; certain students displayed prejudice and sheer antagonism regarding particular faith groups. These sentiments were dispelled through mutual understanding activities in which games, simulations, and focus groups enabled the boys and girls to express their doubts and fears, as well as their hopes and desires.

Thus, a cohort of empathetic teachers of English who had been jettisoned from their safe curricular nest—known as the Approved Materials for Textbooks—into the often stereotype-holding audience succeeded in bringing about a change which, by dint of their tenacity, was perpetuated. Their students created an exhibition of presentations on artifacts and texts representing religions and customs of their own and others' cultures. This exhibition has become a regular feature of the school calendar of activities. There is now an annual exhibit and activity day focusing on the local community and its neighbors.

A college program. Participating in content-based EFL instruction programs, prospective elementary school teachers—native speakers of Arabic, Hebrew, Russian, and French—studied multicultural education, and mentoring, and mentorship. The core content was concerned with knowing the other and knowing oneself, or, as Stuart (2005) calls it, "honoring diversity." Another aspect of our work was the organization of seminars and other preservice and in-service education programs for teachers of English, where we succeeded in getting people together to talk about common concerns, both personal and professional, while creating products collaboratively that could subsequently be used in ESOL classrooms (Jakar, 2006; Jakar & Deeb, 2009; Jakar & Lucas, 2006). A welcome development of those seminars came about because of a fortuitous meeting between Valerie Jakar and Alison Milofsky at a Peace Forum that took place at the TESOL Annual Convention in 2003.

Over a period of 5 years, Milofsky supervised workshops and ongoing programs of work for ESOL teachers using peacebuilding training materials developed at the United States Institute of Peace. The teachers who engaged in the workshops and meetings were from Hebrew- or Arabic-speaking communities in Israeli, Jordanian, and Palestinian locales. The composition of the groups was eclectic: They included orthodox Jews, devout Muslims, and Catholic and Protestant Christians, all of whom were Israeli citizens. Collaboratively, the teachers modified the institute's materials to fit their own contexts. In working together toward a common goal they used the very skills they would eventually be teaching their students. The outcomes of these programs can be witnessed in the schools and the seminars where the students create presentations and mount displays of materials, classbooks, and letters sent from New Zealand, Bethlehem and Aman.

Conclusion

Peacebuilding is a process—an active process—that requires ongoing effort. Regardless of the level at which one works (at the individual level in the classroom or at the institutional level), the experience of self-reflection, of sharing one's humanity and seeing the humanity in others, of honoring each others' stories, of listening in dialogue and being open to a multiplicity of perspectives, creates spaces of possibility in which we can begin to realize peaceful relationships.

References

Deeb, I., & Jakar, V. S. (2009). The book after a book project: Aspects of teaching English as a foreign language. In D. Meier (Ed.), *Here's the story: Using narrative to promote young children's language and literacy learning* (pp. 92–106). New York, NY: Teachers College Press.

Dugan, M. A. (2003, October). Stable peace. In G. Burgess & H. Burgess (Eds.), *Beyond intractability*. Conflict Information Consortium, University of Colorado, Boulder. Retrieved from http://www.beyondintractability.org/essay/stable-peace

Jakar, V. S. (2006). Knowing the other through multicultural projects in school EFL programs. In G. H. Becket & P. C. Miller (Eds.), *Project-based second and foreign language education: Past, present, and future* (pp. 181–194). Chicago, IL: Age Publishing.

Jakar, V. S., & Lucas, E. (2006). Conflict resolution in a troubled region. In J. Campbell, N. Baikaloff, & C. Power (Eds.), *Education in the Asia-Pacific region: Issues, concerns and prospects. Vol. 7: Towards a global community* (Part II, pp. 179–198). Dordrecht, The Netherlands: Springer.

Milofsky, A. (2012). A place of transformation: The role of education in peacebuilding. *Worldview Magazine, 25*(2), 23–24.

Milofsky, A. (2014, June 2). Bringing peacebuilding into the English language classroom [Virtual seminar]. TESOL International.

Milofsky, A. (2011). *Peacebuilding toolkit for educators.* Washington, DC: USIP Press. Available at http://www.buildingpeace.org/train-resources/educators/peacebuilding -toolkit-educators

Oz, Amos. (2002). Between right and right. In *How to cure a fanatic* (pp. 1–35). Princeton, NJ: Princeton University Press.

Shapiro, S. (2002). Towards a critical pedagogy of peace. In G. Salomon & B. Nevo (Eds.), *Peace education: The concept, principles and practices around the world.* New York, NY: Lawrence Erlbaum.

Shonfeld, M., Hoter, E., & Ganayim, A. (2012). TEC Center: Linking technology, education and cultural diversity. *Journal of Educational Technology, 9*(1), 15.

Stuart, J. (2005). Prejudice in the ESL classroom. *TESL Canada Journal, 23*(1), 63–75.

CHAPTER 5

Tension and Harmony

Language Teaching as a Peacebuilding Endeavor

Eastern Mennonite University

In a high-energy performance in 2002, Palestinian Mira 'Awad and Israeli Noa wrestled back and forth with the lyrics of the 1965 Lennon and McCartney hit "We Can Work It Out." Whether the song represents a quarrel between lovers, friends, or even enemies, the heated dialogue signals that stubborn opinions may lead to a permanent separation. Yet hope that things can be worked out persistently flairs up as the title words of the song get repeated at the end of each stanza. As the singers dueled with each other, their bodies were alive with the tension—the optimism and the pessimism—that Lennon and McCartney built into the song, as in their very genes they represented the divisive tensions of the Israeli-Palestinian conflict. Yet all the while they created beautiful harmonies.[1]

Like these two singers, artists, musicians, and actors use their art forms to promote peace without sacrificing the quality of their art. From the iconic anti-war singers of the 1960s and 1970s (Pete Seeger, Judy Collins, John Lennon, and others) to classical musicians in the United Kingdom who play benefit concerts for peace and disarmament to the worldwide network of musicians who "play for change," the passion that peace-loving artists pour into their work may enhance its beauty and impact. Although there may be some fans who wish their favorite musicians would stay of out of politics, most would not be surprised to find artists making music for the cause of peace.

Why should the same not be true for language teachers? Should we not expect people who love other languages and cultures to make peacebuilding an important part of their work? Although there are socially aware teachers within the English language teaching profession, many may not regularly integrate peace and social justice

---

[1] A performance of this song can be viewed on Youtube https://www.youtube.com/watch?v =1FwRyaTvnYg. Mira 'Awad is an Israeli Arab/Palestinian singer, actor, and songwriter and Noa is an Israeli Jewish singer and peace activtist.

content into their daily lessons. In fact, some think or act as if English language teachers should teach only language—period. (e.g., see Gadd, 1998). Publishers of materials for ELT rigorously follow a set of rules summarized by the acronym PARSNIP, which means "no politics, alcohol, religion, sex, narcotics, isms, or pork" (Thornbury, 2010). To ensure marketability across a wide range of countries, published materials should avoid controversial issues, and peacebuilding has political implications that could negatively affect profitability. The result is "what Mario Rinvolucri once characterised as 'the soft, fudgy, sub-journalistic, woman's magaziney world of EFLese course materials'" (as cited in Thornbury, 2010). Some language teachers may believe that by focusing on language learning, teaching a culture, and facilitating travel, they are doing their part for world peace; they may not feel the need to go further to incorporate peacebuilding knowledge, skills, and values into their courses.

A possible reason some language teachers do not permit the music of peace to penetrate more deeply into their teaching is that peacebuilding is not a significant part of their identity. Some people yearn more intensely than others for human well-being and flourishing and have educated themselves in peace and conflict studies. They realize that conflict is normal because it arises from human diversity, and it provides opportunities for creativity and growth. Equipped with an understanding of peace dynamics, they develop a deeper commitment to explore with their students ways to transform conflicts so that relationships do not dissolve into a cacophony of divisions, where communication is cut off, understanding diminished, the truth distorted, and injustice multiplied. A peaceable language teacher shudders at the cycle of violence these circumstances portend.

No matter how single-mindedly a teacher yearns for peace, there is much more to identity than a single dimension like peacebuilding. Identities are complex, multi-layered things. After surveying the literature on identities, Day, Kington, Stobart, and Sammons (2006) offered this summary: "[I]dentities are a shifting amalgam of personal biography, culture, social influence and institutional values which may change according to role and circumstance" (p. 613). Personal, institutional, and professional elements enter into the construction of an identity (Sammons et al., 2007). Data from a study, "Variations in Teachers' Work, Lives and their Effects on Pupils (VITAE)" in the United Kingdom (Sammons et al., 2007), indicate that for long-time teachers personal identity tends to be more fully integrated with professional identity (see Day, Kongton, Stobart, & Sammons, 2006, pp. 605–606). Focused in part on the exploration of links between teachers' identities and the effects on student learning, VITAE sees "identity [as] a key influencing factor on teachers' sense of purpose, self-efficacy, motivation, commitment, job satisfaction and effectiveness" (Day et al., 2006, p. 601). Because we teach out of who we are, including personal and professional values that are central for us, a commitment to peace will be a "key influencing factor" for some teachers.

Therefore, it becomes impossible to discuss identity fruitfully without a "thick narrative" of a teacher's life. Identity is always evolving; we construct and reconstruct our identities in every interaction we have with individuals, social aggregates, and institutions. I can illustrate how peacebuilding emerged as a part of my identity by narrating briefly how I began to develop as a peaceable language teacher.

Identity Narrative

It was a Tuesday morning—shortly after 7:30—and I was the first to arrive at the Intensive English Program (IEP) of Eastern Mennonite University (EMU) in Harrisonburg, Virginia. Classes would not begin until 8:30, so all was quiet as I checked e-mail and started my work for the day. Since my office was located upstairs, I barely heard the office coordinator and students enter the house. When I came downstairs just before 9 a.m., the television in our commons room was on, showing pictures of the New York City skyline and smoke billowing from the north tower of the World Trade Center. In less than 5 minutes, the small gathering of students and staff witnessed along with me the traumatic scenes of a second airplane smashing into the south tower and, about 90 minutes later, the collapse of the north tower.

I had accepted a position as director of the IEP just 2 years prior. The university's commitment to a pacifist position rooted in the Christian faith drew me here. In the words of EMU's mission statement:

> We invite each person to follow Christ's call to
> bear witness to faith,
> serve with compassion, and
> walk boldly in the way of nonviolence and peace.
> (Eastern Mennonite University [EMU], 2014b)

Although I had grown up in a Protestant church that held a "just war" position, for years I had affiliated myself with the minority pacifist advocacy group of my denomination. For years I had screened my investments to avoid supporting the military-industrial complex and used charitable giving as a tool for reducing my liability to paying taxes in support of that complex. I had even begun exposing first-year college writing students to questions about the legitimacy of war through novels and films that were woven into my college writing courses. I had not, however, systematically thought about how I might integrate peacebuilding into my professional practice as an English language teacher. I viewed EMU as the perfect place to begin doing this, though in 2001 I had barely gotten started on the task. The horrors of September 11 added new urgency to this project.

The aftermath of that event brought several changes at EMU. First, our Conflict Transformation master's program began to enroll record numbers of international students from conflict hot spots around the world, most them on Fulbright scholarships. The IEP began offering writing tutorials to these graduate students. As the chief tutor, I read students' analyses of conflicts in their home countries: Nepal, Sri Lanka, the former Yugoslavia, Afghanistan, Kenya, Israel, and Palestine. Working with them on their papers and reading some of the books that they recommended, I gained an informal education in peace and conflict studies.

A second important change that came to EMU was a large grant from Church World Service to establish a trauma-training program to serve caregivers, peace practitioners, and civil society leaders of all faiths (Yoder & Barge, 2011). The Seminars in Trauma Awareness and Resilience (STAR) program began bringing to our campus, several times a year, cohorts of participants from conflict spots all over the world who were seeking training. Initial cohorts included caregivers who directly experienced the chaos and losses in New York City and Arlington, Virginia, on 9/11 as well as Kenyan victims of the bombing of the U.S. Embassy in Nairobi in 1998. In the first 5 years of the program, my colleague Carolyn Yoder facilitated more than 50 week-long training sessions "with nearly 800 people from more than 60 countries" (Yoder & Barge, 2011).

Meanwhile more terror sprang up in the world. In spite of massive demonstrations in the United States and around the world, even in spite of the protest of Pope John Paul II, the Bush administration staged its invasion of Iraq in March 2003. My determination to work for peace intensified. I began to increase my charitable giving—again to deny every tax dollar that I could to the U.S. war machine—and to funnel even more of it to causes that promoted "bringing people together to solve conflicts with words, rather than weapons" (EMU, 2014a). These developments in my personal life would soon begin spilling into professional life because, as Day et al. (2006) write, "teaching demands significant personal investment" (p. 603), and so personal experiences and the sense of identity arising from those play a key role in the professional lives of teachers.

To usher me into the next stage of my development as a peaceable English language teacher, two different groups of persons traumatized by conflict entered my life. One group was the Kurdish immigrants in our town who had fled northern Iraq after the 1991 Gulf War as the regime of Saddam Hussein exacted revenge on the Kurds for the uprising staged with the encouragement, but not the sustained support, of the U.S. government. Many members of our Kurdish community had family members who perished in chemical attacks and whose houses had been bulldozed multiple times by Iraqi authorities. In 2005, four Kurdish men in our community were arrested by the FBI in a series of raids that retraumatized all the Kurdish families in our area, people who had already fled the terrors wreaked by Saddam Hussein. They were charged with felony violations of the (so-called) USA Patriot Act for operating unlicensed money-transfer businesses. One of the men charged and one of his relatives had studied in our IEP, a circumstance that prodded me to join with others in organizing the community (Brulliard, 2006; Shenk, 2008). Many community members agreed that these arrests were part of the general hysteria ensuing from September 11. We rallied the community to stand with our Kurdish neighbors, garnering so much support that the judge in the case publicly acknowledged our efforts and denied the prosecution the stiff penalties being demanded.

The second influential group comprised students in our IEP who had suffered personal traumas: a Kurdish man who barely escaped being buried alive by the Iraqi military; a torture survivor from the Salvadoran civil war; a refugee from the Rwandan genocide; a Kurdish woman whose witnessing of unnamed atrocities emotionally wrecked her. In each case, my staff and I were bewildered about how to help these people whose psychological traumas profoundly affected their ability to learn a new language. We suspected that we should be taking a different kind of teaching approach with them, but we were clueless about what that should be.

By 2008, I finally received the decisive push I needed to focus on appropriate ELT approaches for trauma-affected students. I received an invitation from the English Language Specialist Office of the U.S. State Department to conduct two weeks of workshops for English teachers in Kosovo. An immigrant from the former Yugoslavia, who developed materials for EMU's STAR program for youth (Hart, 2007), mentored me as I designed workshops for Kosovar teachers who endured the traumatic events of 1999, when Serbian police, militias, and military forces attempted to cleanse the territory of its ethnic Albanian majority. Designing and conducting those workshops motivated me to enroll in STAR to learn as much as I could about trauma induced by violence.

The development of the peacebuilding motif in my identity as an ELT professional began in a rather abstract way in my personal life, opposing militarism and war based on my religious faith. The involvement of my country in escalating the violence in Iraq and Afghanistan in the first decade of this century sharpened my responses, just as bloodshed in Syria, Yemen, or Nigeria sparks new peacebuilding impulses in younger English language teachers today. I made decisions to support peace that were limited to my personal affairs and only gradually improvised my commitments to peace so that they began to sound in my professional life. In my role as IEP director, when I encountered persons affected by violence, my rather general commitment to pacifist principles involved human faces. Those encounters drove me to learn more about the roots and fruits of violence. I discovered that by attending to the shocks that learners have experienced through encountering violence—from overt forms of violence to dysfunctional relationships, personal indignities, or unjust social structures—I could begin addressing the prevention of violence.

The shocks of life, including but not limited to clinically diagnosed post-traumatic stress disorder (PTSD), are part of the cycle of violence. People are created in such a way that violence jolts them, and the shocks that they receive may reverberate to produce more violence. Those who are trauma-affected may inflict violence on themselves in the form of unhealthy behaviors such as substance abuse or high-risk behaviors (Levine & Kline, 2007; Yoder, 2005); or, acting out of anger at the shocks they have suffered, they may pursue revenge against those who perpetrated the violence (Bayer, Klasen, & Adam, 2007). They may displace angry feelings onto family members or co-workers (Hinton, Rasmussen, Nou, Pollack, & Good, 2009), and they may pass their resentments and thirst for revenge to the next generation (Audergon, 2004). Groups of people who share a collective experience of being violated feel a solidarity with one another that can have a magnifying effect on aggressive behavior toward perceived enemies, fueling large-scale disruption of peace (Audergon, 2004; Volkan & Fowler, 2009). Violence is a vicious circle that we must break.

In the work of bringing hope, restoration, and healing to traumatized persons, I have found a satisfactory way of envisioning a role for English language teachers in peacebuilding. The elements that I learned while preparing for Kosovo provided the basic tunes for which I continue to improvise a peaceable approach to English language teaching: maintain a sense of safety in the classroom; build a sense of community; allow teachers and learners space to mourn their traumas; foster creative problem solving, especially in relation to conflicts; and open up to learners all avenues of knowing and expression by taking a multiple intelligences approach to teaching (Medley, 2009a, 2010, 2012, in press). In other words, the approach for integrating peace into my teaching has become more of a compassionate concern for the needs of learners, including concern about the shape of the future for them and their children, than a passionate pacifist protest against a militaristic state.

Orientations and Approaches— Communal, Intercultural, and Critical

To begin living the song of peaceable language teaching and harmonizing with it, the first step is to recognize the culture that learners bring into the classroom. Convinced that culture plays an important role in language learning, I have begun to understand that culture includes the personal, social, and political histories of learners and their ancestors. I realize now that "young learners are not disembodied cognitive devices for processing language input, but persons with histories. They are the products of what they have seen, heard, smelled, touched, acted on, and been subjected to—as well as the products of their ancestors' experiences" (Medley, 2012a, p. 112). These complex, multilayered, mysterious beings with their needs and aspirations, with whom we enter into relationship, become the center of the class. Whether they manifest any sense of victimization or not, they have endured their share of tensions. Teachers need to remain open to hearing the stories that these learners have to share—even if this might interrupt the flow of the lesson that has been planned for the day. This is one way of showing compassion for what learners have experienced.

In Osh, Kyrgyzstan, in 2013, Betsy Becker's class for English teachers listened to the song "Fragile" by British singer and social activist Sting (Gordon Matthew Thomas Sumner). Because Becker was open to her students' past traumas, she welcomed their interest in relating the lyrics of the song to interethnic violence that had occurred in their city three years before. She followed up this heavy discussion with a lively physical activity that simulates chaos, which breathed laughter into the class and, afterward, allowed participants to reflect on the similarities between the activity and traumatic situations in life (personal communication).

Paula Huntley (2003) showed similar compassion toward her intergenerational class of Kosovar Albanians who had suffered the horrors of attempted ethnic cleansing two years before. Huntley allowed learners to share their stories through speaking and writing, whether these stories were part of her original lesson plan or not. She instituted a Hemingway book club, where her students very naturally identified with the suffering and the courageous persistence of the protagonist in *The Old Man and the Sea*.

CLASS LETTER WRITING

One activity that I have found effective for creating a caring ethos is a class letter-writing activity that a teacher can manage with even 20 to 40 students (see Medley, 1999). The teacher begins by outlining the procedure for the activity in a letter to the class. An excerpt from that first letter might read like the following:

> About 7 times during this semester you will write me a letter about 250 to 500 words in length. Most of the time, I will give you some questions to answer. Most of the questions will be the same for everyone in the class; sometimes I may ask questions specifically for you as an individual. In addition to answering my questions, you may feel free to write whatever you want.
>
> You will write your letters in an electronic forum. At first, your letters will be private—just between me and you. When I answer the letters, I will compose one letter for the whole class. In my letter, I might mention topics that you bring up or even quote your words.
>
> You will write your next letter in response to my letter to the whole class. Later on in the semester, we could move to a forum where all the letters may be read by every member of the class, but only if that is agreeable to you.

I pose questions to the class to find out their interests, their history as readers and writers, and the challenges they feel in relation to particular assignments. I stay alert for topics students raise that can be turned into questions. For example, when a student asked me about study strategies to help her succeed, I turned that into a prompt: *What study strategies do you find most helpful?* When another commented that it was hard for him to keep his motivation strong, I received excellent responses to the questions *"What do you do to maintain your motivation? What do you do to help yourself when you are discouraged or frustrated? What are some of the blessings you have experienced that give you strength?"* The last of these hints at the importance of having students consider the sources of their resilience.

While traditional letters are less common than in the past, students respond positively to this assignment. As one student, Amina,[2] wrote: "Writing these letters brought us together and made good friends of the people in this class. . . . Knowing what they think can lead to a friendship and respect. For me i [*sic*] would love to do these letters and share it with others. It just makes my life much easier inside and outside of college. . . . I don't read these letters because I have to but I read them for myself to learn from others." The private letters that students write offer them the opportunity to say whatever they want to the teacher. After just a few letter exchanges,

---

[2] Names have been changed. Excerpts from the letters are quoted with the permission of students.

Amina has learned the powerful effects of the letters in creating a sense of mutual respect, friendship, and a community of learning.

She has also quickly perceived that the letters are an expression of care for her and her classmates, as illustrated in her third letter of the semester: "I'm going through the hardest time in my life because of the difficulties I'm facing at home (I really don't want you to share this with my classmates but I really needed to tell you this). . . . I think the writing class is the only class that I feel there are people who care about me and support me." These responses were spontaneous, unprompted. She came into the class having endured many hardships as a teenager in wartime Iraq. She found in her ESL writing class a culture of compassion that responded sensitively and did not ignore the culture that she brought with her in all its rich and heart-wrenching complexity.

INTERPRETIVE FLEXIBILITY IN CONFLICT

The letter activity is one way of acknowledging the cultures that students bring to the classroom while building a caring community. Another way is to give students opportunities to explore what matters to them, the artifacts of culture that they distract themselves with (entertainment media, fashion, food, etc.) and to help them move beyond the superficial to discern how these things affect relationships with others. Conflict is an inescapable part of relationships. Students know this fact well—from conflict with parents, siblings, friends, and lovers extending to conflicts between neighborhoods, ethnic groups, and nations. What they know and care about can draw them into deeper engagement with the new linguistic knowledge and skills they are acquiring (Smith, DeYoung, Uyaguari, & Avila, 2007; Stevick, 1996).

An important step in dealing with conflict in relationships is to cultivate a deep appreciation for the complexity and mystery of human beings. Language learning itself represents an encounter with mystery, complexity, and ambiguity: *Did my word choice and syntax convey the right meaning? Did I understand what my interlocutor really intended to convey?* Therefore, a language teacher who highlights the value of doubting and of developing interpretive flexibility in connection with language learning can naturally extend that to interpersonal relations, thus dissuading students from thinking about relational conflicts in black-and-white terms. Critical language educators call for instruction that de-emphasizes the use of questions with clear-cut, right-and-wrong answers, that prepares students to "recognize and respect" diverse perspectives on issues, and that develops skill in interpretive flexibility (Akbari, 2008; Kumaravadivelu, 2003). Teachers can choose from many activities to help students stretch their ability to entertain doubts and be more flexible in their interpretation of human behaviors.

STRATEGIES FOR WELCOMING DIVERSITY WHILE MAINTAINING SAFETY

General strategies for welcoming diversity in ways that are safe and peaceable include the following:

- Build community through a variety of activities.

- Ask open-ended questions that don't have right or wrong answers.

- Maintain flexibility to allow for students' personal stories when they emerge (but never forced).

- Use various artistic media (music, visual arts, mime, film clips, etc.) to create interpretive tasks and ensure that diverse viewpoints are expressed and respected.

- Invite or introduce other voices into the classroom.

Possible activities for implementing these strategies are numerous; here are five suggestions.

1. Use icebreakers on a regular basis to introduce an element of lightness into the class and to expand personal knowledge among class members.

2. Use games, interviews, and surveys in the classroom that prompt learners to appreciate the diversity of persons in the class—even what could be interpreted as contradictions within persons.

3. Discuss critical incidents. Give students a certain amount of information about an intercultural encounter and ask them to provide diverse interpretations of the encounter, without suggesting that there is "one correct answer." Snow (2001) explains clearly how to use critical incidents, while Storti (1994) provides a collection of incidents to discuss.

4. Use pictures or other visuals that naturally require interpretation: Different beholders see different things in a picture. Using portraits of persons unknown to the students (e.g., upstanding civic leaders or corrupt politicians from other locales or cultures), elicit from the students the personal qualities they discern in the portraits. Unlike with the critical incidents, the teacher knows that the person has done noteworthy things, both good and bad; the students do not yet know this. After offering their interpretation of the portraits, students can do a webquest to find out information to confirm and disconfirm their interpretations of the portraits.

5. Arrange for students to meet, or invite into class for interviews or storytelling, persons who represent marginalized groups, views on topics that diverge from the dominant view of the class, or even groups perceived as hostile (Bierling, 2007). Prepare the class by teaching them and showing them what it means to listen respectfully to those with a different viewpoint. Smith, DeYoung,

Uyaguari, and Avila (2007) use biographical narratives in their language teaching because narratives help bring the meaning of our lives into focus. Although literary texts may have the potential for affecting learners' responses to "others," they do not provide the same ethical motivations as stories of real persons do. Even grammar study, based on the voice of a real person, receives added motivation when students read the story of a person with whom they can empathize, Smith claims. If students fail to use their grammatical knowledge properly, they risk misunderstanding the story of a marginalized person who now has a chance to speak to them (Smith et al., 2007). Access to the vast collection of video and print material on the Internet makes it easy for teachers in ethnolinguistically homogenous schools to invite diverse persons into the classroom, but a text or video image can never substitute for interaction with a real person, because then the relationship becomes two-way. Skype or Zoom could be a way to allow more interaction with these "other voices."

Engaging in activities such as the ones described above, while building up a sense of community, plants a seed in students' minds that they cannot be sure about who people really are. There is much about other people's experiences that remains unknown until people reveal that information. These seeds of doubt need to be tended and nurtured so that students learn to question their first perceptions of others and appreciate how those perceptions are rooted in certain habits of thought and the prejudices about others they have acquired. Prejudices and stereotypes fuel conflicts and are used to justify violence. The language classroom might show how the walls that divide us can be torn down. Language learning itself is an activity that gives us access to people and viewpoints that may not be represented in our culture. When language teachers are attuned to peace, they guide learners in exploring human diversity and revering all beings.

CRITICAL APPROACHES CREATE TENSIONS

Some of the activities described above will create mild tensions in the classroom. For example, in critical incident and picture activities, class members will disagree on how they perceive and evaluate people and situations. These relatively low-stakes disagreements provide opportunities for practicing respectful ways of discussing differences. Tensions may rise in the higher stakes activities that challenge stereotypes by exposing students to marginalized voices. Hearing those voices may arouse dissonances for some class members who feel a sense of loss or threat in letting go cherished stereotypes, learning that what has been taught or modeled in their home may be wrong and that they should relate in a more understanding (if not charitable) way with persons whom they have been taught to ignore, suspect, or hate. The peaceable language teacher, however, finds ways to make room for marginalized persons and voices in course materials (Akbari, 2008). The voices we least want to hear are those that we despise or reject, the voices of our enemies, and yet we must eventually open our ears even to those voices. Peaceable language teachers work to orchestrate these tensions to create harmony.

Because it challenges the widespread belief that violent actions can be redemptive, peace education is necessarily a critical and experiential endeavor. Students may come to class with beliefs such as "the only way to stop a bad guy with a gun is a good guy with a gun" or "we can only achieve peace by *eliminating them*." They learn these principles, not from current affairs programming on public television, but from the potent world of Hollywood films: from *The Hobbit* (2012–2014), *The Hunger Games* (2012–2015), *Inglourious Basterds* (2009), and *War Horse* (2011) (Lavender, 2015). Language teachers concerned about the connection between trauma and violence should be prepared to adopt approaches informed by critical pedagogy. These approaches may include content-based learning that raises awareness about conflict, styles of conflict management, the effects of individual and collective trauma, the cycle of violence, and issues of justice, truth, forgiveness, and reconciliation. Materials published by the U.S. Institute of Peace (USIP) and edited by Alison Milofsky (2011) cover many of the basic concepts of conflict transformation through experiential activities using topics that young people can relate to, but also provide suggestions for stretching them to consider international conflicts. Experiential teaching and learning can be one of the most effective ways of integrating language and peace education. This kind of teaching is especially effective for learners who have born the negative effects of conflict. USIP's *Peacebuilding Toolkit for Educators* (Milofsky, 2011) is freely downloadable in both middle and high school editions. Experienced ESL/EFL teachers will be able to integrate the activities described in these books with language teaching objectives.

TEACHING LANGUAGE AND PEACE ETHICALLY

Part of the tension in being a peacebuilding language teacher is maintaining the integrity of the class as a language class by fully integrating language teaching with the concerns of peace education. If the class is not billed as a language class with a "peace and conflict studies" theme, it would be unfair to students to make the class into that. Negotiating this tension skillfully, however, can allow the harmonies of peace to swell in the lives of learners.

First, we can articulate our justification for including moral and ethical content related to peacebuilding in our language courses. We must be prepared to answer the criticism of some colleagues (and skepticism of students) who insist that the focus should be on language and not on the inner life of learners or their moral responsibilities in the world (Gadd, 1998). The view that linguistic knowledge and skills should be the sole focus seems close to the instrumentalism that Freire (2005) and Macedo (1994) so incisively critiqued in literacy teaching. Once we consider learners as whole persons, then political, social, moral, and spiritual issues come into relief, and values such as nonviolence, justice, or peace become naturally salient. Doug Brown, a steady and credible voice in ELT, asserts that "the objectives of a curriculum are not limited to linguistic factors alone, but also include developing the art of critical thinking" about complex social, moral, or ethical issues (2007, p. 515). In fact, including contro-versial issues in the English language classrooms can lead to "intrinsically motivating content-based language learning" (Brown, 2009, p. 267).

Brown's comment accentuates the idea that every language curriculum requires content. Underlying content is a moral supposition. Smith (2009), for example, refers to the "thinly veiled consumerism of communicative language textbooks" (p. 243)—namely, content that enables language learners to become participants in "the market." Learners, however, are much more than "economic units." They are whole persons who (among other things) engage in conflicts as a part of their everyday life, who have developed particular conflict styles, who are able to manage conflicts more or less well, and who are members of social groups and nations naturally in conflict with other groups and nations. Teachers have a moral responsibility to deal with their learners as whole persons in a world more complex than the commercial one.

The teaching of whole learners must be rooted in their reality. Wholeness takes into account the whole reality faced by learners and the history that they bring to the classroom—including conflicts in which they may be enmeshed. There may be some pragmatic benefits of bracketing off parts of learners' lives to avoid arousing conflict or strong emotions in the classroom. However, in the long run, the benefits of suppress-ing conflict or emotions are outweighed by the benefits of acknowledging learners' particular life histories and situations. The kind of education that brackets off these sometimes "troubling parts" of learners' lives may be one that reproduces structures of inequality and oppresses people, disempowering them because it denies them the tools for addressing and possibly changing their reality. If education brackets off the harms done by violence, then by default it affirms the status quo for the victims and trauma-affected.

In a language classroom oriented toward communication where conflict is part of the curriculum, the peaceable language teacher naturally has the opportunity to orchestrate discussion that is respectful and tolerant of others views. As Brown confirms, language teachers are "responsible for creating an atmosphere of respect," creating a classroom that becomes "a model of the world as a context for tolerance and for the appreciation of diversity" (2009, p. 267), a model of civil discourse. O'Donnell-Allen (2011) carefully defines "civil discourse" as a "thoughtful and thought-provoking exploratory" conversation about "culturally relevant" issues in which the participants recognize the complexity of the issues and "respectfully acknowledge a range" of views and demonstrate an "intentionally empathic" attitude toward others' views (p. 12). She goes on to make the interesting argument that "engaging in civil discourse about culturally sensitive topics is one way of enacting social justice in and of itself . . . [because] language use is itself a form of social action." Quoting Holtgraves (2002), she contends that "to use language . . . is an attempt to alter the world in some way . . . or to commit oneself to a particular depiction of the world" (p. 13). Because of the connection between social justice and peace, O'Donnell-Allen's argument can be extended to peace education in language class-rooms. (See activities 1 & 2 below.)

STRATEGIES FOR TEACHING LANGUAGE AND PEACE ETHICALLY

Some general strategies for promoting critical thinking in caring and ethical ways include the following:

- Model and teach the elements of civil discourse.

- Work to create more egalitarian classroom structures (Harris & Morrison, 1999; Wasson, Anderson, & Suriani, 1999), giving learners opportunities to lead and to feel their voices being respected.

- Use experiential learning opportunities (even ones that arise unexpectedly) to develop moral courage in learners.

- Let the teacher take the role of learner to model for the class how one learns compassion by working with victims of violence who deserve or thirst for compassion.

Implementing strategies to promote critical thinking in caring and ethical ways is a challenging task. The six activities below exemplify that challenge.

1. Give students "tough texts" to read and discuss, i.e., ones that evoke disagreement (O'Donnell-Allen, 2011), with the object of training learners in the art of civil discourse, a way of dealing with conflict that should lead to understanding and not violence. Peaceable language teachers can actively work with students to instantiate this kind of discourse in the classroom. Some suggestions made by O'Donnell-Allen could be adapted for ESL classrooms. Teachers can provide some sentence frames that help learners realize the following speech acts:

   - Disagreeing with or challenging an assertion

   - Drawing into the discussion someone who has withheld comments

   - Responding with (a) an appreciative comment followed by (b) a statement of one's own point of view

   - Respectfully recognizing a range of views

   - Recapping in one's own words a summary of the perspective that another student has just shared in such a way that the speaker can agree with the summary

   These are the kinds of rules for civil discussions that can be taught along with some of the activities mentioned in the previous section, for example, in negotiating different interpretations of critical incidents or pictures and interacting with visiting presenters who may sometimes represent controversial viewpoints.

2. "Disrupt the traditional teacher-student hierarchy" (O'Donnell-Allen, 2011, p. 93) by tasking learners with formulating written norms for their discussions. Learners can be asked to define "controversy/controversial," to distinguish between "argument" and "disagreement," and to describe more specifically

what "respectful verbal behavior/response" looks like. When a student violates a norm or claims that a norm has been violated, then the class members can adjudicate the violation.

3. Explore the difference between aggressive and assertive language (see Bartel, 1999). It is appropriate to use assertive language in dealing with conflicts. Assertive language is honest, direct, and respectful. It is firmly polite and centered on facts related to the issue at conflict. The user of assertive language owns his or her feelings and opinions on the issue without denigrating those who disagree. Aggressive language, by contrast, is designed to put down, humiliate, and dominate others. It is characterized by exaggeration and an accusatory tone. It is more evaluative than factual and comes across as an attack on the ones who disagree with the speaker. Leadership psychologist Cedric Johnson (2013) suggests these analogies that students might begin with as they consider the difference: "aggressiveness is like wrestling; assertiveness is like a dance." The teacher can continue by presenting a series of short scenarios and asking students to formulate two contrasting responses: an aggressive response and an assertive response. Because language teaching is a cross-cultural endeavor, it is important for teachers to help their students explore the boundaries of assertiveness and aggressiveness in their respective cultures.

4. Help learners acquire critical language awareness by doing a comparative close reading of news reports from different perspectives (Kumaravadivelu, 2003) or by comparing visuals. An English teacher in Karachi, Pakistan, Asima Ali (2014) presents her students with contrasting pictures, "one exhibiting serenity and happiness and the other displaying strife and turmoil" (p. 24). She takes the learners through a carefully devised set of activities, eliciting comments from them on various aspects of the two pictures, beginning with objective descriptions, which require the use of accurate nouns, verbs, and adjectives; moving on to a discussion of the emotions and behaviors that promote peace or inflame conflict; and culminating with a discussion of steps required for resolving conflicts, from the very particular one depicted in her visual to conflicts on the national and international level.

5. Exercise students' listening and speaking skills through creating conflict scenarios, role playing them, and then analyzing the conflicts. These should be conflicts that are relevant for students. Sample topics may include these: (a) Students are given a group project to work on, and two strong personalities in the group want the project to go in different directions; (b) A school plans to implement a policy requiring all students to wear a uniform, and students are divided in their opinions; (c) A student has strong reservations about the family's plan for him/her to study engineering. The materials produced by Milofsky (2011) give additional ideas for conflict scenarios If class brainstorming does not yield good results.

6. Teach the skills of conflict analysis (Milofsky, 2011). In a workshop, "Healing the Wounds of Partition," C. G. Modi asks eighth graders in Mumbai, India, to work in groups to depict their perspective on the bloody separation of India and Pakistan in 1949. Each group creates its own tableau by freezing their bodies. These "freeze frames" (Modi, 2014) become the topic for discussion as the viewers give their interpretations of each tableau. He asks the students tough questions such as these:

> "Were Hindus and Muslims the only two communities that suffered during the Partition of 1947? Do we blame the British only because we do not want to take responsibility for our own actions? Is healing truly possible after the intensity of what happened?" (p. 22)

Modi's approach illustrates some of the ideas already presented. He uses a critical pedagogy approach. He brings up a conflict that is distant in time from his eighth-grade learners but which continues to affect their lives in ways they may not realize. The freeze-frame activity not only affords an alternative means of expression and an occasion for interpretive flexibility, but it also provides the class a chance to practice the elements of civil discourse on a tough topic (O'Donnell-Allen, 2011).

Exploring/Enjoying the Tensions from which Harmony Ultimately Emerges

The tensions involved in living out one's identity as a peaceable language teacher provide opportunities for professional and personal growth. Professional growth occurs as teachers notice how the diverse cultures from which students come influence their assessment of behavior as peaceable or not. What appears aggressive or passive aggressive to the teacher may appear peaceable to the student. Learning through interactions with students is one of the most enjoyable tensions teachers experience, since they often enter the profession because they want to be lifelong learners.

The tension between teaching language and fostering peacebuilding skills presents the teacher with a dissonance to resolve. Students must not experience peacebuilding as a distraction from language learning. This tension drives the teacher to discover the linguistic correlates of peacebuilding skills that will be useful to students in their lives beyond the English classroom. Students will appreciate when teachers highlight the reasons for merging language study with peace education. Giving students a rationale for integrating peace and language education may involve sharing how one came to be a language teacher committed to peace. Yet by taking a critical pedagogic approach, teachers will have to cloak their personal views on controversial topics and allow students to develop their own critical thinking abilities as they wrestle with the issues. As Brown (2009) asserts, teachers need to "remain sensitively covert, lest a student feel coerced into thinking something because the teacher thinks that way" (p. 267). To achieve a pleasing harmony, the teacher needs to know how much to reveal of self and how much to conceal.

Finally, there is a tension within the critical education stance itself as one seeks the integration of peace and language education. On one hand, the critical educator wants to elicit critical thinking from students; on the other hand, the peaceable educator who employs critical methodology desires students to change, wants to move them to the point where they see that violence is not redemptive, does not work, and violates human dignity. As Brown (2009) notes, students learn "how to disagree without imposing" their views on others, but teachers who desire to see this kind of critical engagement impose their standards for civil discourse and peace values on the class. "Nevertheless," writes Brown, "this is where one's pedagogy becomes 'critical' in that the teacher's vision of a 'better more humane life' is usually predicated on such basic values" (p. 268) as love, equality, and peace—holistic human well-being and flourishing.

Returning to the point where I arrived through a process of reflection on my identity as a peaceable language teacher, I find myself committed to the proposition that to care about the learners in my charge is to act morally, in accord with my beliefs about human worth. Knowing that violence can and will destroy my students—whether it is self-inflicted in various forms or perpetrated by others—motivates me to ally myself with them to drown out this violence with the harmonies of peace. No matter the tensions I encounter in working out my personal and professional identity as a peaceable language teacher, the optimistic connotations in Lennon and McCartney's lyrics resonate with me: "We can work it out"—ultimately to the benefit of my students and the world in which they will live.

References

Akbari, R. (2008). Transforming lives: Introducing critical pedagogy into ELT classrooms. *ELT Journal: English Language Teachers Journal, 62*(3), 276–283. doi:10.1093/elt/ccn025

Ali, A. (2014). Visuals for peace. *SPELT Quarterly, 29*(4), 24–28.

Audergon, A. (2004). Collective trauma: The nightmare of history. *Psychotherapy and Politics International, 2,* 16–31.

Bartel, B. C. (1999). *Let's talk: Communication skills and conflict transformation.* Newton, KS: Faith & Life Press.

Bayer, C. P., Klasen, F., & Adam, H. (2007, August 1). Association of trauma and PTSD symptoms with openness to reconciliation and feelings of revenge among former Ugandan and Congolese child soldiers. *Journal of the American Medical Association, 298*(5), 555–559. doi:10.1001/jama.298.5.555

Bierling, M. (2007). Legal and illegal immigration: Complex ethical issues for the language classroom. In D. I. Smith & T. A. Osborn (Eds.), *Spirituality, social justice, and language learning* (pp. 89–105). Charlotte, NC: Information Age Publishing.

Brown, D. H. (2007). *Teaching by principles* (3rd ed.). New York, NY: Pearson Education ESL.

Brown, D. H. (2009). Imperatives, dilemmas, and conundrums in spiritual dimensions of ELT. In M. S. Wong & S. Canagarajah (Eds.), *Christian and English language educators in dialogue: Pedagogical and ethical dilemmas* (pp. 265–271). New York, NY: Routledge.

Brulliard, K. (2006, June18). Kurdish defendants find support in town's clasp. *The Washington Post*. Retrieved from http://www.washingtonpost.com/wp-dyn/content/article /2006/06/17/AR2006061700964.html

Day, C., Kington, A., Stobart, G., & Sammons, P. (2006). The personal and professional selves of teachers: Stable and unstable identities. *British Educational Research Journal, 32*, 601–616.

Eastern Mennonite University. (2014a). EMU believes . . . . Retrieved from www.emu.edu /about/core-values/

Eastern Mennonite University. (2014b). EMU mission statement. Retrieved from www .emu.edu/president/mission/

Freire, P. (2005). *Pedagogy of the oppressed: 30th anniversary edition* (Myra Bergman Ramos, Trans.). New York, NY: Continuum.

Gadd, N. (1998, July). Toward less humanistic language teaching. *ELT Journal, 53*(2), 223–233.

Harris, I. M., & Morrison, M. L. (2002). *Peace education* (2nd ed.). Jefferson, NC: McFarland & Co.

Hart, V. (2007). *When violence and trauma impact youth: Facilitator's training manual*. Harrisonburg, VA: Eastern Mennonite University.

Hinton, D., Rasmussen, A., Nou, L., Pollack, M., & Good, M. J. (2009). Anger, PTSD, and the nuclear family: A study of Cambodian refugees. *Social Science Medicine, 69*(9), 1387–1394. doi:10.1016/j.socscimed.2009.08.018

Holtgraves, T. (2002). *Language as social action: Social psychology and language use*. Mahwah, NJ: Lawrence Erlbaum.

Huntley, P. (2003). *The Hemingway book club of Kosovo*. New York, NY: Jeremy P. Tarcher/ Penguin.

Johnson, C. B. (2013, September 20). Does assertiveness negate humility? [Web log post]. Retrieved from http://cedricj.wordpress.com/2013/09/30/does-assertiveness-negate -humility/

Kumaravadivelu, B. (2003). *Beyond method: Macrostrategies for language teaching*. New Haven, CT: Yale University Press.

Lavender, W. (2015). *The worldview of redemptive violence in the U.S.* New York, NY: Palgrave Macmillan.

Levine, P. A., & Kline, M. (2007). *Trauma through a child's eyes*. Berkeley, CA: North Atlantic Press.

Macedo, D. (1994). *Literacies of power: What Americans are not allowed to know*. Boulder, CO: Westview Press.

Medley, R. M. (1999). Channel effects: Two methods of letter writing in the classroom. *Journal of Adolescent and Adult Literacy, 42*(8), 668–675.

Medley, R. M. (2009a, June). Hope for the English language teachers of Kosovo. *Global Issues in Language Education, 72*, 11–13.

Medley, R. M. (2009b). [Review of the book *Spirituality, social justice, and language learning*, by D. I. Smith & T. A. Osborn (Eds.)]. *Christian Scholar's Review, 38*(3), 397–399.

Medley, R. M. (2010). Serving trauma-affected learners in Pakistan. *SPELT Journal, 25*(4), 2–12.

Medley, R. M. (2012, March). A role for English language teachers in trauma healing. *TESOL Journal, 3*(1), 110–125.

Medley, R. M. (in press). *Resilience: The art of bouncing back*. Bloomington, IN: Westbow Press.

Milofsky, A. (2011). *Peacebuilding toolkit for educators.* Washington, DC: United States Institute for Peace. Available from http://www.buildingpeace.org/train-resources /educators/peacebuilding-toolkit-educators

Modi, C. G. (2014, June). Talking peace in the English language classroom. *SPELT Quarterly, 29*(2), 21–23.

O'Donnell-Allen, C. (2011). *Tough talk, tough texts: Teaching English to change the world.* Portsmouth, NH: Heinemann.

Rinvolucri, M. (1999). The UK, EFLese sub-culture and dialect. *Folio, 5*(2), 12–14.

Sammons, P., Day, C., Kington, A., Gua, Q., Stobart, G., & Smees, R. (2007). Exploring variations in teachers' work, lives and their effects on pupils: Key findings and implications from a longitudinal mixed-method study. *British Educational Research Journal, 33,* 681–701.

Shenk, N. G. (2008). *Hope indeed: Remarkable stories of peacemakers.* Intercourse, PA: Good Books.

Smith, D. I. (2009). The spiritual ecology of second language pedagogy. In M. S. Wong & S. Canagarajah (Eds.), *Christian and English language educators in dialogue: Pedagogical and ethical dilemmas* (242–254). New York, NY: Routledge.

Smith, D. I., DeYoung, S., Uyaguari, A., & Avila, K. A. (2007). Of log cabins, fallen bishops, and tenacious parents: (Auto)biographical narrative and the spirituality of language learning. In D. I. Smith & T. A. Osborn (Eds.), *Spirituality, social justice, and language learning* (pp. 107–129). Charlotte, NC: Information Age.

Snow, D. B. (2001). *English teaching as Christian mission: An applied theology.* Scottdale: PA: Herald Press.

Stevick, E. W. (1996). *Memory, meaning, and method: Some psychological perspectives on language learning.* Boston, MA: Heinle.

Storti, C. (1994). *Cross-cultural dialogues: 74 brief encounters with cultural difference.* Boston, MA: Nicholas Brealey.

Thornbury, S. (2010, June 27). T is for taboo. *An A to Z of ELT* [Web log post]. Retrieved from http://scottthornbury.wordpress.com/2010/06/27/t-is-for-taboo/

Volkan, V. D., & Fowler, J. C. (2009, April). Large group narcissism and political leaders with narcissistic personality organization. *Psychiatric Annals, 39*(4), 214–233. doi:10.3928/00485713-20090401-09

Wasson, R., Anderson, R., & Suriani, M. (1999). Integrating a multicultural peacebuilding strategy into a literacy curriculum. In L. M. Forcey & I. M. Harris (Eds.), *Peacebuilding for adolescents: Strategies for educators and community leaders* (pp. 213–226). New York, NY: Peter Lang.

Yoder, C. (2005). *The little book of trauma healing: When violence strikes and community security is threatened.* Intercourse, PA: Good Books.

Yoder, C., & Barge, N. Z. (2011). *STAR: The unfolding story, 2001–2011* [9/11 commemorative ed.]. Harrisonburg, VA: Eastern Mennonite University Center for Justice and Peacebuilding. Retrieved from http://www.emu.edu/cjp/star/sept-11th -commemorative-book/

CHAPTER 6

Healing Colonial Pain
English as a Bridge Between Korea and Japan

Kip A. Cates
Tottori University, Japan

K orea and Japan share a sad history of war, exploitation, and oppression. The future demands a relationship based on peace, friendship, and cooperation. English educators in both countries have a special role to play in overcoming the bitterness of the past and the stereotypes of the present to build a future of peace and mutual understanding.

My involvement with Japan and Korea is both personal and professional. My wife is Japanese; my brother's wife is Korean. I have lived in Japan for 30 years and have visited Korea 30 times. I have been actively involved with student and academic exchanges between these two nations for the past 25 years.

My interest in language as a bridge between people comes from my background and experiences. I grew up in Canada, took part in student exchanges between English-Canadians and French-Canadians, and realized the value of language as a means for making connections between communities. I grew up with stories of fighting against Japan and Germany in World War II and decided in university to specialize in German and Japanese to understand the causes of war and how wars can be prevented. Before coming to Japan to teach English, I spent a year in Europe in the 1970s working with international youth camps that brought together European students with the aim of promoting friendship, respect, cross-cultural understanding, and European citizenship.

Korea and Japan
HISTORICAL ROOTS OF KOREAN-JAPANESE HOSTILITY

The relationship between Japan and Korea is complex, emotionally charged, and constantly changing. These countries share a tumultuous history, which is marked by periods of engagement, mutual attraction, and interaction, as well as periods of suspicion, hostility, and isolation.

The roots of Korea's hostility toward Japan come from Japan's long history of aggression. In the invasions of 1592–1598, Japanese troops under Toyotomi Hideyoshi raped, pillaged, and plundered their way through Korea. Crops were razed, buildings burned, and the economy devastated. Priceless treasures, historical records, and cultural relics were looted or destroyed, and hundreds of skilled Korean craftsmen were taken to Japan as prisoners.

In the 20th century, Korea was forcibly annexed by Japan and occupied as a colony for 35 years (1910–1945). Japan's aim, as described by Breen (1998), was to "annihilate Korean culture and identity, and absorb the people into a greater Japan as second class citizens." Breen and others such as Kim (1970) note that during Japan's occupation,

- 85% of the buildings in Seoul's royal Kyongbok Palace were destroyed;

- 150,000 Korean "comfort women" were forced into Japanese military brothels as sex slaves;

- half a million Korean men were shipped to Japan, with 250,000 put to work in coal mines;

- Korean industry, commerce, and agriculture were exploited for Japan's benefit;

- Koreans were forced to take Japanese names and to worship at Shinto shrines; and

- Korean history and culture were not allowed to be taught in schools, and were replaced with Japanese history and culture, taught by Japanese teachers.

A special feature of the Japanese occupation was linguistic oppression. Japanese was made the official language of Korea while Korean became a "second language" and was eventually banned. Korean pupils received corporal punishment for speaking Korean at school. Leaders of the Korean Language Society were tried in court by the Japanese authorities for compiling a Korean dictionary in the 1940s.

KOREAN ATTITUDES TO JAPAN AND JAPANESE

While Japan's occupation of Korea ended in 1945, anti-Japanese attitudes in Korea have remained strong. These are reflected in various guidebooks and introductions to Korea. For example, Saccone (1994) mentions that "a large number of Koreans still harbor at least some resentment of the Japanese because of the sometimes inhuman occupation" (p. 15) while Hur (1988) mentions, "As a result of the early Japanese invasions and the more recent annexation of Korea, Korean people do not hold Japan or the Japanese in high esteem. Japanese living in Korea have many hurdles to overcome."

Encounters with Koreans described in travel books on Korea also touch on these attitudes:

> Mr. Kwang was a Korean nationalist. He loathed the Japanese for what they had done during the colonial period and was determined his son should grow up with a loathing for them, too. "There is a soap opera on our KBS television about life under the Japanese. It's the only program I force my son to watch. It's too easy for young

people to forget what those Japanese did to us. We can never trust them again. They seem friendly now, but deep down they are not. Deep down, I really hate them for what they have done. They took away our language. They took away our names and made us take Japanese names. They took away our king. They stole our treasures. They ruined our land. I can never forgive them for what they did. I am determined my children will never allow it to be forgotten." (Winchester, 1988, p. 143)

These attitudes have been documented in various opinion polls. In 1995, a survey about Japan's image in seven Asian countries asked, "What words do you think of when you hear the name *Japan*?" Koreans most often mentioned "colonization, World War II, brutality." In contrast, countries such as Thailand and Indonesia mentioned "intelligent, technology, polite" (Yomiuri Shimbun, 1995). Another 1995 survey found that 69% of Koreans polled professed a strong dislike for Japan (Asahi Shimbun, 1995). By 1999, this attitude had dropped slightly to 63%, with a greater number of older Koreans disliking Japan compared to younger Koreans (NHK, 2000). A more recent survey, conducted in 2014, found that only 15% of Koreans viewed Japan favorably, while 79% held negative views (BBC, 2014).

A Korean colleague once explained to me how Korean attitudes toward Japan differed by generation. The grandparents' generation, who had experienced the Japanese occupation, had mixed feelings about Japan. While they directly knew the oppression and brutality, they spoke Japanese, were familiar with Japanese customs, had spent their youth surrounded by Japanese culture, and sometimes sang Japanese songs when drunk. The parents' generation, who only learned about the Japanese occupation second-hand, had a strong hatred of Japan and the Japanese, stronger than that of the grandparents, even though they had no experience themselves. The children's generation, in contrast, had grown up knowing they were supposed to hate Japan, but they were not actually that knowledgeable about or interested in history.

For some Koreans, even positive exposure to Japan cannot dispel this negative image. One of my Korean colleagues, a high school English teacher in Seoul, visited Japan several times and had numerous enjoyable exchanges with Japanese teachers. Yet, when asked about her feelings, she thought carefully before answering, "I like Japanese people, but I don't like Japan."

JAPANESE ATTITUDES TO KOREA AND KOREANS

If historical Korean attitudes to Japan can be described as *bitterness* and *hate*, postwar Japanese attitudes to Korea can be described with the words *ignorance* and *fear*.

Young people in Japan grow up knowing vaguely that Japan did something terrible to Korea, but are unsure of exactly what happened. While schools teach some facts, the full details never quite come out. With this vague knowledge of a brutal past, Japanese youth sometimes find it difficult to interact with Koreans. Many come to feel that history is a millstone around their necks and resign themselves to carrying this burden of the past. Therefore, some are scared of Koreans and avoid encounters, as unpleasant experiences to be shunned.

I once helped arrange a visit by a Korean guest speaker to a Japanese high school. The Japanese students were asked to write about (1) their pre-visit expectations and (2) their thoughts after the visit. A comment from one student ran roughly as follows:

> When we were told a Korean student would come to our class, I wasn't happy at all. I knew Japan had done terrible things to Korea and I was sure the Korean student would spend the whole hour yelling at us Japanese students for what our country had done to Korea in the past. I was really surprised, then, when the Korean student arrived. He spoke fluent Japanese, made funny jokes, and told interesting stories about Korea. We really enjoyed the class. Before his visit, I thought there was no way that Koreans and Japanese could ever be friends. Now, I realize that it's possible.

IGNORANCE VERSUS PREJUDICE

A Japanese tour guide once summarized the challenges of youth exchange between Japan and Korea. Each country, she said, had one major problem to overcome. Japan's problem was ignorance; Korea's problem was prejudice. Japanese young people knew little about Japan's occupation of Korea and were surprised to learn the brutal facts. Their lack of knowledge often shocked and angered the Koreans they met. Korean young people, raised on stories about Japan from their teachers, textbooks, families, and the media, arrived in Japan expecting to be mistreated by arrogant Japanese. When they were lovingly taken care of by generous Japanese families, they were surprised and confused.

English as a Bridge Between Cultures

The English language has a special role to play as "mediator" in promoting communication, understanding, and peace between Korea and Japan. Four major reasons account for English having this role:

1. English is a compulsory subject in both Korean and Japanese schools. In both Korea and Japan, children begin English in elementary school, and continue the study in junior high school, senior high school, and university.

2. English is the only common language between Korean and Japanese young people. In Japan, beginner classes in Korean do not begin until university and are only electives. In Korea, Japanese is a foreign language mainly at university, where it is studied as an elective.

3. English is a politically neutral language for Koreans and Japanese. In Korea, Japanese was imposed as a language of occupation and still has bad connotations for some Koreans. In contrast, English is an international language for global communication in both Korea and Japan, with no negative connotations.

4. English is a language of equality for Koreans and Japanese. In Japan and Korea, young people study English as a foreign language for a similar length of time and attain roughly the same proficiency level. Neither side has the power advantage of being a native speaker.

English Textbooks in Korea and Japan

ENGLISH HIGH SCHOOL TEXTBOOKS IN KOREA

Korean high school English texts have not been shy about dealing with Japan. The generation of Korean texts published for the 1990s contain a number of English lessons on Japan and its history of aggression in Korea. One lesson describes the defeat by Korean naval hero Admiral Yi Sun-Shin of the Japanese invasion of Korea in 1588 (Shin, 1992). Another describes the assassination of Japanese Governor General Hirobumi Ito by Korean patriot Ahn Chung-gun in 1909 (Kang, 1992). Another lesson describes the brutally suppressed Sam-Il independence uprising against Japanese colonial rule in 1919 (Kim, 1992). No lessons in this generation of texts deal with modern Japan, Japanese culture, or Japanese people.

While English lessons such as these were designed to keep Korean students' awareness of Japan's colonial domination alive, not all Korean EFL texts have the same focus. One high school English lesson from the same generation, "The Unforgettable Hour," aims at promoting Korean-Japanese forgiveness and reconciliation (Lee, 1992). This lesson focuses on the experience of one Korean family on August 15, 1945, the day of Japan's defeat in World War II (celebrated each year as Liberation Day in Korea). The lesson includes the following dialog between an American and Korean girl.

> **Dialogue**: Judy (American) and Ha-na (Korean) talk about August 15 in Korea.
>
> Judy: Ha-na, aren't you going to school today?
> Ha-na: It's August 15 today. It's a national holiday.
> Judy: What are you celebrating?
> Ha-na: It's the day when Korea was freed from the Japanese occupation.
> Judy: I see. How long did Japan occupy Korea?
> Ha-na: For 35 years.
> Judy: For so long? Koreans must have had a hard time during that period.
> Ha-na: My grandfather says it was one of the darkest periods in Korean history.
> Judy: I can imagine how happy Koreans were when they were freed from the occupation. Do you have any hard feelings toward the Japanese?
> Ha-na: Most of the older people do, but the younger generation have mixed feelings.
> Judy: You mean you shouldn't blame the young Japanese for what their ancestors did?
> Ha-na: That's right. (Lee [1992], *High School English II: A*, lesson 9, p. 163)

The Korean textbook writers could easily have written this dialogue to strengthen Korean anger at Japan and hostility to the Japanese. Instead, they deliberately wrote the dialogue to end on a note of hope, inserting the final lines to break the generational cycle of hate and hostility toward Japan.

ENGLISH HIGH SCHOOL TEXTBOOKS IN JAPAN

Crown English series. While no authorized Japanese high school texts deal with the Japanese occupation of Korea, one pioneering text does introduce Korea to Japanese students (Crown, 1992). The following excerpt gives a flavor of this lesson.

> Reading Passage (spoken by a Japanese high school girl)
> I have studied English for about two years. I have also studied Korean since last month. Korea is Japan's neighbor. It lies about 50 kilometers from Tsushima across the sea. Korean is quite similar to Japanese in some ways.
>
> **Dialogue**
> Tom: I hear you're studying Korean.
> Kumi: Yes. Who told you that?
> Tom: Ken did. Have you studied it for a long time?
> Kumi: No.
> Tom: How long have you studied it?
> Kumi: Only a month and a half.
> Tom: Is it interesting?
> Kumi: Yes. The word order of Korean is almost the same as that of Japanese. I'm also interested in Korean culture. I've just read a book about it.
> Tom: Is Korean culture quite different from Japanese culture?
> Kumi: Well, the two cultures are the same in many ways, but there are some big differences too.
> Tom: Can you give me an example?
> Kumi: Well, people in both countries use chopsticks. But Korean people usually use spoons to eat rice. In Japan we bring a bowl up to the mouth. That's rude in Korea. (Crown [1992], *New Crown English Series III*, lesson 3, pp. 14–16)

This Japanese high school English lesson was designed to practice a number of grammar points (present perfect: *Have you studied . . . ?*; comparisons: *Korean is the same as Japanese*; contrasts: *In Japan. . . . But in Korea . . .*). As can be seen from the excerpt above, however, the lesson aims to promote interest and understanding of Korea in a number of ways:

- It links the study of one foreign language (English) with the study of another (Korean).
- It emphasizes that Korea is Japan's neighbor "across the sea" (while diplomatically omitting the controversy over the two conflicting names of that sea: the Japan Sea in Japan and the East Sea in Korea).
- It tells Japanese students that Korean is an interesting language with the same word order as Japanese.

- It underlines similarities between Japan and Korea while informing Japanese students of basic cultural differences.

- It includes a map of Korea and the Korean *hangul* alphabet to further stimulate student interest in Korea.

Anyong Korea. A more ambitious Japanese high school English text, designed entirely around the topic of Korea, is the side reader *Anyong Korea* (Nishizawa, Muroi, & Brock, 2001). This book aims to improve Japanese students' English comprehension skills while introducing them to the people, the culture, and the history of Korea. Its 13 units deal with such topics as Korean language, Korean food, Korean traditions, Korean entrance exams, Korean unification, Korean-Japanese high school exchanges, and the Korea-Japan World Cup Soccer championships. Special units focus on Koreans in Japan and on Yu Gwan-Sun, Korea's 16-year old "Joan of Arc" who fought for Korean independence and was tortured to death in 1920 by the Japanese military. Each unit features photos of Korea, a reading passage, vocabulary notes, and English language exercises. The text also includes a map of Korea and a *hangul* Korean alphabet chart.

English Pen-Pal Programs

As educators such as Hinkelman (2002) and Suzuki and Choi (2001) have shown, English pen-pal and key-pal programs can play a special role in promoting mutual understanding between people and countries. My initial involvement in teaching English for Korean-Japan understanding began with an English pen-pal program I set up back in the 1990s.

As a new English teacher in Japan, I learned that my Japanese university had—on paper—a sister relationship with a university in Korea. Seeing my Japanese students' need for extra English writing practice and believing in the importance of promoting Korean-Japanese understanding, I sat down and wrote a "To Whom It May Concern" letter to the English department of our Korean partner university suggesting we start an English pen-pal program between students at our universities. I got no answer. Two years later, the president of our partner university made an official visit to Japan, and I was able to ask him about the letter I had written. The following week, I got a reply. The letter was from a New Zealander teaching English in Korea, who answered more or less as follows:

> Thank you for your letter of 2 years ago, Mr. Cates. The President ordered us to look for it and we found it gathering dust in our files. Your naïve letter shows that you've probably never been to Korea and obviously don't know how much Koreans hate Japan. Your idea of an English pen-pal program is very idealistic, but I'm afraid it will never work.

I wrote back saying that I'd been to Korea, that I understood his point, and that the enmity between our two countries was the reason I was suggesting this program. I said

I realized that my pen-pal idea might not work, but urged him to at least give it a try before giving up. Luckily, my letter persuaded him. The following week he walked into his university English class and announced to his Korean students:

> "I've just received a letter from a Canadian teacher at our sister university in Japan. He wants to start an English pen-pal program. Who would like to have a Japanese pen pal to write to in English? Please put your hands up."

My New Zealand counterpart later related that his Korean students did not know they had a sister university in Japan. He assumed that none of them would be interested in an English program with Japan. Imagine his surprise, then, when 50 Korean students put up their hands and volunteered to take part!

This story illustrates one obstacle to initiating exchange programs in conflict areas: stereotypes and assumptions. My New Zealand colleague in Korea had naturally assumed that the anti-Japanese rhetoric he heard around him every day accurately reflected the attitudes of young Koreans. Yet, unknown to him, many Korean youth were curious about Japan, eager to learn about its economic and technological successes, and interested in making contact with young Japanese, if given the chance. His willingness to announce my "naïve" pen-pal program allowed him to break through his stereotype that all Koreans hate all Japanese.

Two weeks later, I found myself with a box of 50 English letters from Korean students addressed to "My as-yet-unknown Japanese pen pal." Reviewing all 50 Korean letters, I found that most Korean students' letters had little to do with Japan or Korea, and instead were concerned with interests to students their age. These read something like the following:

> Dear Japanese pen pal,
>   Hi! My name is Pak Eun-mi. There are 5 people in my family—my grandmother, my father, my mother, my brother and me. We have a pet cat named Iri. I belong to the computer club at school. My hobby is collecting stamps. My favorite singer is Michael Jackson.

The Japanese students eagerly wrote back to their new Korean pen pals about their Japanese families, hobbies, pets and favorite singers.

A minority of the letters, however, were different and read roughly like this:

> Dear Japanese pen pal,
>   Hi! My name is Kim Ki-chul. I'm 21 years old and a second year university student. When our New Zealand teacher told us about this pen-pal program, I thought this was an excellent chance for us. Japan and Korea share a sad history. It's our responsibility as the young generation in our countries to overcome the past and build a better relationship for the future. I'm looking forward to getting to know you through this program and to working with you on the task of building links of friendship between our two countries.

These thoughtful letters were all from young men who had just returned from Korea's compulsory military service. Because of their experiences, these Korean students had thought carefully about war and peace and had grasped the goals I had for the program.

This first experience of setting up an English pen-pal program resulted in a rich exchange between Japanese and Korean students, accomplishing the dual aims I had set: to improve students' writing skills while building mutual understanding. Over the years, the program led to deeper relations between participants as well as visits by individual students eager to meet their pen pals face-to-face. In 2014, I happened to meet one of the original Japanese students—now in her 40s—who had been part of the first wave of pen pals. Amazingly, she and her Korean pen pal were still writing to each other! They had kept in touch for 20 years, traveled overseas to visit each other, celebrated each other's weddings, had children, then brought their families together to meet and continue their exchange.

Overseas School Visits

Annual school trips to national places of interest have long been a tradition in Japan. These usually involve trips to Tokyo or Kyoto, but destinations often include peace sites such as Hiroshima and Okinawa. In the 1980s, an increasing number of Japanese high schools began taking students on study tours overseas.

According to Japan's Educational Tour Institute (2014), the first Japanese high school trips to Korea were undertaken by two private high schools in 1972. A decade later, in 1982, 60 schools were taking student trips to Korea. Student numbers increased 5-fold after the 1988 Seoul Olympics. At present, the Educational Tour Institute estimates that more than 20,000 students from 170 Japanese schools visit Korea each year.

SHUKUTOKU YONO HIGH SCHOOL

Shukutoku Yono Girls' High School in Saitama Prefecture is a Japanese school that pioneered school trips to Korea. In 1986, the school began annual English study trips to the United States and England for first-year students, followed by a Korea school trip for second-year students with the goal of using English to focus on Japan-Korea relations. The philosophy of the school is that language should be a tool for developing internationally minded women. The first school trips to Korea were significant enough that the school published two books (in Japanese) describing the students' experiences (Shukutoku Yono High School, 1987, 1988). A teacher involved described the program:

> English was chosen as the medium of communication for very practical reasons. Since most Koreans could not speak Japanese and most Japanese had no knowledge of Korean, it was necessary to use a third language—English. For the few

SOCIAL JUSTICE IN ENGLISH LANGUAGE TEACHING

Koreans who did know Japanese, using English was still preferred as it avoided the painful associations of Japanese colonial rule when officials forced Koreans to speak Japanese. In addition, as English was a foreign language for both groups of students, their ability levels were about the same. This reduced pressure and created a more relaxed speaking atmosphere. The only communication problem was the different accents and pronunciation of Japanese and Korean English. This was incorporated into subsequent English classwork.

The changes in language learning motivation for the students were far-reaching. "English for internationalization" became a real concept representing cross-cultural friendship and the overcoming of prejudice—an immediate and highly motivating goal for learning and improving English. (Hinkelman, 1993)

TOTTORI UNIVERSITY

My involvement with Korea-Japan school trips began in 1993 and grew out of the program described above. After several years of Korean-Japanese EFL pen-pal exchanges, my colleagues and I at Tottori University decided to take a group of our Japanese students to Korea. Our first challenge was to justify to the university administration and our Japanese colleagues why our English department was making an overseas trip to Korea, a country that is not English dominant, instead of to a nation like the United States, Canada, Britain or Australia, where English is the lingua franca.

Our second challenge was to design a 10-day trip to Korea that would improve our students' English and promote better Korean-Japanese relations. As leader of the trip, I was faced with some interesting decisions. I could have arranged for our students to visit Korean museums and tourist sights, do homestays with Korean pen-pal families, then return to Japan with a superficial but rosy view of Korea. Instead, I chose a more challenging, 2-part design, which I called "the agony and the ecstasy." To warm up, our Japanese student group spent the first 2 days in Seoul for sightseeing. Then came the "agony": a visit to the Korean Independence Museum in Chonan, featuring graphic displays of beatings, torture, and killings from Japan's brutal occupation period. Our Japanese students were shocked. Next day, we began the "ecstasy": a 3-day homestay with the Korean pen pals and their host families. The day after seeing the horror of what Japan had done to Korea, our Japanese students suddenly found themselves being fussed over and cared for by friendly Korean pen pals and their generous Korean families.

This 3-day period was crucial in terms of language learning and peace education. When we first handed over our Japanese students to the Korean families, we could see that the students were nervous—about going to live with total strangers, about having to speak English for the next three days, and about facing people whose country Japan had so brutally occupied. When we picked them up 3 days later, the scene was a total contrast. The Korean and Japanese young people were now best friends, everyone was crying at having to part with their host families, and our Japanese students were excitedly saying, "I can't believe it. I've been speaking nothing but English for the past 72 hours!" Several Japanese students told us that their visit to the Independence

Museum had enhanced their homestays. Their Korean families were moved that the students had gone to the museum and that they were shocked by what they had seen. Some Japanese students stayed up until late at night with their families, discussing the past, hearing personal stories, and sharing their feelings—all in English.

This new view of English is perhaps best expressed by a Japanese high school student, who shared her ideas in an English speech she gave at a high school competition held before her school trip to Korea:

English and I

"What is English for me?" I thought. "It can't be just a language. Then what am I studying English for?" I really thought and thought. I have never thought of what English means but dreamed that I would be a nice stewardess or a good interpreter some day. But I suddenly hit on another question, "What do I want to get such jobs for? Just for money?" No, by no means do I want to live such a mundane life. Now there is a reason for me to study English.

Our school makes a school trip to Korea every year. And this fall we're going to Korea. The purpose of my studying English is something related with this trip. At first I thought I wouldn't like to go to Korea and wondered why we had to go there. I wished we could have gone to another country in Europe. I was so thoughtless and selfish. I didn't know any of the facts about events which had occurred between Korea and Japan. I never knew the Japanese had done so many terrible things during World War II. I thought, "What in the world will happen when we go to Korea?" I just thought I had no power to improve the relationship between Korea and Japan. But I was completely wrong. I realized it because I had a chance to go to a Korean school in Tokyo. I was surprised that they were more friendly and nicer than I had expected. Whenever I remember it, I am deeply moved even now. One important thing I learned is that things we could do to help are always around us. If we look more carefully, we will be able to find something we can do to help.

When we go to Korea, we will make contact with Korean students and of course they can't speak Japanese. We must talk in English to them. And the reason of "English and I" is now found. English is like a bridge between Korea and Japan. My wish is to make the world smaller. I mean a united world. Though there is a long, difficult road to this goal, I think we can make it some day, if we believe, "Everyone can make the world a better place." English will be a great help for me to try it out. (Minato, 1990)

Conclusion

I began my work promoting Korea-Japan understanding through EFL in the 1990s, a difficult time when relations between the two countries were characterized by hostility and mistrust. Dramatic changes in the following decade were symbolized by the successful co-hosting of the 2002 Korea-Japan World Cup Soccer championships.

The level of mutual interest, understanding, and friendship between Koreans and Japanese manifested through the World Cup were a notable change from the past. Where Japanese culture was once banned in Korea, there arose in Korea a boom in

Japanese music, movies, and pop culture. Where ignorance of Korea once reigned, there arose a boom in Japan for Korean food, movies, and fashion. Where the national flags of Korea and Japan were once raised in opposition, they suddenly flew together in the hands of young Japanese and Korean fans cheering each other's soccer teams. What was once unthinkable suddenly became possible. The first Japanese-Korean love story, *Friends*, a jointly produced TV drama about the romance between a young Japanese woman and young Korean man, was broadcast in both countries and drew a big audience in Japan. Pro-Korean attitudes and the ideal of Korean-Japanese cooperation in Japan got a giant boost when two selfless Tokyo residents—a Japanese photographer and a Korean student in Japan—jumped on the tracks at a local train station to save the life of a man who had fallen and were killed together by an oncoming train. I believe that part of the credit for this transformation of bitterness and antagonism into friendship and understanding was due to English educators in Korea and Japan who see English and English teaching as a means of promoting reconciliation and peace.

Koreans still enjoy Japanese music and pop culture, and Japanese still love Korean films, food, and fashion. Unfortunately, however, relations have temporarily soured again because of new territorial conflicts, unresolved historical issues such as the "comfort women" sex slaves, and as well as provocative statements by politicians. There is still work to be done—an on-going challenge for English language teachers in both countries.

While this chapter has examined the role of English education in promoting better relations between Koreans and Japanese, there are many other examples of how English has helped to promote peace between peoples and countries. Forhan (1996), for example, has described a teacher-training course that brought together Israeli and Palestinian English teachers for professional development and mutual understanding. McCloskey (2014) has reported on the role of English in an international EFL peace camp in Eastern Europe. These examples, and this report on English for mutual understanding between Korea and Japan, show the potential of English language teaching for truly promoting peace.

International friendship, trust, and respect can only be achieved through the actions of dedicated people in countries around the world. English language educators have a special role to play in promoting international understanding by teaching English for peace and by providing opportunities for international exchange—through English—which bring together young people from conflict regions.

References

Asahi Shimbun. (1995). *Han-nichi konjo* [Anti-Japanese attitudes]. Retrieved October 12, 2015, from https://ja.wikipedia.org/wiki/反日感情

BBC. (2014, June 3). Negative views of Russia on the rise: Global poll. BBC World Service. Retrieved August 7, 2014, from http://downloads.bbc.co.uk/mediacentre/country-rating-poll.pdf

Breen, M. (1998). *The Koreans*. London, England: Orion Books.

Educational Tour Institute. (2014). *Kaigai shukgaku ryoko* [Overseas school trips].
    Retrieved August 7, 2014, from http://shugakuryoko.com/chosa/kaigai/

Forhan, L. (1996). Israeli and Palestinian educators collaborate to strengthen EFL programs
    and professional cooperation. *Global Issues in Language Education Newsletter, 22,*
    14–15. Retrieved from http://gilesig.org/newsletter/22col.htm

Hinkelman, D. (1993, May). Overseas tours to research social issues: Language learning
    through experiential education [Special issue on global education]. *Language Teacher,*
    17(5).

Hinkelman, D. (2002, May). *Korea-Japan student exchanges.* Presentation at JALT CALL
    conference, Hiroshima, Japan.

Hur, S. (1988). *Culture shock: Korea.* Singapore: Times Books.

Kim, R. (1970). *Lost names.* Seoul, South Korea: Si-Sa-Yong-O-Sa Press.

McCloskey, M. (2014, March). *Story-telling to prevent another genocide.* Presentation at
    TESOL conference, Portland, OR.

Minato, M. (1990). English and I. Quoted in D. Hinkelman (1993), Overseas tours to
    research social issues: Language learning through experiential education [Special issue
    on global education]. *Language Teacher, 17*(5).

NHK. (1999). *Nikkan wo meguru genzai, kako, mirai* [The past, present and future of
    Japan-Korea relations]. Retrieved October 12, 2015, from https://www.nhk.or.jp
    /bunken/summary/research/report/2010_11/101101.pdf

Saccone, R. (1994). *The business of Korean culture.* Seoul, South Korea: Hollym.

Shukutoku Yono High School. (1987). *Joshi kokosei no mita Kankoku* [Korea as seen by
    high school girls]. Tokyo, Japan: Shingaku.

Shukutoku Yono High School. (1988). *Anyong haseyo Kankoku* [Hello Korea: A high school
    study tour]. Tokyo, Japan: Chikumashu.

Suzuki, S., & Choi, T. (2001, October). *Discourse analysis on the Internet between Korean
    and Japanese high school students.* Presentation at Korea TESOL Conference, Seoul,
    South Korea.

Winchester, S. (1988). *Korea: A walk through the land of miracles.* New York, NY:
    Prentice Hall.

Yomiuri Shimbun. (1995). Nihonjin to kiite omoiukaberu kotoba [Images of Japanese].
    Retrieved October 12, 2015, from http://www7b.biglobe.ne.jp/~g-plan/tokua
    /072107.jpg

KOREAN TEXTBOOKS CITED

Kang, Yong-Se. (1992). *High school English II: A.* Seoul, South Korea: Dong A Press.

Kim, Ki-Hong. (1992). *High school English II: B.* Seoul, South Korea: Hyong Sal Press.

Lee, Mang-Sung. (1992). *High school English II: A* . Seoul, South Korea: Ji Haksa Press.

Shin, Sang-Sun. (1992). *High school English I.* Seoul, South Korea: Ungjinmunhwa Press.

JAPANESE TEXTBOOKS CITED

Crown. (1992). *New Crown English Series III.* Tokyo, Japan: Crown.

Nishizawa, T., Muroi, M., & Brock, S. (2001). *Anyong Korea.* Tokyo, Japan: Sanyusha.

PART III:
POSITIONING
FOR ADVOCACY

CHAPTER 7

Equity and Professionalism in English Language Teaching

A Glocal Perspective

Ali Fuad Selvi
Middle East Technical University, Northern Cyprus Campus

Nathanael Rudolph
Mukogawa Women's University

Baburhan Uzum
Sam Houston State University

Since its inception as a profession and a *bona fide* field of scholarly inquiry, English Language Teaching (ELT) has witnessed numerous efforts to enhance the quality of teaching and learning, and "the goal of raising the status of teaching as a profession" (Zeichner, 2003, p. 499). Such initiatives have contributed to the development of ELT as "a professional activity" defined by a specialized knowledge base contextualized in and developed through both theoretical and practical experience and as "a profession" whose membership is contingent upon entry requirements and standards (Richards, 2008). More specifically, the burgeoning professionalism of ELT has paved the way for the establishment and proliferation of professional organizations at international, national, regional, and local levels. The trend toward professionalism has also led to increased membership in such organizations, professional journals and conferences, professional standards and curriculum frameworks, nationally accredited and internationally recognized teacher education programs in ELT, and policy initiatives influencing ELT activities, including the detailing of professional positions regarding standards and equity in the field.

Collectively, being and becoming an ELT professional in today's glocal (Lin, Wang, Akamatsu, & Riazi, 2002) context means "becoming part of a worldwide community of professionals with shared goals, values, discourse, and practices but one with a self-critical view of its own practices and a commitment to a transformative approach to its own role" (Richards, 2008, p. 5). What is the current state of professionalism in a glocalized profession such as ELT? It goes without saying that professionalism is a construct that may take different definitions, forms, and implementations in different settings around the world. In his assessment of the legitimacy of the TESOL profession, David Nunan proposed four criteria: (1) advanced education and training, (2) an agreed theoretical and empirical base, (3) standards of practice and certification, and (4) advocacy through professional bodies (Nunan, 2001). Despite the progress achieved on the professionalism front over the past few decades, however, ELT is still considered to be a profession with a weak disciplinary basis and low standards of practice and certification (Nunan, 1999a, 1999b) or even a "nonprofession" (Lorimer & Schulte, 2012).

In this chapter, we argue that one key lingering issue hampering the growth of professionalism within ELT relates to the ongoing struggle over the creation of space for innovation, incorporation, collaboration, and inclusivity within the field, theoretically and practically speaking. In order to frame and confront systemic issues influencing professionalism (or lack thereof) through the lens of social justice, the current chapter unpacks alternate, critically oriented conceptualizations of (in)equity in the ELT profession and challenges deeply ingrained notions of legitimacy among ELT professionals. More specifically, it presents the importance of professionalism within the broader discourses of social justice, equity, and diversity. The chapter concludes with practical suggestions and advocacy practices for ELT professionals in a contextually sensitive and glocally constructed manner.

Conceptualizing and Approaching (In)equity in ELT

Within the glocalized field of ELT, there is ongoing debate regarding conceptualizations of language ownership, use, and instruction. Critically oriented scholarship contends that "the Native Speaker (NS) construct," which affords ownership of English (Widdowson, 1994) and default expertise (Canagarajah, 1999) to an "idealized" NS (Chomsky, 1965), has long served as the "bedrock of transnationalized ELT" (Leung, 2005, p. 128) and of second language acquisition theory and research (Firth & Wagner, 1997; Jenkins, 2006a). This "idealized NS" is constructed as the universal linguistic and cultural target for acquisition, use, and instruction regardless of context (Canagarajah, 2007; Medgyes, 1994; Leung, 2005), underpinning dominant approaches to theory, research, pedagogy, classroom materials, assessment, and hiring around the world (Braine, 2010; B. B. Kachru, 1992; Nayar, 1997; Selvi, 2010). The idealized NS has been conceptualized as Caucasian, male, and Western (Amin, 1997, 1999; Braine, 2010; Kubota, 1998, 2002; Kubota & Lin 2009; Motha, 2006). According to Widdowson (2003), this conceptualization has resulted in the privileging of language users and professionals who fit the description of the idealized NS.

In recent years, critical and practical challenges seeking to move beyond the NS construct have appeared, drawing upon sociocultural, postcolonial, postmodern, and poststructural theory (e.g., Crystal, 2012; Firth & Wagner, 1997; Hymes, 1972; Jenkins, 2005, 2006b; B. B. Kachru, 1985, 1992; Medgyes, 1992, 1994; Nelson, 1985; Norton, 1997, 2000, 2010; Pennycook, 1994, 1999; Phillipson, 1992; Seidlhofer, 2004; Widdowson, 1994, 1998). Around the world, Crystal (2012) posits that English is regularly used by approximately two billion individuals. English has been and is being nativized within former colonies, leading to the emergence of a wide variety of World Englishes (B. B. Kachru, 1985, 1992; Y. Kachru, 2005; Rajadurai, 2005). English is being nativized, owned, and employed as a lingua franca in and across a wide variety of contexts by a diverse population of users hailing from varying linguistic, cultural, national, and ethnic backgrounds (Canagarajah, 2007; Crystal, 2012).

Critically, therefore, scholarship has conceptualized the NS construct as a vehicle for the construction, maintenance, and perpetuation of power and privilege within both the field of ELT and the context in which it is situated (e.g., Canagarajah, 2006a; Houghton & Rivers, 2013; Leung, 2005). Scholars have challenged the NS-centric prioritization of linguistic and cultural knowledge for acquisition, and therefore who might be imagined as a valid speaker and instructor of English (Alptekin, 2002; Canagarajah, 1999, 2007; Firth, 2009; Lowenberg, 2000; Norton, 2010; Widdowson, 1994). Practically, scholars are arguing for a move beyond the "myth" (Y. Kachru, 2005) that users will interact in English with Western native speakers, as well as for a move beyond conceptualizations of English instruction, assessment, and use grounded in the NS construct, as such approaches neglect the contextualized uses of English around the globe (Alptekin, 2002; Braine, 2010; Canagarajah, 2006b, 2006c; Leung, 2005; Lowenberg, 2000; Seidlhofer, 2004). Researchers are therefore arguing for a move beyond decontextualized, one-size-fits-all approaches to ELT, and toward approaches that are "more appropriate to the demands of a global, decentered, multilingual and multicultural world, more suited to our uncertain and unpredictable times" (Kramsch, 2008, pp. 405–406). Learners would be "both global and local speakers of English," able to interact with a wide variety of individuals from different linguistic, sociocultural, ethnic, and national backgrounds (Alptekin, 2002; Canagarajah, 2007: Kramsch & Sullivan, 1996). More recent inquiry related to contextualized language teaching has emphasized the inclusion of linguistic and sociocultural knowledge beyond English, drawing upon of teachers' translinguistic and transcultural identities and lived experiences (e.g., Kubota, 2013).

Critical inquiry has resulted in attention to the lived experiences of nonnative English speaker teachers (NNESTs) (Braine, 1999, 2010; Kamhi-Stein, 2004; Llurda, 2005; Mahboob, 2010; Selvi, 2014). This attention has given birth and shape to a groundswell of scholarship and professional activity addressing inequity and the status of "nonnative" English speaking teachers. Such scholarship and activity has flowed both from organized groups within the TESOL International Association and from efforts around the globe extending beyond organizational affiliation.

Within this NNEST movement, conceptualizations of and approaches to theoretical and manifested inequity are not uniform in nature. Scholars, including Menard-Warwick (2008) and Moussu and Llurda (2008), argue that the majority of critically oriented, NNEST-related scholarship has approached (in)equity via a critically oriented set of binaries: NS/NNS and NEST/NNEST. Through this lens, the NS construct is a universal regime of truth (Foucault, 1984) flowing from the West and global ELT into local contexts, maintained in varying degrees by the active discourses of *native speakerism*: "a pervasive ideology within ELT, characterized by the belief that 'native-speaker' teachers represent a 'Western culture' from which spring the ideals both of the English language and of English language teaching methodology" (Holliday, 2006, p. 385). The discourses of native speakerism in turn perpetuate the NS fallacy (Phillipson, 1992), or the belief that native speakers are the most capable and valuable professionals. The perpetuation of the NS fallacy provided impetus for establishing an institutionalized structure—the NNEST Caucus, later becoming the NNEST Interest Section in the TESOL International Association (Mahboob, 2010) to confront its marginalizing effects within the field of ELT.

Apprehended via categorical binaries, critical scholarship conceptualizes a largely uniform, common NNEST (and NEST) experience. Native speakerism and the NS fallacy privilege NESTs and marginalize NNESTs in hiring practices in both ESL and EFL contexts (Braine, 1999; Canagarajah, 1999; Clark & Paran, 2007; Flynn & Gulikers, 2001; Medgyes, 2001; Selvi, 2010). Native speakerism has cultivated an environment in which the professional capabilities and employability of NNESTs may be called into question by all stakeholders in ELT, including themselves (Amin, 1997; Bernat, 2009; Canagarajah, 1999; Kamhi-Stein, Lee, & Lee, 1999; Reves & Medgyes, 1994). Often prompted to study in Western, English-speaking countries to gain some semblance of linguistic and cultural authority (Braine, 2010), NNESTs nevertheless struggle to find employment in ELT (Canagarajah, 1999). In addition, NNESTs may serve as "gatekeepers" (Widdowson, 1994) of a portion of the linguistic and cultural knowledge of the idealized native speaker, though they are yet deficient as per the NS construct (Leung, 2005). In response, scholars have argued for the superiority of NNESTs in English instruction, whether due to their language learning experiences or status as a native speaker of another language (e.g., Medgyes, 2001). Others contend that neither NESTs nor NNESTs are superior, as each possesses unique abilities and experiences that contribute to their professional validity (Mahboob, 2005, 2010).

In concert with reconceptualizing the professional status of NNESTs, scholars have contributed to and drawn from literature challenging oversimplified categories of "native" and "nonnative" (Cook, 1999; Faez, 2011a, 2011b; B. B. Kachru, 1992; Lee, 2004; Modiano, 1999; Paikeday, 1985; Rajadurai, 2005; Rampton, 1990; Swales, 1993) and have proposed alternate nomenclature for teachers of English that attend to and/or celebrate their potentially diverse linguistic and cultural backgrounds (Brady, 2009; Selvi, 2014). In approaching the experiences of NNESTs (and NESTs) via binaries, however, Moussu and Llurda (2008) assert that scholarship is "implicitly accepting the separation between NSs and NNSs" (p. 318) and the relative uniformity of experience within such categories (e.g., Menard-Warwick, 2008).

In recent years, scholars, including Higgins (2003), Menard-Warwick (2008), Motha, Jain, and Tecle (2012), Park (2008, 2012), and Rudolph (2012), have argued that binaries, critical and otherwise, oversimplify and/or neglect individuals' lived experiences negotiating identity, resulting in a failure to provide conceptual space for learner, user, and teacher identity, and their being stripped of voice and agency. Postmodern and poststructural approaches to identity challenge the notion of universal truths and the essentialized, modern self. Language, culture, and meaning are negotiated in interaction (Norton, 2010). Identity is dynamically negotiated and constructed at the interstices of "discourses" (Bhabha & Appignanesi, 1987), which are "systems of power/knowledge (Foucault, 1980) that regulate and assign value to all forms of semiotic activity" (Morgan, 2007, p. 1036). National, ethnic, cultural, and linguistic borders of "us" and "them," "inside" and "outside" are contextually constructed by concomitantly local and global discourses of identity (Bhabha, 1994) and policed by individuals and institutions with a vested interest in maintaining border integrity. It is in the between spaces (Bhabha, 1996) of borders constructed by localized and globalized discourses of being and becoming that individuals assert agency in conceptualizing and negotiating identity (Kramsch, 2012; Morgan, 2004, 2007; Motha, Jain, & Tecle, 2012; Norton, 2000, 2010; Rudolph, 2012) and, in the process, construct borderland spaces of identity (Anzaldúa, 1987).

From a postmodern and poststructural approach, the NS construct, NS-ism, and the NS fallacy are dynamically, fluidly constructed by discourses of "inside" and "outside" and "us" and "them" flowing in and out of globalized ELT and local context. These borders may involve discourses related to gender, ethnicity, nationality, professional role, linguistic and cultural authority, and cultural behavior (Rudolph, Selvi, & Yazan, 2015; Houghton & Rivers, 2013). Such discourses may construct and confine individuals within categories of identity. Rudolph (2012) argues, in a study examining Japanese university teachers' negotiation of translinguistic and transcultural identity in Japan, for instance, that categories related to the "idealized NS of English" and "NS of Japanese/NNEST" have been constructed therein. These categories seek to define who Japanese learners, users, and instructors of English, and who "native speakers," can and/or should be or become. Such categories may limit and/or eliminate space for native speakers whose identities fit with the idealized NS as locally constructed, as well as for non-Japanese NNESTs. Yet, at the same time, individuals may assert agency in negotiating borders of being and becoming, thus adding complexity to conceptual accounts of privilege and marginalization. Native speakerism, from a postmodern and poststructural perspective, is therefore multidirectional and multilocational. A shared, categorical experience does not exist, either for NEST or NNEST. Privilege and marginalization are fluidly constructed in context. Houghton and Rivers (2013), for example, challenge Holliday's (2005, 2006) conceptualization of native speakerism as lacking descriptive power, and instead conceptualize native speakerism as one of many chauvinistic "-isms" (e.g., racism) or discourses of prejudice that combine to contextually construct "Other" (Houghton & Rivers, 2013, pp. 2–3), and therefore "represent a fundamental breach of one's basic human rights" (p. 14). (In the same book, Holliday [2013] reconceptualizes native speakerism, arguing for a postmodern approach to the discourses that perpetuate the NS/NNS and NEST/NNEST binaries, in the interest of cultivating a more equitable field.)

Postmodern and poststructural approaches to identity, and attention to the deconstruction (Derrida, 1976) of discourses of identity to examine their origin and function (Peters & Humes, 2003, p. 111), necessitate reconceptualization of the

NS construct, NS-ism, and the NS fallacy as glocally constructed by discourses of "inside" and "outside," and "us" and "them." Such scholarship attempts to create richer descriptive space for learners', users', and instructors' negotiation of identity, beyond critical, yet essentializing and confining, categories and nomenclature, in the interest of conceptualizing and approaching inequity in the local and the global (e.g., Block & Cameron, 2002; Canagarajah, 2005). As such, we would argue that conceptual and practical approaches to advocacy would be considered in similar fashion: sensitive to context and glocally constructed, in the interest of a creation of space for innovation, incorporation, collaboration, and inclusivity for all, within the field of ELT.

Practical Suggestions

How might teacher educators and teachers, both current and in training, approach contextually sensitive, glocally constructed awareness, advocacy, and activism (Selvi, 2009), in the interest of a creation of space for innovation, incorporation, collaboration, and inclusivity for all? In the following section, we present a few practical suggestions. In doing so, we assert that there is no uniform "NEST" nor "NNEST" experience and that there is fluidity between privilege and marginalization (Baxter, 2002). As a result, we posit there is no one-size-fits-all approach to addressing issues of (in)equity in ELT. We begin by focusing on teacher educators working with prospective teachers and teachers in service, and follow with attention to the classrooms of current practitioners.

Teacher educators might begin by connecting with the individuals in their classroom:

- Who are the teachers in training and/or current teachers in attendance?
- What are their lived experiences negotiating personal and professional identity?
- What are these individuals' worldviews regarding who they and whether their classmates and colleagues can and/or should be or become as users and teachers of English?
- What are these individuals' worldviews regarding who their students can and/or should be or become as learners and users of English?
- What context/s are teachers teaching, or going to be teaching, in, and how do the discourses of privilege and marginalization therein create, limit, or eliminate space in the context?
- For what sort of interaction/s are these teachers (potentially) educating their students? With whom will students be interacting?
- What sort of linguistic, sociocultural, and academic knowledge might therefore be prioritized in the classroom?

These questions may serve as a foundation for tailoring course contents and materials to suit the experiences, dynamics, and needs of the members of each class, and ultimately, the students with whom they work.

In approaching the classroom, teacher educators would dynamically construct a conceptual framework that explores critical theory and research in ELT seeking to move beyond the idealized NS construct and toward reconceptualizing language ownership, use, and instruction for reasons practical and critical in nature. Practically, teacher educators would provide their students with descriptive accounts of the contextualized negotiation of interaction, as tailored to learners' conceptualized and/or expressed goals. In order to do so, both teacher educators and their students would act as ethnographers, seeking to conceptualize who and what (linguistically and socioculturally) is involved in interaction (Hymes, 1972). This approach would involve a focus on English use within and across contexts, in which people from a wide variety of linguistic, cultural, national, and ethnic backgrounds draw upon their complex, hybridized identities in negotiating borders of being and doing in interaction with each other. Critically, teacher educators would attend to the discourses of identity in society/ies (fluidly intertwining with discourses within ELT in the context/s in which teachers are training and/or working or planning to teach) that seek to create, limit, or eliminate space for innovation and incorporation in terms of being and becoming. Teacher educators and their students would conceptualize, contextualize, and address the construction, perpetuation, and maintenance of borders of being and becoming, connecting both to societal discourses of identity in a given society and to the ELT in the context in which it is situated. Teacher educators may incorporate the experiences of course members negotiating identity into the classroom experience. We would argue that cultivating dialogue and conversation among members of such a community and creating safe spaces for discussion are fundamental to conceptualizing and confronting issues of equity. The teacher educator may also choose to incorporate a range of narrative voices elicited from the ELT literature, from other source materials that touch upon the negotiation of borders of being and becoming (such as social justice/civil rights movements and immigrant experiences), or from guest speakers, members of the local community. In addition, teacher educators might invite their students to participate in professional activities that aim to cultivate inclusivity in the field of ELT and the context/s in which it is situated.

As with teacher educators, we would contend that current teachers begin with apprehending the lived experiences and dynamic identities of their students. This includes tailoring course materials and spaces for dialogue (in oral and written form) in and beyond the classroom. Whenever possible, teachers might engage in dialogue with parents and other members of the local community as well. We would argue, as mentioned previously, that teachers should actively pursue a linguistic and sociocultural knowledge of the context in which they and their students live and interact, likely taking them well beyond the confines of ELT and English use.

Teachers can implicitly and explicitly incorporate a reconceptualization of the ownership, use, and instruction of English into materials and instruction in the classroom. This reconceptualization can be reflected in the language that teachers use to describe users of English, the categories of identity they choose to challenge and deconstruct in the classroom, local and global examples of role models and/or individuals negotiating translinguistic and transcultural identity, and they way they approach pedagogy, including the linguistic, sociocultural, and academic knowledge they choose to prioritize, and the way they choose to assess student "achievement" or "proficiency." Doing so may serve to transform the way students view and value their identities as English learners and users, and the way they perceive their peers, teachers, and other members of the context in which they reside. Students may come to value their translinguistic and transcultural identities and those of others, beyond essentialized categories of being.

In the spirit of critically oriented pedagogy (Freire, 1970, 1973), teachers can address discourses of "inside" and "outside" and "us" and "them" in the classroom, prompting students to apprehend their origins (how they were constructed) and functions (how they are perpetuated and maintained). Teachers can create space for students to share their lived experiences and to dialogue with community members (e.g., former students, community leaders, other teachers) to apprehend the complexity of negotiating identity beyond the classroom. Teachers can create action research projects for students, prompting them to conceptualize, confront, and negotiate dominant discourses of identity within their society and the field of ELT related to who they "can" or "should" or "can't" or "shouldn't" be or become concomitantly as English learners and users, and as members of the local community.

In approaching transformative education, both teacher educators and teachers might necessarily practice *critical pragmatism* (Pennycook, 1997). Critical pragmatism is an approach to teaching wherein, while seeking transformative change in classroom practices and professional activities, educators are mindful of two specific issues: (1) the parameters placed around ELT in a given context, stemming from the expectations of all stakeholders involved, and (2) the threat to the linguistic and cultural authority of individuals and institutions that challenging dominant constructions of identity and roles might pose. Teachers are charged with equipping students for participation in context/s as defined by dominant discourses of identity within ELT and the society in which it is located while also challenging those same discourses for reasons critical and practical. Standardized tests grounded in glocalized constructions of an idealized native speaker are one such example of an issue teachers face. If a teacher fails to address such tests, as valued in context, students may suffer lasting consequences, both personally and professionally speaking, as may the teacher himself or herself. In addition, teachers must be aware of the threat to the linguistic and cultural authority of colleagues, administrators, and other local stakeholders that their teaching may actualize. As noted in (Rudolph, 2012), challenging the authority afforded to individuals via categories of identity and roles established within ELT and in the local society can cause teachers to be personally and professionally isolated and marginalized, and may result in career-altering consequences.

Conclusion

Although the notion of professionalism in ELT is neither new nor controversial in theoretical terms, the attained level of professionalism is far from the desired in practical terms. Using this observation as a strong motivation for discussion, we adopt a professional social justice stance to de-/re-construct issues of social justice, equity, and professionalism in the field of ELT. In order to address and overcome the lingering issues of professionalism, practical efforts for equity, social justice, and professionalism should be expanded in terms of "width" (so as to include various stakeholders such as (under-)graduate students, teachers, teacher educators, administrators, material writers, and policy makers) and "depth" (so as to be more sensitive to the glocal contexts and emerging identities of professionals).

The conceptual and practical parameters of advocacy necessitates the adoption of a glocal perspective that maintains, creates, and promotes spaces, discourses, and practices for innovation, incorporation, collaboration, and inclusivity for all. Since there is no "uniform NNEST experience" or "NEST experience" (nor "NS" or "NNS" experience), the fluidity of privilege and marginalization necessitates going beyond categorical binaries and the one-size-fits-all approach. In conclusion, we contend that social justice, equity, and professionalism should be seen as indispensable and nonnegotiable qualities of all ELT professionals and interwoven into their professional identities for the duration of their careers. These ideas and related efforts, however, need to go beyond the categorical and so-called uniform experiences of NESTs and NNESTs (or NSs and NNSs) and be updated in relation to changing professional landscape of ELT as a field and a profession and adapted in relation to contextual dynamics in which they take place. This understanding is in line with Lorimer and Schulte's (2012) conceptualizations of "professional," defined as "a shifting construct that becomes more salient and significant through time as it is continually defined and redefined by all members of the field" (p. 34) and "professionalism" defined as "a practice rather than an end goal" (p. 34). This understanding enables us to view ELT professionals as individuals who embody and bring a unique set of identities and sociolinguistic and professional histories that overlap, coexist, and cross boundaries. Furthermore, it recognizes professionalism to take different forms and features as dynamic processes that spearhead greater systemic benefits to the entire profession.

Today, the field of ELT is defined by the notion of diversity: diversity of populations served; diversity of professionals who comprise the heart and soul of this profession; diversity of teaching contexts and individual program settings; and diversity of knowledge, skills, dispositions, and philosophies that undergird the activity of ELT. Therefore, as a profession whose hallmark is diversity, ELT should intensify its efforts to diversify its theoretical and practical base upon which develops a stronger commitment to the professionalism for the benefit of ELT professionals from all walks of life. As Nunan (1999b) reminds, "it is up to us who are committed to the notion of ELT as a profession to identify and promote those practices around the world that are consistent with this goal" (para. final). Now, it is not a matter of "why" but a matter of "how" and even "how could I possibly not?"

References

Alptekin, C. (2002). Towards intercultural communicative competence in ELT. *ELT Journal, 56*(1), 57–64.

Amin, N. (1997). Race and the identity of the nonnative ESL teacher. *TESOL Quarterly, 31*(3), 580–583.

Amin, N. (1999). Minority women teachers of ESL: Negotiating white English. In G. Braine (Ed.), *Non-native educators in English language teaching* (pp. 93–104). Mahwah, NJ: Lawrence Erlbaum.

Anzaldúa, G. (1987). *Borderlands/la frontera: The new Mestiza*. San Francisco, CA: Spinsters/Aunt Lute.

Baxter, J. (2002). Competing discourses in the classroom: A post-structuralist discourse analysis of girls' and boys' speech in public contexts. *Discourse & Society, 13*(6), 827–842.

Bernat, E. (2009). Towards a pedagogy of empowerment: The case of "impostor syndrome" among pre-service non-native speaker teachers (NNSTs) of TESOL. *English Language Teacher Education and Development Journal, 11*, 1–11.

Bhabha, H. K. (1994). *The location of culture*. London, England: Routledge.

Bhabha, H. K. (1996). Culture's in-between. In S. Hall & P. du Gay (Eds.), *Questions of cultural identity* (pp. 53–60). London, England: SAGE Publications.

Bhabha, H. K., & Appignanesi, L. (1987). *Identity: The real me* (Vol. 6). London, England: Institute of Contemporary Arts.

Block, D., & Cameron, D. (2002). Introduction. In D. Block, & D. Cameron (Eds.), *Globalization and language teaching* (pp. 2–10). London, England: Routledge.

Brady, B. (2009). Message from the outgoing chair. *NNEST newsletter, 11*(1). Retrieved January 2, 2014, from http://www.tesol.org/read-and-publish/newsletters-other -publications/interest-section-newsletters/nnest-newsletter/2011/10/27/nnest-news -volume-11-1-(july-2009)

Braine, G. (1999). *Non-native educators in English language teaching*. Mahwah, NJ: Lawrence Erlbaum.

Braine, G. (2010). *Nonnative speaker English teachers: Research, pedagogy, and professional growth*. New York, NY: Routledge.

Canagarajah, A. S. (1999). Interrogating the "native speaker fallacy": Non-linguistic roots, non-pedagogical results. In G. Braine (Ed.), *Non-native educators in English language teaching* (pp. 145–158). Mahwah, NJ: Lawrence Erlbaum.

Canagarajah, A. S. (2005). *Reclaiming the local in language policy and practice*. Mahwah, NJ: Lawrence Erlbaum.

Canagarajah, A. S. (2006a). TESOL at forty: What are the issues? *TESOL Quarterly, 40*(1), 9–34.

Canagarajah, A. S. (2006b). Negotiating the local in English as a lingua franca. *Annual Review of Applied Linguistics, 26*, 197–218.

Canagarajah, A. S. (2006c). Changing communicative needs, revised assessment objectives: Testing English as an international language. *Language Assessment Quarterly, 3*(3), 229–242.

Canagarajah, A. S. (2007). Lingua franca English, multilingual communities, and language acquisition. *Modern Language Journal, 91*(5), 923–939.

Chomsky, N. (1965). *Aspects of the theory of syntax.* Cambridge, MA: MIT Press.

Clark, E., & Paran, A. (2007). The employability of non-native-speaker teachers of EFL: A UK survey. *System, 35*(4), 407–430.

Cook, V. (1999). Going beyond the native speaker in language teaching. *TESOL Quarterly, 33*(2), 185–209.

Crystal, D. (2012). *English as a global language.* Cambridge, England: Cambridge University Press.

Derrida, J. (1976). *Of grammatology* (G. C. Spivak, Trans.). Baltimore, MD: Johns Hopkins University Press.

Faez, F. (2011a). Are you a native speaker of English? Moving beyond a simplistic dichotomy. *Critical Inquiry in Language Studies, 8*(4), 378–399.

Faez, F. (2011b). Reconceptualizing the native/nonnative speaker dichotomy. *Journal of Language, Identity and Education, 10*(4), 231–249.

Firth, A. (2009). The lingua franca factor. *Intercultural Pragmatics, 6*(2), 147–170.

Firth, A., & Wagner, J. (1997). On discourse, communication, and (some) fundamental concepts in SLA research. *Modern Language Journal, 81*, 285–300.

Flynn, K., & Gulikers, G. (2001). Issues in hiring nonnative English-speaking professionals to teach English as a Second Language. *CATESOL Journal, 13*(1), 151–161.

Foucault, M. (1980). *Power/knowledge: Selected interviews and other writings, 1972–1977.* New York, NY: Pantheon Books.

Foucault, M. (1984). *The Foucault reader* (P. Rabinow, Ed.). New York, NY: Pantheon.

Freire, P. (1970). *Pedagogy of the oppressed.* New York, NY: Continuum.

Freire, P. (1973). *Education for critical consciousness.* New York, NY: Continuum.

Higgins, C. (2003). "Ownership" of English in the outer circle: An alternative to the NS-NNS dichotomy. *TESOL Quarterly, 37*(4), 615–644.

Holliday, A. (2005). *The struggle to teach English as an international language.* Oxford, England: Oxford University Press.

Holliday, A. (2006). Native-speakerism. *ELT Journal, 60*(4), 385–387.

Holliday, A. (2013). Native speaker teachers and cultural belief. In S. A. Houghton & D. J. Rivers (Eds.), *Native-speakerism in Japan: Intergroup dynamics in foreign language education* (pp. 17–28). Bristol, England: Multilingual Matters.

Houghton, S. A., & Rivers, D. J. (Eds.). (2013). *Native-speakerism in Japan: Intergroup dynamics in foreign language education.* Bristol, England: Multilingual Matters.

Hymes, D. (1972). On communicative competence. In J. Pride & J. Holmes (Eds.), *Sociolinguistics* (pp. 269–293). New York, NY: Penguin.

Jenkins, J. (2005). *English as a lingua franca: Past empirical, present controversial, future uncertain.* Paper presented at RELC International Seminar, Singapore.

Jenkins, J. (2006a). Current perspectives on teaching World Englishes and English as a lingua franca. *TESOL Quarterly, 40*(1), 157–181.

Jenkins, J. (2006b). Points of view and blind spots: ELF and SLA. *International Journal of Applied Linguistics, 16*(2), 137–162.

Kachru, B. B. (1985). Standards, codification and sociolinguistic realism: The English language in the Outer Circle. In R. Quirk & H. G. Widdowson (Eds.), *English in the world: Teaching and learning the language and literatures* (pp. 11–30). Cambridge, England: Cambridge University Press.

Kachru, B. B. (1992). *Teaching world Englishes: The other tongue.* Urbana: University of Illinois Press.

Kachru, Y. (2005). Teaching and learning of world Englishes. In E. Hinkel (Ed.), *Handbook of research in second language learning and teaching* (pp. 155–173). Mahwah, NJ: Lawrence Erlbaum

Kamhi-Stein, L. (2004). *Learning and teaching from experience: Perspectives on nonnative English-speaking professionals.* Ann Arbor: University of Michigan Press.

Kamhi-Stein, L., Lee, E., & Lee, C. (1999). How TESOL programs can enhance the preparation of nonnative English speakers. *TESOL Matters, 9,* 4.

Kramsch, C. (2008). Ecological perspectives on foreign language education. *Language Teaching, 41*(3), 389–408.

Kramsch, C. (2012). Theorizing translingual/transcultural competence. In G. S. Levine & A. Phipps (Eds.), *Critical and intercultural theory and language pedagogy* (pp. 15–31). Boston, MA: Heinle.

Kramsch, C., & Sullivan, P. (1996). Appropriate pedagogy. *ELT Journal, 50*(3), 199–212.

Kubota, R. (1998). Ideologies of English in Japan. *World Englishes, 17*(3), 295–306.

Kubota, R. (2002). The impact of globalization on language teaching in Japan. In D. Block & D. Cameron (Eds.), *Globalization and language teaching* (pp. 13–28). London, England: Routledge.

Kubota, R. (2013). "Language is only a tool": Japanese expatriates working in China and implications for language teaching. *Multilingual Education, 3*(1), 1–20.

Kubota, R., & Lin, A. (2009). *Race, culture, and identities in second language education: Exploring critically engaged practice.* New York, NY: Routledge.

Lee, I. (2004). Preparing nonnative English speakers for EFL teaching in Hong Kong. In L. Kamhi-Stein (Ed.), *Learning and teaching from experience: Perspectives on nonnative English-speaking professionals* (pp. 230–250). Ann Arbor: University of Michigan Press.

Leung, C. (2005). Convivial communication: Recontextualizing communicative competence. *International Journal of Applied Linguistics, 15*(2), 119–144.

Lin, A., Wang, W., Akamatsu, N., & Riazi, A. M. (2002). Appropriating English, expanding identities, and re-visioning the field: From TESOL to teaching English for glocalized communication (TEGCOM). *Journal of Language, Identity, and Education, 1*(4), 295–316.

Llurda, E. (2005). *Non-native language teachers: Perceptions, challenges, and contributions to the profession.* New York, NY: Springer Verlag.

Lorimer, C., & Schulte, J. (2012). Reimagining TESOL professionalism: The graduate student perspective. *CATESOL Journal, 23*(1), 31–44.

Lowenberg, P. H. (2000). Non-native varieties and issues of fairness in testing English as a world language. In A. J. Kunnan (Ed.), *Fairness and validation in language assessment: Selected papers from the 19th language testing research colloquium.* Cambridge, England: Cambridge University Press.

Mahboob, A. (2005). Beyond the native speaker in TESOL. In S. Zafar (Ed.), *Culture, context, and communication.* Abu Dhabi, United Arab Emirates: Center of Excellence for Applied Research and Training & The Military Language Institute.

Mahboob, A. (2010). *The NNEST lens: Non native English speakers in TESOL.* Newcastle Upon Tyne, England: Cambridge Scholars Press.

Medgyes, P. (1992). Native or non-native: Who's worth more? *ELT Journal, 46*(4), 340–349.

Medgyes, P. (1994). *The Non-native teacher.* London, England: Macmillan.

Medgyes, P. (2001). When the teacher is a non-native speaker. In M. Celce-Murcia (Ed.), *Teaching English as a second or foreign language* (pp. 429–442). Boston, MA: Heinle & Heinle.

Menard-Warwick, J. (2008). The cultural and intercultural identities of transnational English: Two case studies from the Americas. *TESOL Quarterly, 42*(4), 617–640.

Modiano, M. (1999). International English in the global village. *English Today, 15*(2), 22–27.

Morgan, B. (2004). Teacher identity as pedagogy: Towards a field-internal conceptuali-sation in bilingual and second language education. *International Journal of Bilingual Education and Bilingualism, 7*(2–3), 172–188.

Morgan, B. (2007). Poststructuralism and applied linguistics. In J. Cummins & C. Davison (Eds.), *International handbook of English language teaching* (pp. 1033–1052). New York, NY: Springer.

Motha, S. (2006). Racializing ESOL teacher identities in US K–12 public schools. *TESOL Quarterly, 40*(3), 495–518.

Motha, S., Jain, R., & Tecle, T. (2012). Translinguistic identity-as-pedagogy: Implications for language teacher education. *International Journal of Innovation in English Lan-guage Teaching, 1*(1), 13–27.

Moussu, L., & Llurda, E. (2008). Non-native English-speaking English language teachers: History and research. *Language Teaching, 41*(3), 315–348.

Nayar, P. B. (1997). ESL/EFL dichotomy today: Language politics or pragmatics? *TESOL Quarterly, 31*(1), 9–37.

Nelson, C. L. (1985). My language, your culture: Whose communicative competence? *World Englishes, 4*(2), 243–250.

Norton, B. (1997). Language, identity, and the ownership of English. *TESOL Quarterly, 31*(3), 409–430.

Norton, B. (2000). *Identity and language learning: Gender, ethnicity and educational change*. Harlow, England: Longman/Pearson Education.

Norton, B. (2010). Language and identity. In N. Hornberger & S. L. McKay (Eds.), *Socio-linguistics and language education* (pp. 349–369). Clevedon, England: Multilingual Matters.

Nunan, D. (2001). Is language teaching a profession? *TESOL in Context, 11*(1), 4–8.

Paikeday, T. M. (1985). *The native speaker is dead!* Toronto, Canada: Paikeday.

Park, G. (2008). Lived pedagogies: Becoming a multicompetent ESOL teacher. In J. A. Carmona (Ed.), *Perspectives on community college ESL, Volume 3: Faculty, administra-tion, and the working environment* (pp. 17–30). Alexandria, VA: TESOL.

Park, G. (2012). "I am never afraid of being recognized as an NNES": One teacher's journey in claiming and embracing her Nonnative-speaker identity. *TESOL Quarterly, 46*(1), 127–151.

Pennycook, A. (1994). *The cultural politics of English as an international language*. London, England: Longman.

Pennycook, A. (1997). Vulgar pragmatism, critical pragmatism, and EAP. *English for Specific Purposes, 16*, 253–269.

Pennycook, A. (1999). Introduction: Critical approaches to TESOL. *TESOL Quarterly, 33*(3), 329–348.

Peters, M., & Humes, W. (2003). The reception of post-structuralism in educational research and policy. *Journal of Education Policy, 18*(2), 109–113.

Phillipson, R. (1992). *Linguistic imperialism*. Oxford, England: Oxford University Press.

Rajadurai, J. (2005). Revisiting the concentric circles: Conceptual and sociolinguistic considerations. *Asian EFL Journal Quarterly, 7*(4), 111–130.

Rampton, B. (1990). Displacing the "native speaker": Expertise, affiliation, and inheritance. *ELT Journal, 44*, 97–101.

Reves, T., & Medgyes, P. (1994). The non-native English speaking EFL/ESL teacher's self image: An international survey. *System, 22*(3), 353–357.

Richards, J. C. (2008). Growing up with TESOL. *English Teaching Forum, 46*(1), 2–11.

Rudolph, N. (2012). *Borderlands and border crossing: Japanese professors of English and the negotiation of translinguistic and transcultural identity* (Unpublished doctoral dissertation). University of Maryland, College Park.

Rudolph, N., Selvi, A. F., & Yazan, B. (2015). Conceptualizing and confronting inequity: Approaches within and new directions for the "NNEST Movement." *Critical Inquiry in Language Studies, 12*(1), 27–50.

Seidlhofer, B. (2004). Research perspectives on teaching English as a lingua franca. *Annual Review of Applied Linguistics, 24*, 209–239.

Selvi, A. F. (2009). A call to graduate students to reshape the field of English language teaching. *Essential Teacher, 6*(3–4), 49–51.

Selvi, A. F. (2010). "All teachers are equal, but some teachers are more equal than others": Trend analysis of job advertisements in English language teaching. *WATESOL NNEST Caucus Annual Review, 1*, 156–181.

Selvi, A. F. (2014). Myths and misconceptions about the non-native English speakers in TESOL (NNEST) Movement. *TESOL Journal, 5*(3), 573–611.

Swales, J. (1993). The English language and its teachers: Thoughts past, present, and future. *ELT Journal, 47*(4), 283–291.

Widdowson, H. G. (1994). The ownership of English. *TESOL Quarterly, 28*(2), 377–389.

Widdowson, H. G. (1998). Context, community, and authentic language. *TESOL Quarterly, 32*(4), 705–716.

Widdowson, H. G. (2003). *Defining issues in English language teaching*. Oxford, England: Oxford University Press.

Zeichner, K. (2003). The adequacies and inadequacies of three current strategies to recruit, prepare, and retain the best teachers for all students. *Teachers College Record, 105*(3), 490–519.

CHAPTER 8

Ideological English
A Theme for College Composition

Jennifer Mott-Smith

Towson University

Ownership and Attachment to "Correct" English

There is a basic social inequity that the language forms used by certain social groups are considered superior to those used by others. While some theorists have argued that no one really speaks correct academic forms natively (Bourdieu & Passeron, 1994), that we all learn them in school, others move the emphasis, arguing that, in the U.S. context, correct academic forms are in fact quite close to the vernacular of the white upper middle-class (Lippi-Green, 1997). Having been raised in a white, upper middle-class household, I know that my family and school instilled the value of academic correctness in my language. Books were consulted, for instance, to ascertain the precise meaning of a word, and speech was corrected to adhere to what we learned. We also used nonstandard forms, but always as if they belonged to someone else. Sometimes we used air quotes, but I soon realized that I could deliver a word such as *irregardless* deadpan and without quotes, in the full knowledge that all would recognize it as a joke. Language was often connected with a sense of play. I grew up using the term *hydrophobia*, for instance, to refer to the vegetable crisper in a refrigerator. At some point I parsed the roots of the word and realized that this couldn't possibly be what it meant—at least, not to anyone outside our family. The joke was on me! These jokes brought us together as a family and taught us something about who we were: people who loved language, who could make English do what we wanted, but who respected the rules of what was correct. When we played with *hydrophobia*, it was never a new coinage but remained, always, a joke.

This conflation of linguistic correctness, emotional attachment, and ownership, is, I believe, shared by many upper middle-class families in the United States. I hear it in discussions between moms at my son's school, and see it in the media. Recently, National Public Radio (NPR) aired some listeners' letters describing their linguistic pet peeves, reporting that one listener "hates the phrase, between you and I, instead of you and me. She thinks changes should be accepted only when they add something. She writes, I am saddened when nuances in language are lost" (Cornish & Siegel, 2014). In addition to the emotion of this statement, we can see the presumption of the superiority of the standard form. The implied claim is that this form is better because it is more nuanced. I am left wondering, just what nuance is lost when "between you and me" becomes "between you and I"? And how is it that what begins as a love of language becomes a rejection of some language forms?

The statement of another listener gave further evidence of this superior attitude. On the one hand, he explained, "I do believe English is, and should be, a living language. When I was teaching high school English, I told the kids that it really doesn't matter if you are proper or correct in your language, since the real goal is to be understood." He then went on to argue: "However, people of higher socioeconomic classes speak more precisely, and if you want to pass—that is, join a higher class of people— you will have to learn to sound like them" (Cornish & Siegel, 2014). This statement is an amalgam of sociolinguistic truth (to join a different socioeconomic group, it helps to sound like members of the group) and contradictory linguistic attitudes (It doesn't matter what forms you use so long as you get your point across, versus The forms of the higher classes are better in that they are more precise). Thus, the listener introduced the issue of socioeconomic class into the discussion of language, but he did not problematize the assumption that the language of the higher classes, the academic language that this teacher had likely been teaching, was considered superior not only because it helped students align with an influential group in society but also because it was linguistically better, i.e., more precise. There is little linguistic evidence, of course, that it is more precise, or better in any way.

For those of us from such backgrounds who become teachers working with students from diverse language backgrounds, it may be common to experience such contradictions. Many of us are drawn toward arguments for linguistic diversity as a form of social justice, but at the same time find it hard to let go our early love for the "correct," to let go our ownership of what we know is good English. Too quickly and with some relief, we may seize on Lisa Delpit's (1988) argument that students need to learn Standard English, the code of power, because it will give them social mobility and increased opportunities. Few have the courage to treat blatantly "incorrect" forms with the respect that Lu (1994) described using in her composition classes, in which she "introduce[d] the multicultural approach to student writing style" (p. 449). Lu described an exercise she used to model how academic language may be negotiated rather than reproduced. Leading her students through a close reading of a student-produced text containing the phrase "can able to," she showed her students (and us) how an "incorrect" form can be taken seriously and analyzed as having deep theoretical roots. She showed that idiomatic English is not the only discourse to turn to in making stylistic writing decisions, and argued that English teachers should not ignore the interests students may have in using nonstandard forms.

Standard English as Native Speakers' English

Today, as a professor working with mostly international first-year college students in the United States, I am smack-dab in the middle of the globalizing "knowledge economy" in which English plays such an important role (Altbach & Knight, 2007, p. 303). Frequently, my students see their English education as a stepping-stone to further educational or economic opportunity. Less frequently, but sometimes, they experience an "ambivalent relationship" with English, like the Hong Kong students described by Pennycook (1998), "acknowledging on the one hand that English is a language of colonial authority and a cultural intrusion but on the other hand that it is the language of success and a language one may come to love" (p. 213). My question in developing the course that I describe in this chapter is, How can I help myself and my students develop a more nuanced and critical understanding of the roles that English plays in all of our lives?

Holliday (2005) introduced *native speakerism* as an influential ideology in the field of English language teaching, and an unpacking of this ideology is key to my work in developing this course. For Holliday, native speakerism is "an established belief that 'native speaker' teachers represent a 'Western culture' from which spring the ideals both of the English language and of English language teaching methodology" (p. 6); it is "based on the assumption that 'native speakers' of English have a special claim to the language itself, that it is essentially their property" (p. 8). According to this ideology, I, as a native English-speaking Western teacher, am deferred to as speaking correct English and as having ownership of English, in contrast to my students, who, as linguistic and cultural Others, do not speak correctly or have a similar right to owner-ship. For Holliday, native speakerism is a type of culturalism, which is the combination of an essentialist view of culture, a colonialist ideology, the politics of Self and Other, and reification, a process through which these ideas become seen as natural rather than as socially constructed (Holliday, 2005, p. 23).

Pennycook's (1998) analysis of colonialism helps us understand the colonialist ideology and politics of Self and Other that undergird native speakerism. Based on an understanding of the colonized territory as a place of cultural production, Pennycook looked at colonial relationships between the British and the peoples of Australia, China, India, Malaysia, and Hong Kong, and revealed that English speakers built discourses of *Self* and *Other* into English over time. These discourses were then imported back to Britain and redistributed throughout the British Empire. In demon-strating that English was represented as a superior language in the writings of the colonial period, he demonstrated that languages other than English were understood to be inferior, and that those who constructed their selves in English were seen as British subjects, while those who constructed their selves in other languages were Other. These discourses were informed by discourses of race, class, and foreignness, so that the Other was constructed as a nonwhite, lower class, foreign, nonnative English-speaker. This analysis then helps to account for why upper middle-class white people look down on certain language forms: It is the Othering of the speakers associated with the forms that labels some forms "incorrect."

According to Pennycook, these colonial discourses came to "adhere" to English (1998, p. 7) and inform contemporary relationships, including those between teachers and students. Just as English is seen as the language of progress, democracy, and sophisticated thought, native English speakers are seen as progressive, democratic, and sophisticated thinkers. In contrast, speakers of other languages are seen as the opposite. To the extent that students are discursively constructed as Other through English discourses, it should not be surprising that they experience discursive conflicts when studying English (cf. Canagarajah, 2002, 2006; Lu, 1987).

The course I describe here confronts this situation directly. It provides students with some facts about the historical spread of English and the existence of different varieties of English, encourages them to examine colonialist, culturalist, and native speakerist discourses surrounding English, and asks them to examine their own language experiences in local contexts. In teaching the course, I seek to recognize the diversity of the students' backgrounds; students are not expected to play the role of the essentialized "nonnative English speaker," but rather are expected to make meaning of the texts we read from their particular standpoint. Since English language teaching, particularly in the United States, tends to be neutral about what it is doing, not looking at the enterprise of English language teaching itself, this course challenges the culturalist and native speakerist default position of the Western classroom.

Ideological English: A Democratic Curriculum

Teachers and students enter the English classroom with a variety of experiences and subjectivities that shape the way they think about English. Just as I was raised to embrace my ownership of English and my right to enforce correctness, some of my students grew up believing that the native English speaking teacher is the "ideal teacher," while others embrace the English norms of their own local context. By coming together in dialogue with each other and with critical texts in a democratic classroom, we can disrupt the ideology of native speakerism. This benefits not only English language students, but their teachers as well, as they unpack their own feelings of attachment, ownership, and correctness.

To engage the theme of *Ideological English* in the U.S. context is to engage students and teacher in a democratic dialogue around difference. Ideological English works as a theme for an ESOL writing course in the United States because it is a lived experience of all my students. Having students take a reflexive approach to the learning of English encourages the development of a critical mind. One of the hallmarks of success of the curriculum is the fact that students have applied ideas they encounter to their own lived experiences; for instance, they have drawn parallels between Standard English hegemony and standard language hegemony in their own countries. Thus, students bring their own knowledge to the dialogue, constructing themselves as knowers and resisting the colonialist discourse that positions them as unsophisticated thinkers. I also learn from dialogue with my students, which helps to democratize the classroom. What I learn expands me as a person and also keeps me from burning out as a teacher.

I developed this curriculum for a 14-week first-year college composition course. I include videos and shorter, more accessible texts because several of the reading texts are quite challenging. I also change the texts for each group of students, adding readings on creoles when I have creole speakers, for instance. Here is an overview of the semester.

PART 1: ENGLISH VARIETIES AND LANGUAGE DISCRIMINATION

Goals. Introduce the notion of language varieties by exploring social dialects and the Englishes of nonnative English speakers; explore attitudes toward different varieties; discuss Standard English as a sociopolitical value and language equality as a linguistic value; gain knowledge of language discrimination in the United States.

Texts.

- Louis Alvarez and Andrew Kolker: *American Tongues* [documentary film].
- Langston Hughes: "Judgment Day," "Morning After," and "Refugee in America" [poems].
- Amy Tan: "Mother Tongue" [essay].
- Rosina Lippi-Green: *English with an Accent.* Chapter 11: "The Stranger within the Gates" (pp. 217–239) [nonfiction text].
- ABC News: *20/20 Downtown*: "Are Some People Being Discriminated Against for the Color of Their Voice?" [television broadcast].

To begin the course, we watch a film and then read some short poems in nonstandard English. Here, I have included three poems by Langston Hughes, two of which contain nonstandard forms. Without telling the students that all three poems are by Hughes, I ask them what they think of them. They often think that "Judgment Day" and "Morning After" are not written by the same poet as "Refugee in America." Thus, I introduce the notion of language variety as choice.

Writing assignments. In addition to questions scaffolding comprehension of the reading texts, students probe their own attitudes, experiences, and knowledge, and extend the ideas in the texts. Here are some of the extension writing prompts I have used:

1. What English form do you consider to be correct? What expert source would you go to if you had a question about English? What makes the answer you get "right?"

2. Write about something that interested/surprised/confused you in *American Tongues*.

3. Discuss the Englishes that you know or use (hear, speak, write, or read). How do these Englishes compare with Tan's (1994)? How would you describe each one? What other languages do you use or did you grow up using? In what contexts do/did you use each?

4. Have you ever seen someone equating language ability with intelligence? Explain.

5. How is the language prejudice experienced by nonnative speakers similar to or different from that experienced by speakers of nonstandard English? Discuss real or hypothetical examples of situations that illustrate cases of language prejudice or discrimination.

6. Think about what language varieties and languages are used in your home country, and how they are differently valued. What language prejudice or discrimination exists in your country? Compare the situation to that of the United States, drawing on the texts for support.

PART 2: COLONIAL ENGLISH EDUCATION IN RHODESIA

Goals. Explore the historical spread of English in one colonial context; gain an understanding of personal gains and losses involved in learning English in this context; examine the theme of Ideological English in narrative form; give students the chance to break away from the theme of English by writing on a different theme from the novel if they so choose.

Text. Tsitsi Dangarembga: *Nervous Conditions* [novel].

Writing assignments. Reader response journals culminating in an essay analyzing one theme from the novel.

PART 3: EXTENDING COLONIAL ENGLISH EDUCATION

Goals. Extend examination of English colonial education to Indian and Kenyan contexts; explore English as lingua franca and as an instrument of internalized oppression; consider what it means for people from postcolonial societies to write in English (touching on the ideas of audience, authenticity, contributions to literature); revisit Dangarembga's ideas in nonfiction form.

Texts.

1. Ngũgĩ Wa Thiong'o: *Decolonising the Mind.* Excerpt from chapter 1, "The Language of African Literature" (pp. 4–13) [essay].

2. Alastair Pennycook: *English and the Discourses of Colonialism.* Excerpt: "Education, Control and Language" (pp. 71–75) [nonfiction text].

3. Shashi Tharoor: "A Bedeviling Question in the Cadence of English" [essay].

Writing assignments.

1. What is *colonization of the mind*? What social groups might be said to experience it?

2. Ngũgĩ (1986) wrote, "The physical violence of the battlefield was followed by the psychological violence of the classroom" (p. 9). Did you see this kind of psychological violence in Dangarembga? Explain.

3. Pennycook (1998) argued that among Indians the demand for English language instruction was high, but that the colonial government seemed not to want to meet that demand. Why do you think the demand was so high? Why do you think the British didn't want to meet it?

4. Tharoor (2001) wrote, "Am I not guilty of the terrible sin of inauthenticity?" What could Tharoor be seen an "authentic" or "inauthentic" representative of?

5. Noting that there is a "new generation" of Indian writers who write in English, Tharoor (2001) argued, "Of the many unintended consequences of empire, it is hard to imagine one of greater value to both colonizers and colonized." How do you think this new generation of writers benefits the colonizers (British)? How does it benefit the colonized (Indians)?

6. What role has English played in your home country?

7. Discuss the theme of English in Dangarembga's novel in the context of the Ngũgĩ, Pennycook, and Tharoor readings.

PART 4: BACK TO ENGLISH VARIATION AND THE UNITED STATES

Goals. Appreciate the power of language; explore the ways in which language is tied to culture and identity; explore racism as a discourse that adheres to English; gain exposure to models of negotiation/resistance; have students claim authority over English and strategize around form; have teacher accept the "communicative burden" (Lippi-Green, 1997, p. 71).

Texts.

- Ossie Davis: "The English Language Is My Enemy" [essay].

- Gloria Anzaldúa: From *Borderlands/La Frontera: The New Mestiza.* Excerpt from Ahmad (pp. 437–445) [essay].

Writing assignments.

1. Have you ever reacted physically to someone using a dirty word? Do you believe that words can do people physical harm?

2. Davis (1973) claimed there are 44 positive synonyms for "whiteness" and 60 negative ones for "Blackness." How might this fact affect the lives of Black and White people concretely?

3. Are you convinced that English carries racism within it in the way that Davis (1973) thought it does, due to the historical relationship between Blacks and Whites in the United States?

4. Consider whether we can understand African-Americans as analogous to a colonized people. Can we read Davis as a colonized person speaking back to English, like Ngũgĩ?

5. Discuss a situation in which you experienced or witnessed language discrimination. How might racism or xenophobia have been involved? Is it possible to separate these three?

6. What story does Anzaldúa (2007) tell about her schooling that is similar to Ngũgĩ's (1986)? Do you hear the kind of internalized oppression that Ngũgĩ wrote about in Anzaldúa's text?

7. Anzaldúa (2007) code-switches in her writing. What effects does this have?

8. What choices have you made about the style of English you use? What aspects of your identity do you want to emphasize in your writing? What audiences do you want to reach? What topics and purposes do you care most about?

For this last assignment, I encourage students not to write in academic English, but rather to make strategic choices around linguistic form, finding a rhetorical fit between author identity, audience, writing purpose, and topic. This goal helps students do authentic writing. It is interesting to note that when students write in English that they believe is nonacademic, their writing often flows better than what they wrote previously. I have taken the assignment a step further and accepted it in languages other than English as well. Most students do not have the courage to hand in a paper in another language in English class, but for those who do, the symbolism of the act is profound. Through this act, the student reverses the power relation between teacher as knower and student as learner. This moment, powerful for both of us, forces me to accept what Lippi-Green (1997) has called the "communicative burden" (p. 71). According to Lippi-Green, Standard English speakers often refuse to do their share to make the communication successful when interacting with people with nonstandard or nonnative accents. When I get a paper in another language and need to slog through it or find a translator, the burden is shifted, and I have to temporarily let go my ownership of what I know is good English.

"English in the Globalized Society": A Student Essay

In closing, I would like to share an excerpt from a student paper written for part 3 of the curriculum. Positioning herself against the resistance narrative that emerged in the postcolonial texts, this Korean student explained why it was reasonable and strategic for Koreans to embrace English. Earlier in the paper she conceded that fighting for the language forms of one's own culture is important, but she went on to argue her main point: that in her experience, the influence of English is tied up with the influence of global capital. Koreans, therefore, have an interest and a right to learn English in order to gain monetarily. Here, she made her argument by developing the metaphor of language as a vehicle:

> Tharoor, an Indian Writer who works for United Nations, write in New York Times (2001), 'Language us a vehicle, not a destination.' People who have a good vehicle like BMW don't need to worry about their own vehicle. However, let's think about a guy who has a small, uncomfortable bicycle. He couldn't dump out his old bicycle because it is inherited from their grand, grand, grandfather. He wants to buy one more vehicle like BMW. It is a matter of course. He could be blamed by other family members or could be confused about their own identity if he throws away his first vehicle. However, finally he has two vehicles at the same time.
>
> Tharoor who sees himself as a cosmopolitan Indian with rural roots thinks that the English could tie the family members who are from many differ regions. He wrote in the same article (2001), 'English is the language that brings those various threads of my India together.' The guy who has both BMW and bicycle could give a ride to his family members thanks to the BMW, now. The bicycle is precious one for him, however, it couldn't use for giving a ride over one person.
>
> Ngũgĩ, who was grown up in Kenya during colonization of the Britain, wrote (1986), 'The choice of language and the use to which language is put is central to a people's definition of themselves. (p. 4)' Think about the guy again. Now, his identification could be defined by how much time he use the BMW. If he always uses the BMW and forgets about the bicycle, he is the same with the person who has only the BMW. I think it is the person like immigrants for the language problem. They have their old vehicle; however, they need to use the BMWs because the roads in the big city where they moved are filled with cars. They couldn't be survived with the old, small bicycle. They choose to live there and are forced to use the BMWs.
>
> If he usually uses bicycle and use BMW for special occasions, he is more likely a bicycle-part person. It is the person like my Korean professor in Korea who usually goes abroad to participate the meetings and uses English for communication with foreign scholars. I think most Koreans who live in Korea learn English could be in this case. Some Koreans learn English to sell Korean products to foreigners or to get some information about the better knowledge such as sciences, engineering, and economics. Others learn English to enjoy the movies or music or English-speaking culture. They know it is better to use the bicycles because their old, small bicycle is suitable for thin roads in their hometown. However, when they want to buy something in big cities or to travel other places with wide roads, they could use the BMWs. They know the BMWs are required for their affluent lives.

As a writing teacher, I love this piece for its artistic quality. I am also pleased by the meticulous application of the rules of referencing, which I teach. But I included it here because it exemplifies the type of critical work I look for from students taking this course. Through her extended metaphor, the student engaged in a careful thought experiment, considering various ways Koreans might react to the influence of the

English knowledge economy. She named the gains and losses of making difficult language choices, and connected with her own lived experience by naming her professor as an example. She also recognized the tie between language and identity. The voice of this student came out strong and sure, demonstrating her ownership of English. Isn't that what we, as English teachers, should be reaching for?

References

ABC News (Producer). (2002, February 6). Are some people being discriminated against for the color of their voice? [Television broadcast]. In *20/20 Downtown*. Boston, MA: WCVB.

Altbach, P. G., & Knight, J. (2007). The internationalization of higher education: Motivations and realities. *Journal of Studies in International Education, 11*(3/4), 290–305.

Alvarez, L., & A. Kolker (Directors). (1987). *American tongues: A film about the way we talk* [Documentary]. New York, NY: Center for New American Media.

Anzaldúa, G. (2007). From *Borderlands/la frontera: The new Mestiza*. In D. Ahmad (Ed.), *Rotten English: A literary anthology* (pp. 436–451). New York, NY: W.W. Norton.

Bourdieu, P., & Passeron, J.-C. (1994). Introduction: Language and relationship to language in the teaching situation. In P. Bourdieu, J.-C. Passeron, & M. de Saint Martin (Eds.), *Academic discourse* (pp. 1–34). Stanford, CA: Stanford University Press.

Canagarajah, A. S. (2002). Multilingual writers and the academic community: Towards a critical relationship. *Journal of English for Academic Purposes, 1*(1), 29–44.

Canagarajah, A. S. (2006). The place of World Englishes in composition: Pluralization continued. *College Composition and Communication, 57*(4), 586–619.

Cornish, A., & Siegel, R. (2014, June 4). Letters: Reactions to "Bad English." Retrieved July 7, 2014, from http://www.npr.org/2014/06/04/318888320/letters-reactions-to -bad-english

Dangarembga, T. (1989). *Nervous conditions*. Seattle, WA: Seal Press.

Davis, O. (1973). The English language is my enemy. In R. H. Bentley & S. D. Crawford (Eds.), *Black language reader* (pp. 71–77). Glenview, IL: Scott, Foresman.

Delpit. L. (1988). The silenced dialogue: Power and pedagogy in educating other people's children. *Harvard Educational Review, 58*(3), 280–298.

Holliday, A. (2005). *The struggle to teach English as an international language*. Oxford, England: Oxford University Press.

Hughes, L. (1974). *Selected poems of Langston Hughes*. New York, NY: Vintage.

Lippi-Green, R. (1997). *English with an accent: Language, ideology, and discrimination in the United States*. New York, NY: Routledge.

Lu, M.-Z. (1987). From silence to words: Writing as struggle. *College English, 4*, 437–448.

Lu, M.-Z. (1994). Professing multiculturalism: The politics of style in the contact zone. *College Composition and Communication, 45*(4), 442–458.

Ngũgĩ Wa Thiong'o. (1986). *Decolonising the mind: The politics of language in African literature*. Portsmouth, NH: Heineman.

Pennycook, A. (1998). *English and the discourses of colonialism*. New York, NY: Routledge.

Tan, A. (1994). Mother tongue. In D. McQuade & R. Atwan (Eds.), *The writer's presence: A pool of essays* (pp. 144–149). Boston, MA: Bedford St. Martin's.

Tharoor, S. (2001, July 30). A bedeviling question in the cadence of English. *The New York Times*.

CHAPTER 9

Provincializing English
Race, Empire, and Social Justice

Suhanthie Motha
University of Washington

A still silence suffused the dim classroom, all eyes on the dark-haired girl reading in a soft voice, only the hushed murmur of voices in the hallway seeping in through the closed door.

Marisa concluded: ". . . I don't know what he done after that, but I was happy that I had stayed home. The End."

Ms. Mora allowed the words to settle into her students' ears, then commented, nodding approvingly: "That was a moving story, Marisa. 'I don't know what he *did* after that.' Thank you for reading it to us. And there's the bell. Your final drafts of your narrative essays are due on Monday. Have a good weekend, everyone."

Marisa packed up her books and hesitated by Ms. Mora's desk.

"I really enjoyed listening to your story, Marisa. Do you have a question?"

"Ms. Mora, which one is right, 'I don't know what he *did* after that' or 'I don't know what he *done* after that'? Because my friends all say 'done,' and some of them are American."

"Well, Marisa, it's okay to say 'what he done' when you're talking with your friends, but when you write that sentence in an essay, you should write 'what he did.'"

"Are my friends wrong?"

"No, it's just that different forms of English are appropriate under different circumstances. 'What he done' is a register we use when talking with our friends, and 'what he did' is just a different register that we use when we write for academic purposes. It's not that one is good or bad, they're just different. It's good for you to know both and to be able to use both in the appropriate circumstances. We call that 'code-switching.' It's a good skill to have."

———

"There's something powerful about students seeing their own language within an academic context, in an English classroom," said Mr. Kim, adjusting his projector to cast the solid black letters across the length of the university classroom onto a white screen. "So I use bilingual materials as often as I can, such as pieces by Junot Diaz and Sandra Cisneros. One of my favorites is Gustavo Pérez Firmat's (1995) poem 'Bilingual Blues.' It's a piece grounded in the author's own experience of bilingualism as a contradiction, as both a blessing and a burden. Pérez Firmat mixes his languages together as he writes about his mixed feelings toward his two languages. My sense is that my bilingual students often see themselves in the poem and connect to the author's experience, which makes it meaningful for and relevant to for them."

———

Before Ms. Martin clicked on the key to start the Youtube video of her high school students, she commented:

> I encourage my students to develop their own hip-hop pieces as part of a poetry unit. As homework they first do research, they develop an ethnography of hip-hop so that they know what it looks like, how it sounds, the different forms it takes. Hip-hop is such a wonderful gateway to linguistic hybridity; it offers amazing promise for students to develop understandings of the role of glocalization in their lives. My students are super-invested in hip-hop, it's accessible to them, and it's a perfect site for them to develop linguistic flexibility and sophistication through language mixing and translanguaging. It allows them to participate in a culture they identify with and want to be a part of, and to be a part of a large movement that is meaningful to most of them. It spits in the face of many language ideologies we're trying to reject. And on a basic level, they get to play with words, rhymes, alliteration, rhythm.

Introduction

In this chapter, I argue that many of the pedagogical strategies we as English teachers employ in support of multilingualism, antiracism, and anticolonialism are underpinned by efforts toward "deterritorializing" (Hardt & Negri, 2000) English, or reducing the connectedness between the English language and particular places. While deterritorialization is not an unworthy pursuit, I suggest that these strategies used alone are not always helpful in working toward social justice and can even sometimes serve the opposite end. I propose that deterritorializing efforts would be strengthened by adding an additional layer, that is, provincializing (Chakrabarty, 2000) English, or seeking to support in learners and teachers a critical analysis of the ways in which the language is racialized and colonized, of how learning English changes us, and of how participating in the teaching of English changes the world (Motha, 2014).

Provincializing Language Varieties

All of the three teachers in the illustrations at the beginning of this chapter embrace pedagogical intentions that are specifically antiracist. Ms. Mora is committed to ensuring that Marisa and her friends don't hear their language denigrated in any way. Embedded in the strategy she employs to legitimate the form of English that Marisa is using is a suggestion that varieties of Englishes are different but equal, with an attempt to resist passing any judgment of correctness, superiority, or merit. Marisa is in an ESOL class in a school with a majority African American population, and the form she used is typical of Black English or African American Vernacular English (AAVE). She has learned this particular form, the use of a past participle to denote the past tense, from her peers who speak AAVE.

When Ms. Mora tells Marisa that different forms of English are appropriate under different circumstances, she implies an ideology of "separate but equal," the notion that the forms occupy different social spaces but are equivalent, in other words are "equally good." Is it true that the language varieties are equal? Ms. Mora certainly would like to believe so, and so would I. Perhaps you would, too. However, telling us that they are equal does not make them so and constitutes, to a degree, a form of color blindness or power evasion. Some forms of English can be used only in high-status spaces; others are limited to lower-status contexts or, if they are used in high-status situations, their use is limited, marked, or must be explained. The differing positions that varieties occupy in the hierarchy are racialized, with varieties associated with Whiteness being accorded greater legitimacy than those connected to people who are coded as racial minorities (Motha, 2014). Understanding the sociohistorical context of the teaching of any material is an important part of understanding that content, and this is certainly true of the teaching of the English language. In this example, the two different forms of English in question occupy different social statuses because of their historical attachment within the social imaginary to particular races or places, these two rhyming constructs being inseparable from each other. African American varieties of English have a long and historical anchoring to the African continent, often by way of other geographies, while English is perpetually on some level, even etymologically, connected to England, also often by way of other lands. To imply that all forms of English are equally legitimate is to attempt to deterritorialize them, to sever their connection to place, since these connections play a meaningful role in preserving their inferior or superior social positioning.

Deterritorialization is a popular strategy for English language teachers seeking social justice. Mario Saraceni (2010), for instance, understands English's connections to particular places to be in the process of being ruptured. In his book *The Relocation of English* he describes shifts that he sees occurring in today's globalized context: a shift from English conceptualized as the language of England to English as the language of many countries; a shift from an emphasis on the importance of nativeness in English to the use of English as a second language or lingua franca; a shift from English as owned by native speakers to English owned by those who use it; a shift from English as a monochrome standard to a recognition of a multiplicity of valid Englishes; and a shift from English as vehicle for Anglo-Saxon culture to English as capable of expressing any culture. These trends all walk hand in hand with a desire for deterritorialization in our contemporary world.

Ms. Mora's approach, too, seeks to shift English from a unitary standard to recognition of a multiplicity of valid Englishes, regardless of their racial or geographical origin. It is a pedagogy in pursuit of deterritorialization. This articulation of equality from an adult whose words carry authority can temporarily allow Marisa to believe that her friends' language and her own are legitimate. However, on some level, and eventually probably at a completely conscious level, Marisa is likely to come to realize that newscasters on the television, most of her teachers, individuals she comes in contact with who carry cultural capital or class status, and even the current president of the United States, who is often identified as Black, do not say "I don't know what he done after that" in public settings. It does not serve Marisa well for us as English teachers to try to obscure or even hide from Marisa the differential positionings of language and in particular a history of language discrimination that has been part of a project to subjugate some groups over others.

English is a fundamentally racialized language, irreversibly shaped by its history as an important vehicle during the 500 years of European colonialism across the globe. For this reason, it is impossible to talk about race without talking about empire, meaning both historical colonialism and modern-day patterns of globalization and Western dominance and the interconnections between the two. It similarly makes no sense to talk about empire without talking about race. English is embedded within its legacy of being passed primarily from people coded as White to those understood to be racial minorities, often as a benevolent dispersion of civilization and culture to poor unfortunates who lacked these qualities. The shadow of this legacy continues to lie over the profession today. It is important to remember that while the historical transmission of English was frequently made to appear to be part of a munificent and often sanctified enterprise, it was also often coercive or violent, both literally and symbolically, and it taught people of color that they were inferior.

Even if Marisa's awareness of the unequal status accorded to different language varieties is not explicit in the moment described, she is nonetheless unconsciously taking in messages about worth and value of not only the language varieties, but also the people and groups associated with them. She is being colonized, as it were, perhaps without her knowledge, by unspoken and subtle messages around her. Because the messages are unspoken, they are not easily available for critique and can more smoothly and invisibly lead individuals to internalize oppression (Fanon, 1963; Friere, 1970), to come to unquestioningly accept an essential inferiority of their language ·or culture.

If we cannot obfuscate English's territorialized past, how do we position ourselves to teach the language in ways that do not promote relations of race and empire? This is where the work of Dipesh Chakrabarty (2000) can provide an alternative—or perhaps expanded—approach. Chakrabarty does not write about the English language specifically but rather about colonized thinking. In *Provincializing Europe*, he writes about the project of provincializing or decentering the intellectual footprint left by Europe across the globe, telling us that

> provincializing Europe is not a project of rejecting or discarding European
> thought. . . . European thought is at once indispensable and inadequate in helping

us to think through the experiences of political modernity in non-Western nations, and provincializing Europe becomes the task of exploring how this thought—which is now everybody's heritage and which affects us all—may be renewed from and for the margins. (p. 16)

He suggests that we should not be rejecting European thought wholesale—and in fact, how could we somehow disentangle, at this point in history, European thought from precolonial thought? Rather, he advocates for an understanding of the ways in which European thought is woven throughout everyday life. We cannot remove the effects of colonization, but we can resist their naturalization by refusing to allow them to become invisible, to stay invisible. In the same way, I suggest the application of this notion of provincializing to a crucial element of colonialism: that is, language and, in particular, the English language. I propose a provincialized English.

What would a provincialized English mean for Ms. Mora (and perhaps by now you have realized that I am Ms. Mora, and I have implemented versions of the pedagogies employed by this only slightly fictional character)? One characteristic that racism has in its favor is its invisibility cloak, its ability to remain unnamed and unseen when it is solidly present. In the example above, Marisa used a language form that was racialized because it is associated with people of color in her school context, specifically, African Americans. Ms. Mora's unconscious decision not to mention this racial layer was underpinned by her anti-racist intentions, her desire to deterritorialize the language forms. In actual fact, however, not mentioning race means that she is not able to have an explicit conversation with Marisa about how racialized language ideologies serve to maintain class divisions, perpetuate economic hierarchies, and oppress some groups of people. By overtly naming race, she would have been able to unambiguously challenge the notion that languages are politically and racially neutral. When she claimed that languages are equal, she missed the opportunity to explain that some languages have been erroneously socially constructed to be associated with grammatical inferiority, laziness, and vulgarity when these claims do not hold true in any linguistic sense, and that the social construction of some languages as inferior serves to keep their speakers subjugated in broader society. Naming race would have allowed her to support Marisa's understandings of how these constructions serve particular purposes and to explore Marisa's own options for questioning or resistance, for making informed language choices in a variety of situations. Provincializing English would have meant equipping Marisa with an understanding of how different varieties of English are situated among networks of power within a history of slavery and colonization.

Provincializing Translanguaging

Let us turn now to Mr. Kim. What would a provincialized English have meant for Mr. Kim? The teacher's embracing of literature that includes Spanish in the classroom of his students, most of whom speak Spanish at home, offers a degree of acceptability to the language, and his use of poetry that mixes two languages helps to legitimize translanguaging (Bou Ayash, 2014; Creese & Blackledge, 2010; García & Li, 2014) and code-meshing (Canagarajah, 2011) practices, which are a natural everyday language use but historically not sanctioned within academic contexts. He chooses materials that are meaningful and relevant to students' own experiences, an important curricular decision when we consider Wayne Au's (2008/2009) caution that "when classes are not grounded in the lives of students, do not include the voices and knowledge of communities being studied, and are not based in dialogue, they create environments where not only are white students miseducated, but students of color feel as if their very identities are under attack" (p. 1). Mr. Kim intentionally draws from students' discursive, linguistic, and semiotic resources to develop his teaching, and he honors writing that approaches mixing two languages as a "single integrated system" (Canagarajah, 2011, p. 403).

However, Mr. Kim's teaching can be read as sidestepping the subject of power. The teacher doesn't discuss the reasons that language crossings are, for Pérez Firmat, "un ajiaco de contradicciones," a melting pot of contradictions, within the broad, international context of inequitable relationships among language speakers. He does not engage with questions surrounding Spanish's positionality in relation to English, shaped as it is by centuries of conflict and convoluted power dynamics between the United States and its Spanish-speaking neighbors. Nor does he mention formations of Spanish speakers within the U.S. and global social imaginary, which help shape the meanings attributed to Spanish. These representations have also evolved in a context of political skirmishes between Spanish speakers and English speakers and often of political consequences of U.S. economic and foreign policy in a number of nations in which Spanish is the most popular language. Mr. Kim's pedagogies do address the artificiality of language borders, rejecting the false construction of static boundaries between languages and contexts in which languages can be appropriately used, and eschewing a long U.S. school history of cultivating shame about Spanish and other heritage languages. The poem that he selected, Gustavo Pérez Firmat's "Bilingual Blues," engages with themes that are likely to ring true for his bilingual students, such as the psychological difficulty of living divided between two languages and the feeling of being failed by both languages. Provincializing English might imply a consideration of why bilingualism is the norm in some communities, with speakers moving somewhat unproblematically between languages in everyday interactions, but for Pérez Firmat is a source of "bilingual blues." Provincializing English would mean having students engage with questions about why translanguaging is permissible (and in particular permissible without any kind of explanation) in this poem but not in the writing portion of the SAT, about how the meanings ascribed to different languages create social hierarchies and reinforce class and economic divisions. It might ask students why the author experiences his two languages as a purée of impurities (*un puré de impurezas*), how the notion of languages as pollutants to each other evolved and, more important, what purposes are served when ideologies of linguistic purity gain traction. Blackledge and Creese (2010) have documented sophisticated and deeply communicative translanguaging practices in complementary schools or heritage language schools in the United Kingdom, practices that would not transfer smoothly to traditional public schooling contexts. To provincialize English would mean asking about what makes these practices and these contexts different, and about the role played by race and empire in the constructions of legitimacy in different spaces. I'm sure that you've guessed by now that I am Mr. Kim, too, and I have embraced versions of his pedagogies.

Provincializing Hip-Hop

Finally, let's consider Ms. Martin. Incorporating hip-hop into teaching offers educators an avenue from youth culture directly into schools and back again. Hip-hop embraces, in its very nature, both deterritorialization and insurgency. It promotes deterritorialization by offering us relocated voices, thus challenging connections between place and communication. For instance, in the Youtube video *Hip Hop is Hip Hop* (I thank Awad Ibrahim for introducing me to this clip on his mobile device), we see a cast of hip-hop artists from around the world. A tall, lanky Korean youth clad in black leather bows deeply, respectfully, then points his fingers at the ground, to his right, to his left, at his temples, directly at the camera. He hummer-shakes and spins on his head before the stately statue of Sejong the Great in Seoul's Gwanghwamun Square. He drums out the words, staccato-like, in Korean: "Have you listened to hangul rap before? Sejong the Great created hangul and Korean hip-hop led the way." Scenes change disjointedly, then a woman wandering through a handicraft market in a red baseball cap emblazoned with the words "Indonesian Hustler" swings a sheet of long gleaming midnight hair over her shoulder and points her index fingers skyward, chanting, "Pelogari melodi ekuni amunisi inspirasi [Study the melody full of ammunition and inspiration]." Switching to a wall slick with bright painted graffiti images, a gloomy-eyed man sporting a beard and a black turban sings, "Mere desh india nu karan pesh global hip-hop di race main chalya. [I'm representing my country. India is the race of global hip-hop]." On one hand, these images rewrite what we know about where culture belongs, mapping images and languages of lives far removed from the United States onto spaces that have been constructed as associated with U.S. urban life or Blackness. Hip-hop makes us question our assumptions about where things belong. Are international hip-hop artists being assimilated into U.S. culture, or are they changing U.S. culture by acting upon and appropriating constructions of hip-hop? Is the embracing of hip-hop a form of assimilation or of resistance? In fact, it is both and neither, making a compelling case for the need for provincialized consciousness in order that students make agentive and informed choices about how hip-hop plays itself out in their lives. Hip-hop can be read as having an assimilatory effect. "Is the whole world becoming a stage for American culture?" asks Alastair Pennycook (2007, p. 1), continuing on to muse, "or are there other ways of thinking about this?" Hip-hop can, alternatively, open up possibilities for subversive racialized action by allowing students to identify ways to disrupt norms, such as conventions of monolingualism or

English dominance. Hip-hop can interrupt the broad social veneration of Whiteness that students encounter frequently in many of the spaces they move in and out of. However, unless hip-hop language practices are understood within the constellation of power relationships that English, Blackness, Whiteness, and youth culture mediate, it can serve to arouse in students unconscious desires (Motha & Lin, 2014) for assimilation and acceptance rather than create opportunities for critical questioning.

My attempts at supporting students' ethnography (You guessed it! I am Ms. Martin, too!) was a good first step. Teaching students to be cultural detectives figuring out the mores of the worlds that they are entering is one way to position them to be agentive in discovering values and conventions. However, this exercise is meaningless if the knowledge they construct in the process ultimately teaches them nothing more than to conform, obey, or unquestioningly appropriate the dominant language at the expense of their own. Rather, provincializing English should teach them to understand and critically analyze the effects of translanguaging practices and English language acquisition in general so that their choices are situated solidly within sociopolitical context.

I pause to mention at this point that provincializing English is not a project to teach students to carry out our will, but rather one to support their agency in making informed decisions about what is in their best interests, something that only they can decide for themselves. Sometimes assimilation is strategic. This means that they may not make the choices we would, or even that we wish they would, but that an important part of provincializing English is the ability to make choices with eyes wide open, regardless of what shape those choices ultimately take.

Another piece of provincializing English is for TESOL professionals—teachers, researchers, administrators, teachers educators, and policy makers—to have an understanding of how English works, how it gains status, and what we as an industry do to change or maintain the value that English holds globally.

It is not enough that we simply oppose racism. Over centuries, the processes that sustain racial discrimination have become invisible and difficult to detect, in keeping with the complex functioning of colonial discourses (Bhabha, 1994). Therefore, antiracist pedagogy requires more than simply confronting racism when it is visible. It requires us to be equipped to detect racialized practices and furthermore to support in our students a critical analysis of the English language, its promises, and the practices involved in its teaching industry. Beverly Tatum (2003) likens the cycle of racism to a moving walkway:

> Active racist behavior is equivalent to walking fast on the conveyor belt. The person engaged in active racist behavior has identified with the ideology of our White supremacist system and is moving with it. Passive racist behavior is equivalent to standing still on the walkway. No overt effort is being made, but the conveyor belt moves the bystanders along to the same destination as those who are actively walking. But unless they are walking actively in the opposite direction at a speed faster than the conveyor belt—unless they are actively anti-racist—they will find themselves carried along with the others. (2003, p. 11)

In the same way, no matter how abhorrent we find the invisible racism inherent in some practices of English language teaching, we will avoid reproducing inequities only if we seek out and unrelentingly confront them. Provincializing English requires us as English teaching professionals to problematize all levels of our profession: our classroom practices around the Englishes we teach and our error correction methods; the situatedness of English language learners within our schools, institutions, and policies; the boundaries between school categories; and our global constructions of English.

Of course, learning and teaching English are important and life-changing endeavors. A social justice orientation to TESOL would ensure that as students acquire English, as teachers teach English, they ensure that it is a provincialized English, one with a thorough understanding of how the language is racialized and colonized, of how learning English changes us, how spreading English changes the world, how our classroom-based instructional practices surrounding accent discrimination, native-speaker supremacy, multilingualism, language varieties, and translingualism are connected to global-level economic disparities, empire, and race. A provincialized English would recognize the importance of its situatedness, history, and location in its learners and its teachers.

References

Alim, H. S., Ibrahim, A., & Pennycook, A. (2009). Global linguistic flows: Hip hop cultures, youth identities, and the politics of language. New York, NY: Routledge.

Au, W. (2009). Decolonizing the classroom. *Rethinking Schools Online, 23*(2). Retrieved from http://www.rethinkingschools.org/archive/23_02/deco232.shtml

Bhabha, H. K. (1994). *The location of culture.* London, England: Routledge.

Blackledge, A., & Creese, A. (2010). Multilingualism: A critical perspective. London, England: Continuum.

Bou Ayash, N. (2014). U.S. translingualism through a cross-national and cross-linguistic lens. In B. Horner & K. Kopelson (Eds.), *Reworking English in rhetoric and composition: Global interrogations, local interventions* (pp. 116–130). Carbondale: Southern Illinois University.

Canagarajah, S. (2011). Codemeshing in academic writing: Identifying teachable strategies of translanguaging. *Modern Language Journal, 95*(3), 401–417.

Chakrabarty, D. (2000). *Provincializing Europe: Postcolonial thought and historical difference.* Princeton, NJ: Princeton University Press.

Creese, A., & Blackledge, A. (2010). Translanguaging in the bilingual classroom: A pedagogy for learning and teaching? *Modern Language Journal, 94*(1), 103–115.

Fanon, F. (1967). *Black skin, white masks.* New York, NY: Grove Press.

Freire, P. (1998). *Pedagogy of freedom: Ethics, democracy, and civic courage.* Lanham, MD: Rowman and Littlefield.

García, O., & Li, W. (2014). *Translanguaging: Language, bilingualism and education.* Basingstoke, England: Palgrave Macmillan.

Hardt, M., & Negri, A. (2000). *Empire.* Cambridge, MA: Harvard University Press.

Motha, S. (2014). *Race, empire, and English language teaching: Creating responsible and ethical anti-racist practice.* New York, NY: Teachers College Press.

Motha, S., & Lin, A. (2014). "Non-coercive rearrangements": Theorizing desire in TESOL. *TESOL Quarterly, 48*(2), 331–359.

Pennycook, A. (2007). *Global Englishes and transcultural flows.* London, England: Routledge.

Pérez Firmat, G. (1995). *Bilingual blues: Poems, 1981–1994.* Tempe, AZ: Bilingual Press/ Editorial Bilingüe.

Saraceni, M. (2010). *The relocation of English: Shifting paradigms in a global era.* Basingstoke, England: Palgrave Macmillan.

Tatum, B. D. (2003). *Why are all the Black kids sitting together in the cafeteria? and other conversations about race.* New York, NY: Basic Books.

PART IV:
LANGUAGE RIGHTS, PRIVILEGE, AND RACE

CHAPTER 10

Language Rights and Indigenous Education in Australia

Adriano Truscott
Australian Council of TESOL Associations

Indigenous[1] education in Australia has long been defined by social justice considerations. Indigenous peoples in Australia have linguistic competencies that range
from multilingual to bidialectal, and thus require specialist TESOL education, what
is commonly referred to in Australia as English as an additional language or dialect
(EAL/D). While this has been acknowledged in important national government
documents, particular ideologies have led to Indigenous education in Australia at
the different levels—from federal to local—being conceptualised, implemented, and
assessed against monolingual norms that pertain to the dominant non-Indigenous
culture. Consequently, Indigenous students are often reflected in media and political
rhetoric as perpetually underachieving, thus reinforcing negative racial stereotypes
and distorting potential multilingual educational possibilities by relying on monocultural conceptualisations of educational and social success.

The TESOL profession works to subvert this trend that is as entrenched as it is
counterproductive to improving education outcomes and achieving actual reconciliation between Indigenous and non-Indigenous Australians. Despite being a minority
voice, TESOL advocates, such as the Australian Council of TESOL Associations
(ACTA), have leveraged important gains for recognition of language rights in the
national curriculum and teacher standards.

This chapter will first review Indigenous Education in Australia within a context
of language policy and rights; then it will examine the role of TESOL in the protection
of such rights. Last, I shall consider selected classroom practices that reflect an

---

[1] The term *Indigenous* refers to the Aboriginal and Torres Strait Islander (ATSI) peoples of Australia and both terms are used interchangeably. The term *Aboriginal* is used as a short form for
ATSI. The author acknowledges the diversity of Indigenous peoples' languages and cultures, and
that many prefer being referred to in their own terms; in general discussion, however, collective
terms such as *Indigenous* are required. The term *indigenous*, in lower case, refers indigenous
groups in general outside of Australia.

approach to Indigenous education that simultaneously addresses the need to enhance self-esteem, develop biculturalism, and encourage the Indigenous cultures of the classroom to thrive.

Personal Perspectives

I write as a non-Indigenous educator and linguist who has for more than a decade been privileged to be immersed in the realm of Indigenous language and education rights. I do not speak on behalf of Indigenous peoples, but as someone who observes and disagrees with the enormous impediments for some groups compared to others, and the hegemonic practices that perpetuate social injustice. I speak as an educator who believes that language and literacy practices in schools should include the language of the student in the first instance, as this inclusion leads competence in Standard Australian English. I also speak as someone of bicultural heritage who has been able to visit and work in different countries in both TESOL and linguistics (indigenous language rights and revival), and for whom it is difficult that Aboriginal and Torres Strait Islander students are not being better supported to succeed on their own terms, in a manner that is respectful of their cultural and linguistic human rights.

I feel compelled to write this chapter, as I see a distinct role for TESOL in achieving social justice in Australia. I began teaching English to refugees and migrants in the United Kingdom, and learnt of different cultural and political challenges these groups have faced. After teaching in different countries, I settled in Australia, and found parallels to these challenges in the case of Indigenous Australia. I became involved in language revival, spending my time with elders and their families, learning about their lives, hardships, past experiences, and gaining insight into what is best described as their *cosmovision*—a term used widely by indigenous Andean peoples to reflect their view of life, which is spiritual and strongly related to the past, present, and future. It was soon clear to me that the term *language revival* was insufficient to describe my context, and that it obfuscated the process of profound generational social marginalisation and educational coercion that had lead to languages, and indeed lives, becoming endangered.

I subsequently worked as researcher and teacher trainer for the state Education department, and I researched (mis)communication between Australian Aboriginal English speakers (students) and Standard Australian English speakers (teachers). This research focussed on cultural conceptualisations (Sharifian, Truscott, Konigsberg, Malcolm & Collard, 2012) and explored the depth of how and why different cultures can miscommunicate, particularly when using different dialects of the same language. This research was to profoundly affect my approach to TESOL, enhancing how I practically facilitate intercultural communication in the classroom to ensure critical cross-cultural literacy.

My role included training teachers, health professionals, and lawyers in the subtleties of cross-cultural communication with Aboriginal English and Aboriginal language speakers in professional contexts. It is here that I learned much about the challenges non-Indigenous teachers (particularly non-TESOL-trained teachers) and education departments face regarding the education of Indigenous peoples. In general, understanding of Standard Australian English (SAE), its context, and culture were wrongly assumed to be preexistent in Aboriginal students by virtue of their living in Australia. In other words, Australia was seen as an English-dominant country, so naturally everyone would speak and understand the standard dialect equally and without compromise.

At time the time of writing, I worked as an English as an Additional Language/Dialect (EAL/D) teacher and coordinator at a remote Indigenous community school. In this school, I combined my research, knowledge of Indigenous linguistics, and TESOL pedagogy, in the hope of being an integral part of a culturally balanced, first-language-friendly educational establishment that respected the rights and wishes of its users. The School Council is working to reposition the local Indigenous community at the helm of school decisions alongside the Department of Education and striving to achieve what our community desires: the centrality of language and culture in their children's learning and total well-being.

Indigenous Make-up of Australia

At the time of the last census in 2006, people of Aboriginal and Torres Strait Islander (ATSI) origin made up 2.3% of the population, or around 455,000 people. It is a young population, with over half aged 21 years old or less (compared to 37 years old for the non-Indigenous population). According to the Australian Bureau of Statistics (ABS, 2006), 86% of all ATSI people reported speaking English at home, the majority of whom would be speaking Aboriginal English (MCEETYA, 2006). The remainder speak one or more Indigenous languages. Many communities are multilingual, but the decline of Indigenous languages has been marked: In 1788, there were some 250 to 300 languages in use, a number comparable to the 300 or so spoken "north of the Rio Grande" in the United States (Mithun, 2001, p. 1); today there are around 20 fragile languages that continue to be transferred intergenerationally (AIATSIS & FATSIL, 2005). This pervasive deterioration of Indigenous languages reflects an increase, not of Standard Australian English (SAE), but of English-based creoles and mixed languages (Simpson, Caffery, & McConvell, 2009). Children, especially in remote areas, will be learning SAE and therefore will require EAL/D instruction. As debates on Indigenous education centre on the remote regions of Australia, where Indigenous students make up the majority of the classrooms, so shall this paper focus on remote education.

Brief Chronology of Language Rights Issues

Wherever the European has trod, death seems to pursue the aboriginal. We may look to the wide extent of the Americas, Polynesia, the Cape of Good Hope, and Australia, and we shall find the same result.

— *Charles Darwin, 1839 (as quoted in Nicholls, 2005, p. 42)*

The arrival of the British in Australia during the late 1700s brought massacres, disease, and a range of often devastatingly different concepts of social, cultural, and environmental phenomena such as institutionalised government systems, pastorization of land, landownership, and the introduction of domesticated animals. In time, the British would also adopt a perhaps distorted Darwinian belief that Indigenous peoples were destined to die out, which justified their assimilationist approaches. Gary Foley (1997), a Gumbaingiggir (Aboriginal) activist and academic, noted that in 1937, the first conference of the Australian Commonwealth and State Aboriginal authorities passed the "Destiny of the Race" resolution, declaring

> [t]hat this conference believes that the destiny of the natives of aboriginal origin, but not of the full blood, lies in their ultimate absorption by the people of the Commonwealth, and it therefore recommends that all efforts be directed to that end.

Ostler (2005) reminds us that invaders and imperialists, such as the Ottomans or the Vikings, were not always monolingually motivated. Unlike other invaders in history, the British, like the Spanish invaders of the Americas, were intolerant of indigenous languages and emphatically, unquestionably, and often violently imposed the privileged language variety. This imperial monolingual expansion coincided with the development of the western European nation state. Consequently, despite some sporadic missionary attempts,[2] schooling was largely adopted to this end, with families often forcibly separated and languages prohibited both by churches and by governments. Thus, the loss of language rights was for many years devastating.

It was only from the 1970s, whilst riding a wave of pro-Indigenous rights activism and awareness inspired by the U.S. civil rights movement (Mosler & Catley, 1998), that the federal government started to take Indigenous languages seriously. In 1972, it introduced bilingual programs in the Northern Territory (NT) and Western Australia (WA). (A chronology of the bilingual school history of the NT can be accessed at http://www.abc.net.au/4corners/special_eds/20090914/language/chronology.htm) Even though the bilingual programs were subtractive, i.e., they went from L1 (first

---

[2] German missionaries became the first outsiders to create the first mother tongue education school in 1839 in the Kaurna language (Simpson, 2010). While this particular school was closed by the government after only 5 years, its impact on language rights was enduring: Documents uncovered from that time have led to a bold revival of the language in Adelaide, South Australia.

language or mother tongue) only, to L1/L2 (the second or additional language), to exclusive L2, they fostered the use of Indigenous languages, Indigenous employment and empowerment. In 1989, 21 bilingual programs were running in the NT (DEET, 1991). That year, Lajamanu School (in the NT), which had been running a Walpiri/ English bilingual program since 1982, had topped all government-run Aboriginal schools in the Department of Education's own standardised English testing.

However, funding cuts in the name of economic savings (see Nicholls, 2005, for a detailed analysis) and improvement of English literacy test scores, even though they were on par with or better than those from non bilingual schools (Silburn, Nutton, McKenzie, & Landrigan, 2011), eventually lead to a decision to dismantle bilingual programs in 2008. Advocacy groups mounted considerable pressure on the federal and territory governments to take account of all available evidence and reconsider the decision, pointing to the overwhelming benefits of an appropriately resourced bilingual model in developing English competency, maintaining Indigenous languages, and supporting cultural well-being. A key research paper by Simpson, Caffrey, and McConvell (2009) summarised the three interrelated rights-based matters at stake:

1. Children have a right to an education that allows them access to the dominant language and wider society.

2. Communities have a right to decide how their children are educated.

3. Communities, especially Indigenous, have a right to maintain and strengthen their Indigenous languages.

This research paper was important, since it stressed the rights implications of the dismantling decision and documented the events leading up to it. Policy continued to fall short, however, as Simpson (2010) observed:

> Too often, educators and policy-makers confuse teaching a second language and a first. They fail to recognise the great divide between these two, and think that the approach used for teaching a second language can be taken over directly into Indigenous language and culture classes for first language speakers. (p. 27)

One area where Indigenous education equates to a social justice issue is when (mis) understandings of language acquisition and literacy learning are conflated by policy makers, and even some teacher educators, who fail to understand that literacy-centric programs (such as those which focus on phonics, decoding, and other reading skills) are not appropriate for EAL/D students who are experiencing a dramatic (and often confronting) intellectual and sociocultural shift by acquiring new linguistic forms and cultural ways of being. In Australia, we routinely revert to a "back-to-basics" approach that focuses on phonics and decoding, and favour commercially driven programs rather than evidence-based pedagogies. These former approaches may well be suitable for L1/D1, rather than L2/D2 learners. Often they exclude key aspects of second language acquisition (SLA), such as syntax, vocabulary, pragmatics, and sociocultural under-standing, including cultural conceptualisations. Reduction of SLA to L1 literacy-centric resources and teaching not only undermines evidence based TESOL approaches, but equates to what Murray (2003) called "minimalisation of the pedagogy" (p. 4).

Invisibility and Misrepresentation of Indigenous EAL/D Learners

Indigenous learners not perceived to be EAL/D learners are disadvantaged in at least three ways:

- They are not being given the appropriate pedagogy to succeed in their acquisition of English language.

- They are being denied an important part of their identity and expression and the opportunity to use their own language(s) to develop themselves in the school setting.

- They are effectively being doubly misrepresented as English language speakers, who are learning their own Aboriginal language on the side (L2), rather than being seen as learning English as an additional language/dialect.

The needs of Indigenous EAL/D learners are being obscured through a distortion of language by policy makers and decision makers: for example, *literacy* is being used to mean literacy in SAE only, rather than a skill that is developed through language and is gained in any language; *language* is being used to mean languages other than English that are learned as L2.

In 2009, the Australian Human Rights Commission's Social Justice Report acknowledged that the linguistic rights of Indigenous children who speak Indigenous languages as their mother tongues were largely not being recognized through appro-priate schooling. Although linguistic rights are recognized in principle in Australia (it is a signatory to the UNDRIP, the UN Declaration on the Rights of Indigenous Peo-ples), debates on language lead to the funding of Indigenous languages in two separate ministerial portfolios: in heritage (language revival programs that work outside of schools and receive limited funding and thereby can have limited long-term impact); and in education, categorised as a Language Other than English (LOTE) subject. If the school chooses to teach the language, and if indeed resources are available, then the language is taught *ab initio* as a secondary language just as "foreign" languages are, even if students already speak the language. Generally, Indigenous languages as LOTE have had limited success beyond raising awareness amongst non-Indigenous learners of the existence of the languages themselves.

In terms of targeted education funding, Indigenous students are again not rec-ognised as language learners. Instead, they are granted funds based on Indigeneity, which may be spent on a range of programs. For example, ACTA's (2014) *State of*

EAL/D in Australia 2014 found cases of school principals, who control how funding is spent, being unfamiliar with EAL/D needs and spending funding on programs and support not related to EAL/D. Conversely, the majority of EAL/D learners, who are refugees or new arrivals, usually attend an intensive English program for an average of 6 to 12 months and are then introduced to mainstream classes.

Similarly, Indigenous students' additional language learning needs are not considered in national English literacy testing, and they are often commented on as "underachieving" in documents that use a language that is unfamiliar to them (Wigglesworth, Simpson, & Loakes, 2011). Siegel (2010) notes that Australian Aboriginal English speakers are generally not recognized as learners of an additional dialect (Standard Australian English). They are treated as D1 users (speakers of SAE as a first dialect), are accused of being careless, and even misdiagnosed as having speech impairments and/or cognitive delays. Similar deficit phenomena have been noted in Canada for First Nation children (Bell & Bernhardt, 2012) and speakers of American Indian English (Siegel, 2010), whose natural process additional language acquisition may be held against them.

Rarely, if ever, are Indigenous learners acknowledged for being aspiring multilinguals with much to offer a nation that is trying to mature in its relationship with its First Peoples. This severe systemic misrepresentation and underestimation of students' potential and EAL/D learning requirements exacerbate the current situation where Indigenous students on average have lower literacy levels (in any language) than their non-Indigenous peers. Furthermore, across the country, and despite the most recent report on Indigenous languages in schools for Indigenous students (Parliament of Australia, House of Representatives Standing Committee on Aboriginal and Torres Strait Islander Affairs, 2012) explicitly recommending EAL/D pedagogy for Indigenous EAL/D students, we are experiencing a dismantling of EAL/D teams in state and territory education departments (ACTA, 2014), putting more pressure on TESOL advocates to demonstrate why teachers should resist "monolingual instructional assumptions" (Cummins, 2005, p. 588).

In spite of local, national, and international research and experience and being a signatory to the UNDRIP, the role of first language in the development of the additional language/dialect continues to be confused, distorted, and obscured by the monolingual ideology displayed by education policy makers and decision makers, among others. However, there are schools across Australia that excel in Indigenous EAL/D education. By employing a range of practices that recognize first language and respect cultural knowledge and integrity, both inside and outside the school, they forge a path towards educational advantage, appraising and celebrating Indigenous EAL/D learners as aspiring multilinguals.

TWO-WAY EAL/D: A MODIFIED TESOL PEDAGOGY FOR INDIGENOUS EDUCATION

> The current system does not take into account our Yolngu Garma curriculum or Yolngu "both Ways" pedagogy and curriculum. Our job as educators is to convince the people who control mainstream education that we wish to be included. Until this happens assimilation is still the name of the game, and reconciliation is an empty word, an intellectual "terra nullius."
>
> —*Marika (1998) (quoted in Murray, 2003, p. 22)*

Kerwin and Van Issum (2013) observed that Indigenous "epistemology and ontology is rarely considered to be a viable tool in the dominant education system." This imbalance is precisely what TESOL in Indigenous education avoids by building from the knowledge base of the children and their community. Indigenous and non-Indigenous educators working together, where possible, allows for a TESOL approach that counters the potential for overdominant Western epistemologies to ensure a bicultural or two-way (Indigenous/non-Indigenous) pedagogy (explained below).

WORKING TWO-WAY

While the term *two-way* is commonly used in bilingual discourses (See Creese & Blackledge, 2011), it has also been used in a range of Indigenous education contexts in Australia, mainly in the Northern Territory (see McConvell, 1982, and Harris, 1990) and then in Western Australia (see Malcolm et al., 1999, and the teaching resource *Tracks to Two-Way Learning* [Western Australia Department of Education 2012]). Harris (1990) defined "two-way Aboriginal schooling" as "a strategy to help make the matter of choice real in both worlds; to provide opportunity for the primary Aboriginal identity to stay strong, though changing, and thus continue to be the source of inner strength and security necessary for dealing with the Western world" (p. 48). The Western Australian Department of Education adopted an approach whereby "both Aboriginal and non-Aboriginal students and educators mutually explore their knowledge about cultural difference, language variation and how different conceptualisations can interact to change meaning" (Sharifian et al., 2012, p. 71). A two-way model needs to be situated throughout community (families), school, and classroom levels. Because the model is based on different groups working together, it is important for community to be consulted and to be actively engaged, such as by being employed in the school or being involved in planning school events. To this end, the *Tracks to Two-Way Learning* comprehensively documents steps to achieve this approach, which penetrates all levels of school life, from curriculum and assessment, to learning resources and staffing. It combines a broad and deep Indigenous presence education with EAL/D pedagogy.

While two-way may still be a loaded term in some areas, I shall adopt this latter Western Australian definition and approach to describe my own practice, as it allows for more opportunities for cross-cultural learning in the heterogeneous contexts in which most schools operate. After the first bilingual cuts of 1998, the term *two-way* replaced *bilingual* in the NT as the more politically correct term, given successive governments' aversion to the concept. Such is the stigma of bilingual in ATSI contexts that a decade later, teachers and public servants, mainly in the NT and WA, would be discouraged from using the term in public discourse. See Nicholls (2005) for in-depth discussion.

Indigenous communities are as spread out as they are diverse. Consequently, the term *two-way* should always be locally contextualised: it may involve

- a local Indigenous TESOL teacher who speaks the students L1, but works alone or with a trained teacher-linguist (mainly EAL context);

- a non-Indigenous TESOL teacher teaching with (or without) an Indigenous teacher (who may be employed as an Indigenous education assistant) working in a linguistically and dialectally heterogeneous classroom (mainly EAL/D context).

In homogeneous classrooms where languages or creoles are spoken, the very few bilingual programs that remain (fewer than five) have followed a variation of a two-way model, which is a transitional approach to second language acquisition, known as the *step model* program. Usually, the first 4 years are spent developing L1 literacy and numeracy skills and other subjects in L1. Over this time, English is increasingly introduced, orally at first. At Year 4, students transition to learning L2 literacy: Their L1 literacy skills are transferred to L2 using TESOL pedagogy to the point where students are learning predominantly in SAE in the latter primary years.

Systematised EAL/D practice in the heterogeneous classroom, with Aboriginal language and Aboriginal English speakers, is still developing, though it is very much the aim of the aforementioned *Tracks* document. Whilst pedagogy for dialect and language learning can be similar (Siegel, 2010), differences between then are based on perceptions of ownership, "false friends," assumptions and expectations (particularly of SAE speakers towards dialect speakers) about learning abilities, self-awareness as language or dialect learners, and motivation to learn. (These topics are treated in detail in Western Australia Department of Education and Training [2009], p. 45.)

To test the validity of two-way practice, Malcolm and Truscott (2012) investigated three schools in different settings with a majority Aboriginal students: fringe metro-politan, fringe rural, and a rural/remote school. They produced a two-way framework that plots how the principal and Aboriginal and non-Aboriginal educators and students can interact along four dimensions, briefly summarised as follows:

- Relationship building. This first dimension acknowledges the essential role of cross-cultural relationships and cultural sharing and valuing between Aboriginal and non-Aboriginal people, be they teachers and students or between students themselves.

- Mutual comprehension building. The second dimension emphasises the importance of mediating when there is a breakdown in communication. It includes insuring that the classroom is safe for students regardless of background, and that all are included. Aboriginal educators play a key role of acting as cultural interpreter and may assist non-Aboriginal teachers in developing a passive knowledge of the students' language(s). Equally, this may be required for a non-Aboriginal teacher to make explicit the non-Aboriginal cultural context.

- Repertoire building. The aim of the third dimension is to embed language diversity in the learning and achieve an additive bidialectalism/bilingualism. Core to this is the development in literacy in the first language/dialect.

- Skill building. The fourth dimension relates to developing SAE competence to access further learning. Differences between dialects need to be explored, and assessment needs to reflect achievement in both dialects/languages.

Once the necessary conditions have been met in terms of classroom practice, the EAL/D repertoire and skill building can be developed along three interlinked principles.

Convergence.

- Exploring cognate relationships and commonalities between the Aboriginal English and SAE.

- Locating where language varieties overlap and meaning is transparent: for example, when pragmatics, lexical items, and cultural conceptualisations carry the same meaning.

Divergence.

- Adopting a contrastive approach to grammar learning, where the home language is described and compared with that of the target language (TL) and differences are learned. As with the convergence principle, students' language and knowledge is valued and the TL added to the students' linguistic repertoire.

- Locating where language varieties overlap, but can cause misunderstandings: for example, when the same words have a similar meaning but different cultural conceptualisations.

Code switching.

- Practicing switching from one code to another when necessary.

- Using bilingual dictionaries when possible and developing of multilingual texts for different purposes.

While code switching has often been seen as problematic, it has also been argued to be a valuable skill in cross-cultural communication (Creese & Blackledge, 2011), and may never be used in some multilingual classrooms where codes are kept separate (see Cummins, 2005). Indigenous students are required to code-switch to engage with school curricula, non-Indigenous teachers, and school guests (and we get lots of these in remote schools!). In the following section, I use my own practice to exemplify these concepts.

Case Study: A Heterogeneous Classroom

My class consists of up to 16 Aboriginal English speakers (six of whom are competent in a home language, others having varying levels of receptive and productive proficiency). There is also one non-Indigenous student whom I have on a parallel program. All students speak Aboriginal English (referred to by the children in my class as Martu English, or ME); up to half the class members speak and have a receptive competence in at least one Aboriginal language (Martu Wangga, a communilect spoken in the area; and/or Ngaanyatjarra), and all are learning SAE. The children range between the ages of 9 to 12 years old.

Integrated teaching of EAL/D happens throughout the curriculum. Planning is based on local phenomena, Dreamtime stories, and cultural events, and these are connected to nonlocal phenomena of the Australian Curriculum. Students are academically assessed in SAE, and they are beginning to also be assessed in the home language as our school moves towards a whole-school practice on multilingual assessment. The high teacher turnover in remote schools and the shortage of EAL/D teachers make training in two-way EAL/D practice quite challenging. However, the school council is looking to embed this practice in policy so that it becomes a priority for new teachers.

Other aspects of pedagogy include these factors:

- Discussion and oral language in general are encouraged in home language and at punctuated moments and specific times in SAE.

- Language (target language and specific registers of subjects) and learning are scaffolded.

- Home language is displayed around the room on students' work samples and content area posters.

- Books are available in SAE as well as Indigenous languages and Aboriginal English, including books made by the class.

CONVERGENCE

This concept is particularly important for Aboriginal English speakers, as they will already have a linguistic grounding in the TL, more so than speakers of an English-based Aboriginal creole and significantly more so than speakers of Indigenous languages. The skill being developed is knowing (and predicting) when and where convergence and divergence occur, because they may happen simultaneously. For example, a new teacher introduced herself to my class, explaining how she enjoyed camping. She raised interest in the class by asking "Who likes camping?" and "Have you ever been camping?" As she continued to describe how she enjoyed going with family and friends, the children nodded and agreed. When describing how she went walking, they nodded, but then looked confused when she talked about hiking (a word they were not familiar with). Whilst the words *camping* and *walking* and their basic meanings converged between SAE and ME, their underlying conceptualisations differed dramatically. However, both groups were not fully aware of where this divergence lay. I invited the class and teacher to brainstorm their notions of camping on a Venn diagram, so we could see where the concepts overlapped or not. It was apparent that there was a chain of minor miscommunications that had the potential for overall misunderstanding. The teacher then showed images of what she was referring to, revealing concepts that were foreign to or unexpected for the students and assumptions not considered by the teacher. Some of the discussion is summarised in Figure 10.1; cultural conceptualisations are documented at length in Sharifian, Truscott, Konigsberg, Malcolm, and Collard, 2012. Had the non-Aboriginal student been present, he may well have identified the conceptual mismatch, as he has become accustomed to do, and alerted the teacher. During these processes the non-Aboriginal student is developing a passive competence in Martu English and is equally developing bicultural competence.

DIVERGENCE

Divergence might be discussed when the opportunity arises (such as when Microsoft Word marks Martu English phrasing or wording as incorrect or when we come across concepts that are not symmetrically translatable), or during a set explicit instruction time. Students have notebooks where they note down the grammar points and add to

Non-Aboriginal teacher's conceptualisation of camping	Aboriginal students conceptualisation of camping
Use of specialist hiking equipment, such as walking poles, boots, backpack with water and snacks, and extra clothes just in case.	Family take a gun (to shoot kangaroos), but they usually would not carry anything with them whilst walking.
Walking in with friends and family in a line (as she showed in her photos) to get from one place to another.	Walking with peers, looking for things, and then going in a circle back to the camp. Friends are usually family members.
Family in this instance was a sister, but she usually went camping with mother, father, and siblings (the Western nuclear family).	Family includes aunties and uncles, *grannies* (reciprocal term in ME for both grandparent and grandchild), cousins (who culturally can be akin to siblings).
On this occasion, the teacher was walking in green, damp, and undulous countryside.	Invariably the land is dry, with red sand, and relatively flat. There may be a water hole or creek where they are camped.

Figure 10.1. Mismatch in cultural conceptualisations.

Grammar point	Martu English (ME)	SAE
Possessive marker: Noun + ku	Take anybodyku chair	Take anyone's chair
Generalized 3sg subject pronoun Zero "be" copula	E right	He/she is right

Figure 10.2. Examples of dialectal divergence between Martu English (ME) and Standard Australian English (SAE).

them as other examples arise. Figure 10.2 shows two examples of divergence between ME and SAE.

CODE SWITCHING

We reinforce this skill through discussion, role plays, and authentic communication scenarios such as when answering the class phone or engaging with school visitors. This skill is covered when discussing convergence and divergence matters as we ponder over when different codes may be used, such as at the solitary local community shop, which is run by non-Indigenous people. We implicitly consider the sociocultural use of language and consider context-appropriate ways of addressing miscommunication. These discussions, which may be planned or otherwise, are opportunities to co-construct knowledge and explicitly consider cross-cultural communication and making meaning.

Conclusion

Social justice in Australia concerns all people being allowed to make the choice about who and how they want to be. For Australia's Indigenous peoples, a range of human rights issues, particularly those relating to language, has persisted for more than 200 years (Australian Human Rights Commission, 2009). Through TESOL pedagogies, many educators and activists are trying to facilitate a form of education that allows Aboriginal and Torres Strait Islander peoples to develop bicultural competence to choose when and how to engage with the wider world on their own terms. This form of education explicitly requires Indigenous involvement and recognizes Indigenous students as developing bicultural children who need to be acknowledged and suitably appraised as language learners, not simply failing as English literacy students.

The TESOL profession in Australia has advocated use of English language learning pedagogies throughout Indigenous education, and has influenced key advances in the recognition of Indigenous linguistic education rights. EAL/D is increasingly acknowledged as best practice in a range of documents, such as government reports (such as MCEETYA, 2006) and reviews (Buckskin, 2009), mandated documents (ACARA,

2011), and teacher training manuals (Price, 2012); yet the positive impact of this broad acknowledgement is undermined by distorted rhetoric that elevates literacy over language learning. Furthermore, it is countered by education policy that appears to be influenced by ideological discourses, derived from a monolingual habitus (Gogolin, 1994), that are deficit driven, remedially focussed, and, worse still, founded on evidence that is inappropriate and immeasurably limiting in terms of developing critical cross-cultural literacy. Consequently, in spite of the best intentions in education and reconciliation, contemporary education practice continues to reproduce itself in its own monolingual image.

TESOL in a two-way EAL/D form is in a privileged position: It can go some way towards offsetting the social injustices of the past and present. It has an obligation to Australia's Indigenous peoples to ensure that English can be learnt in a manner that is not invasive, but emancipatory. We have already seen how community people and TESOL practitioners and other language experts combine to achieve positive learning outcomes and in both Indigenous and non-Indigenous worlds. However, we work in an educational environment that is mainly unaware of the potential of empowered bicultural learners and has yet to envisage the true reconciliatory potential of a thriving multicultural Australia. TESOL, through the Australian Council of TESOL Associations, has a major role in achieving this awareness, but will need to work with other national bodies to make this possible and leverage systemic change at the national level. In terms of Indigenous Australia, TESOL must lead in creating a space where English is understood to be multifaceted, part of an ecosystem, and owned equally by Indigenous and non-Indigenous groups. TESOL must insist that policy makers and decision makers use the correct language to describe language learners, rather than robbing them of their right be who they are and submerging them in deficit discourses. Skutnabb-Kangas noted "both Indigenous and minority education could be organised so as to promote high levels of multilingualism. This would give better results in school achievement, learning of the dominant language, and issues around identity" (2009, p. 341). As long as we have the resource of multilingual peoples, monolingual education standards, practices, and ideologies will not suffice.

References

Australian Bureau of Statistics. (2006). *Population characteristics, Aboriginal and Torres Strait Islander Australians* (Catalog No. 4713.0). Commonwealth of Australia.

Australian Council of TESOL Associations (ACTA). (2014). *State of EAL/D in Australia 2014* [Draft report]. Retrieved August 2014 from http://www.tesol.org.au/Advocacy /Surveys

Australian Curriculum, Assessment and Reporting Authority (ACARA). (2011a). *English as an Additional Language or Dialect teacher resource: EAL/D learning progression.* Sydney, Australia: Author.

Australian Curriculum, Assessment and Reporting Authority (ACARA). (2011b). *English as an Additional Language or Dialect teacher resource: EAL/D overview and advice.* Sydney, Australia: Author.

Australian Department of Education. (2014). *Programme guidelines flexible literacy for remote primary schools.* Canberra, Australia: Author. Retrieved from http://docs .education.gov.au/system/files/doc/other/remote_flexible_literacy_-_programme _guidelines_web_accessible_version.pdf

Australian Department of Education, Employment & Workplace Relations (DEEWR). (2008). *Media release: New report on Indigenous language in schools.* Canberra, Australia.

Australian Human Rights Commission. (2009). *Social justice report 2008.* Retrieved from https://www.humanrights.gov.au/our-work/aboriginal-and-torres-strait-islander -social-justice/publications/social-justice-report

Australian Institute of Aboriginal and Torres Strait Islander Studies & Federation of Aboriginal and Torres Strait Islander Languages. (2005). *National indigenous languages survey report 2005.* Canberra, Australia: Department of Communication, Information Technology and the Arts.

Bell, J., & Bernhardt, B. M. H. (2012). Standard English as a second dialect: A Canadian perspective. In A. Yiakoumetti (Ed.), *Harnessing linguistic variation to improve education* (pp. 189–225). Bern, Switzerland: Peter Lang.

Buckskin, P. (2009). *Review of Australian directions in indigenous education 2005–2008.* Adelaide, Australia: David Unaipon College of Indigenous Education and Research University of South Australia.

Creese, A., & Blackledge, A. (2011). Ideologies and interactions in multilingual education: What can an ecological approach tell us about bilingual pedagogy? In C. Hélot & M. Ó Laoire (Eds.), *Language policy for the multilingual classroom* (pp. 3–21). Bristol, England: Multilingual Matters.

Cummins, J. (2005). A proposal for action: Strategies for recognizing heritage language competence as a learning resource within the mainstream classroom. *Modern Language Journal, 89*(4), 585–592. doi:10.2307/3588628

Foley, G. (1997). Australia and the Holocaust: A Koori perspective. Retrieved from http:// www.kooriweb.org/foley/essays/essay_8.html

Gogolin, I. (1994). *Der monolinguale Habitus der multilingualen Schule.* Münster, Germany, and New York, NY: Waxmann.

Harris, S. (1990). *Two-way Aboriginal schooling: Education and cultural survival.* Canberra, Australia: Aboriginal Studies Press.

Kerwin, D., & Van Issum, H. (2013). An Aboriginal perspective on education: Policy and practice. In R. Jorgensen, P. Sullivan, & P. Grootenboer (Eds.), *Pedagogies to enhance learning for indigenous students.* Singapore: Springer.

Lo Bianco, J., & Aliani, R. (2013). *Language planning and student experiences: Intention, rhetoric and implementation.* Bristol, England: Multilingual Matters/Channel View Publications.

Malcolm, I., & Truscott, A. (2012). English without shame: Two-way Aboriginal classrooms in Australia. In A. Yiakoumetti (Ed.), *Harnessing linguistic variation to improve education* (pp. 227–258). Bern, Switzerland: Peter Lang.

Malcolm, I. G., Haig, Y., Königsberg, P., Rochecouste, J., Collard, G., Hill, A., & Cahill, R. (1999). *Two-Way English: Towards more user-friendly education for speakers of Aboriginal English.* Perth, Australia: Education Department of Western Australia and Edith Cowan University.

McConvell, P. (1982). Supporting the two way school. In J. Bell (Ed.), *Language planning for Australian Aboriginal languages.* Alice Springs, Australia: Institute for Aboriginal Development.

Ministerial Council on Education, Employment, Training and Youth Affairs (MCEETYA). (2006). *Australian directions in Indigenous education, 2005–2008.* Carlton South, Australia: Author.

Mithun, M. (2001). *The languages of native North America.* Cambridge, England: Cambridge University Press.

Mosler, D., & Catley, R. (1998). *America and Americans in Australia.* Westport, CT: Praeger.

Murray, F. (2003, June). *Looking back on the journey forward: Scenes from the rear vision mirror as we journey onto new horizons.* Keynote delivered at Literacy North: New Literacies—Expanding Opportunities. Cairns, Australia.

Nicholls, C. (2005). Death by a thousand cuts: Indigenous language bilingual education programmes in the Northern Territory of Australia, 1972–1998. *International Journal of Bilingual Education and Bilingualism, 8*(2–3), 160–177.

Ostler, N. (2005) *Empires of the word: A language history of the world.* London, England: Harper Collins.

Parliament of Australia, House of Representatives Standing Committee on Aboriginal and Torres Strait Islander Affairs. (2012). *Our land, our languages: Language learning in Indigenous communities.* Canberra, Australia: Commonwealth of Australia.

Price, K. (Ed.). (2012). *Aboriginal and Torres Strait Islander education : An introduction for the teaching profession.* Port Melbourne, Australia: Cambridge University Press.

Sharifian, F., Truscott, A., Konigsberg, P., Malcolm, I. G., & Collard. G. (2012). *"Understanding stories my way": Aboriginal-English speaking students' (mis)understanding of school literacy materials in Australian English.* Perth, Australia: Department of Education Western Australia.

Siegel, J. (2010). *Second dialect acquisition.* Cambridge, England: University of Cambridge Press.

Silburn, S. R., Nutton, G. D., McKenzie, J. W., & Landrigan, M. (2011). *Early years English language acquisition and instructional approaches for Aboriginal students with home languages other than English: A systematic review of the Australian and international literature.* Darwin, Australia: The Centre for Child Development and Education, Menzies School of Health Research.

Simpson, J. (2010, September). Mother-tongue medium education: Lessons from the Australian backlash. In Lewis & Ostler (Eds.), *Reversing Language Shift: How to Re-awaken a Language Tradition. Proceedings of the Conference FEL XIV.* Carmarthen, Wales.

Simpson, J., Caffery, J., & McConvell, P. (2009). *Gaps in Australia's indigenous language policy: Dismantling bilingual education in the Northern Territory.* Australian Institute of Aboriginal and Torres Strait Islander Studies (AIATSIS), 24 [Research discussion paper]. Canberra, Australia.

Skutnabb-Kangas, T. (2009). What can TESOL do in order not to participate in crimes against humanity? *TESOL Quarterly, 43*(2), 340–344.

Western Australia Department of Education. (2012). *English as an Additional Language or Dialect for Aboriginal students: Tracks to two-way learning.* East Perth, Australia: Author.

Western Australian Department of Education and Training. (2009). *ESL/ESD progress map: English as a Second Language, English as a Second Dialect. Professional Guidelines.* Perth, Australia: WestOne Services.

Wigglesworth, G., Simpson, J., & Loakes, D. (2011). NAPLAN language assessments for Indigenous children in remote communities: Issues and problems. *Australian Review of Applied Linguistics, 34*(3), 320–343.

CHAPTER 11

Student Voices Inform Practice

Perceptions of Linguistic and Cultural Discrimination

Elisabeth L. Chan

Northern Virginia Community College, Alexandria

My personal journey into social justice issues within TESOL began in graduate school. I enrolled in a seminar on radical pedagogy, where my professor listed possible topics of interest for the semester. My ears perked up at "race in TESOL." Being of a racial minority from a city with historical racial tensions, I wanted to learn about how race could be examined within the field of TESOL.

Reflecting on my childhood, my views on race relations were rather simplistic: There was White, there was Black, and there was Other. That view was reinforced by the standardized testing at school, which always began with asking me to identify myself as White, Black, or Other.

Asking a test taker to indicate his or her race prior to completing an assessment can negatively affect the success of the student because of stereotype priming, wherein the student's anxiety is raised by the risk of confirming a negative stereotype about oneself (Jamieson & Harkins, 2011; Steele & Aronson, 1995). That is not to say that any overt or purposeful differential treatment took place during the standardized testing I describe here, but rather this one example shows how a young learner may be introduced to socially constructed categories of difference in school. This three-category system of White, Black, and Other corresponded to how Asians were historically viewed in the U.S. South, as if there were a linear spectrum from White to Black and Asians were in the middle, where their race was malleable depending on the social situation and viewed as closer to White or closer to Black, but always Other (Bow, 2010).

A similar request for self-identification occurred in daily life as well. Classmates would often ask where I was from. I told them I was born in America. Because this response did not align with their perceptions of where I must really be from, they would ask where I was *really* from or ask where my mother was from. I would proudly answer America in either case. When they again did not get the answer they expected, they would then inquire about my first language. I had to respond that I only spoke English, that I spoke English to my parents, and I spoke English to my grandparents. In addition to being positioned as a foreigner by peers, every so often my elementary school would get a student whose first language was not English. I have a vivid memory of school administrators finding me and asking if I spoke that language. Each time, I would tell them that I only spoke English. As an educator now, I understand that administrators were doing their best with limited ESL resources. However, the repeated necessity to assert my American and English-speaking identities subconsciously began to shape the association between race and language in my young mind. This form of microaggression delivers an "underlying message to many Asian-American citizens . . . that they are not true Americans and never will be" (Forrest-Bank & Jenson, 2015, p. 143), or in other words are "perpetual foreigners" (Nadal, 2013). (*Racial microaggression,* a term coined by Charles Pierce, refers to minor discrimination which people of color experience on a daily basis, delivered knowingly or unknowingly and/or when racism is dismissed as nonexistent [Forrest-Bank & Jenson, 2015].)

As my cultural and racial identities continued to evolve, I preferred to be identified as "American," and even admit being uncomfortable when referred to as "Chinese." However, I resignedly identified as "Asian" as a middle ground because I had been labeled that way by others, even though I only spoke English, had never been to Asia, and had not been taught much about traditional Chinese culture from my parents. My experience is similar to Wu's experience (2003) as he states, "In most instances, I am who others perceive me to be rather than how I perceive myself to be. Considered by the strong sense of individualism inherent to American society, the inability to define one's self is the greatest loss of liberty possible" (p. 8).

When I attended graduate school in Hawaii, it was an eye-opening experience to be part of the racial majority, where nearly 50% of the population is Asian or Pacific Islander. I faced my own perceptions of what it meant to be "Asian," and for the first time, I was not the "Asian," but the "Southerner." I was suddenly positioned as an expert on a region of the United States where I had grown up, compared to being positioned as an expert on a region of the world, Asia, of which I was not an expert. Gone were the questions about what it was like to "be Asian" and in their place were questions about what it was like to "be Southern." While I found it peculiar that I had to leave the American South to be considered Southern, it was refreshing to be perceived in a different way. I later self-identified as "Asian American" rather than "Asian" or "American," and I expect that my identity will continue to shift and evolve. As a result of this journey, I learned that understanding the variances in perceptual frames (as coined by Fujimoto, 2006) through which I and others view my identity can be viewed as educational opportunities for one to learn about how others view the world.

As I began my graduate school research on race in TESOL, my professor suggested I read the *TESOL Quarterly* special topic edition on *Race and TESOL* (Kubota & Lin, 2006). Themes of race, culture, and language and how they intertwine were fascinating to me. I branched out and read books and articles from other areas of study, such as sociology, anthropology, and philosophy. Books such as *English with an Accent* (Lippi-Green, 2011) became my lens as I tried to piece together these ideas. After completing my graduate studies, I have continued researching discrimination and perceptions of race, language, and culture in TESOL. This interest led me to become involved with TESOL International Association by serving on the Diversity & Inclusion Standing Committee, as well as chairing the Social Responsibility Interest Section.

In addition to this, I discuss my racial, linguistic, and cultural identity with my ESL students because of misperceptions about my linguistic capabilities and expertise of the English language. For example, I have had students ask to switch to another section because they want an "American" teacher. I believe dealing with these perceptions is an important part of my students' education in addition to their language studies. By learning how to navigate these situations, they will be better prepared to not only adjust to other professors' classes but also learn how to assert their own cultural identities and identities as English users. I am privileged to have the freedom to discuss these topics with my students and to challenge them to expand their definition of being American or being an English speaker.

In my opinion, to better understand your own cultural identity, you should place yourself in a situation where everything you think you know about how the world works is challenged. If you open your eyes and your mind to accepting and respecting these differences, you begin to slowly realize who you are and the similarities you share with that new environment and its people.

Similarly, I believe many individuals become interested in studying and working with social justice issues after having a personal experience with a form of injustice. The source of that injustice and the path one takes to understand and react to it leaves a permanent impression upon the way he or she views the world. If one has never experienced the self-doubt, self-loathing, or self-questioning from perceived discrimination, then it is complicated to genuinely understand why discrimination is an issue or the fervor and the passion with which people fight against it. However, it is vital that educators, administrators, and other stakeholders understand the important effects that experiencing or perceiving discrimination may have on the success of international and immigrant students, as well as the retention and recruitment of new students by word of mouth.

Relevant Literature

English language learners who study at universities in the United States bring with them various background knowledge, language and life skills, and cultural norms. Adjusting to the expectations of a foreign country is a daunting task for any traveler and pushes individuals to navigate unfamiliar environments. Furthermore, all students, whether domestic or international, must deal with stress from multiple sources, such as work, school, family, and friends. For international students, the added level of acculturative stress establishes inimitable issues based on language proficiency difficulties, cultural adaptation, homesickness, and perceived discrimination (Tung, 2011). Students' perceptions of discrimination are particularly interesting because this distinctive stressor differs from general stress (Wei, Ku, & Russell, 2008). In addition, a student's merit is not the sole determiner of his or her academic and career success. An individual's gender, race, abilities, and other socially constructed categories of difference play a role as well (Grant & Zwier, 2011).

It is imperative that administrators, instructors, students, and other stakeholders take into account international students' nonacademic experiences in addition to their academic ones. According to Lee (2010), whether students feel that they have received nondiscriminatory treatment is the most salient factor when making recommendations to others about attending their university. With this in mind, it is important to note that international students were found to be more likely to experience or perceive discrimination when compared to U.S.-born students (Poyrazli & Lopez, 2007).

Because the bases of perceived discrimination are varied and people's perceptions are somewhat subjective, it is crucial to have the opportunity for open dialogue. Educators are in a pivotal position to either silence race talk or encourage it. If it is silenced in the classroom, students are less likely to talk about it in the future, reducing the chance for systemic change and furthering gaps, inequities, and patterns of privilege and oppression (Castagno, 2008). To help address these inequalities, research in critical pedagogy and critical multiculturalism can be applied in the field of TESOL, wherein power structures in local and global communities are questioned to foster equality and social justice. Furthermore, principles of Critical Race Theory can be applied to culture and language, namely, that racism is ingrained in society, shifting its form according to the dominant group, and that anti-essentialist stances, noncolor-blind policies, and counter-storytelling are necessary (Kubota & Lin, 2006).

In the United States, it is viewed as taboo to discuss race in many social situations; the mention of or allusion to race can sometimes spark heated arguments or cause people to quickly change the topic. However, objections to categorizing people may be less noticeable or receive less opposition when people comment or differentiate based on language and culture. These references can appear, at times, to be a more socially acceptable practice (Lippi-Green, 2011; Nadal, 2013) and have increasingly stood in as a proxy for race (Lippi-Green, 2011; van Dijk, 1997). An example of this is the call from U.S. Republican politicians for immigrants to "speak American," which garnered a large amount of airtime and media attention in September of 2015. At the same time, opposition to this point of view and the voices of sociolinguists and other experts were noticeably absent within the same media sphere.

Linguistic discrimination, or linguicism, can be defined as "ideologies and structures, which are used to legitimate, effectuate, and reproduce an unequal division of power and resources between groups which are defined on the basis of language" (Phillipson, 1988, p. 339). Users of nonstandard dialects or accents can be perceived as being unintelligent and even socially unacceptable (Ng, 2007). In Niu and Rosenthal's (2009) study on trust discrimination, nonfluent English speakers were less trusted when compared to the fluent-English speakers. The study of linguicism is important, with implications for a wide range of fields and levels of society. At a national level within the United States, one area linguicism appears is in the English-only movement (Pac, 2012), which includes political pushes for a subtractive model of English learning and for English to be the official language of the United States. In the context of a U.S. university, ESL international students reported that because of their level of language proficiency, they faced exclusion from classmates' social groups and aversion from professors, leading to diminished self-confidence (Lee & Rice, 2007). Linguicism also has lasting effects on one's access to higher education, a meaningful career, and emotional well-being (Meyer, 2009; Murillo & Smith, 2011). By not having a full opportunity to gain assistance with schoolwork from peers or professors, these students may be placed at an academic disadvantage with fewer tools to succeed.

Discrimination based on culture is termed *neo-racism,* which "rationalizes the subordination of people of color on the basis of culture . . . while traditional racism rationalizes it fundamentally in terms of biology. Neo-racism is still racism in that it functions to maintain racial hierarchies of oppression" (Lee & Rice, 2007, p. 389). As with the English-only movement in the United States, mentioned above, neo-racist attitudes are also present at a national level, where some people with rigid stances on immigration insinuate that immigrants who are not prepared to completely assimilate and give up their home cultures are threats to the unity of the nation (Lawton, 2013). Lee and Rice (2007) reported that international students in U.S. universities experienced a range of discrimination based on their home cultures, ranging from feelings of unease, which they found difficult to articulate, to direct verbal insults from professors. The students' perceptions, or in some cases misperceptions, of discrimination against their home cultures are internalized, similarly resulting in distance from social groups, decreased motivation, and decreased access to means to succeed academically.

To better understand the extent to which my students face differential treatment based on race, language, and culture, I conducted a qualitative study focused on international students' perceptions of race, language, and culture in the United States of America (Chan, 2008). I surveyed 56 international students of varying genders (24 male, 32 female), ages (17–30+), home countries (African, Asian, Middle Eastern, European, Central and South American, Caribbean), degrees (40+ majors), classifications (18 bachelor degrees, 17 masters, 21 doctorates), and years studying in the United States (1–11 years). My main areas of interest were these:

- What preconceptions of race, culture, and language did the international students hold before coming to the United States? How did those change after arriving?

- What experiences have they had with racism?

- What differential treatment, either positive or negative, have they had in the United States due to having different linguistic and cultural backgrounds?

My goal of the study was to learn more about how moving to the United States changed international students' perceptions of Americans' views of the students' home countries and also to determine what could be done to improve the students' acculturation process in order to increase student retention and recruitment through student recommendations.

The data showed four notable themes. First, there was a significant change in international students' perceptions of Americans' knowledge and opinions. Sixty-six percent of participants believed Americans had a negative view of their home country before they (the students) arrived in the United States for their studies, but 75% of them changed their minds after arriving. Of those 75%, half added that they now believed Americans had a positive view of their home countries and only 17% added a negative view. Secondly, most of the international students lacked accurate knowledge and awareness of discrimination in general. Thirty-five percent of the students reported that they knew nothing of racism or believed that it no longer existed in the United States. It is important that students are aware of potential discrimination, since "one can be oppressed unknowingly but offense requires (logically or conceptually) the awareness and acknowledgment of its victim" (Gay, 1997, p. 46). Third, in response to the question specifically asking about racism, 47% of students reported differential treatment based on language and culture—despite having two separate questions, each asking about differential treatment by language and by culture, respectively. This response suggests that while research shows linguicism and neo-racism as proxies for racism, the international students are using *racism* as an umbrella term to describe any type of perceived discrimination. Last, nearly all the students reported facing challenges to their intelligence and acceptance because of race, language, and culture. In fact, only 4% of the students reported having faced no differential treatment at all based on race, language, or culture. Examples of differential treatment included on-campus struggles due to the international students' racial, linguistic, and cultural differences with other students and professors, as well as with challenges getting on-campus jobs or scholarships.

These results have several implications for schools and programs, including reforming pre-orientation and cultural orientations (Khawaja & Stallman, 2011; Ramburuth & Tani, 2009; Smith & Khawaja, 2011; Ych & Inose, 2003, as cited in Nilsson, Butler, Shouse, & Joshi, 2008), providing designated support systems and peer systems (Curran, 2003; Lee & Rice, 2007; Ly, 2008; Nilsson et al., 2008; Smith & Khawaja, 2011), educating faculty and staff on critical language teaching and intercultural communication (Alfred, 2009; Charles-Toussaint & Crowson, 2010; Hung & Hyun, 2010; Lee, 2010; Nilsson et al., 2008), and incorporating diversity and intercultural issues into the classroom (Curran, 2003; Glass, 2012; Briscoe, 2003, as cited in Grant & Zwier, 2011).

Classroom Practices

Within an ESL context at the university level, there are countless ways to incorporate social justice themes into the classroom and align them with a program's objectives to prepare its students for the rigors of university life. Numerous activities can be used in the classroom to challenge students' ways of thinking to broaden their knowledge and increase their awareness of social justice and social responsibility issues. When implementing such activities, it is important for the facilitator and participants to avoid essentializing the people, languages, and cultures discussed. However, the issues should not be avoided altogether. In fact, classes that incorporate global issues and peace-related content have shown an increase in students' participation, attendance, interest and excitement about the course, and motivation (Kruger, 2012).

Because research indicates that not only international students but also the local community members need to broaden their knowledge and awareness of racial, linguistic, and cultural discrimination (Alfred, 2009; Charles-Toussaint & Crowson, 2010; Curran, 2003; Glass, 2012; Hung & Hyun, 2010; Lee, 2010; Nilsson et al., 2008; Briscoe, 2003, as cited in Grant & Zwier, 2011), an emphasis is placed on making each activity reach beyond the confinements of the classroom to interact with the local campus community. The activities in which students engage within their ESL classrooms have massive potential to effect change in the world when they bring outside participants into the classrooms and encourage the ESL students to extend themselves beyond the classroom door. By increasing their cultural competence and linguistic capabilities, students will be better prepared to navigate real and perceived discrimination in their daily lives, whether it is overt or subtle.

In a beginner-level activity, "Cultural Myth or Truth," students practice both grammar and test-taking skills while challenging themselves and others to confront stereotypes and their perceptions of their own culture and that of others' cultures. Present tense is one of the first grammar points ESL students study. Additionally, in the EAP setting, students are introduced to common test-taking skills, such as true/false questions. This particular activity can be adapted to individual, pair, and group work. It can use as many or as few materials as you have available.

In this simple activity, students write true or false statements in the present tense about their home country, culture, or language. Then others are asked to guess whether those statements are true or false—"myths." Here is an example: "All Americans eat hamburgers." Even when students know this is a common cultural stereotype, the class members can make a connection between their opinion of this statement and cultural myths, such as "Saudis live in tents in the desert" or "Malians ride elephants to school" or "Japanese language is the same as Chinese." All of these, by the way, were created by ESL students based on their personal perceptions of what Americans know about their home countries. Students may make statements about their cultures and languages.

This activity can be powerful within the classroom, but consider also using it as a dialogic tool on campus. For example, every year a large number of U.S. universities celebrate International Education Week, an initiative of the U.S. Department of State and U.S. Department of Education. During this week, universities often host cultural festivals at which students experience other cultures through food, clothing, dance, and colorful, inviting posters with cultural facts. It is just as easy to create a poster with cultural facts and myths. By creating a critical dialogic opportunity, stereotypes of both the ESL students and their booth visitors can be challenged. My ESL students have often been surprised when visitors answer their cultural truth or myth questions correctly. This in turn broadens their own ideas and perceptions of how others perceive them. The key is to make the exchange of knowledge a two-way street.

The second activity, "Challenging Perceptions Through Photographs," is better used at an intermediate to advanced level. In this activity, students practice the academic skills of making inferences and explaining one's opinions during group discussions. The instructor should choose one particular social justice issue to address and find one image to represent this issue. For example, to begin a discussion on linguistic racial profiling (coined by Romney, 2010), you might show an image of a Caucasian man and an Asian man looking at one English textbook. The prompt question for this activity is "What do you see in this picture?" Students should make lists of what they see. They can also compare their ideas in pairs or groups. For instance, a student might write that two men are looking at a book, but another common response is that the Caucasian man is helping the Asian man with his English; however, it could easily be the other way around. Therefore, after the lists are created, the instructor can facilitate a separation of actual descriptions of the image from the students' perceptions or inferences of what is happening. Then ask students to provide reasons for their perceptions and inferences. This exercise can lead to a discussion about the importance of challenging perceptions and keeping an open mind.

This activity can be modified to a simpler version by giving a caption to the image. Using the same image mentioned above, an instructor may add the caption "Tom is helping Ken with his English homework." Then the instructor may ask students, "Who is Ken?" and "Who is Tom?" Many students will respond that Ken is the Asian male. A similar follow-up discussion can then be started, which incorporates the idea of inferences and reasons for the students' beliefs.

As with "Cultural Myth or Truth," this activity can be adapted to share students' own photographs with the community. Students can take their own photographs and create posters that pose the same question to visitors, thereby creating a dialogue between the ESL students and the community around an important social justice issue.

A third activity explores the burgeoning use of technology and gaming in the ESL classroom. Role plays have shown to increase students' awareness, knowledge of, and skills in dealing with social responsibility (Hunger, 2013). Similarly, students can learn about social justice issues through gaming, especially those in which the player takes on a first-person role, assuming the character's identity and making choices that lead to different outcomes. Multiple studies (Gentile et al., 2009) substantiate the fact that an increase in prosocial gaming, where young people are required to help each other in games, leads to the increased likelihood that they will help their community members, including friends, family, and even strangers, in their real lives. Many free games are available to Internet-accessible classrooms. One example is mission-us.org (Mission US | THIRTEEN, 2015). Students learn about U.S. history, such as slavery in the 19th century and immigration in the early 20th century, in an interactive environment with audio-supported text, where their choices determine the fate of their characters. Teacher resources are provided, including learning goals, vocabulary, and pregame and postgame activities that connect the topics to current events and relevant global issues, such as human trafficking or tense race relations. The future use of gaming in the ESL classroom has vast potential to create socially responsible communities.

Conclusion

Some may say that we are all the same and color-blindness should be our ultimate goal, yet is it morally just to not acknowledge the fact that there are people—either in the majority or in the minority—who have faced or overcome discrimination? By whitewashing our views of race, culture, and language, we lose the spectacular wonder of our differences, the benefits of what we can achieve when we work together with people with different backgrounds and perspectives. Therefore, discrimination must be explicitly and proactively considered. Hence, my personal journey and personal interest in social justice within TESOL is to educate and ask people to question the beliefs that they hold, and to always be open-minded to how perceptions of differential treatment may affect their students and colleagues, not just negatively but also positively.

References

Alfred, M. (2009). Nonwestern immigrants in continuing higher education: A sociocultural approach to culturally responsive pedagogy. *Journal of Continuing Higher Education, 57*(3), 137–148.

Bow, L. (2010). *Partly colored: Asian Americans and racial anomaly in the segregated south.* New York: New York University Press.

Castagno, A. (2008). "I don't want to hear that!": Legitimating whiteness through silence in schools. *Anthropology & Education Quarterly, 39*(3), 314–333.

Chan, E. (2008, March). *Linguistic and cultural discrimination of international students: Working towards harmony.* Research-oriented presentation presented at the TESOL International Association Annual Convention & English Language Expo, Dallas, TX.

Charles-Toussaint, G. C., & Crowson, H. M. (2010). Prejudice against international students: The role of threat perceptions and authoritarian dispositions in U.S. students. *Journal of Psychology, 144*(5), 413–428.

Curran, M. E. (2003). Linguistic diversity and classroom management. *Theory into Practice, 42*(4), 334–340. Retrieved from http://www.jstor.org/stable/1477397

Forrest-Bank, S., & Jenson, J. M. (2015). Differences in experiences of racial and ethnic microaggression among Asian, Latino/Hispanic, Black, and White young adults. *Journal of Sociology & Social Welfare, 42*(1), 141–161.

Fujimoto, D. (2006). Stories through perceptual frames. In A. Curtis & M. Romney (Eds.), *Color, race, and English language teaching: Shades of meaning* (pp. 37–48). Mahwah, NJ: Lawrence Erlbaum.

Gay, W. C. (1997). Nonsexist public discourse and negative peace: The injustice of merely formal transformation. *The Acorn: The Journal of the Gandhi-King Society, 9*(1), 45–53. Retrieved from http://acorn.sbu.edu/xSpring97/Spr97-Nonsexist%20Public%20 Discourse.pdf

Gentile, D. A., Anderson, C., Yukawa, S., Ihori, N., Saleem, M., Ming, L. K., . . . Saka-moto, A. (2009). The effects of prosocial video games on prosocial behaviors: International evidence from correlational, longitudinal, and experimental studies. *Personality and Social Psychology Bulletin, 35*(6), 752–763.

Glass, C. R. (2012). Educational experiences associated with international students' learning, development, and positive perceptions of campus climate. *Journal of Studies in International Education, 16*(3), 228–251. doi:10.1177/1028315311426783

Grant, C. A., & Zwier, E. (2011). Intersectionality and student outcomes: Sharpening the struggle against racism, sexism, classism, ableism, heterosexism, nationalism, and linguistic, religious, and geographical discrimination in teaching and learning. *Multicultural Perspectives, 13*(4), 181–188. Retrieved from http://dx.doi.org/10.1080/152109 60.2011.616813

Hung, H. L., & Hyun, E. (2010). East Asian international graduate students' epistemological experiences in an American university. *International Journal of Intercultural Relations, 34*(4), 340–353.

Hunger, I. (2013). Some personal notes on role plays as an excellent teaching tool. *Science and Engineering Ethics, 19*, 1529–1531.

Jamieson, J. P., & Harkins, S. G. (2012). Distinguishing between the effects of stereotype priming and stereotype threat on math performance. *Group Processes & Intergroup Relations, 15*(3), 291–304.

Khawaja, N. G., & Stallman, H. M. (2011). Understanding the coping strategies of international students: A qualitative approach. *Australian Journal of Guidance and Counseling, 21*(2), 203–224. doi:10.1375/ajgc.21.2.203

Kruger, F. (2012). The role of TESOL in educating for peace. *Journal of Peace Education, 9*(1), 17–30.

Kubota, R., & Lin, A. (2006). Race and TESOL: Introduction to concepts and theories. *TESOL Quarterly, 40*(3), 471–493.

Lawton, R. (2013). Speak English or go home: The anti-immigrant discourse of the American "English only" movement. *Critical Approaches to Discourse Analysis Across Disciplines, 7*(1), 100–122.

Lee, J. J. (2010). International students' experiences and attitudes at a U.S. host institution: Self reports and future recommendations. *Journal of Research in International Education, 9*(1), 66–84. doi:10.1177/1475240909356382

Lee, J. J., & Rice, C. (2007). Welcome to America? International student perceptions of discrimination. *Higher Education, 53*, 381–409. doi:10.1007/s10734-005-4508-3

Lippi-Green, R. (2011). *English with an accent: Language, ideology and discrimination in the United States.* New York, NY: Routledge.

Ly, P. (2008). Caught between two cultures. *Diverse Issues in Higher Education, 25*(14), 24–25.

Meyer, R. (2009). Portraits, counterportraits, and possibilities. In J. C. Scott, D. Y. Straker, & L. Katz (Eds.), *Affirming students' rights to their own language: Bridging language policies and pedagogical practices* (pp. 54–67). New York, NY: National Council of Teachers of English/Routledge.

Mission US | THIRTEEN. (2015, February 1). Retrieved March 1, 2015, from http://www .mission-us.org/

Murillo, L. A., & Smith, P. H. (2011) "I will never forget that!" Lasting effects of language discrimination on language-minority children in Colombia and on the U.S.-Mexico border. *Childhood Education, 87*(3), 147–150.

Nadal, K. (2013). *That's so gay! Microaggressions and the lesbian, gay, bisexual, transgender community.* Washington, DC: American Psychology Association.

Ng, S. H. (2007). Language-based discrimination. *Journal of Language and Social Psychology, 26*(2), 106–122. Retrieved from http://jls.sagepub.com

Nilsson, J., Butler, J., Shouse, S., & Joshi, C. (2008). The relationships among perfectionism, acculturation, and stress in Asian international students. *Journal of College Counseling, 11*, 147–158.

Niu, J., & Rosenthal, S. (2009). Trust discrimination toward social dominant and subordinate social groups. *North American Journal of Psychology, 11*(3), 501.

Pac, T. (2012). The English-only movement in the U.S. and the world in the twenty-first century. *Perspectives on Global Development and Technology, 11*(1), 192–210.

Phillipson, R. (1988). Linguicism: Structures and ideologies in linguistic imperialism. In T. Skutnab-Kangas & J. Cummins (Eds.), *Minority education: From shame to struggle* (pp. 339–358). Avon, England: Multilingual Matters.

Poyrazli, S., & Lopez, M. D. (2007). An exploratory study of perceived discrimination and homesickness: A comparison of international students and American students. *Journal of Psychology, 141*(3), 263–280.

Ramburuth, P., & Tani, M. (2009). The impact of culture on learning: Exploring student perceptions. *Multicultural Education & Technology Journal, 3*(3), 182–195. doi:10.1108/17504970910984862

Romney, M. (2010). The colour of English. In A. Mahboob (Ed.), *The NNEST Lens: Non Native English Speakers in TESOL* (pp. 18–34). Tyne, England: Cambridge Scholars Publishing.

Smith, R. A., & Khawaja, N. G. (2011). A review of the acculturation experiences of international students. *International Journal of Intercultural Relations, 35*, 699–713. doi:10.1016/j.ijintrel.2011.08.004

Steele, C. M., & Aronson, J. (1995). Stereotype threat and the intellectual test performance of African Americans. *Journal of Personality and Social Psychology, 69*(5), 797–811.

Tung, W. (2011). Acculturative stress and help-seeking behaviors among international students. *Home Health Care Management & Practice, 23*(5), 383–385. doi:10.1177/1084822311405454

van Dijk, T. (1997) Political discourse and racism: Describing others in western parliaments. In S. H. Riggins (Ed.), *The language and politics of exclusion: Others in discourse* (pp. 31–64). Thousand Oaks, CA: SAGE.

Wei, M., Ku, T., & Russell, D. W. (2008). Moderating effects of three coping strategies and self-esteem on perceived discrimination and depressive symptoms: A minority stress model for Asian international students. *Journal of Counseling Psychology, 55*(4), 451–462. doi:10.1037/a0012511

Wu, F. H. (2003). *Yellow: Race in America beyond black and white.* New York, NY: Basic Books.

CHAPTER 12

Understanding Privilege

Considerations for Teaching and Teacher Training Toward Social Justice

Heidi J. Faust

University of Maryland Baltimore County (UMBC)

Heidi's Story

Returning tonight from a community march in Baltimore to keep Langston Hughes Elementary School, an anchor in the economically disadvantaged African American community of Park Heights, from closing, the topic of this chapter weighs heavily on my mind. Just a few weeks having passed since riots erupted in Baltimore following the murder of yet another unarmed Black man by police,[1] the pending closing of 26 predominantly African American schools in the city feels especially raw. I've never had to worry about my school being closed, or walking through unsafe neighborhoods, or going to school having had nothing to eat at home. I've never had to even *think* about that. And that right there . . . is *privilege*.

As a White, middle-class educator from the small suburbs of Pennsylvania, in the United States, I had been raised in a community where most of the people I encountered on a daily basis looked like me, spoke the way my parents taught me to speak, and lived similarly to the way I lived. Of course there was diversity, even in that small community, but it was relatively invisible to me at the time. This is not an uncommon experience for many White people in rural and suburban towns throughout the United States. I believed whole-heartedly in treating people equally and in the idea of "colorblindness," which some scholars consider to be a form of racism in

---

[1] On April 27, 2015, riots broke out in the city of Baltimore, following peaceful protests of police brutality related to the death of Freddie Gray, an unarmed Black man who was arrested and subsequently died of a severed spine related to the arrest. This happened amid great economic distress among African American communities in Baltimore, and shortly following other episodes of police brutality toward unarmed Black men in other cities across the United States. The outcry for social justice related to race, economics, and education in Baltimore has received little media attention, compared to the day of the riots. As of June 2015, the city is slated to close 26 schools, a move that will affect primarily African American communities in Baltimore.

itself (Bonilla-Silva, 2003), meaning that I minimized race with the belief that it didn't matter. Like many of my fellow Caucasian U.S. citizens, I thought that racism was just something that happened on an individual basis, by prejudiced and ignorant people. I had bought into the "American"[2] mantra that everyone can work their way up from the bottom, if they work hard; and so I often struggled to understand why some students and parents of culturally and linguistically diverse backgrounds weren't as successful economically and academically as the White middle-class people I had grown up around. I knew there was more to this issue, but unaware of my own privilege, and unaware of the histories of others that had not been a visible part of my education, my focus was centered on helping diverse students and parents conform to the expectations of the dominant culture, without understanding all the invisible barriers and conflicts of interest that were occurring behind the scenes. I was unaware of the bigger picture of how race, class, gender, religion, ability, sexual orientation, and other aspects of people's identities affected their access to opportunities and resources in systematic ways, because I had always been a part of the dominant group. Even when I was not in the majority, I was often in a position of power: as a teacher, a consultant or a trainer, or in some cases, just because I was White.

That said, I have always been a fan of crossing borders and a seeker of diverse experiences. I was always the first to sign up for a field trip to anywhere, the immediate ambassador to the new kids and exchange students in school. I've always worked among special populations of students, as a special education teacher and an ESL teacher, and as a diversity trainer and consultant. In my journey as an educator, I signed up for *every* training on diversity that was offered, did my student teaching at a Native American residential school, and deliberately applied to teach in diverse urban schools and programs. Additionally, I have traveled in more than 40 countries, participated in foreign homestays and exchanges, and worked with teachers and students from all over the world. I tell you this not to impress you, but to share the urgency of this situation: In these experiences, I still carried with me my own cultural lens, and in most experiences my privilege followed me as well and informed my interpretation of those experiences along the way. For example, when I visited an indigenous market in Guatemala, I was excited to practice my Spanish and learn about the culture. I felt as though I was increasing my intercultural knowledge through visiting and chatting with vendors. When a friend kindly reminded me that the women I was chatting with all morning were *working* and that I was distracting them, *and* not buying anything, I realized that I had viewed this interaction through my own perspective, but not

---

[2] I put the term *American* in quotes, because in the United States it is standard to refer to oneself as an American. With that comes a host of nationalistic traditional values related to the history and the Constitution of the United States. I do wish to acknowledge that the term *American* has different meanings across geographic and spatial ideologies. For example, I once had a student who said, "I am from the heart of America—El Salvador. It's right in the middle," in which American might refer to anyone from the extended North Central or South American continents.

theirs. What a privilege it was to be traveling in another country, developing my world knowledge, shopping for beautiful things, and making new friends, yet all the while I'd had such a limited understanding of the reality of the women I was interacting with. I am thankful for my friend's intervention, but how else might we understand the dynamics of privilege when we don't always have a friend to set us straight? Those with less privilege are not likely to tell us, and would we believe them if they did?

The diversity programs I attended had focused on celebrating cultures, food, fun, festivities, etc., but had never really taken a critical look at issues such as privilege and intersecting cycles of oppression. Topics of race, class, language, and power were taboo: too political and too sensitive, and therefore carefully omitted or glossed over in favor of the warm and fuzzy celebrations of "heroes and holidays" (Banks, 1990).

The point, therefore, is that educators like myself can easily have *exposure to* without *awareness of* the deeper factors that affect access to participation in academic and economic opportunities. In reflection, I think about how dangerous it is to have such opportunity and so little awareness. Much harm can come from the decisions educators have the power to make when they are not informed, even if they think they are acting on the best interest of the student. But awareness doesn't always come easily, even when the opportunity is right in front of you.

I will explain my struggle with coming to understand privilege, and more recently the challenge of how to help other educators to understand it as well. In the fall of 2009 (15 years into my career as an educator and, I would argue, 15 years too late . . .) I attended the *Summit for Courageous Conversations About Race* and the pre-summit training *Beyond Diversity,* with the intention of coming back and training other educators as part of a countywide initiative of the local K–12 schools I was working with. During this training, I really understood for the first time what *White privilege* is, how it is institutionalized in U.S. schools, curriculum, workplaces, hidden expectations, and assumptions. I began to understand that racism occurs on a daily basis in the omission of the history and accomplishments of non-Whites (Gorski, 2015), in the value placed on production of a "Standard American English" not only in instruction, but across social and professional settings (Bonfiglio, 2002), in the representation of Whites vs. people of color in the media, and so on. I began to see it all around me, in all the places I thought were just normal. Privilege had allowed me to see these systems and values associated with them as normal, rather than dominant or exclusive; to ignore the advantages I had had in navigating the system of education and the workforce; and worse yet, to work on false assumptions and expectations of others who did not have the same privilege. My immediate reaction was grief. I felt guilty for having been a cheerleader for a White middle-class dominated system that ignores the barriers experienced by marginalized students, when all along I thought I had been a champion for my students' success. I realized that I had unintentionally caused potential harm to these students and their families. I had to do something, I had to reflect on how Whiteness affected my thinking and educational practices; and as a teacher educator, I felt compelled to help other educators to understand *White privilege* (McIntosh, 1988).

To my surprise, this task was not met enthusiastically by many White colleagues, many of whom felt attacked by the idea of White privilege. This is understandable given that in general, White people in the United States have not had to think about race or see themselves as White in their daily lives, and they may have had little experience in developing a White-racialized identity (Helms, 1990). More likely, they see themselves as "American"; and so much about the institutionalized Whiteness in schools is validated and viewed as "American" and just *normal*. With that in mind, the charge of accepting and understanding White privilege seemed, to many White educators, like a sudden, unfair accusation, an anti-American attack on the status quo (Wise, 2008). Even some of my dear friends and colleagues, whom I had known to be caring champions for diverse students, made comments about how they were tired of diversity training that made them feel bad about being White. Trainings they had been to that addressed White privilege were having the opposite affect. They were shutting people down and creating resentment. I wrestled with this in my heart and my brain, searching for a way to keep White educators at the table while also honoring the importance of understanding privilege and the way it created opportunities for some students and barriers for those who do not represent the dominant group.

This questioning led me to have many discussions with colleagues and diversity trainers. What I learned is that privilege is complex, and it is tied to power, and to focus the conversation only on Whiteness can often undermine antiracist efforts (Lensmire et al., 2013) as well as miss the bigger picture of how privilege operates. Over the past several years I have come to expand my understanding of privilege in a more holistic way that is inclusive of many populations and allows for multiple entry points to the conversation, since privilege is associated with power that is delineated along intersectional axes of race, class, gender, religion, ability, and sexual orientation (Collins, 2010). Below I will share a broad understanding of privilege and how it operates in educational settings. Through this understanding of privilege, I will then provide classroom activities and training activities that can be used to build awareness of privilege and create opportunities for dialogue. The goal of this discussion and the activities that follow is ultimately to help educators recognize and reduce barriers and increase opportunities for participation and success of marginalized groups, and to help students build respect and awareness of the experiences of various diverse groups. I believe strongly that we must continue to investigate Whiteness and White privilege in the United States in order to understand the way that racism and privilege are institutionalized, but we must also have an awareness that differing levels of privilege affect all people across diverse contexts.

Understanding Privilege Within ELT and Teacher Training

In U.S. K–12 schools, statistics estimate that 80% to 90% of the teaching force consists of White middle-class teachers, many of whom are teaching growing numbers of immigrants and English learners from diverse backgrounds. Without an awareness of how privilege operates, teachers' "logic" may be based solely on the assumptions of White, middle-class, standard English speaking knowledge and values. Similarly in classrooms worldwide, the assumptions of the dominant group reproduce privilege for those in power and create barriers for those in marginalized groups.

SO, WHAT IS PRIVILEGE?

Privilege is the unearned advantages (McIntosh, 1998), opportunities, or access to resources granted to an individual or group based on power and status. The operative word here is *unearned*. Many will balk at this notion and retort that they *do work hard* for their resources and power and status and that privilege had nothing to do with their access to success. And yes, many hardworking people have privilege. Having privilege doesn't mean you don't work hard; but it does mean that people without privilege must work harder to get the same result, because they must overcome additional barriers that a privileged person does not have consider. If you liken obtaining a goal to running a marathon, privilege in this metaphor would provide a smooth, clear road to run. Running a marathon is hard work, so anyone who does it deserves credit for that hard work. Now consider running the marathon without that smooth, clear road. Without privilege the road has some additional hurdles that have to be jumped, maybe more for some than others, depending on their identities. Runners would need more energy to complete the marathon on this road, and it might slow or disrupt runners' ability to finish as quickly, or at all, and might also affect their motivation. In this metaphor, the privileged person, having not experienced those hurdles, may wonder why the same marathon seemed so much harder for those with less privilege. Sometimes judgments and stereotypes emerge when the expectations are based on the dominant group's experience without considering the hurdles that other groups encounter in completing the same task. Now imagine, not a marathon, but a person's ability to do a good job at work or at school. How are invisible hurdles having an impact on members of various groups? Who has easy access to resources and opportunities and who must work harder or is possibly excluded from the same access? The hurdles may be economic, such as not having transportation, materials, or even sufficient food to eat. They may be physical, related to health and the ability to access places and input; they may also be social, such as low expectations and unfair discipline policies that may be related to gender/ability/race and/or socioeconomic status. Cultural and ethnic hurdles may exist that are related to finding appropriate food or negotiating the integration of genders in social spaces. When understanding how privilege works, members of the dominant group can begin to see the hurdles that were once invisible. The next step is then to work toward removing those hurdles or barriers within the system.

Privilege affects access to power and resources. In understanding how these barriers and opportunities are created, it is helpful to consider Cullinan's (1990) discussion of three presumptions of privilege: *innocence, competence,* and *worth.* Let's explore what is meant by each of these, and how they might operate in terms of benefits (privilege) or barriers (oppression).

The presumption of *innocence* is afforded to those with privilege because they are believed, from the first, to be well-intentioned. When a privileged person is pulled over by a police officer for speeding, that person may be let go with a warning because it is believed that s/he just made a simple mistake. Those without privilege may be automatically regarded as suspicious, even when they are not doing something wrong. Ferguson's (2000) study of a multiracial elementary school found that young Black students were punished more frequently and harshly than White students for the same infractions. While White boys were perceived as "just being boys," Black boys were viewed as "dangerous" and more frequently disposed to be criminals. This perception had a direct impact on the life chances of these students and influenced an early pattern of incarceration for Black males. As educators we must consider the implications of our perceptions of students related to discipline and the presumptions of innocence associated with privilege.

Next, the presumption of *competence* speaks loudly regarding who is believed to be capable and able to do a task well. Who is considered for advanced opportunities? Who is recommended for scholarships? Who is recommended for gifted programs and, conversely, who is the recipient of tragically low expectations? Who is overlooked for opportunities? Which populations are over-referred for special education? Whose thinking is discredited or believed only when validated by a person of the dominant group?

Finally, we look at the presumption of *worth*. Who is worthy of the best schools, the best teachers, the nicest materials? These options often come down to economics, but we can also consider these questions: Where are the landfills? The nuclear waste sites? The best grocery stores and the worst? And how do all of these factors compound to affect our students? The simple answer is that the more nondominant identity groups the student is a member of, the more ways in which he or she is being affected by the barriers associated with not having privilege. Likewise, those who are consistently members of the dominant groups have more and more benefits that are just presumed to be normal.

Now that we've begun to consider how privilege operates, let's consider some key points about privilege.

1. *Everyone has varying levels of privilege across identities, situations, and environments.* For example, privilege is associated with membership in dominant groups related to race, class, gender, religion, ability, sexual orientation, and language, to name a few. Each aspect of our identity may bring associated privilege in certain contexts, and likewise can create barriers or oppression when those aspects of our identity fall outside the norm. Psychologists would consider the experiences of *In-groups* and *Out-groups* (Brewers, 1999).

2. *Privilege shifts and is tied to various aspects of our identity and context.* For example, as a native speaker of English, I have a certain amount of credibility in the field of English language teaching, just because I am a native speaker. I may be viewed to be more credible than I actually am, just based on my accent. In this context, I am assumed to be *competent*. However, when I was studying Spanish in Costa Rica,

I was a beginner and was discouraged from doing a more challenging final presentation about my experience learning the indigenous use of medicinal plants in the rainforest because it would be too hard for me, even though I was perfectly capable of doing this project. In this context, people responded to me in a childlike tone and underestimated my intelligence because I sounded simple in Spanish. Here I did not have the privilege of being a member of the dominant language group. I was not presumed to be as competent in this setting as I am in my own context. In this way, you can see how privilege shifts across context, but you can also see what Cullinan (1999) refers to as the *presumption of competence*. Likewise, in U.S. schools, parents and students are often infantalized, i.e., treated as if they were children, thus underestimating their competence and diminishing their power and status. This shift can be dramatic, especially for parents and students who had privilege in their home contexts and then lose that privilege when they immigrate to the United States, or other countries. Schools with limited resources also may rely on the student to interpret and communicate essential knowledge to their parents, thus giving the student the power of an adult, making it more difficult for parents who do not speak English to access unbiased information about their child's progress in school and limiting their access to communication with the school. Additionally, there is power and privilege in conforming to the dominant language and, furthermore, conforming to the standard accent of that language. Lippi-Green (2011) explains of language politics in the United States, "People with unacceptable accents are encouraged to get rid of them by enrolling in a class. The people who show their allegiance to home and region by means of language are expected to understand that they are subordinate, intellectually and culturally, to their neighbors. The fact that the stereotypes which underlie this reasoning are imaginary formations is irrelevant; their power is still real, and they are effective" (p. 225). The power associated with a dominant language cannot easily be underestimated, as in international contexts, where privilege may be associated with English or the dominant language of the region; those from language minority groups may experience similar barriers to participation, such as lack of access to meaningful information and the expectation to function under a different set of cultural and social norms; and all the presumptions of privilege as stated above may apply.

3. *Oppression can be compounded by intersecting identities that are marginalized.* Oppression can be compounded through the intersectionality of marginalized identities. Patricia Hill Collins (2000) discusses the amplified impact of this intersectionality in women of color who are also living in poverty as socioeconomic status race and gender collide to create challenges related to access to employment, healthcare, transportation, education for themselves and their children, and having a political voice. Disempowered across these axes of identity, their voices are not represented in studies, politics, or curriculum, and decisions affecting their livelihood are made by those in power who are responding based on experiences of the White middle-class and upper-class male perspective. In my high school English classes, tensions were sometimes felt between students of Puerto Rican and Dominican descent. My initial thought was that these students had much in common, coming from the Caribbean

Islands, sharing the Spanish language, and so on. Their socioeconomics status and cultural and linguistic diversity presented many challenges for both groups. But I soon realized that there is privilege associated with Nation. Students from Puerto Rico had U.S. passports and could move freely between the U.S. mainland and the island, whereas the Dominican students had another layer of barriers to overcome related to their immigration status. While both groups experienced marginalization related to race, language, and socioeconomic status, the students from Puerto Rico used their citizenship to claim membership in the dominant group and to further marginalize the students from the Dominican Republic. This is interesting not only in understanding how privilege or marginalization can be compounded, but also in understanding how some marginalized groups may gain power in ways that further marginalize others with less privilege. Race, class, language, and immigration status in the United States in particular can exponentially compound the barriers faced by English learners and their parents in navigating the education system, accessing information, preparing and applying for higher education and careers, and other tasks they face.

Privilege and marginalization shift as one changes social settings. This change can be as simple as moving from one social group (i.e., church) to another (i.e., work). The implications are larger for those who are changing nations. Consider how race/class/gender and other identity aspects can change the privilege and marginalization of individuals in this example from Purkayastha (2012):

> I will begin with a simple example that focuses on women of color. A Ugandan Black immigrant and a Ugandan Indian immigrant—whose family lived for many generations in Uganda before being forcibly evicted by Idi Amin—are both racially marginalized, though in different ways, in the United States. While both share the effects of gendered/racialized migration policies that would prohibit or slow the process through which they might form families in the United States, their experiences differ in other ways. The Ugandan Black migrant is likely to experience the gamut of racisms experienced by African Americans, while the Indian Ugandan is likely to experience the racisms faced by Muslims and "Muslim-looking" people in the United States, and they may share other structural discriminations experienced by Asian Americans (Narayan and Purkayastha 2009). These similarities and differences are consistent with racist ideologies, interactions, and institutional arrangements in the United States. But if both return to their home country Uganda, they would encounter a different set of privileges and marginalization in this Black-majority country; the Black Ugandan migrant is advantaged here (though the other intersecting factors would together shape her exact social location). If both visit or temporarily live in India, the Indian-origin Uganda-born person may experience the privileges associated with the dominant group in the country. However, if she is a Muslim or a low-caste Hindu, she might experience a different set of social hierarchies. (pp. 58–59)

In Purkayastha's example, you can see various elements of identity contributing to privilege across contexts, race and ethnicity, religion, class, gender, and other aspects. This situation becomes further complicated when also considering social issues and perceptions related to sexual orientation and ability. In classrooms around the world, privilege may shift based on where power is located, but there will always be students in the in-groups associated with those identities and those in the out-groups who are marginalized. One of the first steps in addressing this inequity/division along the lines of privilege to provide more equitable opportunities is to develop awareness related to the *opportunities* and *barriers* that may be associated with different levels of privilege in your context. Self-reflexivity is essential; as McIntosh (2012) cautions, those who write about privilege tend to "hide their own relation to the subject." So we must first begin with ourselves, noticing the privileges and/or marginalization we have experienced.

> Many people who think they are writing about privilege are in fact writing only about deficits, barriers, and discrimination, and cannot yet see exemptions, assumptions, and permissions granted by privilege. I am convinced that studies of oppression will not go anywhere toward ending oppression unless they are accompanied by understanding of the systems of privilege that cause the systems of oppression. (McIntosh, 2012, p. 204)

Bringing multiple perspectives into the discussion is essential. This approach helps us identify the systems of privilege and marginalization at work and validates different counterstories and experiences of nondominant groups. Next the goal is to find ways to reduce the barriers to redistributing opportunities more fairly. The following activities will consider both what can be done by the teacher, as well as what activities might engage students. It is important to note that these are sensitive topics, so there must be trust and care given to make sure participants feel emotionally safe and not further alienated for their comments or participation. Creating some ground rules is helpful. Sample ground rules might include: *Be an active listener. Welcome diverse perspectives. Speak from your own experience. Everyone deserves to feel safe and understood.*

Classroom Practices and Training Activities[3]
at the Teacher Level

An important first step is to understand how privilege or lack of it creates insider/outsider status, and also how it creates opportunities and barriers. The *Identity Circle*, shown in Figure 12.1, can be used as an activity for self-reflection in teacher training and with students, depending on their age and language proficiency. The image can be simplified, and participants can write their own identity circles rather then using the ones in the example.

---

[3] Many activities in this chapter have evolved after discussions and collaborations with colleagues Rachel Carter, Shawntay Stocks, and Felix Burgos. We have used them in collaborative trainings for preservice teachers and at TESOL conferences. I would be remiss in not citing them for their expertise and feedback.

Identity Circle

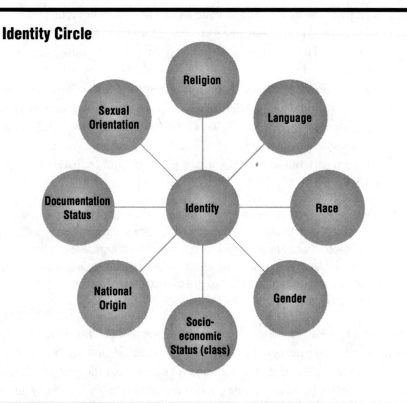

Figure 12.1. Identity circle. Reprinted with permission from Faust, Stocks, & Carter, 2014.

ACTIVITY #1. INSIDER/OUTSIDER

In Activity #1 Insider/Outsider, using the Identity Circle (Figure 12.1), consider the various aspects of your identity. For each aspect of your identity, think of times it has made you feel like an insider, and times it has made you feel like an outsider. For each aspect of your identity consider what opportunities or benefits you gained by membership in this group, and what if any barriers were created by it. Take language, for example. What benefits have you gained by speaking the language(s) you speak? In what ways has that language caused obstacles or limited opportunities for you? How about abilities or disabilities? In what way has your religion made you stand out or blend in? Provide time to think and write about the various aspects of identity. Then, share with a partner. Debrief with the whole group (Faust, Stocks, & Carter, 2014).

ACTIVITY #2. AWARENESS: RECOGNIZING/NAMING/RESOLVING

The Overcoming Barriers chart (Figure 12.2) can be used to brainstorm and also as a discussion starter. Consider in what way each of these aspects has provided opportunities for you or created barriers in your education, your job, and other areas of your life. Then consider the same for your student(s). Which groups are afforded

Identity Group	Opportunities	Barriers	Consequence(s)	Solutions
RELIGION				
ECONOMICS				
LANGUAGE				
RACE				
GENDER				
SEXUAL ORIENTATION				
ABILITY				

Figure 12.2. Overcoming Barriers chart.

opportunities in the current system and which ones are not? Where are there issues that affect student learning and opportunity? Through this process, how might you reduce barriers? create opportunities?

For example, as a Christian, in a mostly Christian community, I had all of my religious holidays as school holidays. School procedures did not conflict with my values, and the food we ate was not problematic. However, a Muslim student in my school would have had to be absent on school days for religious holidays, and school policies of coed gym class and the type of gym uniform we wore (shorts were required for girls) may not have aligned with religious values of more traditional students. This may have affected a student's participation and grading. A solution might be to not give important tests or assignments during other religious holidays, to expand the gym uniform policy to allow pants or alternative clothing. If we go to the chart to consider economics (social class), we might consider the cost to buy books and materials, or to buy materials for school projects, or to buy or rent an instrument for band practice. Students without economic privilege may not participate. One way to remove that barrier would be to provide loaner instruments and extra project supplies for all students. Students with money may have extended opportunities to further develop themselves, while students who are not economically privileged may not only not participate, but then must also compete with their peers for jobs and opportunities later. This privilege then reproduces itself as economically advantaged students continue to reap benefits, while those without encounter more hurdles.

As we go deeper into these considerations, we might explore which groups are represented in our curriculums and which are omitted. We may consider the presumptions of privilege in terms of who is disciplined more heavily, which students are expected to succeed, and so on. Once we have become aware of how privilege is operating in our context, we can create some solutions to those barriers and also recognize and redistribute the privileges afforded to some and not others.

ADDITIONAL TEACHER CONSIDERATIONS

When a dominant group is in power, there is often the "danger of a single story" (Adichie, 2009), which can result in a curriculum that tells the stories of those in power and highlights the achievements of those from the dominant group while inevitably invalidating the diverse experiences and achievements of others. This is a privilege that reproduces privilege. Teachers can disrupt this in a number of ways. One way is *teacher as facilitator*. As a facilitator of learning, rather than a deliverer of "knowledge," the teacher can incorporate the knowledge and experiences of many groups into the classroom. As the teacher cocreates knowledge with the students, students can access the diverse funds of knowledge (González, Moll, & Amanti, 2005) from various communities and populations. Repositioning marginalized students as assets can create a shift in privilege and opportunity. This move shifts teachers from deficit thinking toward strengths-based thinking. Surfacing the experiences of others through counterstories and multiple perspectives helps expand the worldview of traditionally privileged students and reposition marginalized students as insiders.

Redefining boundaries is another way to blur the lines of insiders and outsiders. In this work, the goal is to redefine what "WE" means in a class, in a school, in a community. Often the "WE" refers to the dominant group as we discuss history, achievements, perceptions, cultural norms, and so on. "WE" is the in-group, so to speak. Mixing students into groups across social boundaries is important. Creating new in-groups can occur with team building, establishing new "norms" that the class creates together, and coming together around common goals. The direct teaching of content related to privilege (i.e., the definition, the presumptions) may also bring students together in creating awareness and class goals around social justice.

Classroom Practices and Training Activities at the Student Level

Building awareness is a great place to start. This can be done even with younger students with simple insider/outsider activities. Students may discuss a time they felt that they belonged and a time that they felt left out. They can tell why and perhaps state what would have made them feel included. Introducing some classroom conversations around this topic can be supported through a variety of activities. Students can learn vocabulary to support these conversations. Listening and speaking skills can be developed, and extending these activities into reflective writing also supports language development. For lower proficiency levels, the charts and graphic organizers and sentence starters are a helpful support. Consider the two examples that follow.

ACTIVITY #3. COURAGEOUS CONVERSATIONS

Use the following sentence starters to facilitate conversations around various topics such as belonging, privilege, and various aspects of identity, or create your own sentence starters, depending on the age group and language level. These talk stems can be used in teacher training as well. An alternative to having this conversation is to give students sticky notes or note cards and have them write their answers. They can then post them on a wall or bulletin board quietly. This is more safe emotionally and socially and somewhat anonymous. Then the class can read all the things that make the class feel safe, like they belong, and so on.

I feel like part of the class (school, community . . .) when . . .

I don't feel like part of the class (school, community . . .) when . . .

I feel (safe, valued, validated, understood, accepted, included, etc.) when . . .

I don't feel (safe, valued, validated, understood, accepted, included, etc.) when . . .

A time someone presumed I was (competent) based on my (race/class/ability/ etc.) was . . .

A time someone presumed I wasn't (competent) based on my (race/class/ability/ etc.) was . . .

Analyzing stocks and flows is one tool for thinking about systems, which can be used for problem solving (Senge et al., 2012). This adapted version of the *bathtub* metaphor can be used with students to consider what contributes to a situation and what takes away from it. For example, one might consider: What fills your bathtub? What drains it? Consider the next activity.[4]

ACTIVITY #4. THE BATHTUB (STOCKS AND FLOWS)

In this example we will consider the concept of *belonging*. Students will consider all the things that make them feel like they belong. This is what fills their bathtub. Then students will consider those things that make them feel like they don't belong. This is what drains it. After the students have identifies both what drains and fills their bathtub, they discuss how to increase the things that fill their bathtub, and how to reduce the things that drain it. See Figures 12.3 and 12.4.

Figure 12. 3. Stocks and Flows Bathtub Metaphor. Reprinted with permission from Lucas, 2012.

---

[4] Teachers may consider changing the metaphor of a bathtub if this concept is one that students may not connect to. In developing regions with limited access to water or luxuries, another metaphor might be considered based on the context of the students.

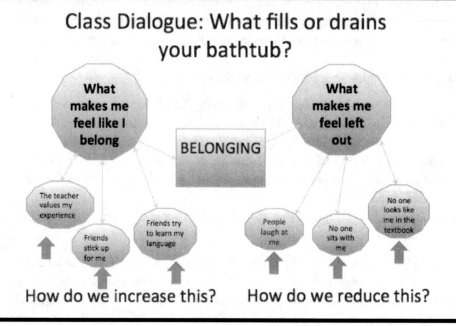

Figure 12.4. Sample response to the Bathtub Metaphor. Reprinted from Faust & Burgos, 2014.

As we consider how to increase factors that contribute to a sense of belonging, we may work on teaching students how to stand up for others, giving them some language for dealing with bullies or prejudiced comments and actions. We may work on reducing factors that take away from a sense of belonging by creating class norms such as *Reach out to a person who is alone.* We may encourage students to bring in examples of role models, stories, and other sources from their own lives to expand on the text.. One activity that honors the lives and context where students live is writing about their experiences.

ACTIVITY #5. "WHERE I'M FROM" POEMS

"Where I'm from" poems[5] (Lyon, 1999) can be framed in different ways. Simple in format, they can elicit the rich cultural and contextual experiences of students and bring them into the classroom. Have students complete the prompts to write their own "Where I'm from" poem.

---

[5] Lyon's original "Where I'm from" poem can be viewed on her website, http://www.george ollalyon.com/where.html, along with links to an oral reading of it. There are many examples online of adaptations for these poems that can be used with language learners.

Example format.

> I am from (name three things in your backyard or around your home)
>> That's where I'm from
> I am from (name three things your mother or family members say)
>> That's where I'm from
> I am from (name three foods you eat) That's where I'm from
> I am from (name three memories you have) That's where I'm from

My example.

> I am from Christmas trees,
> brokedown tractors, and
> stray cats
> That's where I'm from

> I am from *That's the way the cookie crumbles*
> *Look me in the eye when I'm talking to you,* and
> *Kannst du miche fange?*
> That's where I'm from

> I'm from Nana's Chicken potpie (the kind with homemade noodles),
> shoofly pie, and
> ring bologna
> That's where I'm from

> I am from baseball games in the hot summer sun,
> Playing rummy with mom mom, and
> Night drives through the backroads in dad's pickup truck, spotting deer.
> That's where I'm from

Representing the rich variety of experiences and perspectives of our students and community is an important step toward inclusive classroom practices. As we work with students to create more equitable classrooms we can help them build awareness of inequalities in their daily lives and community. Creating informal and formal structures to support this change begins with building awareness and vocabulary to both recognize and discuss these issues. Helping students to become allies for those who are marginalized is another way to address this challenge. One example is to organize and train students to be ambassadors who welcome new students. One ESL teacher I worked with created an ELL Ambassador program with fourth graders in her school. They welcomed new English Learners to the school and helped them learn the culture and expectations. Other examples include the creation of safe spaces, where marginalized students may convene, discuss relevant experiences and issues, and feel that they have a space where they can be comfortable. In the interest supporting students with sensitive issues related to gender and sexual orientation, some faculty have posted "safe space" stickers on their doors, or even published a faculty "out list" so that students have role models on the faculty and safe places they can go related to LGBTQ concerns. Rethinking the representations of the various groups in our classes, schools, and communities within our curriculum and space is important. Ask the questions Who is represented here and how are they portrayed? Who is not represented here? Why?

Conclusion

As we reflect on the big ideas of the chapter, we must remember that everyone has varying levels of privilege and that privilege shifts across contexts. The first step begins with evaluating our own experiences and considering how the presumptions of privilege (innocence, competence, and worth) have provided opportunities and barriers in our own lives and in our classrooms. We must not stop there. We must move beyond awareness to action, implementing practices that reduce barriers and that examine and redistribute existing privilege toward a more socially just practice.

DISCUSSION QUESTIONS FOR TEACHERS

1. Who in my context is afforded the presumptions of innocence, competence, and worth? Who is not? What does that mean for my students?

2. In what ways does privilege create opportunities for certain students? What barriers exist for students who don't have that privilege? How can this be compensated?

3. How does my own privilege affect my view of the world? In what ways have I experienced opportunities? Barriers? How does this experience affect the assumptions I make about my colleagues? My students?

DISCUSSION QUESTIONS FOR STUDENTS

1. When is a time you felt like an insider, or part of the group? What did that do to help you? When is a time you felt like an outsider, or not part of the group? How did it affect you?

2. Consider the language you speak. Was there a time it made you feel like an insider or an outsider? What happened? What do you want other students to know about this? What do you want your teacher to know about this?

3. What do you want from others when you feel like an outsider? What would make you feel like an insider?

4. What can you do to help others? What do you need from others (to participate, feel included, meet your goals, etc.).

References

Adichie, C. N. (2009). *The danger of a single story* [TED Talk.] TEDGlobal. Retrieved from http://www.ted.com/talks/chimamanda_adichie_the_danger_of_a_single_story

Banks, J. (n.d.). *Approaches to multicultural curriculum reform.* Retrieved from http://onnetwork.facinghistory.org/wp-content/uploads/2013/05/Banks-Approaches-to-Reform.pdf

Bonfiglio, T. P. (2002). *Race and the rise of standard American.* Berlin, Germany: Mouton de Gruyter.

Bonilla-Silva, E. (2003). *Racism without racists: Color-blind racism and the persistence of racial inequality in the United States.* Lanham, MD: Rowman & Littlefield.

Brewers, M. B. (1999). The psychology of prejudice: Ingroup love and outgroup hate? *Journal of Social Issues, 55*(3), 429–444. doi:10.1111/0022-4537.00126

Collins, P. H. (2000). Black feminist thought: Knowledge, consciousness and the politics of empowerment (2nd ed.). New York, NY: Routledge.

Collins, P. H. (2010). The new politics of community. *American Sociological Review, 75,* 7–30.

Cullinan, C. (1999). Vision, privilege, and the limits of tolerance. *Electronic Magazine of Multicultural Education.* Retrieved January 15, 2014, from http://www.eastern.edu/publications/emme/1999spring/cullinan.html

Faust, H. J., & Burgos, F. (2014, November). Building cross-cultural communities: Classroom activities and discussions for creating a culture of respect. *No one left behind: Integrating multicultural perspectives in the English classroom.* 41st annual PRTESOL Convention, Ponce, Puerto Rico.

Faust, H. J., Stocks, S., & Carter, R. (2014, November 4). *Race and privilege in the classroom, part II: Classroom strategies.* Collegial Conversations Series. University of Maryland Baltimore County, Department of Education.

Ferguson, A. A. (2000). *Bad boys: Public schools in the making of Black masculinity.* Ann Arbor: University of Michigan Press.

González, N., Moll, L. C., & Amanti, C. (2005). *Funds of knowledge: Theorizing practice in households, communities, and classrooms.* Mahwah, NJ: Lawrence Erlbaum.

Gorski, P. (2015). Stages of multicultural curriculum transformation. *Multicultural curriculum reform.* Retrieved from http://www.edchange.org/multicultural/curriculum/steps.html

Helms, J. E. (1990). *Black and white racial identity: Theory, research, and practice.* New York, NY: Greenwood Press.

Lensmire, T. J., Mcmanimon, S. K., Dockter Tierney, J., Lee-Nichols, M. E., Casey, Z. A., Lensmire, A., & Davis, B. M. (2013). McIntosh as synecdoche: How teacher education's focus on white privilege undermines antiracism. *Harvard Educational Review, 83*(3), 410–431.

Lippi-Green, R. (2012). *English with an accent: Language, ideology and discrimination in the United States* (2nd ed.). New York, NY: Routledge. Retrieved from http://www.eblib.com

Lucas, T. (2012). *Systems thinking tools for teachers* [PowerPoint]. Class presentation, University of Maryland Baltimore County, Baltimore, MD.

Lyon, G. E. (n.d.). Where I'm from. Retrieved from http://www.georgeellalyon.com/where.html

Lyon, G. E. (1999). *Where I'm from, where poems come from.* New York, NY: Absey.

McIntosh, P. (1988). White privilege: Unpacking the invisible knapsack [Excerpt]. (Reprinted from *Independent School,* Winter 1990.) Wellesley College Center for Research on Women, Wellesley, MA. Retrieved from http://www.deanza.edu/faculty /lewisjulie/White%20Priviledge%20Unpacking%20the%20Invisible%20Knapsack.pdf

McIntosh, P. (2012). Reflections and future directions for privilege studies. *Journal of Social Issues, 68*(1), 194–206.

Purkayastha, B. (2012). Symposia on the contributions of Patricia Hill Collins: Intersectionality in a transnational world. *Gender & Society, 26*(1), 55–66. doi:10.1177/0891243211426725

Senge, P. M., Cambron-McCabe, N., Lucas, T., Smith, B., Dutton, J., & Kleiner, A. (2012). *Schools that learn: A fifth discipline fieldbook for educators, parents, and everyone who cares about education* (2nd ed.). New York, NY: Crown Business.

Wise, T. J. (2008). *Speaking treason fluently: Anti-racist reflections from an angry white male.* Brooklyn, NY: Soft Skull.

CHAPTER 13

Racializing Justice in TESOL
Embracing the Burden of Double Consciousness

Shelley Wong
George Mason University

Rachel Grant
City University of New York–College of Staten Island

Yet for so long, indigenous peoples from across the globe have been unable
to speak, to contribute to the solutions of the problems facing humanity. . . .
As our cultures disappear with the wilderness that sustained us, we are a
vast library, a repository of knowledge, intelligence, and an understanding
of the earth that is being lost to the world.

—*Ingrid Washinawatok*

Freddie Gray, Walter Scott, Eric Garner, Michael Brown, Tamir Rice, John
Crawford, Jonathan Ferrell, Jordan Davis, Trayvon Martin . . . Emmett Till.
What do we have to do to stop these senseless fatal attacks upon black
male bodies? Police body cameras, indictments, guilty verdicts and even
DOJ (Department of Justice) reports are not enough. . . . We must examine
the *racialized culture* that is America." (emphasis added)

—*Kelly Brown Douglas, CNN News*

he voices of the two women of color who open this chapter, Ingrid Washinawatok
O'Peqtaw-Metamoh (Flying Eagle Woman) and Rev. Dr. Kelly Brown Douglas,
professor of religion at Goucher College, in Baltimore, Maryland, provide a spiritual dimension to a central problem for all of us in TESOL who already care deeply
about social justice and want to know how we can *counter* racism when it seems so
deeply entrenched and ingrained in our culture, thinking, and way of life. What can
we do when our students are victims (or perpetrators) of bullying, racial profiling,
and racial attacks? How do we engage in antiracist practices in our classrooms and

communities when our classrooms may be as racially divided and polarized as the communities and societies in which we work? How do we promote racial justice when racial and economic divisions between haves and have-nots seem to be growing?

Ingrid Washinawatok (1957–1999) was a member of the Menominee Nation from Wisconsin, in the United States. Washinawatok was a Native American community activist who worked to bring recognition of American Indian struggles for education, land, and sovereignty to international arenas such as the United Nations. She was invited to Colombia, South America, by the U'wa Indians to assist them in developing a traditional school that would protect their culture. She was murdered in Colombia working for Indigenous peoples' democratic and human rights, land, and sovereignty. Although she was only 41 years old when she was killed, her life's work for the survival of Indigenous people lives on through the struggles of Indigenous people to promote heritage language education and protect their communities from environmental racism. (See chapter 21 on environmental justice herein.)

Rev. Dr. Kelly Brown Douglas, an Episcopal priest and university professor of religion, directs attention to the historic dehumanizing perception of black male bodies as property rather than conscious human beings when she writes, "The 21st century version of the black body as chattel is the criminal black body. The fact that there are more black men imprisoned today than were enslaved in 1850 signals that the transformation from chattel to criminal is complete when it comes to the black male body. . . . the notion that criminals are black males and black males are criminal has been subtly but firmly implanted within the American mind" (Douglas, 2015). In addition the criminalization and negative portrayals of Black males in popular culture such as cartoons and Hollywood movies and (White) mainstream U.S. news media may have influence around the world in countries where ESOL students have little direct experience with people of African heritage and descent.

In this chapter we will address "racializing TESOL," or the process of racialization or becoming conscious of the significance of race and racism in TESOL, by discussing intersecting definitions of race, racism, whiteness, colorism, and other hierarchies of difference such as gender, class, (dis)ability through the concept of double consciousness. Next we will share our own family histories, and finally we will discuss pedagogical implications for racializing TESOL and discussing what it might mean to "embrace" the burden of double consciousness in our classrooms and communities.

Definitions of Race

Race is a "socially constructed" system of categorization that has no basis in biological reality (Omi & Winant, 1986). Nineteenth century and 20th century studies of brain size or body shape that attempted to show the racial superiority of "white," "Aryan," or European bodies have been discredited (Gould, 1981; Selden, 1999). There are as many differences within any of the so-called "races" with respect to skin color, type of hair, and other features to make biological categorization of the "races" problematic. But while there is no biological basis for "race," racial tagging and *racism* exist as part of U.S. culture. As Henry Louis Gates Jr. (1986) writes, race

> pretends to be an objective term of classification, when in fact it is a dangerous troupe.
>
> The sense of difference defined in popular usages of the term "race" has both described and *inscribed* differences of language, belief system, artistic tradition, and gene pool, as well as all sorts of supposedly natural attributes such as rhythm, athletic ability, cerebration, usury, fidelity and so forth. The relation between "racial character" and these sorts of characteristics as been inscribed through tropes of race, lending the sanction of God, biology, or the natural order to even presumably unbiased descriptions of cultural tendencies and differences. (p. 5)

Racism is a social fact and a historical reality embedded in our literature, culture, and national consciousness (Bell, 1992). We are socialized into accepting racial categorizations and racism, the ideology that supported and was engendered by the African slave trade, slavery in the Americas and colonialism and imperialism in Africa, Asia, Australia and the Pacific, and Latin America and the Caribbean. Racism continues through war, military conquest, inequitable distribution of social and economic resources, and political injustice.

The phenomena of "double consciousness" was first introduced by Dr. W. E. B. Du Bois (1903/1961) in his path-breaking book *The Souls of Black Folk.* Originally published in 1903, the book was written 40 years after slavery was abolished. Although the system of slavery had ended formally, Black people were neither free nor equal and did not enjoy the democratic rights of citizenship of White people. Du Bois described double consciousness as looking at oneself through the eyes of the other and measuring one's soul by the tape of another world as a marginalized permanent outsider to a country that had previously held Black people as personal property rather than persons with rights. It was not the situation of the colonial master who imposed his language and culture on the natives whose land he conquered and occupied (Memmi, 1970); but it is the situation of those who are the former slaves and the colonized. *The Souls of Black Folk* speaks to the moral dilemma poised by being of two worlds. A contemporary example of this duality is provided by the hyphenated ethnic identity of being Chinese-American or Mexican-American. The American Psychological Association no longer hyphenates these terms—now Chinese American or Mexican American. This change in punctuation is to be commended. Symbolically, the elimination of the "hyphen" signals a more holistic rather than divided representation of personhood. The historic ethnic duality between people of color and White people is a historical division rooted in slavery, European conquest, and colonialism. The dominant American identity is White, while the American or Black American is deemed "less than ideal" or not a true American.

The world is divided into "marked" and "unmarked"; "unmarked" is English, White, the Anglo core. Double consciousness is having the awareness that one is measured by the standards of the unmarked Anglo American or the White European American core group. In reality the White "mainstream" is not homogeneous. Within the White core, historic differences existed between the Irish, the Italians, and the core Anglos. Many Italian Americans or Eastern Europeans experienced bigotry akin to racial prejudice because their darker skin and hair were associated with "dirtiness," ignorance, and inferiority. The history of White people reflects not only the invention of "race" as Irish became White, but the praising of whiteness for economic, scientific, and political purposes (Painter, 2010).

Language teaching—especially for children who are of working-class origin or racial or religious minorities—accounts for the issues of double consciousness and reflects sensitivity to the complexity of racial and other forms of social identity. Positive views of one's personhood and social identity are important to academic achievement (Wong & Grant, 2007).

Racism and colonialism can lead to denigration of one's ethnic, cultural, or racial identity, self-hatred, or being ashamed of one's background. In addition, marginalized students may think that learning academic English is a betrayal of their native language and culture or in conflict with promoting their home language, culture, and community (Ladson-Billings, 2000). If we are unaware of the power relations involved in the teaching of English to indigenous students or students who are products of a colonial legacy, we may be in danger of unwittingly participating in cultural and linguistic genocide.

Feminist standpoint theorist Nancy Naples (1996) posed a traditional debate in ethnographic research that is relevant to researching race in TESOL and educational research: Is it more effective to conduct fieldwork from the position of an "insider" or an "outsider" to the communities being studied? Naples is critical of taking a binary approach, in which "insiders" and "outsiders" are fixed or static categories. She points out that "outsiderness" and "insiderness" are "ever-shifting and permeable" (1996, p. 83). Yet when it comes to race, while insider/outsider boundaries may be shifting and dynamic, the historic strength of racism is a permanent feature in U.S. culture, institutions, and society. Racism is still the glue that holds our society together—despite its tremendous disparities in wealth, income, and opportunity (Bell, 2004).

The 21st century has seen the election of the first indigenous and African American presidents after 500 years of colonial conquest beginning with Christopher Columbus. Bolivia elected the first indigenous president, Juan Evo Morales Ayma, in 2006. When President Barack Hussein Obama, an outsider, became the supreme insider and was elected the first African American U.S. president, many heralded his historic victory as "the end of racism" and the beginning of a new era of racial acceptance. To some, this victory signaled that the United States had entered into a post-racial society and that race and racism could no longer be used as an excuse for lack of achievement of African Americans (Dixson, 2013; Milner & Self, 2013).

A nativist movement across the country challenged Obama's insider status. Members of this movement demanded that Obama show his original, handwritten certificate of birth and alleged that he had been born in Kenya, which would mean that he was not qualified to be president. An outsider, first as a presidential candidate and later after being elected, Obama has repeatedly responded publicly by producing official documents from the state of Hawaii that prove that he was born in the United States. However, the "Birther Movement" has questioned the authenticity of those papers.

Obama's insider/outsider experience is not unlike the experiences of many racial and ethnic people today whose legitimacy is questioned, including my grandmothers, who were born in the United States but not afforded the rights of other U.S. citizens. In order for outsiders to become successful insiders they must *embrace* the burden of double consciousness. This is particularly true of people who have suffered historically under slavery, colonial occupation, exclusion and internment, Jim Crow racial discrimination and segregation.

Family History I

I am fifth-generation Chinese American. The earliest members of my family to come to the United States from China are from my mother's family; the first generation came in the 1850s, during the California Gold Rush, to work in the mines and on the railroads.

On my father's side, my *Yen Yen* (Cantonese Toishan dialect for paternal grandmother) Alice Mar was born in 1901 in Weaverville, a gold-mining town in northern California. Her father would carry supplies from San Francisco to Weaverville by horseback to sell to the miners.

It was not easy to be Chinese in those days. Some of the White miners grew jealous of Chinese miners who were staking claims and set fire to the row of houses where the Chinese lived to drive them out of Weaverville. All the houses burned to the ground except for my grandmother's house—the last house in the row; it was spared because of a change in the wind. After this incident, my grandmother's family decided to move to Sacramento, California, where my grandmother was able to go to school for the first time at age 12.

My *Yeh Yeh*, or paternal grandfather, was born in China. He came to the United States at the age of 15 and worked as a houseboy in Sonoma, California. After he met my grandmother and they got married, they tried to buy some property under her name, since she had been born in the United States and was a U.S. citizen. To their surprise, they learned that they couldn't buy the land because she had forfeited her citizenship by marrying someone who was not a U.S. citizen. My grandmother had to hire a lawyer and had to take citizenship classes to get her citizenship back (Wong, 2006).

My grandmother bore four children, but only two children survived, my father, Delbert, and my uncle, Ervin. During World War II, my dad and my uncle wanted to enlist in the military. In those days the Marines didn't accept any non-Whites. Before being accepted into the Army Air Corps, my father was turned down by the Navy. African Americans served in completely segregated units in the Air Corps, while

Asians and Latinos served with Whites. Among 360 flying officers, my father was the only Asian. Stationed in England, my father flew 35 bombing missions over Germany. Casualty rates for the bomber crews were high. Only 3 of the 18 navigators who went through training with my father completed their required 30 missions. The other 15 were shot down, and several were taken as prisoners of war.

My Uncle Ervin joined the Army out of high school and was killed in a training accident. He was 19 years old. My grandmother joined the Gold Star Mothers, an association of mothers whose sons who had died while serving in the armed forces, and she continued to be active in her chapter in Bakersfield for years. But despite being born and raised in the United States and losing her son during World War II, she was always treated as a foreigner in the land where she was born, never as a citizen.

My grandmother and my parents, like many other "outsiders" in the United States—those who have gone before us, such as Native Americans, African Americans, Latinos, and Asian Americans, and those from diverse racial and ethnic backgrounds today, such as Arab Americans of all faiths, Muslim Americans, and Sikhs—have been subject to double standards which relegated them to second-class citizenship, even though they worked, contributed, and sacrificed in the same ways as White Americans have. This experience of double consciousness is still evident in how we as people of color, as gay, lesbian, bisexual, and transgendered as religious minorities, and as undocumented residents who have committed no crimes but are demonized with the label "illegal aliens" respond to the crisis in education and society today.

Family History II

I am one of six children born to African American parents who took part in the Great Migration of southern Blacks to northern industrial cities during the 1930s and 1940s. I was born and spent the first 17 years of my life in a midsize city in northeastern Ohio. My family lived on one of three streets that stretched the length of the city. However, our street was more special than the others because it was named for the 22nd and 24th president of the United States, Grover Cleveland. Cleveland Avenue was said to have been where President Cleveland once owned a home. Cleveland Avenue was noteworthy to me for another reason. My family had the distinction of being the first "Negro" family allowed to purchase a home on this avenue of the president.

In many ways my childhood was typical of Black Midwestern girls growing up during the 1950s and 1960s. My father was the oldest of nine children who attended high school, but was the only one not to graduate. Like many African Americans of his generation, he volunteered for military service. My father served in the Navy at the same time that my uncles Nathaniel and Richard were in the Army and my uncle Robert served in the Air Force. My mother, the youngest of 15 children, was the first in her family to earn a high school diploma. After marrying, my father worked in a factory and my mom stayed at home to raise the children, until her youngest child was in first grade. When my mother did go to work, like most African American women of her time, she performed domestic "day work" for a number of White families.

My siblings and I attended integrated schools in a school district where the school board and superintendent all were White. In elementary school there were several African American teachers, but in high school there was only one. Throughout school all our principals were White and male; in high school there was one African American female counselor. As was typically for many smaller cities in northeast Ohio during the 1950s and 1960s, our schools were integrated, but our churches were segregated. Unofficially, we had "colored" parks and "White" parks, and Blacks and Whites bought clothing and groceries in the same stores. To my memory my parents voted in every election, but all of the mayors, city council members, policemen, and bus drivers were White.

From my childhood and youth in Middle America, I carry with me the memories and experiences that influence who I am, what I do, and how I conduct my personal and professional lives. Like other adults I carry a treasure trove of experiences that shape and define both my private and my public "self" as a raced, gendered, and classed individual. Growing up, I witnessed the daily telecasts of the violence visited upon Blacks in the U.S. South as they marched for voting rights, fair housing, equal education, and basic human rights. However, talk about race and racism took place within the private space of our home because, after all, "we didn't have those problems in the North." Both born in Alabama, my parents talked about what it was like growing up in the Jim Crow South, and they helped their children understand that although we lived among Whites and sat next to them in school, there were certain "understandings" Blacks needed to have in order to be safe "up North." During the recent killings of unarmed Black men by White policemen and what feels like, at least to me, the never-ending assault on Black life, I find myself repeating one of my parents' basic understandings: Simply put, for Blacks to be safe in this country, we must remember that Black life does not hold the same value as White life, so we must at all times be aware of what we say, where we go, and how we behave, because if something happens to you at the hands of a White person, in all likelihood nothing will be done about it. The experiences my parents shared and their guiding principles, their way of reinforcing Du Bois' "double consciousness," provides a historical framework that informs who am I as a raced, gendered, and classed individual. Randall Robinson (2000) in his powerful book, *The Debt* states, "No people can live successfully, fruitfully, triumphantly without strong memory of their past, without reading the future within the context of some reassuring past, without implanting reminders of that past in the present" (p. 27).

Of course, many childhood experiences provide the context for understanding both race and racism and help me understand the historical and situational nature of these concepts. However, for Americans of African decent race is not merely a social construct; race is a lived experience. We sense it, we smell it, we see it, we taste it, and, finally, we know it. I believe that the understandings and experiences are part of the essential framework that shapes my identity as a person of color and determines which theories and pedagogies inform my work as a literacy and language researcher/educator.

In the Unites States and other countries many issues related to race remain unresolved: in particular, issues that are legacies of past injustices to Native peoples, African Americans, and people of color who immigrate to this country. Racism evolved as a concept designed to ensure that Europeans could sustain economic, political, and social privileges. As a socially and culturally constructed factor, race can affect privileges and subsequent discrimination based on a person's physical character- istics. Through its various institutions (e.g., schools, military, legal system), dominant groups impose their will, ensuring placement at the top of society as systems are set in place to perpetuate their control. Because schools are uniquely positioned as the one place where everyone in a society must "pass through," schools remain a crucial tool for sustaining long-standing practices and traditions of privilege and discrimination. Hegemonic ideologies of language, and relationships among language, race, and national identity, have played an important role in schooling in the United States.

Critical Race Theory (CRT) helps us understand, explain, and address multiple levels of discrimination that affect students in school and the larger society. CRT has become helpful to many educational scholars who analyze racial injustice in schools as it is played out through educational issues, policy, and ideology. CRT acknowledges the significant role of various forms of discrimination that impede achievement of Black students and other members of subordinated racial or ethnic groups. Given that immigrants and U.S.-born English learners also are members of marginalized groups, failing to consider the interrelatedness of analytic categories may weaken the ability of local and national efforts to achieve social, economic, and educational equity for English learners and others. The categorization of populations according to social and cultural criteria is closely linked to race and language identity. The relative importance of language and race in the United States has become the growing preoccupation in education discourses and can be seen in the changing construction of immigration difference and the use of raced-based arguments in calls for immigration restriction. A connection between U.S. identity and the English language has become firmly cemented in the public consciousness, and the United States has become hegemoni- cally constructed as a White, English-speaking nation. Efforts to explore the complex- ity of how teachers teach and children learn necessitates the use of critical theory and methodological tools for examining the links between race and language, race and gender, race and social class, and so on (Wong & Grant, 2014).

Conversely, while schools serve as a mechanism for sustaining the hegemony of White and dominant American English prominence, they also offer great promise for changing the status quo. Education lies at the heart of what is needed to raise awareness and promote opportunities for addressing race for two distinct reasons. First, education is directed toward the development of human personality to its fullest. Second, "full realization of human capacities contains within itself the mandate to educate towards respect for the human rights and fundamental freedoms of others" (Dhillon, 2011, p. 250)

Embracing the Burden of Double Consciousness: Transforming Educational Practices

W. E. B. Du Bois' concept of "double consciousness" can be a tool for racial, linguistic, and cultural outsiders—for anyone who has been identified as "the problem" or has been demonized or treated as less than human. First, it helps us to address the problem of cultural capital and language loss, a problem for indigenous students, students from former colonies, and speakers of "less prestigious" languages. In the United States, whether our student's home language is a world language such as Spanish, French, Arabic, or Chinese or a language on the verge of extinction, such as Native American languages, we as TESOL and multilingual multicultural leaders must be concerned with memory for the home language and the new language (Wong, 2011).

Second, the concept of double consciousness can be embraced through using Critical Discourse Analysis (CDA) to work with and between two kinds of discourse—the "little d" discourse and Big "D" Discourse, between the discourses of the oppressed and the dominant Discourse (Gee, 1990; Luke, 1996; Pennycook, 1994). Using CDA involves working through and between the more linguistic discursive aspects of teaching students to read and write, such as subject-verb agreement or the correct register, and the political and ideological aspects of teaching literacy. Working between two kinds of discourse involves critical readings of history, culture, and ideology. It involves comparing various genres and perspectives and reaching back to collective memories that are suppressed by dominant Discourses.

Double consciousness enables language learners to understand and affirm where they came from, to appreciate those elders and ancestors who went before them—the indigenous people, the former slaves and plantation workers—and to criticize "false consciousness" the taken-for-granted views of the dominant Discourse that lead to self-hatred and to being ashamed of parents and grandparents because they speak English with an accent or ashamed of having "two moms" as parents. Double consciousness is an important concept for ethnic and women's studies that seek a multivoiced writing of history from the grass roots. Embracing the burden of double consciousness entails recognizing and working from one's marginalized and privileged identities to be allies of and advocates for and with those who are the most exploited, oppressed, alienated, and vulnerable.

Du Bois' theory of double consciousness and the transformative role of intellectuals address the questions "Knowledge for whom? Or whom does knowledge serve?" (Wong, 2011). He called on the world to "listen to the striving in the souls of black folk." A historian and sociologist, Du Bois examined the condition of African American people 100 ago, 100 years after slavery ended, and asked why the nation had "not found peace from its sins," why freed men and women had "not found freedom in their promised land." He said the problem of America was the color line.

Education must be extended to all; knowledge, like private property, must not be kept only in the hands of the wealthy. We can guard knowledge like the master craftsmen and guilds in a feudal society or we can work to democratize knowledge, extend it to serve all people and work to dismantle the forces in education that reproduce inequity.

Posing the question "Knowledge for whom?" helps us consider what our students need in order to succeed; when we pose this question, do our best to answer it, and cause our classrooms to reflect those answers, we pave the way toward increasing the numbers of disenfranchised people who participate in all levels of education.

In *The Souls of Black Folk*, Du Bois (1903/1961) described "double consciousness":

> After the Egyptian and Indian, the Greek and Roman, the Teuton and Mongolian, the Negro is sort of seventh son, born with a veil, and gifted with second-sight in this American world—a world which yields him no true self-consciousness, but only lets him see himself through the relation of the other world. It is a peculiar sensation, this double-consciousness, this sense of always looking at one's self through the eyes of others, of measuring one's soul by the tape of a world that looks on in amused contempt and pity. One ever feels his two-ness, an American, a Negro; two souls, two thoughts, two unreconciled strivings; two warring ideals in one dark body, whose dogged strength alone keeps it from being torn asunder. (pp. 16–17)

The greatest tragedy in our school districts today is that we have kindergarteners who enter the schools speaking a hundred different languages, and instead of supporting and building on this tremendous resource, we squander it. By the time these children leave school, most of them will have lost their native languages. Sadly, many do not acquire English at a level of proficiency needed for them to go to college, and yet they have lost the ability to speak their native language to their parents. What a terrible waste this is when we need skilled bilingual people in every profession, in every field. The greatest impact that we can have on the next generation is to promote bilingualism and respect for the languages and cultures of all of the children and families.

Many of the immigrant parents whose children enter U.S. classrooms will themselves be unaware of the problem of linguistic genocide and language loss of the home language. They want their children to learn English and to do better in school. They themselves may not know English and worry that because they don't speak English that they won't be able to help their children succeed in school.

The single most important lesson that we as TESOL professionals can share with these parents is that they should continue to speak the home language with their children.

The challenge for us as teachers is to teach English as an *additional* language. We need to have an additive, not a subtractive, approach to language learning. We need to build on and support the home language of children, not to replace the home language with English.

As we anticipate the future, asking how we can support the many home languages and cultures of our students, we can draw from lessons of the women's movement as we look to the future and ask, "How can things be different?" We can draw from the importance of consciousness raising to rely on the power of consciousness-raising sessions. The women's movement said "the personal is political," asking that we reflect on the hierarchies and the differences in gender, racial, and class inequalities and how they affect us in our personal lives. The idea that "the personal is political" asks us to draw a connection between gendered roles and systematic, institutional patterns of inequality and how that system works personally in our daily lives. To "the personal is political" we would add "professional." As TESOL professionals, we have a responsibility to use our professional knowledge and expertise in the service of our students, their families and the multilingual communities of which they are a part.

By enhancing our professionalism, we as teachers can be better advocates for racial, linguistic, and ethnic minority students. For example, teachers can be proactive with their principals and directors, offering to lead workshops and in-service programs on how to honor home languages and cultures and how to work with parents who speak different languages to incorporate their wealth of knowledge and their funds of knowledge into school curriculum. The quality of being professional lends credibility as we become change agents to make school institutions and the culture of the classroom more responsive to the multilingual realities of our students.

Yuri Mary Kochiyama (2004), the great civil rights Asian American activist who worked with Brother Malcolm X and was with him when he was assassinated, remembers one of the lessons she learned from him. Kochiyama was a Sunday school teacher and also worked with children when she was a young woman in the 1940s. After being a community activist, she as a movement elder passed on this thought, from Brother Malcolm, to the younger generation:

> It is more important what you teach a child to love than what you teach a child to know.
> Let us go forward, teaching our children to love.

References

Bell, D. (1992). *Faces at the bottom of the well: The permanence of racism.* New York, NY: Basic Books.

Bell, D. (2004). *Silent covenants: Brown v. Board of Education and the unfulfilled hopes for racial reform.* New York, NY: Oxford University Press.

Dhillon, P. (2011). The role of education in freedom from poverty as a human right. *Educational Philosophy and Theory, 43,* 249–259.

Dixson, A. D. (2013). Introduction. In A. D. Dixson (Ed.), *Researching race in education: Policy practice, and qualitative research* (pp. xv–xxi). Charlotte, NC: Information Age.

Douglas, K. B. (2015). Seeing God in the face of Freddie Gray. CNN News. http://www.cnn.com/2015/04/28/living/god-freddie-gray/

Du Bois, W. E. B. (1961). *The souls of black folk.* Greenwich, CT: Fawcett Publications. (Originally published 1903, Chicago, IL: A.C. McClurg.)

Gates, H. L. (1986). *"Race," writing and difference.* Chicago, IL: University of Chicago Press.

Gee, J. (1990). *Social linguistics and literacies: Ideology in discourses.* London, England: Falmer Press.

Gould, S. J. (1981). *The mismeasure of man.* New York, NY: Norton.

Kochiyama, Y. (2004). *Passing it on: A memoir*. Los Angeles, CA: UCLA Asian American Studies Center Press.

Ladson-Billings, G. (2000). Racialized discourses and ethnic epistemologies. In N. Dezin & Y. Lincoln (Eds.), *Handbook of qualitative research* (2nd ed., pp. 257–277). Thousand Oaks, CA: Sage.

Luke, A. (1996). Text and discourse in education: An introduction to critical discourse analysis. *Review of Research in Education, 21*, 3–48.

Memmi, A. (1970). *The colonizer and the colonized*. Boston, MA: Beacon Press.

Milner, H. R., & Self, E. A. (2013). Studying race in teacher education: Implications from ethnographic perspectives. In A. D. Dixson (Ed.), *Researching race in education: Policy practice, and qualitative research* (pp. 3–29). Charlotte, NC: Information Age.

Naples, N. (1996). A feminist revisiting of the insider/outsider debate: The "outsider phenomenon" in rural Iowa. *Qualitative Sociology, 19*(1), 83–106.

Omi, M., & Winant, H. (1986). *Racial formation in the United States*. New York, NY: Routledge.

Painter, N. (2010). *The history of White people*. New York: W.W. Norton.

Pennycook, A. (1994). Incommensurable discourses? *Applied Linguistics, 15*, 115–138.

Robinson, R. (2000). *The debt: What America owes to blacks*. Middlesex, England: Penguin Putman.

Seldon, S. (1999). *Inheriting shame: The story of eugenics and racism in America*. New York, NY: Teachers College Press.

Washinawatok, I. (n.d.). Ingrid Washinawatok el-Issa reflects on working toward peace. Retrieved from www.scu.edu/ethics/architects-of-peace/el-Issa/essay.html

Wong, S. (2006). Perpetual foreigners: Can an American be an American? In A. Curtis & M. Romney (Eds.), *Color, race, and English language teaching: Shades of meaning* (pp. 81–92). Mahwah, NJ: Lawrence Erlbaum.

Wong, S. (2011). *Dialogic approaches to TESOL: Where the ginkgo tree grows*. New York, NY: Taylor & Francis/Routledge

Wong, S., & Grant, R. (2007). Academic achievement and social identity among bilingual students in the U.S. In J. Cummins & C. Davison (Eds.), *The international handbook of English language teaching* (Vol. 2, pp. 681–691). New York, NY: Springer.

Wong, S., & Grant, R. (2014). Critical race, feminist/womanist & post-colonial perspectives for peace making in multilingual multicultural classrooms. In R. Oxford (Ed.), *Language of peace in a global* society (pp. 29–51). Charlotte, NC: Information Age.

PART V:
GENDER AND SEXUAL ORIENTATION JUSTICE

CHAPTER 14

Gender Sensitization as a Learning Outcome

Kirti Kapur

National Council of Educational Research and Training,
New Delhi, India

The title of this chapter is a reflection of my journey as a woman and an education-ist. Reams have been written about India largely being a patriarchal society. It is an undeniable truth that "She" is subsumed in "He." Segregation of sexes in all-female spaces and all-male spaces is unquestioned in many areas, be it public transport, academic institutions, lines in buffets, or seating areas in public functions or concerts. This separation is accepted without questioning, and extends to roles at home, at the work place, and in social situations as well. As one among three sisters, I may not have borne the brunt of the infamous preferential treatment of a male child over female siblings, but I was acutely aware of how unfortunate my parents were considered for having no male heir.

In school too there was an unsaid code of conduct: separate seating for girls and boys, absence of group activities that encouraged interaction between the sexes, and allocation of vastly different activities for girls and boys during leisure and games. Boy Scouts led strategic activities and Girl Scouts learned about good moral conduct. My cognition that the rules were different for different sexes, and unfairly so, would not have found expression had it not been for my college degree. There, exposure to English literature and polemic works by women authors opened my eyes to the structures that operate and sustain gender discrimination. I was able to discern how access to a certain kind of vocabulary could help me articulate my opinions and think beyond what was prescribed culturally and socially.

In the 1970s and 1980s, Gender Studies was emerging as a specialized field. Women writers were standing shoulder-to-shoulder with male counterparts, and other professions too had starting inducting women. Yet, prejudice remained; and working women, considered an anomaly or a minority to be indulged and not celebrated, were relegated to the background. As a young teacher in 1980s in India I realized that classrooms are but microcosms of the social institutions that perpetuate gender hierarchies. I grew interested in how texts were written and selected. I made an effort to collect writings, articles, and books written by women or featuring women as positive role models. I also began consciously adopting gender-neutral terms and encouraged my students to do so. I encouraged girls to participate in listening and speaking and to collaborate with boys wherever possible. Over the years I began using language as a tool to reduce that gap that I witnessed and experienced in the classroom.

Following from these experiences, in this chapter I propose that positioning gender sensitization as a learning outcome of an English language class can empower learners to become critical users of language. In addition, it promotes social justice through a more nuanced understanding of how gender is constructed through language use.

Social Justice and ELT

Social justice, gender studies, and English language teaching (ELT) are three domains of knowledge that have been addressed extensively in their own right. A vast body of work addresses issues and challenges pertaining to each. Bringing these domains of knowledge together and addressing them in relation to one another is a crucial and relevant step towards ensuring holistic development and responsive education. The questions to deliberate upon, therefore, are: What is social justice? How is gender equity placed in the paradigm of social justice? How do teachers and materials developers integrate these aspects into ELT?

Irrespective of their origin, operational definitions of social justice assert that differences in caste, race, class, and gender should not curtail individuals from developing their potential to its fullest. In socioeconomic terms, empowering individuals to realize their skills optimally would entail ensuring that benefits of development, including mobility, are accorded to all individuals and communities equally. The United Nations Educational Scientific and Cultural Organization (UNESCO) regards education as means to achieving "economic and social progress for all people without discrimination." UNESCO defines social justice as based on equal rights for all peoples. It proposes that education aimed at sustainable development can promote social justice globally. Using this measure, educators too must (re)examine the goals and outcomes of learning a subject or language. When education is visualized as a means of awakening social justice, change can be affected in all its components: policy, curriculum, instruction, learning, and assessment. In his seminal text *Pedagogy of the Oppressed*, Paulo Freire (1970) encourages educators to use critical pedagogy as means to creating awareness about equity because "it is the means through which people discover each other" (p. 109).

Making students aware of and involved in the welfare of marginalized communities would entail adoption of constructivist methods wherein learners' participation and their views were given primacy. Specifically, in ELT this can be achieved by inculcating competencies such as critical thinking, creative problem solving, and collaborative decision in the teaching learning process. In fact, ELT relates easily and fruitfully to developing social justice because it has the scope to foster independence of thought, sensitivity to others' well-being and feelings, and creativity and flexibility in responding to new situations, besides ensuring language acquisition. Further, language in itself cuts across the curriculum and is a means for expression of self, maintaining culture, and providing context.

Gender and the World of Words

The intersection of various social factors can produce fairly complex gender outcomes. Cultures, lifestyles, values, and languages shape how gender relations and identities are created. Educators also need to be critically conscious of how gender-based inter-actions affect the experiences of students; they cannot afford to neglect or disregard these interactions. As Androulla Vassiliou (2010) notes, "despite the existence of comprehensive legislative frameworks, gender equality is yet to be achieved . . . With regard to education and training, gender differences persist in both attainment and choice of courses of study. . . . [These] . . . can also negatively affect economic growth and social inclusion" (p. 3).

The interrelation between gender and language or discourse is particularly relevant to ELT because English language has emerged as a lingua franca in many developing and underdeveloped countries. Here linguistic assertion and gender sensitive discourse can go a long way in addressing gender exclusion promoting social justice. Unfortunately, the "cult of the apron" dominates most instructional materials, and women are shown less often and in a fewer set of roles. The term was coined by A. P. Nilsen in her 1975 study *Women in Children's Literature,* which observed that majority illustrations in award-winning texts in the United States showed women wearing aprons. The women are usually passive and are depicted in domestic or conventional spaces. Language used in reading materials is highly leading as well and promotes gender stereotypes. The study "Gender Differences in Educational Outcomes" (2010), conducted by the Eurydice network for the Swedish Presidency of the Council of the European Union, contains several examples from review of research literature on gender and education that highlight gender differences. The study notes, for example, that the term *cameraman* is used uncritically instead of the gender-neutral *cameraperson,* and "boys are said to 'laugh' while girls 'giggle'" (p. 26). It is therefore incumbent upon ELT scholars and practitioners to adopt strategies that prevent isolation resulting through language. As the poet Rosenberg (2004) asks:

> why is it
> she, would hold both she and he
> but he, is only he?
> and why is it
> her, would claim both her and he
> yet him, is only him?

Feminist linguistic approaches to language and gender take into account socio-economic events and politicocultural processes, since they structure and affect the use and outcomes of language use. Mellor (2011), for example, discusses four models correlating gender and language: deficit model, dominance model, cultural difference model, and discursive model. The deficit model, based on the arguments contained in Otto Jesperson's book *Language: Its Nature, Development and Origin* (1922), identifies women as deficient communicators in comparison to men, especially at the workplace. This model is the result of socially imposed hierarchies and gendered bias towards competencies and roles that women can assume. Women are not encouraged to play with the normative standards of expression operational in a particular society and are therefore restricted cognitively and creatively. They are also socialized into using terms of reference that essentialise them as deferring and inexperienced. It is important to note that ELT classrooms are likely to be situated in societies and regions where all or at least one of the models may be applicable. Therefore, providing students opportunities to speak, listen, engage, express, and create can in themselves be the very learning outcomes that foster gender parity and equality.

The dominance model, as Mellor notes with reference to Robin Tolmach Lakoff's *Language and Woman's Place* (1975), moved away from characterizing female speakers to critically evaluate language used by male speakers. The model was used to identify and enlist strategies of domination adopted by men to circumvent, counter, and silence women speakers. These included overlapping, raising one's pitch, using language that objectifies and intimidates women, and dismissing women's arguments as ineffective or invaluable. ELT practitioners can use this model to undertake a discourse analysis of instructional design, classroom interactions, and curricular provisions, and identify areas for improvement in terms of gender neutrality and inclusiveness. The Eurydice study (2010) quoted above also notes that, ironically, language learning itself is considered a feminine pursuit. ELT professionals therefore need to argue for reexamination of such gendered attribution to disciplines.

The cultural difference model perceives differences in women's and men's communication patterns positively. The model, described in Deborah Tannen's *You Just Don't Understand: Women and Men in Conversation* (1990), proposes that in same-sex conversations, certain linguistic codes are used that are characteristic of women and men. This approach does not presuppose any hierarchies between women's and men's use of language but locates the differences as resulting from practiced culture. It also suggests that a bicultural tolerance can improve gender relations. The fact that expression, and therefore meaning-making, results from subcultures of gender can be used productively by English language teachers in identifying and responding to varied learning styles, forms of expression, and levels of participation.

The discursive model can be applied to all the poststructuralist works that examine the construction of gender, language, and social relations as a product of existing power structures. It is recognized that "sex as well as gender is socially constructed, but this is rarely discussed in public domains" (Coates, 1998, p. 502). Masculinity and femininity are therefore to be understood in relation to "the asymmetrical dominance and prestige which accrues to males" (Sattel, 1983, p. 119). Besides sociological origins of gender, the impact of economic conditions on gender roles and stereotypes can also be accessed under the rubric of this model, thereby providing teachers a theoretical paradigm to encourage exploration of existing cultural frameworks and construction of identities. This would make an ELT class an input-rich source for examination of self, society, and power.

Gender in Education

In India, concerns about adequate representation of gender in education acquired centre stage in the 1970s with the publication of the *Report of the Committee on the Status of Women in India.* The report, brought out by the Ministry of Education and Social Welfare in 1974, led to a reconceptualization of prevalent discourses on issues of gender and economic well-being, political participation, law, health and family welfare in India by highlighting gender disparity prevalent in social institutions in the country. The report underscored that welfare policies of the government in post-independence India did not help improve the overall status of women in Indian society. Consequent discussions and debates culminated in shifting the focus from viewing women as a passive welfare category to critical actors of development related to agriculture, industries, and myriad other service sectors. In academics, concern for reflecting women's contribution in all disciplines and making the curriculum gender-inclusive gained momentum in the late 1970s and has continued since then.

India's *National Curriculum Framework–2005* states that "we need to recognize that rights and choices in themselves cannot be *exercised until central human capabilities are fulfilled.* Thus, in order to make it possible for marginalized leaders, and especially girls, to claim their rights as well as play an active role in shaping collective life, education must empower them to overcome the disadvantages of unequal socialization *and enable them to develop their capabilities of becoming autonomous and equal citizens*" (NCERT, 2005, p. 6).

In this context, UNESCO organized in 1982 a meeting of experts on women's studies to gauge the degree of emphasis on women's perspectives being visible in different disciplines. The findings of the workshop highlighted that women's perspectives were "missing in the domain of Social Sciences particularly in subjects like Sociology, History, and Political Science. In subjects like Economics, Psychology, and Education, too, gender sensitive perspectives had yet to be integrated" (NCERT, 2014, p. 1).

Gender (in)equality in school education is further affected by issues such as difficult access to schooling for girls and cultural preference for a male child. Girls generally drop out of school earlier than boys because of social pressures as well as lack of basic infrastructure such as safe transportation or passage to schools, toilet complexes (especially after onset of menarche), and textbooks and learning materials. In this regard, ELT alone cannot bridge gaps and reforms at the systemic level. However, there is great demand for ELT, driven by a utopian desire for a shared language of communication across the globe. This is further accelerated by the fact of globalization. Digital technology and multinational companies have almost dissolved national boundaries, and the English language is regarded as a ticket to upward mobility across sections of society. Albeit limited by other factors, the ability to positively affect lives of many young persons and adults across the globe using ELT cannot be denied.

ELT for Change: Methods and Approaches

Introducing the idea of gender equality in an ELT classroom must not be seen as painting everyone with the same brush. A monocultural framework will be counter-intuitive to the idea of gender equality. Constructs of gender affect both boys and girls and are the result of various psychological, cultural, and social conditions. Consequently, parity in representation of gender can be achieved by ensuring multiplicity of genres, plurality of texts, and opportunities for discourse on perspectives. The *Position Paper of National Focus Group on Teaching of Indian Languages* (NCERT, 2006a) suggests, "it is extremely important that textbook writers and teachers begin to appreciate that the passive and deferential roles generally assigned to women are socio-culturally constructed and need to be destroyed as quickly as possible. The voices of women in all their glory need to find a prominent place in our textbooks and teaching strategies" (p. 3). In fact, regarding diversity as a resource in instructional design has the potential to help bridge differences stemming from other social hierarchies besides gender.

Cooperative work or collaborative activities such as group discussions, role plays that challenge traditional roles, team reports, peer-moderated rewriting of ends of stories, and quizzes can foster respect of different viewpoints as well as inculcate greater understanding of the need to share physical, psychological, and social space equally across gender. Studies have in fact shown that "peer relationships among learners are largely determinant of the outcomes of schools" (Boykin, Tyler, & Miller, 2005, p. 521). Also, "teachers' perceptions of male- and femaleness are crucial for their relations with pupils and can be an important factor in generating gender equity in schools" (Education, Audiovisual and Culture Executive Agency, 2010). "Sexual division of labour in the social process of schooling" (Humm, 1989, p. 95), such as classroom and playground dynamics, friendships, and teacher-student interactions, must be avoided at all costs. Using a metacognitive approach to gender inclusiveness can therefore enable teachers to facilitate reflection on causes and implications of differences of gender.

Ensuring discussions raises students' familiarity with alternative discourses of gender and sexuality and enhances their ability to reflect critically on both verbal and nonverbal behaviors. These discussions can also lead to a dismantling of power structures within the classroom, and this lends scope for critical pedagogy. In addition, well-planned units and lessons can help develop knowledge on a range of issues related to gender, such as legal rights, social systems, and positive role models. Collaboration and social interaction can provide authentic contexts for various components of ELT and facilitate situated learning. Materials developers should in fact seek to correlate inputs with students' cultures and provide knowledge about the widest possible range of groups and gender identities. Diversity in learning styles can also be addressed through the use of wide-ranging cues—visual, auditory, and tactile—which in turn will enhance and accelerate language learning as well, since they "reinforce memory" (ELT Well, 2014, p. 1). Other strategies would entail the use of gender-inclusive terms, alternative pronouns such as "he or she," and symmetrical phrases to include both females and males. Use of gender-neutral language, which recognizes that *man* is not an adequate representation and therefore employs alternatives such as *human beings, humans, humanity, person,* and *individual,* should also be encouraged. Teachers should follow and encourage adherence to a basic checklist that dismantles and discourages allocation of passive and deferential roles to women. This would entail avoiding language that has innuendo and is offensive, discriminatory, or derogatory.

The same consideration must be extended to the selection of materials, illustrations, and activities. For example, you can refer to images in the lesson "The Fun They Had" (NCERT, 2006b, p. 7) and the lesson "Quality," in *Honeycomb* (NCERT, 2007b, p. 81) that are gender neutral and depict a healthy interaction among both genders in a classroom setting via the website www.ncert.nic.in.

As you would have observed, the activity-prompts also encourage cooperative learning through pair/group work. Activities such as these give both girls and boys equal opportunity to share their ideas as well as to learn from each other. Activities may also be thematically structured around issues of gender equality. An appropriate example in this regard would be a short story, "Bholi," by noted Indian author K. A. Abbas. (*Bholi* in Hindi is a gendered reference to innocence. It means *innocent girl.* The masculine form of the term would be *bhola.*) A narrative about a neglected girl child, the story highlights a girl child's right to education. Not only is the selection of the text gender sensitive, post-reading activities have scope for discussion on socio-cultural barriers faced by girls in their pursuit of education. A sample activity from the short story "Bholi," in the NCERT textbook *Footprints Without Feet* which promotes gender sensitization among learners is given below.

> *Talk About It.* Bholi's teacher helped her overcome social barriers by encouraging and motivating her. How do you think you can contribute towards changing the social attitudes illustrated in this story? Also, should girls be aware of their rights, and assert them? Should girls and boys have the same rights, duties and privileges? What are some of the ways in which society treats them differently? When we speak of 'human rights', do we differentiate between girls' rights and boys' rights? (NCERT, 2007a, p. 62)

Critical literacy necessitates that learners be taught how to examine texts used in the classroom as well as those circulating in popular culture for gender representations and bias. Teachers must foster a classroom environment conducive to discursive interactions of students with each other. Peer-moderated discussions supervised by teachers may "encourage students to reflect on their own experiences, confront social inequities, and make changes in themselves and the world around them" (Beck, 2005, p. 395). These discussions may include analyzing gender relations and construction of privilege, contemplating various gender categories, as well as considering approaches of communities other than their own. In this regard, it is also imperative that teachers themselves contemplate their students' identities and if their voices and needs are being addressed. They must not lose sight of the fact that "language learners are themselves constantly engaged in constructing and reconstructing their identities in specific contexts and communities" (Schmenk, 2004, p. 515).

Emphasizing the Particular

Despite the glaring gaps in gender equality across cultures and learning contexts, we must acknowledge that research in creative and inclusive pedagogy has helped dissolve some boundaries. For example, writings by women are part of many main-stream texts without the sometimes alienating label: feminist writings. Yet, there are discussions and activities that detail the nuances and characteristics of writing specific to women, including neocriticism that details the circumstances of their creation. This enables students to imagine alternative ways of looking at the dynamics of gender besides the conventional one-versus-the-other approach.

In the Indian context, bringing multilingual perspectives into an ELT class can offer unparalleled opportunities for teachers to engage with cross-cultural differences and the social construction of gender and sexuality. Exposure to diversity in approach, address, and roles across communities and cultures can help learners develop insights into gender-specific practices and even gender-neutral and gender-sensitive language. Here, teachers' backgrounds and exposure to debates on gender also become part of the equation. They way they frame questions, define issues, and evaluate responses are inextricably linked to their own place in a culture with its particular and unique gender relations.

However, these deliberative practices can only be fruitful if there is institutional support and interest. Policy documents that guide school systems should reiterate the importance of gender sensitization, and school administrators must be open to the idea of a constructivist and postmodern approach to teaching and learning. Only political will combined with community support can enable the ELT classroom to become an effective space for learners to engage with the local community on issues of social justice such as gender inclusiveness and adopt measures for positive change.

Conclusion

In order to encourage appropriate policy measures and adoption, the UN General Assembly declared the years 2005–2014 as the decade for Education for Sustainable Development (ESD). The key aim of ESD is to produce informed and responsible citizens who are able to address local and global issues pertaining to social justice. Today, at the cusp of a new decade, we must pause and reflect on how social justice can be further achieved through curricular reform. Perhaps some of the answers lie in integrating the components of social justice at all stages of school education, including ELT.

"Our commission as teachers includes the goal of helping learners to become informed of the issues that intrinsically affect their lives" (Brown, 1994, p. 177). Teachers of ELT must aim to help their students achieve not only academic competence but also social consciousness. The use of pedagogy focused on social justice and multiculturalism can enable students develop a keener awareness of and sensitivity to the positives of sociocultural diversity, including gender. In addition, since language and literacy enhance self-esteem, ELT can help address existing gender based divisions. A language classroom is indeed a potent place to make a bid for more humane and inclusive world.

References

Beck, A. S. (2005). A place for critical literacy. *Journal of Adolescent and Adult Literacy, 48*(5), 392–400.

Boykin, A. W., Tyler, K. M., & Miller, O. (2005). In search of cultural themes and their expressions in the dynamics of classroom life. *Urban Education, 40*(5), 521–549.

Brown, H. D. (1994). Teaching global interdependence as a subversive activity. In J. E. Alatis (Ed.), *Educational linguistics, cross cultural communication, and global interdependence* (pp. 173–179). Washington, DC: Georgetown University Press.

Coates, J. (Ed.). (1998). *Language and gender: A reader.* Oxford, England: Blackwell.

Educational, Audiovisual and Culture Executive Agency. (2010). *Gender differences in educational outcomes: Study on the measures taken and the current situation in Europe.* Brussels, Belgium: Education, Audiovisual and Culture Executive Agency.

ELT Well. (2012). Cuisenaire questions. Retrieved August 2, 2014, from www.eltwell.co.uk.

Freire, P. (1970). *Pedagogy of the oppressed.* New York, NY: Herder & Herder.

Gorman, T., White, J., & Brooks, G. (1987). *Pupils' attitudes to writing.* London, England: NFER-Nelson.

Humm, M. (1989). *The dictionary of feminist theory.* Hemel Hemstead, England: Harvester Wheatsheaf.

Jesper, O. (1922). *Language: Its nature, development and origin.* London, England: Allen & Unwin.

Lakoff, R. (1975). *Language and woman's place.* New York, NY: Harper and Row.

Mellor, B. (2011). Deficit, dominance, difference and discursive: The changing approaches to language and gender. *Diffusion, 4*(2), para. 1.

National Council of Educational Research and Training (NCERT). (2005). *National Curriculum Framework–2005.* New Delhi, India: MHRD.

National Council of Educational Research and Training (NCERT). (2006a). *Position paper of national focus group on teaching of Indian languages.* New Delhi, India: Author.

National Council of Educational Research and Training (NCERT). (2006b). The fun they had. In *Beehive* [Class IX English textbook]. New Delhi, India: Author.

National Council of Educational Research and Training (NCERT). (2007a). Bholi. In *Footprints Without Feet* [Class X English textbook]. New Delhi, India: Author.

National Council of Educational Research and Training (NCERT). (2007b). Quality. In *Honeycomb* [Class VII English textbook]. New Delhi, India: Author.

National Council of Educational Research and Training (NCERT). (2014). *Gender analysis of NCERT primary textbooks of Classes I to V: Marigold.* New Delhi, India: Author.

Rosenberg, D. J. (2004). *Gender.* Retrieved August 2, 2014, from www.authorsden.com

Sattel, J. W. (1983). Men, inexpressiveness and power. In B. Thorne, C. Kramarae, & N. Henley (Eds.), *Language, gender and society* (pp. 119–124). London, England: Newbury.

Schmenk, B. (2004). Language learning: A feminine domain? The role of stereotyping in constructing gendered learner identities. *TESOL Quarterly, 38*(3), 514–524.

Tannen, D. (1990). *You just don't understand: Women and men in conversation.* New York, NY: Bantam.

Vassiliou, A. (2010). Preface. *Gender differences in educational outcomes.* Brussels, Belgium: Education, Audiovisual and Culture Executive Agency.

CHAPTER 15

Exploring Perceptions of Gender Roles in English Language Teaching

Mayra C. Daniel
Northern Illinois University

Melanie Koss
Northern Illinois University

Teachers of English have long understood that they do more in their work than share the syntax, grammar, and lexical components of a language. Osborn (2008) proposes that English language educators need to "reform and expand language curricula and instruction along the lines of a critical approach to language education, pedagogically oriented toward an examination of issues related to the role of language in discourses, in discrimination, and in ideology" (p. 18). Indeed, English language teaching (ELT) requires teachers give students access to the ways of being to those for whom English is a first language. Teachers need to carefully select curricula that will prepare learners to confidently and effectively interact in English-dominant environments.

Schools need to provide safe and productive third spaces for plurilingual learners (Bhabba, 1994). Thus, in the English classroom teachers will want to focus on developing high levels of intercultural competence in students (Sercu, 2011). Effective instructional models acknowledge the personal nature of language use and how this is affected by attitudes and cultural norms. ELT focused on social justice issues helps learners gain a grasp of the implicit cultural messages that are necessary to interact positively in English-dominant societies.

Some topics addressed in ELT require educators to strike a balance between introducing students to ideas that may shock them because they conflict with their cultural norms, and sharing the ways social justice differs across environments. The topic of gender requires walking a fine line because English learners often experience cultural mismatches as they struggle to understand what is appropriate and not offensive in different English-dominant nations. Therefore, the ELT classroom needs to offer

an approach to language and education that strives to (a) understand the relationship between power and knowledge; (b) theorize the role of language in production and reproduction of power, difference, and symbolic domination (in particular in educational context); and (c) deconstruct master narratives that oppress certain groups—be they immigrants, women, or minority members . . . and devalue their linguistic practices. (Norton & Pavlenko, 2004, p. 2)

Definitions and understandings of gender roles vary significantly across cultures and countries even when speakers share the same language. In the English language classroom, gender-identified behaviors that differ across cultures may obscure the meaning of speech interactions for learners. Students' religious beliefs, socioeconomic status, prior education, their nation's history, and their country's degree of tolerance and acceptance of difference are important factors that contribute to the learning environment (Nieto, 1996; Norton & Pavlenko, 2004). To understand the impact of curricular choices on perceptions of gender roles in ELT, it seems necessary to examine the cultural influences and perceptions that English learners might bring to the classroom. In addition, it is also important to consider how classroom tasks influence English learners' language use and contribute to their views of gender in English-dominant cultures (Cameron, 1996).

In this chapter, the authors explore how English learners' understandings of gender roles in English-dominant societies develop as they study English. They address the ways curriculum contributes to the development of new forms of interpersonal knowledge, and consider the use of authentic children's and young adult literature as an effective medium for instruction.

Social Justice in ELT: Gender Awareness

Gender socialization begins the moment a human being takes his/her first breath, and continues to be shaped within the home, the neighborhoods, and the countries of residence of the person throughout his/her life span. In the English classroom, it is important that English learners have opportunities to explore gender roles across cultures through authentic literature. This cannot be accomplished from a Eurocentric perspective. Fang, Fu, and Lamme (2003) explain what can go wrong when instruction reflects a colonial discourse. They tell us that when "sharing literature for personal interpretation and reflection is not incorporated, and there is no discussion of the artistry of writing or illustration, the author's role in constructing the text, or cultural authenticity" (p. 290), will be missing and instruction will likely overlook the cultural nuances, truths, and/or inaccuracies present or absent in text. Authentic literature leads English learners to make unexpected discoveries that highlight power relations in ELT and helps them understand the intersections of language, culture, class, race, and gender (Maher & Ward, 2002). Classroom communities that empower English learners do so because they support their unique backgrounds by fostering an awareness of social justice issues (Nieto, 1996) such as gender discrimination and how it is perpetuated in different racial, cultural, and sociocultural contexts (Nieto & Bode, 2007). Classroom conversations that lead English learners to identify stereotypical assumptions of gender roles and representations promote social justice in ELT by ensuring students' voices are heard (Chapman, Hobbel, & Alvarado, 2011).

Attitudes Toward Gender Roles Internationally

Attitudes and beliefs around gender roles, defined as "beliefs regarding the appropriate roles for men and women" (Schutz, Tufis, & Alwin, 2010, p. 184), are complex and differ across countries and cultures (McInnes, 1998; Zvonkovic, Greaves, Schmiege, & Hall, 1996). They are multidimensional and address issues such as power (e.g., Larsen & Long, 1988), manifestation (e.g., Larsen & Long, 1988), and area of conceptual development and socialization (e.g., Kortenhaus & Demarest, 1993). Numerous studies have sought to measure gender role attitudes (Braun, 2008; Constantin & Voicu, 2014; Halman, Sieben, & van Zundert, 2011; Inglehart & Norris, 2003), and the results vary from country to country. What are consistent are the areas of study that include identifying the traditional family model (e.g., Cunningham, Beutel, Barber, & Thornton, 2005; Kroska & Elman, 2009), divisions of labor within a family (e.g., Alwin, 2005), and gender depictions apparent in general society (e.g., Bergh, 2006; Pfau-Effinger, 1993). Since conceptions of gender vary across cultural lines, English learners might note cultural mismatches when studying literature from countries where English is the dominant language, and must challenge their own thinking as they learn not only language but also cultural information. Enhanced understanding of such cultural differences will assist in English language development.

Praxis: Eliminating Gender Bias

Chapman, Hobbel, and Alvarado's (2011) research offers implications for social justice in ELT and suggests ways to eliminate gender bias from the curriculum and challenge it in society. They propose that gender differences need to be celebrated and their existence and power noted beyond the school setting. A contextually situated curriculum provides the medium that helps English learners understand gender role differences and identify ways to enhance intercultural competence in ways that affect language learning. It contributes to classrooms where students can safely address their worries as they look for similarities and differences that do not place individuals in the category of *the other* (Bhabba, 1994). A social justice instructional approach teaches English learners through different genres of children's and young adult literature.

Why Children's and Young Adult Literature?

The educational value of using literature for language learning has long been an accepted practice worldwide. "There has been an increasing awareness of the significance of integrating literature in EFL/ESL curriculum" (Amer, 2003, p. 63). Quality literature is authentic; it encourages examination, discussion, and interaction; and it can present multiple layers of meaning. Additionally, children's and young adult literature "provides a wonderful opportunity for children to see language in action" (Winch, Johnston, March, Ljungdahl, & Holliday, 2004, p. 402). Carter and Long (1991) and Lazar (1993) discuss multiple models of teaching literature to English learners, one of which is the cultural model. The cultural model views text as a cultural product, specifically, a product that provides insight into the culture in which it was created. This model encourages the study of a text by looking at how the culture is presented in terms of social, political, and historical viewpoints. A rich exposure to and examination of quality literature offers both teachers and students opportunities to broaden their understandings both of the world and, specific to this chapter, of gender roles.

In many cultures, stories, both print and oral, are an important and effective means of sharing cultural values and expectations. Children's and young adult literature specifically "present a microcosm of ideologies, values, and beliefs from the dominant culture, including gender ideologies and scripts" (Taylor, 2003, p. 301). As children's books model and teach cultural values and attitudes (Crisp & Hiller, 2011; Taylor, 2003), looking at how males and females are depicted will provide insight into the culture in which they are written. As described by Kortenhaus and Demarest (1993), "the characters portrayed in children's literature mold a child's concept of socially accepted roles and values, and indicate how males and females are supposed to act" (p. 221). Therefore, using children's literature from a particular English-dominant country/culture in ELT classrooms depicts instances of gender roles of that country/culture, allowing students to identify and challenge their own ideas of gender and compare and contrast such ideologies across cultural lines. Mitchell (1996) believes that students who never examine and challenge gender roles they see may assume traditional gender roles are consistent across cultures. This belief system may impede students' learning of the English language, as content within the books of study may not match students' current conceptual understandings.

Selecting Literature for Use in the English Classroom

When beginning to consider using children's and young adult literature in ELT, teachers must first identify their own cultural conceptions of gender, their knowledge of the gender roles inherent to the English language country of origin of the books they're considering using as curricular materials, and their own comfort level in using literature that portrays gender roles potentially at odds with their personal views. Some questions teachers might want to ask themselves include: What do I already know about the gender roles common in the country from which the literature was published? What are my biases toward these gender roles? How do they conflict with the gender roles in my culture that I am accustomed to? How comfortable am I in discussing these gender roles in a room full of students? Can I put aside my own biases and teach gender roles of other countries objectively? How much cultural background will my students need to comprehend the text enough so their personal knowledge does not stand in the way of learning English?

Once teachers are comfortable with their own knowledge and biases, the next step is to select literature to use. Remember that English learners are students engaged in ongoing processes of constructing and reconstructing their identities for English-dominant worlds (Schmenk, 2004). The challenge is finding literature that is accessible and engaging, and with appropriate content and language. Picture books are great place to start, as they allow readers to be scaffolded by "reading the pictures" (Vardell, Hadaway, & Young, 2006). Using picture books will allow English learners to connect words and vocabulary to the pictures, which in a book with strong gender role depictions assists in cultural understandings. When seeking picture books to use, look for titles with varied artistic styles and illustrations that work together with the text to support students' understanding and to aid them in developing visual literacy. When looking for chapter books, select titles that have high-interest topics with an accessible reading and vocabulary level.

A number of resources are available to help you find quality children's and young adult literature. Look for literature that has won awards or that is included on lists from professional organizations, such as the American Library Association (www .ala.org). Some particularly relevant awards that identify high-quality books from a given year are the Caldecott Medal (picture books), the Newbery Medal (children's chapter books), the Printz Award (young adult books), and the Sibert Medal (nonfiction). Other lists available on this site include Notable Books for Children, Popular Paperbacks for Young Adults, and Quick Picks. Additionally, numerous professional journals have websites that provide articles and book recommendations, including *Booklist, BookLinks, Horn Book Magazine*, and *School Library Journal*.

In addition to print texts, online resources provide full-text digitized versions of children's and young adult literature for use in classroom and library settings. One such online site is the subscription service Tumblebooks (http://www.tumblebooks .com). The service provides access to hundreds of well-known and quality picture books, chapter books, and nonfiction books and includes a language-learning component. Each title includes the reading level of the title and provides a narrated animated version of the book. The book's illustrations are used, and the words are highlighted as the text is read aloud. This oral aspect allows students to hear the rhythm of the English language as well as the word pronunciations. There is also a feature called "word help" that allows the viewer to click on a word and have it repeated and broken down into syllables for added pronunciation assistance.

Classroom Applications

When Shor wrote *Education is Politics: Paulo Freire's Critical Pedagogy* (1993), he methodically led the reader to examine a pedagogy centered on the goal of critical consciousness. Using authentic literature in ELT places teachers on a path that "problematizes generative themes" from English learners' lives and, because of its participatory nature, is "situated in student thought and language" and thus leads them to decode "thematic problems" in their world. It is critical and democratic because classroom conversations lead students to explore what they know and what they need to know through dialogue that "is constructed mutually" (p. 33).

In your work, once you select appealing titles and prior to bringing the literature into the classroom, plan how you will work with students to analyze books for the gender role depictions they contain. When bringing children's and young adult literature published in English-dominant countries into the classroom, begin by discussing gender roles in general with your students. The teacher might begin a lesson through critical questioning that leads the English learners to brainstorm issues related to gender bias. Chapman et al. (2011) encourage questions such as "What concerns you? Which of these issues concerns your family and your community? Do these same issues distress the world on a global level?" (p. 540). To follow up on this train of thought, a teacher might ask students to develop definitions for terms such as *intercultural competence, bias, diversity, affirmation, critique,* and/or *solidarity.*

Next, discuss how different cultures accept different gender roles in society, and discuss how those gender roles can affect the meaning of a text. Share books that have strong nontraditional gender roles present, and then ask students to identify the gender roles they noticed within the book. Sunderland, Cowley, Rahim, Leontzakou, and Shattuck (2002) call this action identifying the "gender critical point," or the specific section of a text in which gender roles are apparent and accessible to students for unpacking and analyzing. Ask students if the behavior of the characters in books is the same as or different from the gender roles they are familiar with in their culture. If the behaviors are different, ask the learners how knowing the different gender roles of the culture group might affect their English language learning.

LESSON EXAMPLE: *THE PAPER BAG PRINCESS*

One example of a children's book with strong gender roles perfect for use in the English language learning classroom is Munsch's *The Paper Bag Princess* (1992). At first glance this picture book appears to be written for young learners. However, it is a story that will serve as a lovely and amusing backdrop appropriate for engaging adolescents and adults in examining gender stereotypes. The narrative surprises, pleases the reader, and challenges normative assumptions of gender characteristics and power. Munsch entices the reader's exploration of the fallacies of generalized assumptions about being strong and weak. The reader meets a valiant, cunning, and brave princess who is very different from the prince who fears his shadow.

A teacher would begin the lesson asking the students to compare and contrast the qualities of princes and princesses by using a Venn diagram. This task is an opportunity for the teacher to introduce new vocabulary, and for students to share the language they know and identify cognates, examine ideologies transmitted through language, and explore their own and their culture's biases (Ogle & Correa-Kovtun, 2010). This initial exploration will reveal assumptions about gender roles that automatically place the male in the role of the leader and savior. It is important for English learners to realize that even books that depict females as spunky and intelligent often couch sexist notions of behavior that perpetuate gender inequalities. A possible second step in the lesson is a reader's theatre application that involves student volunteers acting out the roles of the main characters in the book while the teacher reads aloud the narrative. After this, a whole-group in-depth exploration of the attributes initially assigned to the prince and princess allows students to discuss the societal norms that led to their initial assumptions. Last, the students examine how the descriptors they first assigned to the prince and princess may have privileged one gender over the other in their culture and in English-dominant societies.

LESSON IDEA: *THE HUNGER GAMES*

The Hunger Games (Collins, 2010), a best-selling young adult novel from the United States, challenges gender norms and will challenge English learners to think about gender roles in a dystopian society. Although not set in the real contemporary world, this novel, having been written by an American as a commentary on the world today, depicts a strong woman capable of taking care of not only herself, but also her male companion. It is a fast-paced novel with short, readable chapters that capture readers' attention and leads them to root for the strong heroine. The book is set in a future society ravaged by war, and Katniss, the female protagonist, must support her family by hunting for food and maintaining the household. Her country holds an annual Hunger Games, a televised "reality show" that pits contestants against each other to the death until one person remains. That remaining person achieves glory and money for his/her district. Katniss is one of her district's two delegates, and she bands together with Peeta, her fellow delegate, to challenge the premise of the game. Her traditionally masculine skills of hunting, resourcefulness, strength, perseverance, and athletic ability, among other things, contrast with Peeta's gentler manner to challenge traditional gender roles.

To begin a lesson, the teacher would ask students to make a list of traditional gender roles for females and males using a T-chart or other graphic organizer. Then, after reading *The Hunger Games*, students will identify the gender role characteristics of Katniss and Peeta. Next, the teacher asks students to differentiate between stereotypical characteristics and characteristics that do not conform to traditional gender stereotypes (i.e., Katniss "acting" to show the audience that she is in love with Peeta [stereotypical] versus Katniss's prowess as a hunter [nonstereotypical]). English learners may read this book and immediately return to moments in time when their sisters, mothers, or grandmothers energized them because they demonstrated a strength they never would have thought possible within their circumstances. Other English learners might explore this book and note the support that Katniss gives Peeta and how their collaboration provides them the strength to overcome their society's assumptions of what makes a winner.

Curricular Suggestions for Teachers

The following books are a few additional examples of titles that are both appropriate for young and adolescent English language learners and have significant gender role content reflecting aspects of English-dominant countries' cultures. Using these or similar books, teachers can plan instruction to help learners discover, examine, and challenge gender role stereotypes across their worlds. When planning lessons, ask yourself these questions:

1. Do the characters in this book represent masculinity or femininity in ways that may surprise my students?

2. What will I need to do to bridge gaps in knowledge for my students before, during, and after they read this book?

3. How will the characters in this book help the students go beyond arbitrarily defined binary constructions of gender?

4. Will this book provide students a bridge to greater intercultural understandings of gender that cross from their world to those of English-dominant societies?

5. What community-based activities might be appropriate extension activities to support this narrative and add concreteness to the learning?

6. What other books might I include in a unit of study focused on gender equity?

7. How will I take my students from intellectual engagement to critical consciousness that results in active advocacy?

PICTURE BOOKS

- Bradley, K. B. (2006). *Ballerino Nate*. New York, NY: Dial.
- Codell, E. R. (2011). *The Basket Ball*. New York, NY: Abrams.
- Hoffman, M. (1991). *Amazing Grace*. New York, NY: Dial.
- Richardson, J., & Parnell, P. (2005). *And Tango Makes Three*. New York, NY: Simon & Schuster.
- Zolotow, C. (1985). *William's Doll*. New York, NY: Harper & Row.

SHORT CHAPTER BOOKS

- Barrows, A. (2007). *Ivy and Bean*. San Francisco, CA: Chronicle.
- de Paola, T. (1979). *Oliver Button is a Sissy*. New York, NY: Houghton Mifflin Harcourt.
- Howe, J. (1996). *Pinky and Rex and the Bully*. New York, NY: Atheneum.
- Messner, K. (2011). *Marty McGuire*. New York, NY: Scholastic.
- Wyeth, S. D. (1998). *Tomboy Trouble*. New York, NY: Random House.

CHAPTER BOOKS

- Atkinson, E. (2013). *From Alice to Zen and Everyone in Between.* New York, NY: Carolrhoda.

- Federle, T. (2014). *Better Nate Than Ever.* New York, NY: Scholastic.

- Levine, G. C. (1997). *Ella Enchanted.* New York, NY: HarperCollins.

- Levy, D. A. (2014). *The Misadventures of the Family Fletcher.* New York, NY: Delacorte.

- Turnage, S. (2013). *Three Times Lucky.* New York, NY: Penguin.

YOUNG ADULT NOVELS

- Blackman, M. (2011). *Boys Don't Cry.* London, England: Corgi/Random House.

- Kemp, G. (2006). *The Turbulent Term of Tyke Tiler.* London, England: Faber.

- Lockhart, E. (2007). *Fly on the Wall: How One Girl Saw Everything.* New York, NY: Delacorte.

- Lockhart, E. (2008). *The Disreputable History of Frankie Landau-Banks.* New York, NY: Hyperion.

- Roth, V. (2014). *Divergent.* New York, NY: HarperCollins.

Conclusion

Without question, TESOL educators in this millennium have an increased level of awareness of the impact of cultural norms in ELT and of the links between gender, social identity, and English language acquisition. We recognize that teacher advocates who create safe spaces and foster questioning build classroom communities that empower learners. Tasks such as collaborative exploration involving teachers and students focused on the implicit messages in books as those described in this chapter give voice to English learners (Norton & Pavlenko, 2004) as they acquire cultural and linguistic knowledge (Shor, 1993). Thus, as we look to the future we cannot but consider the need to give learners ownership of their literacy development. Indeed, to create equitable ELT classrooms, "teachers, researchers, and teacher educators need to take into account individual learners and their respective positioning in particular social and cultural contexts" (Schmenk, 2004, p. 514).

References

Alwin, D. (2005). Attitudes, beliefs, and childbearing. In A. Booth & A. C. Crouter (Eds.), *The new population problem: Why families in developed countries are shrinking and what it means* (pp. 115–126). Mahwah, NJ: Erlbaum.

Amer, A. N. (2003). Teaching EFL/ESL literature. *Reading Matrix, 3*(2), 63–73.

Bergh, J. (2006). Gender attitudes and modernization processes. *International Journal of Public Opinion Research, 19*(1), 5–23.

Bhabba, H. K. (1994). *The location of culture.* New York, NY: Routledge.

Braun, M. (2008). Using egalitarian items to measure men's and women's family roles. *Sex Roles, 59*(9/10), 644–656.

Cameron, D. (1996). The language-gender interface: Challenging co-optation. In V. L. Bergvall, J. M. Bing, & A. Freed (Eds.), *Rethinking language and gender research: Theory and practice* (pp. 31–53). New York, NY: Longman.

Carter, R., & Long, M. (1991). *Teaching literature.* London, England: Longman Group.

Chapman, T. K., Hobbel, N., & Alvarado, N. V. (2011). A social justice approach as a base for teaching writing. *Journal of Adolescent & Adult Literacy, 54*(7), 539–541.

Collins, S. (2010). *The hunger games.* New York, NY: Scholastic.

Constantin, A., & Voicu, M. (2014). Attitudes towards gender roles in cross-cultural surveys: Content validity and cross-cultural measurement invariance. *Social Indicators Research.* Retrieved from http://www.ulib.niu.edu:2359/article/10.1007/s11205-014-0758-8/fulltext.html

Crisp, T., & Hiller, B. (2011). Telling tales about gender: A critical analysis of Caldecott medal-winning picture books, 1938–2011. *Journal of Children's Literature, 37*(2), 18–29.

Cunningham, M., Beutel, A. M., Barber, J. S., & Thornton, A. (2005). Reciprocal relationship between attitudes about gender and social context during young adulthood. *Social Science Research, 34*(4), 862–892.

Fang, Z., Fu, D., & Lamme, L. L. (2003). The trivialization and misuse of multicultural children's literature: Issues of representation and identification. In D. L. Fox & K. G. Short (Eds.), *Stories matter: The complexity of cultural authenticity in children's literature* (pp. 284–301). Urbana, IL: National Council of Teachers of English.

Goshen, I. (1997). ESL with children's literature. *English Teaching Forum Online, 35*(3). Retrieved from http://exchanges.state.gov/forum/vols/vol35/no3/p14.htm

Halman, L., Sieben, I., & van Zundert, M. (2011). *Atlas of European values: Trends and traditions at the turn of the century.* Leiden, The Netherlands: Brill.

Inglehart, R., & Norris, P. (2003). *Rising tide: Gender equality and cultural change around the world.* New York, NY: Cambridge University Press.

Kortenhaus, C. M., & Demarest, J. (1993). Gender role stereotyping in children's literature: An update. *Sex Roles, 28*(3/4), 219–232.

Kroska, A., & Elman, C. (2009). Change in attitudes about employed mothers: Exposure, interests, and gender ideology discrepancies. *Social Science Research, 38*(2), 366–382.

Larsen, K. S., & Long, E. (1988). Attitudes toward sex-roles: Traditional or egalitarian? *Sex Roles, 19,* 1–12.

Lazar, G. (1993). *Literature and language teaching.* New York, NY: Cambridge University Press.

Maher, F. A., & Ward, J. V. (2002). *Gender and teaching.* Mahwah, NJ: Erlbaum.

McInnes, J. (1998). Analyzing patriarchy capitalism and women's employment in Europe. *European Journal of Social Science Research, 11*(2), 227–248.

Mitchell, D. (1996). Approaching race and gender issues in the context of the language arts classroom. *English Journal, 85*(8), 77–81.

Munsch, R. (1992). *The paper bag princess.* Toronto, Canada: Annick Press.

Nieto, S. (1996). *Affirming diversity: The sociopolitical context of multicultural education.* (2nd ed.). White Plains, NY. Longman.

Nieto, S., & Bode, P. (2007). *Affirming diversity: The sociopolitical context of multicultural education* (5th ed.). Boston, MA: Allyn & Bacon.

Norton, B., & Pavlenko, A. (2004). Gender and English language learners. Alexandria, VA: TESOL.

Ogle, D., & Correa-Kovtun, A. (2010). Supporting English-language learners and struggling readers in content literacy with the "Partner Reading and Content, Too" routine. *Reading Teacher, 63*(7), 532–542.

Osborn, T. A. (2008). Teaching world languages for social justice. *Journal of Christianity and Foreign Languages, 8,* 11–23.

Pfau-Effinger, B. (1993). Modernization, culture part-time employment: The example of Finland and West Germany. *Work, Employment & Society, 7*(3), 383–410.

Schmenk, B. (2004). Language learning: A feminine domain? The role of stereotyping in constructing gendered learner identities. *TESOL Quarterly, 38*(3), 514–523.

Schutz Lee, K., Tufis, P., & Alwin, D. (2010). Separate sphere or increasing equality? Changing gender beliefs in postwar Japan. *Journal of Marriage and Family, 72*(1), 184–201.

Sercu, L. (2011). The acquisition of intercultural competence: Does language education help or hinder? In G. Zarate, D. Levy, & C. Kramsch (Eds.), *Handbook of multilingualism and multiculturalism* (pp. 45–50). Paris, France: Editions des Archives Contemporaines.

Shor, I. (1993). Education is politics. In P. McLaren & P. Leonard (Eds.), *Paulo Freire: A critical encounter* (pp. 25–35). New York, NY: Routledge.

Sunderland, J., Cowley, M., Rahim, F., Leontzakou, A. C., & Shattuck, J. (2002). From representation towards discursive practices: Gender in the foreign language textbook revisited. In L. Litosseliti & J. Sunderland (Eds.), *Gender identity and discourse analysis* (pp. 223–255). Amsterdam, The Netherlands: Benjamins.

Taylor, F. (2003). Content analysis and gender stereotypes in children's books. *Teaching Sociology, 31*(3), 300–311.

Vardell, S. M., Hadaway, N. L., & Young, T. A. (2006). Matching books and readers: Selecting literature for English learners. *Reading Teacher, 59*(8), 734–741.

Winch, G., Johnston, R. R., March, P., Ljungdahl, L., & Holliday, M. (2004). *Literacy reading, writing, and children's literature.* Melbourne, Australia: Oxford University Press.

Zvonkovic, A. M., Greaves, K. M., Schmiege, C. J., & Hall, L. D. (1996). The marital construction of gender through work and family decisions: A qualitative analysis. *Journal of Marriage and Family, 58*(1), 91–100.

CHAPTER 16

Walking in the Words of "the Other" Through Ethnodramatic Readers Theatre

Carter A. Winkle

Barry University

For lesbian, gay, bisexual, transgender, or queer (LGBTQ) English language teachers and academics (TESOL professionals), the intersections of their multidimensional and socially constructed identities affect how they perform—literally and figuratively—in classrooms, academic conferences, and in the world. And in these performances, LGBTQ TESOL professionals are often making moment-by-moment decisions about the degree to which they are "out," self-disclose as other-than-heterosexual (Clark Cummings, 2009; Ellwood, 2006; Nelson, 2004, 2009), or—as I prefer to think of it—living openly as their authentic selves. This was perhaps never truer for me, personally, than when I experienced *The Bite of the Teacher's Pet* (Winkle, 2010) while facilitating an intermediate writing course for adult second-language learners who were engaged in composition topics—which escalated into full-class discussion topics—related to my own marginalized identity as a gay man. The results were unintended and painful encounters within and around the *discursive faultlines* (Menard-Warwick, 2009) of sexual orientation.

Julia Menard-Warwick (2009) describes discursive faultlines as contentious discourses that are triggered when interlocutors, often from different social positions, contest each other's cultural representations—and as a result draw on their personal discourse systems to represent the issue from their own perspectives. She asserts, however, that "these tensions are pedagogically valuable because they index the cultural areas that need to be explored in order to work toward interculturality" (p. 30). While a few of my students expressed support for people with marginalized sexual identities during our class discussions vis-à-vis marriage equality and adoption by same-sex couples, the vast majority remained in strong opposition. As had been my fear, some of my most favored students—the "teacher's pets"—were among the vocal opposition.

Nearly jumping out of her seat was Trudy, shouting, "Never! Never, never, never! Same sex must not raising children. Parents—or adopted parents—should be model. Same sex don't have decent behavior or morality. Will lead children to abomination and malediction!" A woman of 30 from Haiti, Trudy was someone I considered to be the perfect student. She was a hard worker. She arrived on time with homework completed and contributed actively to class discussions. I liked Trudy. I knew Trudy liked and respected me. The sting, however, of hearing these words from a student with whom I'd felt such an affinity was extremely painful.

Throughout my ESL teacher-preparation program—a master's degree in applied linguistics—I was generally unprepared to encounter and navigate classroom discourses around issues of gender and sexual identity such as the one I had with Trudy. Indeed, the program's requisite "Cross-Cultural Issues in TESOL" course focused primarily on our understandings of constructs such as race, ethnicity, enculturation, and ethnocentrism. And while these are all worthy and important topics, those related to marginalized identities—those that are manifest on both the teacher and the student sides of the lectern—were absent.

The predominance of this chapter consists of an *ethnodrama* (Saldaña, 2011), or playscript (re)constructed from research field-text which I believe provides opportunity for preservice and in-service TESOL professionals to engage in critical dialogue around issues of gender and sexual identity in TESOL. The purpose of this *arts-based research* (Leavy, 2009) project has been to empirically collect, co-construct, analyze, and ethno-theatrically (Saldaña, 2011) (re)present the lived experiences of six TESOL educators from routinely marginalized professional (Jenks & Kennell, 2011) and social (Nelson, 2009) groups as they navigate relationships with peers, administrators, and students. Data for this inquiry were autoethnographic first-person narratives written by research participants responding to prompts that had them consider critical incidents related to their lives as TESOL professionals and their identit(ies) as sexual/gender minorities. I then analyzed these first-person narratives—as participant-composed field texts (Clandinin & Connelly, 2000)—for the purpose of identifying shared or contradictive ideas, perspectives, or experiences. To facilitate the illumination of intersections and divergences of experience, I transformed the participant-composed narratives through both individual (monologue) and collective (dialogue) *restorying* (Ollerenshaw & Creswell, 2002) and the purposeful construction and interweaving of *cross-cutting, bantering,* and *choral exchange* dialogue (Saldaña, 2011, pp. 105–111) through the narrative genre of ethnotheatric performative texts. As a means to attending to *transactional validity* (Cho & Trent, 2006), participants were provided with member-checking opportunity to review and give clarifying feedback to the reconstructed texts via e-mail and, additionally, during rehearsals and following a live readers theatre presentation of the ethnodrama at the *TESOL 2014 International Convention and English Language Expo* in which the participants themselves performed their stories (Winkle et al., 2014).

The ethnodrama may be "performed" as a readers theatre with players standing at music stands, as indicated in the script. It may also be read aloud by nonperformers (e.g., in-service or preservice TESOL educators, students of research methods, academic conference attendees, etc.) as a means of enacting or embodying the lives of the research participants—walking in the words (Smith, 2005) of the other—and, thus, using the shared experience of readers theatre as a mediating artifact (Vygotsky, 1978) or heuristic for exploring social phenomena (Chambers & Davis, 2012; Donmoyer & Yennie-Donmoyer, 2008). The aim of this arts-based research project has been to "raise significant questions and engender conversations rather than to proffer final meaning" (Barone & Eisner, 2012, p. 166) while fostering a stance of respect, empathy, and relativity concerning differences in sexuality, culture, and gender. It provides no answers, raises many questions, and provokes dialogue. While there has been research in the area of LGBTQ students in second-language learning contexts (Kappra & Vandrick, 2006; Nelson, 1999, 2002, 2009; and others), this work contributes to scholarship exploring the lived experiences of TESOL professionals (Clark Cummings, 2009; Nelson, 2004; Vandrick, 2009; Winkle, 2010; and others) within marginalized sexual-minority and gender-minority social groups working within a professional academic field which is, itself, at the margins of the academy (Jenks & Kennell, 2011). Beyond its scholarly significance in illuminating the experiences of the research participants, the ethnodrama itself—as artifact—contributes pedagogically as praxis: a research-based tool for use in teacher preparation, human resources development, and research methods teaching in graduate educational settings.

In the pages that follow, the ethnodrama, *Walking in the Words of LGBTQ English Language Teaching Professionals through Ethnodramatic Readers Theatre* (Winkle, 2014), is presented in its entirety. A brief inventory of discussion prompts for use in teacher-preparation and professional development activity concludes the chapter, and I invite readers to imagine for themselves other pedagogical uses for the ethnodrama in their own teaching contexts.

Walking in the Words of LGBTQ English Language Teaching Professionals Through Ethnodramatic Readers Theatre

NOTES FOR THE PLAYERS

1. Occasionally an individual player's speaking is "joined" by one or more of the other players when such utterances represent shared experiences. A small hand symbol (✋) appears to alert the readers in advance: a reminder to prepare for the unison speaking (which is gray-shaded). In the example below, VALENTINA is joined by RUTH and LINDA for the shaded portion of her dialogue:

   VALENTINA: Many of my adult ESL students say they have come to the United States for "Freedom." Do they really feel free here? ✋

   VALENTINA (+ *RUTH and LINDA*): Teachers of English to those entering U.S. society teach our students much more than English.

   VALENTINA (*continued*): We are role models; we bring our own experiences, cultures . . .

2. The final word, clause, or sentence of some passages is intended to be spoken in unison with the speaker who follows. In the example below, the <u>underlined</u>

portion of the first speaker is also gray-shaded for the second speaker: Below, CALVIN should say the words "a teacher" at the same time that VALENTINA speaks them:

> **VALENTINA:** . . . an activist, an immigrant's daughter, a second-language learner, a teacher-

> **CALVIN:** -a teacher, genderqueer, African American, androgynous, pansexual, seeming to be a somewhat feminine man—

THE PLAYERS

CALVIN—Human, a TESOL professional
JAVIER—Human, a TESOL professional
LINDA—Human, a TESOL professional
MANUEL—Human, a TESOL professional
RUTH—Human, a TESOL professional
VALENTINA—Human, a TESOL professional
and PETER—an audience member who speaks one line from his seat

TIME

It is the present.

PLACE

Here. There are seven music stands arranged in a slight semicircle in the performance space.

Walking in the Words of LGBTQ English Language Teaching Professionals through Ethnodramatic Readers Theatre

(As the lights rise, the players—VALENTINA, MANUEL, LINDA, CALVIN, RUTH, and JAVIER—who have been sitting in various locations among the audience members, rise and approach the performance space/stage. While moving into place, Javier nervously queries Ruth.)

JAVIER *(to Ruth in a stage whisper)*: Does my hair look all right?

> *(RUTH silently reassures JAVIER.)*

JAVIER *(continues, to Ruth)*: Aye, Ruth, you never know who's out there. Maybe I'm gonna meet my Prince Charming this year.

> *(There is silence as the players each position themselves behind one of the seven music stands arranged in a semicircle in the performance space. The center music stand is left unoccupied. They open their scripts.)*

MANUEL (*after a brief pause*): "Are you married, Mr. Suarez? Do you have a girl-friend? What did you do last weekend?" In a language classroom, we are constantly asking our students to use their personal experiences—their own lives to explore vocabulary and syntax as they construct sentences, paragraphs, and persuasive essays, as well as their developing second-language identities. But I have always been very careful about how I talked about my own identity—my own personal life in the classroom.

RUTH: "Mr. Suarez, do you have any children?"

CALVIN: "Are you a man or a woman?"

JAVIER: "You keep talking about 'your friend,' Mr. Suarez, but is that your girlfriend, or what?"

LINDA: "Wasn't that you I saw at the gay bar downtown?"

VALENTINA: "What does your wife do for a living?"

MANUEL: "Why do you wear a ring if you aren't married?"

ALL (*except Manuel*): "Soltero y maduro, maricón seguro!"

MANUEL (*simply*): If you are older and still a single man, you have to be gay. (*Brief pause.*) Coming from a Latin American country to teach in the southeastern United States meant not only getting used to a new culture, but also to the fact that I would have to redefine myself as a Latino immigrant man who used to self-identify as "homosexual."

JAVIER: Y what are you now, Tia?

MANUEL: Among many things, I am a queer of color. (*pause*) I had always felt oppressed in my home country for not following ✋

MANUEL (+ *CALVIN and JAVIER*): -male-female gender performance binaries,

MANUEL (*continued*): -especially since I tended to act more effeminate than most boys my age. Where I'm from, everyone thinks that—if you're gay—well, then you must want to be a woman, you like to be penetrated, and you will most likely end up getting AIDS. We're seen as promiscuous molesters of children—or that we're inter-ested in having sex with every male we encounter.

Language is so important. In Spanish, the words queer and gay don't really have accurate translations, so people use the existing derogative words like marica, cueco, loca, joto, puto, pato, del otro lado—just to name a few. This pushes many gay people to become victims of gender discrimination. And since sexual identity also intersects issues of class and race, things are even more complicated, leaving psychological scars. So, many oppressed gays and lesbians hide their sexual orientation in order to gain acceptance within the larger group. Others, like me, leave their parents' home and even their home countries looking for a safe place while the rest get trapped in majoritarian discriminatory assumptions about gay or queer people.

I moved to the United States in 1999 hoping to find a more tolerant environment where I could work as a teacher and pursue higher education. Where I ended up was in the rural south. My excitement fell apart when I quickly learned that my skin color, strong accent, and gender performance would be scrutinized and tested all the time. Soon I learned that everybody who looked like me or who looked like my mostly Spanish-speaking students was considered "Mexican." For the non-Hispanic locals, what "being Mexican" meant was "wet back," illiterate, stupid, illegal, drug dealer, abusive-

JAVIER (*interjecting*): Hey!

MANUEL (*continuing*): -drunk, macho, party animal, and—maybe sometimes— "rico y suave."

JAVIER: Okay, well the rico y suave part is maybe true.

MANUEL: Within the school, I could say that I did hold status with some- with a few of the teachers and some students and their families, but outside—in the dominant community—I suffered the same types of discrimination that most immigrants of color suffer in this country. Right along with my students, I felt the pain they felt, and 🖐

MANUEL (+ *ALL*): -I experienced again what it meant to be the "other"

MANUEL (*continued*): -in what was supposed to be my safer adopted home. But I was now twice the other: once for being "Mexican" and again for being gay.

My students and their families—for the most part—seemed to ignore my sexual orientation, though I did have times when 🖐

MANUEL (+ *JAVIER*): -students made nasty comments about gays and lesbians

MANUEL (*continued*): -just to see my reaction. But as the teacher—and as a legal immigrant—I was seen as being of a different social status within the local Latino community. But- 🖐

MANUEL (+ *CALVIN and RUTH*): -I never really talked about my sexual identity in front of my students,

MANUEL (*continued*): -though, looking back, I think I realized that they all knew I wasn't straight. Yeah, I always tried to hide my sexual orientation from my students and many of my colleagues. There were several gay and lesbian teachers in the school, but we never talked about it. I was always afraid that I would get into trouble— rejected or even fired—for being gay, even though my district ESL coordinator was gay. At work he pretended to be a strong and strict White man, but at the bar, we were just the same. But no, I never really felt pushed to talk about my sexual identity with my students. I'm not sure it would have been safe for me to do that.

RUTH: Not too long ago I returned to New York City from four years teaching in Japan expecting to feel liberated, let out of the closet, and free again to do as I pleased in the ESL classroom. In Japan, when I informed the director of my program of my sexual orientation, she suggested that I "keep it a secret forever." If you know me at all, you'd know that that wasn't going to happen. But I did come to understand her perspective. In the small city in Japan where I worked, such a revelation would have brought an assembly of local television, radio, and newspaper reporters to campus, and I would quickly have become the most famous foreigner in town: and not in a good way. Still, I wanted to explore what it would mean for me to be my authentic self while teaching: ✋

RUTH (+ *LINDA, MANUEL and VALENTINA*): -being able to talk about my life and my partner without editing or dancing around the pronouns I used.

RUTH (*continued*): Of course, I knew that I wasn't going to go in there on the first day of class and announce to my students—outside of any context whatsoever—"Good morning, everyone. You may have noticed my short hair and comfortable shoes; well, in fact, I am a lesbian—"

VALENTINA: -a lesbian, a writer, an activist, an immigrant's daughter, a second-language learner, a teacher-

CALVIN: -a teacher, genderqueer, an African American, androgynous, pansexual, seeming to be a somewhat feminine man-

JAVIER: -a somewhat feminine man, a former kindergarten teacher, a Disney Princess, a language instructor, a gay man-

MANUEL: -a gay man, a queer of color, a teacher-educator, effeminate, partnered to a man-

LINDA: -partnered to a man, married, feminine, bisexual, liberal, and well-educated English language teaching professional.

RUTH: Yes, all that: all the aspects of my own complex human identity, which includes my sexual identity. But I also didn't want to imply to my students that I had, well, simply happened to have chosen a novel for our course that happened to have a protagonist who seemed to be questioning his sexual orientation because, well, it was just one of those topics that I couldn't get enough of. Instead, I decided I would wait for the golden moment where I could reveal this part of myself in context.

I had read a lot of the literature related to coming out as an act of self-disclosure, and I shared concerns that in doing so in an arbitrary or decontextualized way, I would not only be giving up heterosexual privilege and authority, but I would be inviting my students to apply to me all of the labels and stereotypes they have in their minds about what a lesbian is, what a lesbian looks like, what a lesbian does, and finally, to attribute anything I do that offends or frightens them to the fact of my being a lesbian. I hoped that waiting—waiting until the students themselves recognized that the "queer issue" was an important one in the novel and possibly in their own lives—that waiting might also mitigate the artificiality and sense of "wrongness"—of something that seemingly required a purposeful "disclosure" unrelated to course content. So, I would wait, then: wait for that "golden" moment when I would disclose my sexual identity to my students in the context of someone else's story, within the curriculum of the course.

LINDA: I remember deciding that I wouldn't lie: I wouldn't "advertise" my sexual identity, but if asked, I would tell the truth to my students. That was years back when I used to self-identify as a lesbian woman. But now, clearly I see that I unintentionally come out nearly every day as straight, even though I'm not. But as a feminine woman married to a masculine man, it happens, despite my actually being bi. This assumption bothers me because I care very much about avoiding heteronormative stereotypes. ✋

LINDA (+ *ALL*): I can't help but use examples from my life when I teach,

LINDA (*continued*): -and my husband is such an enormous a part of that life. So I'm perceived by many, I think, as being 100% heterosexual. One of the struggles of being bi is that your sexual identity tends to get masked by whichever kind of relationship you happen to be in. And so now I am frequently reminded of how edited my life was with my students back when I was with my ex: a woman I loved and with whom I shared two dogs, many friends, "not-in-laws," and a fairly happy home for nearly eight years.

That break-up was a doozy. We'd been together since college, had moved in together, shared a life together, and suddenly—or honestly, not so suddenly—it was over. I was grateful to friends I had at work who let me cry in the teacher break room and invited me out on the weekends, but in class with my students, I plastered on the best smile I could muster. I had moments where I was kind of angry that this breakup wasn't getting the same respect that a divorce would get, because it sure felt like one. Regardless of marriage laws in my state, and the sex of my partner, maybe I would still have plastered on that smile in front of my students. But it sure would have been nice to have felt that I could have, you know, apologized for my occasional flakiness and short nerves in class, having the socially allowable excuse of going through a painful divorce. I was glad that I could, at least, share this loss with my coworkers, and for that, I am incredibly grateful.

CALVIN: I am incredibly grateful and feel fortunate to work in a public university with an explicitly stated nondiscrimination policy for sexual orientation, gender identity, and gender expression. I was certainly never more appreciative of this than the day I walked into the director's office and told him that I would be transitioning the following semester. At the time I was still riding the high of having recently told my immediate supervisors about my decision, and that these meetings had gone rather well. So, as I headed to the director's office for my appointment, I walked down the hallway with positive, crackling energy.

The director was, understandably, caught off-guard by my announcement. He later told me he had thought I just wanted a quick meeting about plans for the upcoming holiday party. But rather than cupcakes and streamers, I just came in, sat down, looked him in the eyes, and told him outright that I was transgender—that I would be changing my name soon—and that I hoped he would do the business of informing the faculty and staff of my transition. I would be lying if in all my adrenaline-fueled confidence there wasn't a hint of dread mixed with mischief as I mentally scrolled through the possibilities of what he might be thinking. ✋

CALVIN (+ *RUTH and VALENTINA*): It was just so intensely liberating to be so straightforward about who I am and what I want.

CALVIN (*continued*): Ultimately, the director himself wasn't able to make the announcement because my transition somehow qualified as "health information" in the eyes of Human Resources, and so I would have to do it myself. I decided I would send an email to the entire listserv, waiting until just a couple of days before winter break so people could know about my transition as they were preparing to go on vacation and sort of forget about it, let it sink in, make a bunch of jokes about it, or whatever they personally needed to do.

The liberation sort of faded in and out, replaced with utter vulnerability—especially when I sat at my computer, opened up the draft email I had already written and rewritten and proofread to no end. The Subject title was "Notice," and I had kept the tone as matter-of-fact as possible. I took a swig of my coffee and clicked Send: another gulp of coffee, staring at my screen, mentally folding myself into a little ball as I tried to go on with my work. Then the first new email alert pops up.

JAVIER (*as Calvin's colleague*): I love your new name, Calvin. Just wanted to let you know how much I admire your courage in sending this email out to everyone. Good on you.

CALVIN: And then another and another.

LINDA (*as Calvin's colleague*): Even though we don't know each other well, I wanted to let you know just how much I respect and support you. Sending good vibes your way.

VALENTINA (*as Calvin's colleague*): Thank you for trusting us. I have to confess that I will miss the old you. I think I am going to grieve that loss a bit, but I want you to know that am so happy for you—if you're happy and 100% sure about this next step.

CALVIN: I had over a dozen replies. Most responded with support and congratulations—even from those who I'd only ever spoken to in passing or people I wouldn't have expected to be so accepting. Some responded with questions—some maybe a bit awkward—but it was so affirming and humbling that there was so much positivity. I don't want to paint a picture that coming out was perfectly smooth and wonderful with all of my coworkers—but it was positive overall. I was able to relax, just a bit, into this new phase of my professional life.

MANUEL: -this new phase of my professional life was about to end. When I look back, I think one of the final pushes that caused me to leave the oppressive public school system was when one of my vocal Mexican students, Carlos—who had been in trouble with me for skipping school and disrespectful behavior—was having a conversation with one of his buddies about his home town in Mexico: Guadalajara. When I overheard this, I shared with them that I had always wanted to visit that part of Mexico, since I had heard good things about it.

JAVIER (*as Manuel's student*): You know, Mr. Suarez, a lot of *gay* people like to live in Guadalajara.

MANUEL: I quickly realized that Carlos was trying to offend me with his comments. And then he shouted,

JAVIER (*as Manuel's student*): Soltero y maduro, joto seguro!

MANUEL: Carlos was trying to hurt me with his words, and he did. By this time I was already nearing the end of my doctoral studies at university, about to collect data for my dissertation research thesis, and so I decided to quit my job. It wasn't easy, financially or emotionally. I missed my students and their families—and it was then that I truly began to recognize all that they had given me. It was they who, for the most part, 🖐

MANUEL (+ *LINDA and VALENTINA*): -accepted and respected me without regard to my sexual orientation.

MANUEL (*continued*): They helped instill in me my own sense of agency and helped me see that I had become a leader and advocate in the community. But at the same time I also realized that I had to leave the public school system in order to fulfill my goal of earning my PhD: one of the reasons that drew me to this country in the first place. 🖐

MANUEL (+ *LINDA and JAVIER*): I needed to find freedom from the oppression I felt in K–12 education.

MANUEL (*continued*): My hope is that things will be better in higher ed. So, I've been teaching part-time in an adult ESL program at the local community college in order to supplement what I earn through my graduate assistantship, teaching undergraduate preservice teachers. I defended my dissertation thesis earlier this month, and so I hope now to find a place in academia. Still, I worry if I will find a position in higher ed that will provide the level of emotional and academic freedom which will allow my authentic and free voice to be heard and, I hope, valued.

VALENTINA: Many of my adult ESL students say they have come to the United States for "freedom." Do they really feel free here? 🖐

VALENTINA (+ *LINDA and RUTH*): Teachers of English to those entering U.S. society teach our students much more than English.

VALENTINA (*continued*): We are role models; we bring our own experiences, culture, philosophies, and politics to students. Among all the struggles immigrant students experience adjusting to the U.S. or any country, learning to speak the language correctly is minor. Can we really understand the culture of another person? Do we ask our students to give up values, traditions, dreams, in order to fit into the U.S. or other English-dominant countries? How do we actually help our students articulate their deepest thoughts and needs? They come to a classroom setting, familiar to us, but not them, and again they feel they don't belong. And if our student is lesbian, gay, bisexual, or transgender—or if they have a son or daughter who is—this is a further complication in their lives as immigrant others.

Working with my adult ESL students, I explain some of these difficulties through my own experiences as "the other" when appropriate: as a child of immigrants from a no-longer-existing Yugoslavia; as one who, herself, struggled with the English language as a child and adolescent. I share the ways in which I was changed by becoming who I am today—a lesbian, a writer, an activist, a teacher. As their teacher it is my job to show them how crucial language is to their own identities. Teachers do not give students the gift of language; they find it themselves. We give them opportunities. We give them opportunities to struggle with a new language which will have an impact on how they experience this new cultural and linguistic world in which they find themselves.

RUTH: So, I found myself deciding I would wait for the golden opportunity. Informed by my reading related to outing oneself in the classroom, as it were, I decided to remain . . . neutral . . . about the novel's protagonist's apparent struggle with his sexual identity. Neutral? My problem with this approach is that my students know I have a passionate position on every issue that comes up in our discussions. 🖖

RUTH (+ *ALL*): How could I possibly be neutral?

RUTH (*continued*): Still, I decided to wait for that "golden moment" for self-disclosure, if one arose. Otherwise, I would refrain from bringing up my own sexual identity in the class conversation, merely helping my students develop as writers and critical thinkers in the context of the novel we were discussing. In the beginning, class discussions centered primarily on the socioeconomic differences students noticed between themselves and the characters in the novel.

MANUEL (*as Ruth's student*): This book is about rich people.

VALENTINA (*as Ruth's student*): James's father must be important. He could only have lunch with his father if he made an appointment with him.

RUTH: But then came a moment when I considered intervening: when a student shyly asked about a dialogue between the protagonist and his father during their lunch appointment.

CALVIN (*as Ruth's student*): I keep thinking about James's family; it is like a crazy family. What holds my mind: a father told his son that it's okay for James if he is gay. That is really bad.

RUTH: "Bad in what sense?" I asked, wondering if this was my golden moment. My heart was pounding, my palms sweating.

CALVIN (*as Ruth's student*): How could he ask him that question?

RUTH: "This is New York. Parents want to know exactly what's going on with their children. We talk about everything," I said. But the student was struggling with what he would say next. He couldn't express his indignation on behalf of the young protagonist in the novel. I waited for him to go on. Finally, he blurted out . . .

CALVIN (*as Ruth's student*): What he said about the pasta!

RUTH: In the novel, the father comments to his son that he should never order pasta as a main course. "It's not manly." But what I thought would be my golden moment suddenly slipped away as the conversation quickly spiraled to a discussion of food from the students' home cultures.

I later wrote in my journal: 🖐

RUTH (+ *ALL*): Is my coming out even relevant?

RUTH (*continued*): How much do I, a 60-year-old lesbian, have in common with an 18-year-old gay boy who is just discovering his sexuality? Do I tell them I have been through a similar struggle? As an 18-year-old, alienated in the affluent suburbs of New York City, I fell in love with my best friend; we slept together; I discovered myself; she wanted to die, tried to kill herself, and was institutionalized? Wouldn't that be going too far? Where do I stop once I've started?

During our discussion of the end of the novel, one of the students suggested, quietly, that perhaps we all had feelings like James did sometimes. But then another student said,

JAVIER (*as Ruth's student*): It is all right for a woman, but for me, it is sick.

RUTH: Here, finally, was a moment where I felt I must intervene. "I think it's fine," I told him. "For men or for women. It may not be fine for you, personally, but it's fine."

The students all smiled at me benignly. Did they know? Should I tell them? Instead I told them something my dissertation adviser had said to me 20 years earlier. I asked, "Do you know what a continuum is?"

LINDA (*as Ruth's student*): Yes. Connected. In chemistry. Like rainbow.

RUTH: "Exactly. Maybe we are all somewhere on the continuum." And I drew a semi-circle on the board. "Somewhere between 100% heterosexual and 100% homosexual." And I wrote these words at the opposite ends of my continuum. "Maybe that's okay." Then one of my male students firmly declared,

JAVIER (*to Ruth, as her student*): Well, I am over there. 100% heterosexual.

RUTH: "That's fine. That's fine. But maybe we are not all over there with you. Not every minute of every day. And maybe that's OK."

(*After a brief pause*)

JAVIER (*to audience, as himself*): Actually . . . I am . . . 100% homosexual.

(*sensing the audience's confusion*)

No, no, no. This is *my* story now. Pay no more attention to Ruth. She's done. Just look at me.

(*stage-whispering to RUTH*)

I love you Ruth,

(*after a moment, JAVIER continues slowly*)

Well, I think that—You know, I think that everything relates to the fact that I am— maybe I am afraid of my true self.

   (*pause*)

I was born in a place where there are two roles for everyone: working in the oil fields, if you're a man, and a teacher, if you're a woman. I guess I didn't fit there, so I moved to a bigger town: one that had a gay-friendly reputation. Would you believe it; it was worse. It's kind of ironic, but being gay in Guadalajara, Mexico, is a super big challenge. Even though it is one of the gayest cities in the country, it is also one of the most religious. I found a job at the local American School, which was fine, but it was nothing compared to the language institute where I had worked before. As far as my students were concerned, everything was great. 🖐

JAVIER (+ *ALL*): I believe I touched the lives of my students more than just teaching them grammar.

JAVIER (*continued*): The real problem was with their parents—who felt the idea of having someone "like me" teaching their children was not appropriate at any level. It wasn't easy for some parents to see an effeminate dude with long hair teaching their children. Look, I am aware that I am super feminine: the way I sound, the way I walk, and the way I emphasize it. But this is me.

CALVIN and **RUTH**: This is me.

MANUEL: Este soy yo.

LINDA and **VALENTINA**: This is me.

JAVIER: In my teen years, my parents took me to a shrink. What was wrong with me? He suggested I should hide my femininity—become discreet. I told him, "You can turn me into Schwarzenegger, but inside I can't change." I stopped going.

Once upon a time I isolated myself from life and from the world and, most painfully, from my own family. I see myself differently now. I recently read that Hans Christian Andersen wrote a love letter to another man, and that he then adapted it into his famous tale, *The Little Mermaid.* Aye, yes; I think I now see myself as one of the Disney Princesses: Disney's Little Mermaid— half girl from the waist up—willing to give everything up for love, yes—but on my own terms and with a well-placed tiara.

LINDA: Still living my "happily ever after," and before the break-up with my ex- girlfriend, I had gone back to university to get my master's in applied linguistics. I then ended up getting hired in the ELI there after graduation and, at the university, 🖐

LINDA (+ *RUTH and VALENTINA*): -things felt safer as a lesbian working in higher education,

LINDA (*continued*): -but I still wasn't especially out. The pattern repeats: out in grad school with my peers, out with some close colleagues—sure, but in my first year as an adjunct with no real job security, was I out to my students? Not so much.

PETER (*a voice from the audience*): Excuse me. Excuse me, Linda. I thought you said you were *bi*sexual?

LINDA (*to audience*): That's my husband.

 (*to Peter*)

I'm getting there, Peter.

 (*then, to audience*)

Honestly, I really don't get overly concerned with labels. So then—and—Here it comes, Peter—<u>then</u> I met and fell in love with the wonderful, open-minded, and supportive man who is now my husband: Peter.

And with that came a new freedom that I wasn't looking for and didn't really expect. It was only after I was "safe" in my heterosexual relationship that I did workshops on heterosexism for my colleagues and, even now, when I do them at our institute and beyond, I question whether or not I should come out. I wonder if being out will add more power to what I am saying—

VALENTINA: Hey look. Our esteemed colleague is queer and we didn't even know it. She must really understand these issues.

LINDA: —or if it will detract—

MANUEL: The only reason she's interested in this stuff is because she's queer herself. She's just interested in self-preservation.

LINDA: I've done it a few different ways and am still unsure of the best approach. Honestly, I feel invisible in the queer community most of the time. There was a time when I could pass a woman on the street and with a small look we both knew we were in the same family. I tried that while out with my husband several times—

 (*to Peter*)

—<u>early</u> in our relationship—out of habit—and the returned look from the woman was one of indifference. Had I lost that part of my identity? I don't try anymore, at risk of being misinterpreted as judging. I miss going to Pride festivals, but the last time I went I felt I didn't fit. It wasn't for me anymore, at least not the way that it was when my girlfriend and I rode with Dykes on Bikes.

Gay students on campus have no reason to seek me out—beyond the Safe Zone Ally sticker on my window—and we don't run into each other at gay events like Raj and I did several years ago. I had been out with friends at a gay bar during Pride week and ran into a student from our program, Raj. He was Saudi and gay, and neither of us had "known" about each other until that moment. He told me I was the first person he met at the English language institute, and he remembered my being nice but serious at orientation. We became friends, and he told me his story. I was one of the only people at the ELI who knew, and I felt proud to be able to support him in that way. But those things don't seem to happen anymore. Now-

LINDA (+ *CALVIN, JAVIER, and MANUEL*): I go back and forth about how "out" I would be-

LINDA (*continued*): if I were in the market for a new job. Right now, on my CV, I proudly list my involvement with the LGBTQ Forum here within the TESOL organization, and I name the workshops and presentations I have done to raise awareness about heteronormativity in ESL. My workplace is very supportive. But, when I think about potential future job searches, I wonder about editing out that involvement for certain job markets, particularly overseas. There is a part of me that wants to keep it in my CV to ensure I wouldn't end up in a place that wouldn't have hired me for that, but another part that thinks I might do whatever I "needed" to do to get a job. It would feel like selling out, but I think I could get to a place where I would make that choice more easily than I'd like to admit or want to confess. And so, here I am, in this presentation, telling my story with my long hair and heels, confessing that I don't know how or if to come out, and feeling unsure of how "out" I should generally be in the world.

VALENTINA: Coming out or being out in the world: Making public what is feared and risking ridicule or castigation is a demanding undertaking. It is a decisive step, a step in favor of life. The process of making public what is most private is the job I am doing with collecting and publishing interviews and coming out stories of queers in Russia. Sometimes these interviews chronicle moments of the first time individuals thought about their "coming out" as an event. Some interviewees felt transformed by the interview itself.

In my explorations, I am becoming aware of how slow and varied the process is. It is worth representing, including the history and customs of a people. Do I have a right to write about all this? Should I be publishing a book of interviews of people telling me about their most intimate stories and hidden lives? While I listen to them, I comprehend parts of my own sexual history and family and social dynamics. I, too, become more public. What is generally considered very private even in U.S. society is made public in order that sexual minorities can be liberated. 🖐

VALENTINA (+ *ALL*): Queer people have been forced to be secretive about our sexuality and our lives to survive.

VALENTINA (*continued*): To counteract the homophobia in society, we reveal our same-sex orientation in our art and activism, by the way we dress, and finally in "coming out." This is the beginning of all of our freedom. We all have the right to live openly as our authentic selves.

CALVIN: The first day back from the holiday break, I went over and over in my mind what I was going to wear, how I would walk, and how I would talk. As I had just barely started taking testosterone, my voice and body were basically the same as they always had been. Already part of my wardrobe was my binder, which is like a tight polyester tank top that gives you a flatter chest. And even though I had been wearing binders to work for a while, I had still been consistently gendered female by others. So I knew the binder itself would not be enough. I decided to wear a dress shirt and tie even though it might seem like I was trying too hard, and a pair of women's jeans. I wore plain black earrings—everything black and grey—and a black beaded bracelet. The jewelry made me feel like myself, and like I could sort of very, very quietly state that gender norms are silly, and it's quite all right to break them if you like. I added a new canvas satchel to replace my giant purse and a steel coffee mug in place of my hot pink one—which I now do bring sometimes, because, why not? I was ready. I rehearsed to myself, "Okay. So the first day I go in, I write my name on the board, 'Calvin Bowen,' and then I tell them they can also call me 'Cal,' and then we move on." It could have gone every which way but smooth, but as luck would have it, the first day was—fine—mundane, even. Work was just work and I felt that the semester would be all right after all. I have ✋

CALVIN (+ *LINDA and RUTH*): -tried to find a balance between honesty about myself and maintaining my own privilege,

CALVIN (*continued*): -which is not something I am proud of, but it is the truth. I have used the privilege of being able to "pass" as cisgender—as male—to hide my queer identity. Once, while teaching, however, when discussing an article about trans* rights that a student had brought in, I outed myself to the entire class—a relatively small group of students I had been teaching for a few months. They were polite about it, though some were visibly uneasy. One student started to ask questions about medical modifications I had done, which gave me a chance to educate the students on what questions are and are not appropriate to ask a trans* person whom they don't know very well. The student who had seemed most flabbergasted by my revelation did not return the next session. I know all about correlation and causation, but ✋

CALVIN (+ *JAVIER and MANUEL*): I can't help but wonder if that student just wanted to get away from the abomination that is me.

CALVIN (*continued*): I would love to reach a point where I can come right out on day one of class and say: "My name is Calvin Bowen. You've probably heard that I used to identify as a woman, and it's true—but I prefer you use neutral or masculine pronouns for me now. I'm looking forward to working with you this semester." I'm not there yet, but I have become more comfortable bringing my whole self into the classroom. My immediately visible identity as African American, my less visible identities as an atheist, as a liberal, as a pansexual, as a transgender person—whether I mention them explicitly or not, ✋

CALVIN (+ *ALL*): I think my students can benefit from the perspective of someone like me,

CALVIN (*continued*): -and I feel incredibly lucky that I have the chance to bring this perspective to them—perhaps change some minds.

JAVIER: Ay, Ruth, I've changed my mind about my Disney Princess. I am not the Little Mermaid anymore. I am the new one, Elsa, the Snow Queen from the movie *Frozen*. Like me, Elsa was born with a beautiful and amazing gift, but the gift is dangerous if she lets fear control her.

If you haven't seen it yet—and you should—you need to know that Elsa was born with these powers—something she and her sister see as natural and normal. And this is just like me and my sister: for my sister, my being gay was just me being Javier—her hermanito. Then, in the movie, Elsa's powers accidentally hurt her sister—which is just like with me: my being gay caused some of my sister's schoolmates to bully her for having a gay brother. This then causes Elsa to be scared of using her gift and makes me afraid to be myself because being myself was hurting not only me, but the ones I love.

I know that I am very lucky to have parents who may not always understand—may wish things were different—that I was different—but who I know deeply love and support me, in spite of the fact that they have been hurt collaterally by the fact that they have a gay son.

I can super relate to the story of *Frozen* when her parents try to help her control her gift and tell her to "conceal it, don't feel it, don't let it show," as this was exactly what my parents used to tell me, to protect myself. "Keep it hidden!" And that psychiatrist shrink they sent me to?! Ay, my parents could have saved a lot of money and just sent me to a Disney matinee for five pesos!

I have given up teaching . . . for the moment, and I go back and forth about what to do about it. I used to teach for an organization that was full of gay people: full of them, but maybe they weren't as gay as me. Administration would limit me from visiting other towns to teach English because I was considered "too gay" for the students, and I would get complaints about the way I talked and walked, and all of that kind of discouraged me from teaching. Perhaps I could have been a happier teacher if I had hidden myself from the world.

At this time in my life—and I moisturize a lot, so you may think I am younger than I actually am—I am planning to go back to school for my master's in TESOL or applied linguistics: hopefully in the United States. Maybe it would be better for me to teach adults—and teach them in a country that is, maybe, a little more progressive. I don't know. But, it looks like I'll be a student again.

And maybe I'll be your student, or your student, or your student. You know—this isn't all about queer ESL teachers. ✋

JAVIER (+ *ALL*): We are all going to have gay or queer international students in our classrooms.

JAVIER (*continued*): We have gay students in our ESL classes—or in teacher-preparation classes if you teach in higher ed. You have gay students, and you have gay students, and you.

And if you teach in a master's program in TESOL . . . well, you might even get to have me.

As Elsa the Ice Queen would say, maybe it is time for me to just "let it go" and start concentrating on me—on *being* me. (*Brief pause.*) I just want to be me.

217

(JAVIER closes his playscript and crosses to position himself behind the "empty" music stand at center. After a moment, he addresses the audience.)

This space. This empty space is—for me—being held for the new generations of LGBTQ international teachers and students who feel silenced and without a voice as they leave their home countries to seek a better education and a freer life.

(JAVIER then exits the performance space and sits among the audience as VALENTINA crosses to the empty stand for her final statement. This movement and speaking pattern is repeated by the remaining PLAYERS as they deliver their final lines and exit the performance space to sit among audience members.)

VALENTINA: For me, I hold this space for the queer community of Russia who are being aggressively oppressed.

RUTH: This empty space is here to honor of all of the gay English language teachers whose voices we have lost to AIDS.

MANUEL: This spot is for my Latino and Latina students who once thought about committing suicide after feeling rejected by parents, relatives, and peers.

CALVIN: This stand is for those who give up a little piece of themselves every time someone calls them "sir" or "miss," or who don't think they can or should ever come out. This stand is to remind you that you do have a place in this community.

LINDA: This is for my high school girlfriend who had to leave home at 17 because she was gay and for all the "invisibles" in the queer community.

(As LINDA exits the performance space to sit among the audience, the lights dim, leaving only the center music stand illuminated.)

END

What follows is a brief inventory of discussion prompts that may facilitate productive dialogue for preservice and/or in-service TESOL educators and administrators. Several are conducive to the development of role-playing activity.

1. What does sexual identity or gender identity have to do with language teaching?

2. *"Chris told his husband Albert to wash the dishes."* Grammar curriculums (and generally all ESL curriculums) are heteronormative: that is, the situations and language use presume a heterosexual orientation. What are some implications for grammar instruction vis-à-vis a more open discourse around LGBTQ issues and people? What do you know about gender-neutral pronouns that some transgender individuals are adopting (i.e., subject: zie; object: zir; possessive determiner: zir; possessive pronoun: zirs; reflexive: zirself)?

3. How can sexual and/or gender minority (1) international students, (2) teachers, and (3) administrators be supported in our teaching and learning contexts?

4. It what ways might LGBTQ issues be integrated into ESL curriculum from a social justice perspective? Should they be? Should they not be? What would be the justification?

5. You are a program administrator or a colleague of an LGBTQ teacher. International students (or their parents) have come to you to complain about the LGBTQ colleague and request that they be placed with a different instructor. How would you respond?

6. What do you see as some of the challenges LGBTQ teachers (and students) face in K–12 settings as compared to higher educational settings? What about the LGBTQ parents of children in K–12 settings?

7. What do you see as some of the challenges LGBTQ teachers (and students) face in traditionally "queer-hostile" environments (e.g., some rural, international, or parochial settings)?

8. What is the job of the TESOL professional beyond teaching the English language?

9. Of all of the play's characters, with whom did you most (or least) identify? Why?

10. With the understanding that the play's narratives are drawn from the lives of actual English language teaching professionals, what was *your* experience "walking in their words"?

References

Barone, T., & Eisner, E. (2012). *Arts based research.* Thousand Oaks, CA: Sage.

Chambers, J. R., & Davis, M. H. (2012). The role of the self in perspective-taking and empathy: Ease of self-simulation as heuristic for inferring empathic feelings. *Social Cognition, 30*(2), 153–180.

Cho, J., & Trent, A. (2006). Validity in qualitative research revisited. *Qualitative Research, 3*(3), 319–340.

Clandinin, D. J., & Connelly, F. M. (2000). *Narrative inquiry: Experience and story in qualitative research.* San Francisco, CA: Jossey-Bass.

Clark Cummings, M. (2009). Someday this pain will be useful to you: Self-disclosure and lesbian and gay identity in the ESL writing classroom. *Journal of Basic Writing, 28*(1), 71–89.

Donmoyer, R., & Yennie-Donmoyer, J. (2008). Readers theater as a mode of qualitative data display. In G. Knowles & A. Cole (Eds.), *The arts in qualitative research.* Thousand Oaks, CA: Sage.

Ellwood, C. (2006). On coming out and coming undone: Sexualities and reflexivities in language education research. *Journal of Language, Identity, and Education, 5*(1), 67–84.

Jenks, F. L., & Kennell, P. (2011). The quest for academic legitimacy. In M. A. Christison & F. L. Stoller (Eds.), *A handbook for language program administrators* (2nd ed., pp. 177–195). Miami Beach, FL: Alta Book Center Publishers.

Kappra, R., & Vandrick, S. (2006). Silenced voices: Queer ESL students recount their experiences. *CATESOL Journal, 18*(1), 138–150.

Leavy, P. (2009). *Method meets art: Arts-based research practice.* New York, NY: Guilford.

Menard-Warwick, J. (2009). Co-constructing representations of culture in ESL and EFL classrooms: Discursive faultlines in Chile and California. *The Modern Language Journal, 93*(1), 30–45.

Nelson, C. (1999). Sexual identities in ESL: Queer theory and classroom inquiry. *TESOL Quarterly, 33*(3), 371–391.

Nelson, C. (2002). *Queer as a second language: Classroom theatre for everyone* [Spotlight Session, a featured presentation]. TESOL Convention, Salt Lake City, Utah.

Nelson, C. D. (2004). A queer chaos of meanings: Coming out conundrums in globalized classrooms. *Journal of Gay and Lesbian Issues in Education, 2*(1), 27–46.

Nelson, C. D. (2009). *Sexual identities in English language education: Classroom conversations.* New York, NY: Routledge.

Ollerenshaw, J. A., & Creswell, J. W. (2002). Narrative research: A comparison of two restorying data analysis approaches. *Qualitative Inquiry, 8*(3), 329–347.

Saldaña, J. (2011). *Ethnotheatre: Research from page to stage.* Walnut Creek, CA: Left Coast Press.

Smith, A. D. (2005). *Four American characters* [TED Talk]. Retrieved from http://www.ted .com/talks/anna_deavere_smith_s_american_character/transcript?language=en#t-6585

Vandrick, S. (2009). *Interrogating privilege: Reflections of a second language educator.* Ann Arbor: University of Michigan Press.

Vygotsky, L. S. (1978). *Mind and society.* Cambridge, MA: MIT Press.

Winkle, C. A. (2010, March 27). *The bite of the teacher's pet: Sexual identity inquiry in an ESL composition class.* Paper presented in the ILGBTF Forum Academic Session, "Supporting Lesbian, Gay, Bisexual, and Transgender ESL Teachers and Students," at TESOL's 44th Annual Convention and Exhibit, Boston, MA.

Winkle, C. A. (Ethnodramatist). (2014). *Walking in the words of LGBTQ English Language Teaching professionals through Ethnodramatic Readers Theatre* [Playscript]. Barry University, Miami Shores, FL.

Winkle, C. A., Archer, L., Cummings, M. C., Franeta, S., Reyes, R., Rios-Vega, J., & Royal, K. (2014, March 28). *Performing our stories through autoethnodramatic narratives: The ILGBTF Forum colloquium.* ILGBTF Forum presentation at the 48th Annual TESOL Convention and Exhibition, Portland, OR.

PART VI:

WORKING ACROSS BORDERS / ADVOCATING FOR STUDENTS

CHAPTER 17

When Nobody Seems to Care

Preparing Preservice Teachers for English Language Learners in Texas Classrooms

Baburhan Uzum
Sam Houston State University

Mary Petrón
Sam Houston State University

On June 10, 2014, the Mexican American Legal Defense and Educational Fund (MALDEF) filed suit on behalf of the League of United Latin American Citizens (LULAC) against the State of Texas (LULAC v. State of Texas, 2014). According to the suit, the state was not doing enough to meet the needs of English language learners in Texas public schools and was in violation of the U.S. Federal Equal Education Opportunities Act of 1974. Data for the lawsuit was taken from the state's own accountability system. There is a 40-year history of civil rights lawsuits dealing with the education of English language learners in Texas. This latest lawsuit alleges that the state fails to provide adequate support and supervision of ESL programs, particularly at the secondary level. Weak monitoring of the educational progress of English language learners in Texas fails to hold districts accountable. Furthermore, the ESL teacher certification process is woefully inadequate in the state, with teachers requiring little training or education. Although only two school districts in San Antonio are named in the case, it is acknowledged that many Texas school districts have similar problems.

Texas is a minority majority state: Only 44% of the population is non-Latino White, according to 2013 population estimates (U.S. Census Bureau, 2013). Latinos represent the largest ethnic group in the state, comprising about 38% of the population (U.S. Census Bureau, 2013). Approximately 51% of the K–12 public school population is Latino (Texas Education Agency, 2013). Texas does have a more diverse teaching workforce in public schools than the United States as whole. While 84% of teachers in the United States are non-Latino White (Feistritzer, 2011, p. 11), approximately two thirds of the teachers are White in Texas (Ramsay, 2014). These percentages are similar to those in our education preparation program, where 69% of preservice teachers are White (Enterprise Services, 2013).

In Texas, 1 out of every 6 public school children is an English language learner (Texas Education Agency, 2013). Ninety-two percent of English language learners are Spanish speakers and 89% are economically disadvantaged (Morgan & Vaughn, 2011, p. 5). The majority of English language learners are increasingly concentrated in high poverty and high minority schools, facing the triple isolation of language, economics, and race/ethnicity (Heilig & Holme, 2013, p. 616). At the 6–12 grade levels, 70% of the English language learners have been in ESL programs for more than 5 years and are considered long-term English learners (LULAC v. State of Texas, p. 11). According to the preliminary analysis of the Texas English Language Proficiency Assessment System (TELPAS) data from the 2013–2014 school year, more than 1 out of every 2 ELL students (56%) in grades 3–12 failed to advance at least one proficiency level (LULAC v. State of Texas, p. 16).

The failure of Texas schools to address the academic progress of English language learners is as lacking as their attempts to address their English language development. Recent accountability statistics from state exams are alarming. For example, at the 6th-grade level in the 2012–2013 school year, the percentage of all students who met the state standard in reading was 72%, while only 37% of English language learners as a subgroup did (LULAC v. State of Texas, p. 17). State exams at other grade levels in other subjects, such as math, science, and social studies, also show negative results. Significant differences exist between the total number of students who met the standards and the total of number English language learners who did (p. 17). Furthermore, the four-year graduation rate of English language learners in Texas is 58%, opposed to 86% for all students in the state (Stetser & Stillwell, 2014, p. 8). Like many districts in the state, the public school district near our university has failed to make adequately yearly progress for English language learners.

ESL Teacher Certification in Texas

Despite this disturbing picture, ESL teacher certification requirements for general in-service classroom teachers continue to be lax in Texas; neither course requirements nor in-service hours are required. Teachers must simply pass the ESL certification exam. Many districts have implemented cram sessions for the exam. Few colleges of education in Texas require specific coursework for preservice teachers in the area of ESL. The college of education where we work requires all elementary and middle school teacher candidates to seek ESL certification and take three courses in working with culturally and linguistically diverse children: multicultural education, second language acquisition, and ESL methods. Yet this commitment to English language learners appears to be superficial at best even at our institution, which is recognized in the region for the quality of teacher preparation it provides. High school preservice teachers only take the course in multicultural education. Furthermore even in the elementary/middle school teacher preparation program, no field experience dedicated to working with English language learners is required. Field experience refers to an institutionalized component of a course that involves working directly with children in the public schools. This field experience does not exist for ESL courses because the assumption is that preservice teachers will have the opportunity to work with English language learners during other field experiences in literacy block, content methods, and student teaching. Unfortunately, there is no actual mechanism for ensuring that ESL-specific experiences take place; nor is there any guarantee that the mentor teachers in whose classrooms preservice teachers are placed have significant training in working with English language learners. As stated previously, a Texas teacher may be certified by simply passing an exam.

Our own college of education data indicate that teacher candidates fail to adequately address the needs of English language learners and that they recognize their limited preparation in the area of ESL. Furthermore, many of our colleagues in the college of education readily admit their own professional knowledge base in ESL is lacking. A recent comment from one professor is typical of their comments and queries: "I don't really know much about working with LEP students. What can you tell me about the ELPS?" (LEP stands for Limited English Proficiency and is used by the Texas Education Agency to refer to English language learners. ELPS are the English Language Proficiency Standards adopted by the State of Texas in 2007.) In other words, the content presented in the ESL courses is not necessarily being reinforced in general teacher preparation courses. It is rather like many education textbooks where English language learners are relegated to a chapter rather than integrated throughout.

Service Learning for Equity in Education

It is in this environment that we work as professors of ESL education. Our commitment to social justice for English language learners is based in our own life experiences. Mary Petrón began her teaching career as a high school Spanish teacher. She first became involved with ESL because the ESL teacher on the campus was also the football coach. His teaching consisted of having students watch ESPN day in and day out. She listened to ELL students' growing frustration and began teaching them survival English. She soon realized the lack of commitment to English language learners that existed in many public school settings. This understanding of the plight of ELL students deepened when she adopted two older children from El Salvador who also received ESL services. She has dedicated her personal and professional life to improving ESL programs through teacher education and civic engagement projects. Baburhan Uzum was raised in a rural city in Turkey and spent many of his weekends and all of his summers doing farmwork in his nearby village. He was first exposed to English in middle school, as a foreign language class, and was fascinated by the sound of an unfamiliar language and the fact that it would allow him to interact with new people. Almost immediately, he realized that English would provide access to further education and the opportunity to experience the world outside of Turkey. Grateful for these opportunities that would have otherwise been unavailable to him, Uzum pursued a career in teaching English as a way to offer the same chances to other less privileged populations in Turkey and in the United States.

In effort to improve the educational experience of ELL students, we advocate strongly at the administrative level for increased integration of ESL content at all levels of teacher education coursework and dedicated ESL field experiences for preservice teachers. Field experiences help preservice teachers make connections between the teacher education course content and the realities of classrooms. These practical link-ages make education theories more accessible, understandable, and useful to preser-vice teachers. According to situated learning theory, through learning by doing, "the individual learner is not gaining a discrete body of abstract knowledge which (s)he will then transport and reapply in later contexts. Instead, (s)he acquires the skill to perform by actually engaging in the process" (Lave & Wenger, 1991, p. 14). Field expe-rience not only includes a comprehensive understanding of content (e.g., education theories), but also an acute awareness of the local context, including "the conceptions and preconceptions that students of different ages and backgrounds bring with them" (Shulman, 1986, p. 9). Therefore, practical experiences enable preservice teachers to perform the roles and duties of a teacher and develop a professional perspective that understands and values the diverse needs and interests of their students.

The importance of local context brings into question the appropriateness of "best practices" in each and every setting (Lortie, 1975). Instead of looking to create gold standards of education, many researchers argue for the need to go beyond the search for "best method" and work toward developing a teacher's capacity to devise peda-gogical practices to address the needs of the local context (Gordon, 2004). Teachers should develop the ability to create their own methodology based on the needs of a local context rather than following predetermined best practice guidelines that are supposedly designed to fit all (Kumaravadivelu, 2006).

Although the importance of field experiences has been established in the literature, our program still does not have a formal field component. Advocating for the addition of this field experience is important, but the wheels of change move slowly. Action was needed immediately. Consequently, we looked to service learning to provide the experiences with English language learners that our preservice teachers desperately needed. Service learning is already strongly supported and promoted at the institu-tional level at our university. In other words, we found a way to circumvent the limited scope of the existing curriculum by using service learning to provide our preservice teachers with an opportunity to meet the needs of the community and engage with ELL students in the public school classroom.

Service learning has the potential for addressing social justice issues, including systemic educational inequities for English language learners in the area of teacher preparation. We define *service learning* in accordance with the definition provided by Berger Kaye (2010):

> Service learning can be defined as a research-based teaching method where guided or classroom learning is applied through action that addresses an authentic community need in a process that allows for youth initiative and provides structured time for reflection on the service experience and demonstration of acquired skills and knowledge. (p. 9)

Service learning must be carefully planned and executed in order to achieve an authentic learning experience for students as well as to produce positive outcomes in the community. According to Bollin (2007), service learning should originate in community needs. Students must have the opportunity to apply content they are learning in the formal classroom to community settings. Finally, students need to reflect on these community experiences so as to connect classroom learning to community learning through a formalized structure. Service learning is inherently constructivist, since students are actively participating in authentic and meaningful community projects (Rodriguez, 2013).

In an effort to provide our preservice teachers with the much-needed opportunity to work with ELL students and address the pressing needs of our local community, we integrated a service learning project into the ESL methods classes. This project was designed in collaboration with a local middle school located in a low-income school district with limited resources. The middle school also has a history of poor academic outcomes among the ELL population. As a result of the field experience, preservice teachers had the opportunity to teach a class with English language learners for the first time and reflect on their teaching experience. The field experience via service learning contributed to the professional development of preservice teachers by creating a space for innovation, collaboration, and exploration of social justice issues related to English language learners. At the same time, they provided a valuable service to ELL students in the local community.

Discussion

The service learning project supported the preservice teachers' development of a social justice perspective by providing a venue to establish a professional identity that values equity in education (Hawkins & Norton, 2009; Kaur, 2012); negotiate and reflect on prior beliefs about English language learners; interact with a diverse group of students; and develop context specific methods and strategies to address the needs of English language learners. In designing this service learning project, we believed that four critical components had to form an integral part of the experience. First, the project needed to be done in collaboration with the teachers in the middle school so that the needs and interests of both sides were discussed and addressed in an equitable manner. Second, middle school teachers had to be afforded the opportunity to make curricular choices based upon their most pressing needs. They would choose the content objectives to be covered in the classes. Third, preservice teachers would contribute their developing knowledge of ESL methods by teaching these objectives using the SIOP method (Echevarria, Vogt, & Short, 2000). We teach this method because of its strong research base and acceptance in U.S. public schools. Finally, we wanted preservice teachers to reflect on the experience in a way that forced them to think about social justice issues in the education of English language learners in Texas.

We recognize the limited nature of the service learning project; however, there is evidence that preservice teachers gained an understanding of the diverse needs of English language learners and the importance of context specific methods and strategies as part of an equitable learning environment for ELL students. Preservice teachers' reflections indicated that their field experience through service learning had a powerful impact in three major areas: interaction with diverse populations, recognition that limited English proficiency did not mean limited cognitive ability, and understanding of the necessity to differentiate instruction because of language proficiency. With respect to diversity, the experience brought preservice teachers into contact with English learners for the first time. Typically, when we ask students in our classes what programs existed for ELL students in the schools they attended, they state that they did not know because they did not have contact with these students. This situation is not unusual, considering segregation patterns in Texas (Heilig & Holme, 2013). Consequently, many of the preservice teachers initially expressed a fear of teaching English language learners, as is evident in the following quote:

> I was so nervous and scared to mess up teaching ELL's before entering the classroom. I thought I couldn't teach ELL's because I didn't know how to speak their native language . . . . After being in the classroom, I realized this was not the case.

The experience served to humanize ELL students in a way that textbooks and videos could not and enabled preservice teachers to see beyond any language barriers.

Preservice teachers also recognized that language proficiency and cognitive ability are distinct entities. In other words, the ability to think critically is independent of one's proficiency in English. One preservice teacher was particularly articulate in stating the epiphany she had with respect to this issue:

> These students [English language learners] can still be challenged because critical thinking is not necessarily a language objective. All students can think critically even if they are not native English speakers. That is why the complexity of the language can be reduced, but not the intellectual demands.

The "dumbing down" of the curriculum and failure to promote higher levels of thinking is a serious issue with ELL students, as noted in the literature (de Jong, Harper, & Coady, 2013; Verplaetse & Migliacci, 2008). The realization that English language learners can think critically is an important step in meeting their academic needs. As Danling Fu (2004) stated, "We need to understand that they are as intelligent as other students of their age" (p. 10).

Finally, preservice teachers grasped the importance of differentiating instruction to accommodate for language proficiency. They understood it was a difficult but necessary proposition, as noted by the following quote in a preservice teacher's final reflection:

> I have learned that there is so much to do with ESL students. This is related to differentiated instruction, giving them more time, and using a lot more visuals, among many other things. From the experiences I have had in an ESL classroom, I had to make adjustments to my lesson so that the students understood the material more. Would it have been easier to stick with my lesson? Yes. Would it have been easier to not pay attention to their needs? Probably. However, this is not a good way to teach! You have to expect the unexpected and that is definitely true when it comes to an ESL class. You have to tweak your lessons and add and take away some material. For any lesson, you need to be willing to change if you see that the students are struggling.

The recognition that they needed to make accommodations for ELL students was uppermost in the teachers' minds. They frequently discussed lessons that failed because they did not scaffold the content in accordance with ELL students' proficiency and those that were successful as a result of on-the-spot changes they made. They also made frequent note of the importance of knowing what the English language proficiency level of a student was.

Practical Implications for Teacher Educators

The bleak picture of ELL students in Texas, evidenced by the statistics, is not uncommon in the rest of the United States (Kim, 2011). Teacher educators dedicated to social justice cannot wait for colleges of education to catch up with changing demographics. It is critical that teacher educators themselves develop opportunities to engage preservice teachers as part of the solution. Service learning presents itself as viable and practical alternative in the absence of formal field experiences. In order to design and implement a successful service learning project with English language learners, we suggest that teacher educators keep in mind the following steps, which guided our service learning project. First, they must be aware of the local context for ELL students. This means it is necessary to leave the university and immerse themselves in local public schools. Second, teachers must be asked what they need rather than told what they should do. Third, preservice teachers should collaborate with classroom teachers at every stage of the project. They must put community needs at the forefront of their practice. Finally, reflection should be a key component for all: preservice teachers, classroom teachers, and teacher educators. Every stakeholder should be afforded a venue to discuss process, outcomes, challenges, successes, and failures.

All in all, while this service learning project certainly did not provide the extensive field experience that we wished was present in the educator preparation program, it represented an attempt to plant the seeds of change. Rather than waiting for administrative solutions, we worked within the existing system and our primary sphere of influence: preparing the next generation of teachers. We encourage other ESL teacher educators to look for similar service learning and community engagement projects. As is evident in the statistics we presented at the beginning of this chapter, English language learners cannot wait for colleges of education or state education agencies or school districts to do what is needed.

References

Berger Kaye, C. (2010). *The complete guide to service learning* (2nd ed.). Minneapolis, MN: Free Spirit.

Bollin, G. (2007). Preparing teachers for Hispanic immigrant children: A service learning approach. *Journal of Latinos & Education, 6*(2), 177–189.

de Jong, E., Harper, C., & Coady, M. (2013). Enhanced knowledge and skills for elementary mainstream teachers of English language learners. *Theory into Practice, 52*(2), 89–97.

Echevarria, J., Vogt, M. E., & Short, D. (2000). *Making content comprehensible for English language learners: The SIOP® Model.* Needham Heights, MA: Allyn & Bacon.

Enterprise Services. (2013). *Sam Houston State University Cognos report.* Retrieved from http://www.shsu.edu/dept/it@sam/enterprise-services/making-requests.html

Feistritzer, C. E. (2011). Profile of teachers in the US 2011. National Center for Education Information. http://www.ncei.com/Profile_Teachers_US_2011.pdf

Fu, D. (2004). Teaching ELL students in the regular classroom at the secondary level. *Voices from the Middle, 11*(4), 8–15.

Gordon, D. (2004). "I'm tired. You clean and cook." Shifting gender identities and second language socialization. *TESOL Quarterly, 38*(3), 437–457.

Hawkins, M., & Norton, B. (2009). Critical language teacher education. In A. Burns & J. Richards (Eds.), *Cambridge guide to second language teacher education* (pp. 30–39). Cambridge, England: Cambridge University Press.

Heilig, J. V., & Holme, J. J. (2013). Nearly 50 years post–Jim Crow: Persisting and expansive school segregation of African American, Latino/a, and ELL students in Texas. *Education and Urban Society, 45*(5), 609–632.

Kaur, B. (2012). Equity and social justice in teaching and teacher education. *Teaching and Teacher Education, 28*(4), 485–492.

Kim, J. (2011). *Relationships among and between ELL status, demographic characteristics, enrollment history, and school persistence* (Research Report No. 810). Retrieved from http://www.cse.ucla.edu/products/reports/R810.pdf

Kumaravadivelu, B. (2006). TESOL methods: Changing tracks, challenging trends. *TESOL Quarterly, 40,* 59–81.

Lave, J., & Wenger, E. (1991). *Situated learning: Legitimate peripheral participation.* New York, NY: Cambridge University Press.

Lortie, D. (1975). *Schoolteacher: A sociological study.* Chicago, IL: University of Chicago Press.

LULAC v. State of Texas. Civil Action No. 6:14-CV-138. (D. Texas. 2014). http://www.scribd.com/doc/229268862/Complaint-Filed-by-LULAC-MALDEF-against-Texas-Education-Agency-other-districts

Morgan, G. P., & Vaughn, S. (2011). *A review of high school completion rates and drop out prevention for students identified with limited English proficiency: A report to the 82nd Texas Legislature.* Austin: Texas Education Agency.

Ramsay, M. C. (2013). Employed teacher demographics 2009–2013. Retrieved from Texas Education Agency website: http://www.tea.state.tx.us/index2.aspx?id=5033&menu_id=886&menu_id2=794

Rodriguez, A. D. (2013). Bilingual and ESL pre-service teachers learn about effective instruction for ELLs through meaningful collaboration. *GIST Education and Learning Research Journal, 7,* 12–34.

Shulman, L. S. (1986). Those who understand: Knowledge growth in teaching. *Educational Researcher, 15*(2), 4–14.

Stetser, M., & Stillwell, R. (2014). *Public high school four-year on-time graduation rates and event dropout rates: School Years 2010–11 and 2011–12* (NCES 2014-391). Retrieved from U.S. Department of Education, National Center for Education Statistics website: http://nces.ed.gov/pubsearch/pubsinfo.asp?pubid=2014391

Texas Education Agency. (2013). *Snapshot 2013: Summary tables state totals* [school district profiles]. Retrieved from http://ritter.tea.state.tx.us/perfreport/snapshot/2013/state.html

U.S. Census Bureau. (2013). *State & county quickfacts: Texas.* Retrieved from http://quickfacts.census.gov/qfd/states/48000.html

Verplaetse, L. S., & Migliacci, N. (2008). Making mainstream content comprehensible through sheltered instruction. In L. S. Verplaetse & N. Migliacci (Eds.), *Inclusive pedagogy for English language learners: A handbook of research-informed practices* (pp. 127–165). New York, NY: Lawrence Erlbaum.

CHAPTER 18

Pedagogies, Experiences, Access, Collaboration, and Equality (PEACE)

Reforming Language Pedagogies to Promote Social Justice for Undocumented Immigrants

Christine E. Poteau
Alvernia University

This chapter begins with the journey of the author's immigrant family as a principal source of influence on the author to pursue studies in the fields of social justice and language education. While the author's family story represents an isolated experience of a "documented" family, nevertheless it unmasks a context that many immigrants face. With a review of the current state of the undocumented immigrant as a linguistic minority, the chapter includes research on the misperceptions and misrecognitions of undocumented individuals and interdisciplinary pedagogies that serve to promote global social justice learning. Within the constructs of an interdisciplinary framework, this chapter examines the role of intercultural competence skill development in transformative social justice education using collaborative service-learning models and interactive online tasks. Challenges and benefits of these pedagogical methods are also addressed in the chapter. Exploring the roles of each in the formation of a global life-long learner, specific classroom practices of service-learning and online tasks that incorporate self-reflection, critical thinking, meaningful interactions, and collaboration are reviewed.

———

With tears in her eyes, a former graduate student approached me after our English as a Second Language (ESL) certification course to express how a child of a refugee family that fled a war-torn nation forever altered her pedagogical and social justice perspectives. During an undergraduate linguistics course, another student courageously shared with our class the story of her undocumented parents' struggle to remain in the United States with her. Her parents' dream was to provide their daughter with a safe home environment and educational opportunities. In response to her personal family story, one student trembled and cried to admit that her grandparent refused to shop in certain stores because of the Spanish-speaking customers who frequented the shops within her community. This student also noted that prior to the beginning of the undergraduate linguistics course that included serving undocumented families, she firmly believed that the increasing number of minority language speakers in the region was the fundamental reason for economic downturns. She was proud to admit that her experiences in the course and serving undocumented families transformed her perspectives on social justice practices and human life. As a result of her personal transformation, she chose to continue serving undocumented families after completing the course.

Poignant moments such as these represent personal and meaningful metamorphoses. It is difficult to pinpoint a decisive moment that led to my studies in social justice and language pedagogies. Growing up with an immigrant mother from Brazil who experienced inequalities unquestionably inspired me to pursue global studies and issues surrounding linguistic minorities.

My family's journey began with my Ukrainian grandparents and eldest aunt (an infant at the time), who were left with no other option but to flee the only nation they had ever known, seeking refuge in a camp in Austria during World War II. While residing in the camp, my grandparents had their second child. Leaving Austria, they fled to Brazil, where my mother was born and raised. My grandparents' work in Brazil was often not enough to provide sufficient nourishment for their three daughters, a painful childhood memory shared by my mother and aunts. Although my mother's childhood in Brazil was not free from hardship, the embracing and spirited community was truly uplifting. From the neighborhood dog, Gringo, greeting my mother at her school window to playing with neighborhood children in the street, the simple childhood experiences that she found gratifying were brought to an abrupt stop when she became an immigrant on her 13th birthday.

As a young Brazilian immigrant in the United States, my mother worked in a sweatshop during her summer vacations to help purchase a house and provide for her family. She attended public schools in an urban community that did not offer ESL classes or any form of academic support for nonnative speakers of English. Consequently, at the age of 13, she was placed into a first-grade classroom and faced discrimination from teachers and classmates. Difficult experiences such as these bolstered her self-determination to learn English, and she did so by studying a dictionary and reading any books she could find. Reflecting upon this difficult experience with my mother affected how I take into account the unique backgrounds and learning styles of each and every student in my classroom. This has also affected my research on how educators across disciplines can work collaboratively to facilitate learning experiences and improve our pedagogical practices with a common goal of promoting global social justice.

The challenges my family experienced, coupled with the meshing of cultures and languages, enabled me to a gain a deeper understanding of diversity. The unique learning experiences linguistic minorities encounter and the pedagogies we implement should serve to support our students in their effort to become lifelong learners. As a victim of discrimination and a witness of racial and ethnic prejudices against my mother and peers during my formative years, I learned and continue to learn how to approach language pedagogy. Helping learners experience language as a form of culture can support and encourage social justice practices.

My informal knowledge also stems from my experiences in urban public schools during my preteenage years. During my youth, I was fortunate to be exposed to and learn from my multicultural and multilingual family and community. Nevertheless, attending elementary school and a few months of middle school in an urban public school system was also a difficult experience. The academic support systems were underfunded and dedicated and creative educators were faced with an immeasurable pedagogical task. My parents' decision to move from our urban home to a suburban community flipped my world upside-down, experiencing two completely different worlds within one region.

My middle and high school experiences in a nationally ranked blue ribbon school district in an affluent suburb helped pave the way for my initial stages of personal involvement within social justice studies. This school system provided me with an exceptional academic program, extraordinary educational resources, and the oppor-tunity to meet many international students. However, it also exposed me to the harsh realities nonnative speakers face in secondary school settings: a world of isolation and the discrimination new students can face entering another community. Although my personal experiences cannot compare to the struggles many nonnative speakers face in a new nation, I have, nevertheless, felt the powerful discriminatory actions and words from others. Shoved into a locker by two older male students while gathering my books and verbally ridiculed for my urban roots are just a few examples of my experi-ences as a new student in a suburban middle school. These personal experiences have, undoubtedly, transformed my pedagogical approaches that enabled me to examine the learner as critical participant in the formation of a collaborative learning environment, which radiates a co-construction of knowledge-building and diverse experiences from each member.

With a determination to study the complexities of social justice and diversity through language and pedagogical studies during my undergraduate career, I opted to major in Spanish and minor in linguistics and education. By observing classes in ESL and Spanish in affluent suburban to underrepresented secondary schools, I gained additional formal theoretical knowledge of academic and social inequities. My grad-uate studies in Spanish applied linguistics and collaborations with faculty and peers from around the world triggered my profound research interest in interdisciplinary pedagogies, intercultural competency, linguistic minorities, social justice, and affective factors in Second Language Acquisition (SLA). Additionally, my teaching experiences and learning from my high school, undergraduate, and graduate students in disciplines including ESL, Spanish, and linguistics in urban and suburban settings furthered my research interests. My personal background and my teaching and research experiences resulted in my commitment to promoting social justice in all of my classes. Social justice pedagogies begin in my classes by guiding students to explore beyond the classroom and textbook contexts and examine the social justice issues surrounding immigration and language in local and global contexts.

Accordingly, the subsequent section will review three primary areas: the role of the undocumented immigrant as linguistic minority; social justice education; and intercultural competence skill development and service-learning pedagogies.

Relevant Literature

Natural disasters, poverty, wars, and violence narrowly exemplify conditions that can precipitate immigration. According to a study from the Pew Research Center, reports from U.S. Homeland Security indicate that the number of unaccompanied children detained at the U.S. border has almost doubled in less than one year as a result of extreme poverty in Guatemala and escalating drug and gang violence in El Salvador and Honduras (Gonzalez-Barrera, Krogstad, & Lopez, 2014). While the Spanish-speaking population currently represents a linguistic minority in the United States, Chandler (2014) notes that the population is "the fastest growing immigrant group" in the nation, evidencing the urgent need to develop equitable access to educational resources (p. 1).

It is also equally important to note that undocumented minors come from other nations, including (but not limited to) Bangladesh, Brazil, Canada, China, Croatia, France, Ghana, Indonesia, Iran, Israel, Nigeria, Pakistan, the Philippines, and Taiwan (Chan, 2010, p. 29). Each group encompasses different official languages and dialects and a multitude of unique cultures. Many undocumented individuals in the United States face obstacles, including "poverty, assimilation, language barriers, violence in their community or home environment, lack of access to health care, and mental health issues" (Eusebio & Mendoza, n.d., p. 5). In the same vein, Chung, Bemak, and Grabosky (2011) report that intolerance has ensued as a result of "discussions about undocumented groups [which] include myths and stereotypes of immigrants that consist of the wide-sweeping misperceptions that most immigrants have entered the U.S. illegally; are taking non-immigrants' jobs; misusing resources and services; hurting the economy" (p. 88). These misperceptions, in turn, impede global progress and prevent social recognition.

Recognition, according to Honneth (2003), "locates the core of all experiences of injustice in the withdrawal of social recognition, in the phenomena of humiliation and disrespect" (p. 134). Curricula that lack recognition of a learner's language background, for instance, can impede literacy development. Research consistently shows that educating linguistic minority children in a second language (L2) prior to a child's development of a first language (L1) can result in detrimental effects (e.g., developmental, psychological, linguistic), emphasizing the need for additive L2 learning (as opposed to L1 replacement) (Cummins, 1984; Hickey & Ó Cainín, 2001; Magga, Nicolaisen, Trask, Dunbar, & Skutnabb-Kangas, 2005; Ovando, Combs, &

Collier, 2006). For instance, Yoshikawa's (2011) study on early development of illegal immigrants' children revealed that these children exhibited substantially low language and cognitive developmental levels because of numerous factors, including a lack of opportunities for L1 development. Thus, there is a growing need to provide supportive learning environments through bilingual and multilingual forms of instruction.

Although the development of bilingual and multilingual programs may be viewed as an insurmountable task, Magga, Nicolaisen, Trask, Dunbar, and Skutnabb-Kangas (2005) identify several countries that have implemented these types of programs in an effort to provide pedagogies that encourage multilingualism and, at the same time, lead to high academic achievement levels and increased support for learners' identity expression. Thus, there is an increased global need to promote cultural and linguistic awareness and develop innovative curricula that encompass social justice education. As defined by Bell (2007), *social justice education* refers to "an interdisciplinary conceptual framework for analyzing multiple forms of oppression and a set of inter-active, experiential pedagogical principles to help learners understand the meaning of social difference and oppression both in the social system and in their personal lives" (p. 2). Hence, social justice education diversifies learners' experiences via encouraging social recognition, self-reflection, collaborative dialogue, and development of critical thinking skills, each of which allows learners to meaningfully build upon their inter-cultural competence skills.

Intercultural competence has been defined as the "effective management of interaction between people who, to some degree or another, represent different or divergent affective, cognitive, and behavioral orientations to the world" (Spitzberg & Changnon, 2009, p. 7). Intercultural competence extends beyond awareness and entails cultural sensitivity and effective use of intercultural skills that contribute to social justice practices. Intercultural competence includes critical thinking skill development and self-reflection to evolve from an ethnocentric perspective by means of critical evaluation of an intercultural context for effective communicative practices. From social recognition to critically examining societal power imbalances and individual attitudes, thoughts, and actions within diverse social contexts, language educators can transform educational experiences with a goal of engaging all participants by design-ing cross-cultural classroom environments that integrate the cultural and linguistic complexities of an interaction.

For example, in an ESL classroom setting, learners can self-reflect on the role of language and culture in professional contexts in both their native homeland and the United States. Following this critical self-reflection, learners can participate in role-play exchanges with native speakers of English in professional contexts. These interactive exchanges can help learners apply learned cultural and linguistic practices in an interaction. As a concluding activity, learners and native speakers can collectively reflect on the role of social differences in interactions and generate strategies that can eliminate oppression in professions and society. These tasks provide supportive con-texts for individual transformation by linking social justice education to intercultural competence skill development. Connecting these two frameworks in the classroom can enable all participants to examine diverse social and oppressive conditions within and outside of the classroom context.

These types of intercultural competence building strategies serve as a key element in social justice foreign language and L2 education (Lojacono, 2013). Broadly defined, *foreign* language (FL) contexts principally refer to an environment in which the learner lacks exposure to the target language outside of class (e.g., French class in the United States), whereas L2 contexts are those that refer to exposure within and outside of the classroom setting (e.g., ESL class in the United States). While many FL classes in the United States serve as either core requirements or optional coursework, one important role of L2 classes is to develop L2 proficiency for academic and/or professional success. Nevertheless, some FL and L2 educators share a common goal of reforming educational programs and promoting social justice awareness through increased intercultural competence skill development.

Since FL and L2 educators often serve as a learner's first encounter with the target language (Hawkins & Bonny, 2009), educators can co-construct interactive classrooms that extend beyond the classroom context to include diverse cultural values and linguistic norms within societies to enhance intercultural skill development (as in the previously reviewed role-play example). Moreover, institutions that offer both FL and L2 courses are ideal learning spaces to connect all learners in a multitude of intercultural tasks that address and apply social justice practices. Bridging the FL and L2 context gaps by using collaborative exchanges between learners within each group is one way that FL and L2 educators can encourage a community of lifelong learners while fostering social justice learning and developing learners' intercultural competence.

Constructing this community of FL and L2 learners within a *transformative social justice* framework, "calls on people to develop a process of social and individual conscientization" (Torres, 2008, p. 7). Within this framework, Paulo Freire's (1979) use of the concept of *conscientização* represents a "método pedagógico de libertação dos camponeses analfabetos" (a pedagogical method that liberates illiterate peasants) (p. 8). In essence, this means that through education the illiterate can be freed from oppression. In both FL and L2 contexts, *conscientização* begins by exposing learners to social oppression to raise awareness of marginalization of linguistic minorities with primary goals of actively involving all learners to develop new perspectives on language as culture and to collaboratively engage in solutions to combat oppression in society.

Transformative social justice learning facilitates social transformation and self-reflection and enables learners to understand and learn about themselves and the world while "promoting positive cross-national and cross-cultural understanding" (Osborn, 2006, p. 17). As in the previous role-play example, connecting FL and L2 learners within and outside of the classroom context facilitates a global understanding of individual experiences. This can help reshape attitudes toward undocumented individuals through these meaningful learning experiences for learners in FL and ESL studies. In light of the current research on social justice learning, the following section will explore two classroom practices (SL and online tasks) that promote social justice learning.

Classroom Practices

From isolated to inner-city communities, globalization has touched all aspects of societies around the world. Nevertheless, social justice within the global community has not been easily practiced. The classroom practices reviewed in this section serve to encourage learners within and outside of the classroom context to seek new collaborative experiences as lifelong learners.

Service learning (SL) can function as a path for all participants to engage in meaningful discourse. SL can be defined as "a course-based, credit-bearing educational experience in which students (a) participate in an organized service activity that meets identified community needs and (b) reflect on the service activity in such a way as to gain further understanding of course content, a broader appreciation of the discipline" (Bringle & Hatcher, 1995, p. 112). SL enables learners and community members to become active participants, benefitting all involved in a co-construction of diverse and meaningful experiences.

Research (Green, 2001; Hale, 1999; Overfield, 1997; Pak, 2010) on SL has revealed numerous advantages in language learning, including students' and community members' increased development of the target language and cultural cognizance. Additionally, SL can serve to develop linguistic and cultural understandings of segregated community members. Research (Gunnarsson, 2013; Roberts, 2007) indicates minimal opportunities for L2 cultural and linguistic development for immigrants with low-paying jobs, since these individuals face increased isolation from majority language groups in these particular workplaces. Thus, SL offers meaningful opportunities to learn from one another through active engagement among all participants.

SL has also faced critical analyses (Hesford, 2005), since it can also present challenges without methodical task development. Nevertheless, SL can be an effective tool that can offer cultural and linguistic interactive exchanges and promote development of FL and ESL skills.

As noted in the previous section, SL can have a powerful effect on learners and community members. In many ways, SL is a pedagogical tool that integrates a form of performative instruction, which uses "unique elements in each classroom [to create] space for change, invention, [and] spontaneous shifts" (Hooks, 1994, p. 11). As a performative pedagogy, SL allows students and community members to collaboratively incorporate personal perspectives in spontaneous and continuous dialogue that can, in turn, promote social transformation. SL can take place in various contexts that help learners and community members in a reciprocal and global learning process. For these reasons, the author implements SL pedagogical methods in university courses with an ultimate goal of promoting social justice in linguistics and FL studies. Students in these SL courses are assigned to serve at a U.S. Homeland Security facility housing undocumented families.

During the SL, students are given an option to complete various interdisciplinary tasks that address their major field of study with specific guidelines provided by the educator. Interdisciplinary tasks can include FL and/or L2 instruction and health literacy initiatives. This SL program can be implemented in various university courses including ESL, FL, health sciences, law, and teacher education. Depending on the course, numerous interdisciplinary tasks can be implemented to help prepare students for SL tasks and achieve predetermined course goals.

Prior to beginning SL, for example, have students identify five pertinent concepts on social justice. Specifically, students write what the concept of *language* signifies to them. Next, students define *culture*. Then, ask students to explain whether these two particular concepts are connected and how they are (or are not) related. Following this, students define the concept of *identity* and discuss whether this term correlates with the previous two. After defining these concepts, students define the concepts of *immigrant* and, finally, *justice*. The purpose of the specific, one-by-one ordering of these concepts is to avoid any potential influence on their reflections about the subsequent concept. Students share their definitions in pairs; then the class gathers to reflect and discuss the five concepts. After their SL, each student revises his or her definitions of the five concepts and shares this new knowledge and experience with the class.

Throughout their SL program, students keep journals in which to reflect on their daily experiences and make connections to course topics. In the journal, students also include newly learned cultural and/or linguistic elements and questions and/or comments about their SL and the course. At the end of the semester, they submit their SL journals and conduct a research investigation in which each student posits a research question (based on the course and SL program) for their final research paper. Students' research included topics on various forms of oppression, its consequences on society, and methods that seek to improve current conditions.

Research examples included the effects of educational policies on linguistic minorities in the United States and the European Union, factors that influence language attitudes and legal rights implications in the United States, and comparative analyses of linguistic minorities and healthcare policies in the United States, the United Kingdom, and Canada. The course and SL enabled students to identify specific research areas of interest that allowed them to examine human experiences across societies. Students who participated in the SL reported positive learning experiences serving undocumented adults and children. The undocumented adults and children looked forward to meeting with students on a daily basis to share their personal stories and struggles to immigrate to the United States.

The undocumented children, for example, excitedly anticipated the arrival of students. As their guide, I help my students create SL activities for undocumented children and adults that U.S. Homeland Security facility officials authorize as acceptable. For example, undocumented children's SL activities included reading exercises and writing summaries based on my students' personally selected children's books in English. Following these exercises, the children reflect on creating their own short narrative or reflect on one of their favorite books in written and oral forms in English.

Depending on the course, these activities are also completed in Spanish to further undocumented children's L1 development and also promote social recognition of the target language. This step also supports FL students with additional Spanish language practice. Adult activities have included oral and written activities on a variety of topics including (but not limited to) soccer, music, health literacy, and personal background information on their native homeland and journey to the United States. Most of the undocumented families at the facility noted that they attempted to escape domestic abuse situations or crime-infested communities or wanted to provide academic opportunities for their child or children. For example, one individual from South America noted that he came with his 15-year-old daughter to try to provide her with a better quality of life in the United States. His wife had already reached the United States, prior to their arrival. He and his daughter were detained at an international airport and sent to the facility. While these difficult experiences can never be erased, he and a number of adults at the facility noted that the residents looked forward to the SL activities and interactions. These encounters were the only possible interactions the residents had with the community. Many students said that these encounters contributed to intercultural skill development and also cultivated new learning experiences that fostered a socially just environment. Without SL, access to the outside world is impossible for the residents, just as it is impossible for students to access and become exposed to undocumented individuals' perspectives and experiences.

These are just a few types of several SL program interactions that cannot be duplicated in a classroom context. Students shared their perspectives at the end of the semester and noted how the SL served as a transformative experience that altered their perspectives on the role of language in society. Students learned that language is a complex form of culture that shapes an individual's identity. Students who themselves are immigrants or whose parents are recent immigrants also expressed how working with undocumented families transformed their perspectives on the undocumented individual.

Incorporating online resources is another way to promote lifelong learning outside of the classroom environment. Online tasks create collaborative learning spaces, helping learners "transmit their skills and knowledges to fellow students and teachers alike" (Kahn & Kellner, 2008, p. 29). For example, integrating songs from various websites (e.g., SoundCloud, iTunes) featuring vernacular English and dialects of English not only can serve to broaden students' understanding of English varieties but also can contribute to global tolerance and social justice awareness through exposure to cultural and linguistic diversities in the ESL classroom setting (Poteau, 2012). Additionally, students can practice listening and reading skills while gaining cultural knowledge of unique instruments within a song. Students and educators can incorporate global music in the classroom and share personal interests while practicing writing skills. As an online task, links to specific music videos can be posted on a course blog or online discussion board to give learners a way to gain visual exposure to various cultural elements (e.g., communities, instruments). After watching the music video, students can post comments and questions on a course blog or online discussion board. Students can also post their own links to music videos on a course blog or discussion board describing how the song embodies an aspect of their culture.

As a social justice pedagogical approach, this task embraces an inclusive and collaborative learning environment that allows learners to incorporate personal cultural elements. Class members gain opportunities to address social identity misrepresentations and eradicate stereotypes. After each student posts a music video link, students can stream the videos and post comments and questions on the blog or online discussion board to reflect on cultures, human identities, and societies. With a social justice aim, songs can promote tolerance of multicultural identities and increase cultural awareness by shaping a community of learners who recognize and value diverse social identities in our global community. This activity consists of a series of collaborative tasks that diversifies learners' cultural experiences with exercises in listening, reading, and writing.

For example, I integrate music and cultural videos from around the world in FL and L2 contexts, some of which include footage of the *favelas* (impoverished communities throughout Brazil) and instruments that are unique to Brazil. In FL and L2 contexts, music and videos can serve as powerful tools that provide learners with meaningful experiences of social justice issues in lyrics and/or visual imagery. Depending on the course, translations of song lyrics may need to be provided. After class discussions on the music, students post their own links on our discussion board with descriptions of their posted musical video and its social justice importance. Following this, peers are asked to respond to each other by posting comments and questions about the song, instruments, artists, region, or anything that sparked curiosity, and about how the selected piece influenced their thoughts on social justice and diversity.

Using online links to poems in FL and L2 classrooms is another task that offers diverse experiences and perspectives on immigration and social justice. Songs and online links can foster collaborative and meaningful learning environments, since many FL and L2 texts feature limited authentic connections to global societies. Hence, while many ESL texts highlight isolated cases of immigrant stories, online resources can offer educators a wide array of useful and pertinent resources. For example, in Gulliver's (2010) review of the immigration success stories provided in 24 ESL texts used in government-funded language classes in Ontario, he concludes that "these stories of newcomers legitimate the pain that newcomers experience by representing these hardships as inevitable but transitional economic struggles and character-building experiences that will transform them into hard-working and successful members of the national community" (p. 741). He argues that educators are responsible for implementing resources and employing pedagogies that consider diverse immigrant experiences that do not delineate a single experiential pattern. Similarly, Taylor (2006) highlights various forms of cultural racism in ESL curricula that marginalize students by presenting culture as otherness and failing to take into account cultural diversities of English language learners. Thus, online resources can provide educators with a multitude of appropriate literary texts that foster a collaborative learning environment that encourages learners to actively participate and share personal perspectives.

Examples of poems on social justice for university-level courses in ESL include those written by undocumented Asian American college students, which can be found on *Hyphen Magazine: Asia America unabridged* website; Jimmy Santiago Baca's "Immigrants in our own land"; and Christy Namee Eriksen's "What does an illegal immigrant look like?" As a pre-reading exercise, students can develop their own interpretations of what they expect to read and learn, beginning with the title of the selected poem. As students read the selected poem, students can list new words presented in the poem to increase vocabulary development and begin analysis of the poem. Analysis can include identifying tone, imagery, symbolic elements, and structure. Next, students can reflect on the selected poem and share their thoughts (e.g., identifying contrasts between experiences) with the class on oppression and social justice issues presented in the poem. As a closing activity, students can write their own poem to creatively express their personal story on oppression and social justice, which they can share with peers during class or by virtually posting their work on a privately maintained online class blog or discussion board.

The classroom practices reviewed do not serve simply to build cultural or linguistic appreciation. These practices serve also to build socially just and tolerant global societies that enable all to flourish in an equitable and impartial community.

Conclusion

While educators are aware of misrecognition and administrative academic tracking errors (Callahand, 2005; North, 2006; Sharkey & Layzer, 2000) because of an individual's linguistic background, it is possible to collaboratively implement new interdisciplinary programs that provide each learner with equitable learning environments. As SL programs can offer students a multilingual, multicultural approach to social justice learning through intercultural competence development, online resources can also serve to encourage a diverse learning opportunity to explore and reflect. Cultivating a social justice learning environment with an interdisciplinary approach promotes global lifelong learning. Taking the classroom to the community with SL and bringing learners together in virtual contexts serve to provide pedagogies, experiences, access, collaboration, and equality (PEACE) in our globally changing world.

References

Bell, L. A. (2007). Theoretical foundations for social justice education. In M. Adams, L. A. Bell, & P. Griffin (Eds.), *Teaching for diversity and social justice* (pp. 1–14). New York, NY: Routledge.

Bringle, R., & Hatcher, J. A. (1995). A service learning curriculum for faculty. *Michigan Journal of Community Service Learning, 2*(1), 112–122.

Callahan, R. M. (2005). Tracking and high school English learners: Limiting opportunity to learn. *American Educational Research Journal, 42*(2), 305–328.

Chan, B. (2010). Not just a Latino issue: Undocumented students in higher education. *Journal of College Admission*. Retrieved from http://www.nacacnet.org/research/KnowledgeCenter/Documents/Marketplace/NotJustLatino.pdf

Chandler, M. A. (2014, July 8). Growing number of kindergarteners are Hispanic. *The Washington Post*. Retrieved from http://www.washingtonpost.com/blogs/local/wp/2014/07/08/growing-number-of-kindergarteners-are-hispanic/

Chung, R. C. Y., Bemak, F., & Grabosky, T. K. (2011). Multicultural-social justice leadership strategies: Counseling and advocacy with immigrants. *Journal for Social Action in Counseling and Psychology, 3*(1), 86–102.

Cummins, J. (1984). *Bilingualism and special education: Issues in assessment and pedagogy*. Austin, TX: Pro-Ed.

Eusebio, C., & Mendoza, F. (n.d.). The case for undocumented students in higher education. *Educators for Fair Consideration (E4FC)*. Retrieved from http://e4fc.org/images/E4FC_TheCase.pdf

Freire, P. (1979). *Conscientização: Teoría e prática da libertação*. São Paulo, Brazil: Cortez e Moraes.

Gonzalez-Barrera, A., Krogstad, J. M., & Lopez, M. H. (2014). DHS: Violence, poverty is driving children to flee Central America to U.S. Retrieved from the Pew Research Center website: http://www.pewresearch.org/fact-tank/2014/07/01/dhs-violence-poverty-is-driving-children-to-flee-central-america-to-u-s/

Green, A. E. (2001). "But you aren't white": Racial perspectives and service learning. *Michigan Journal of Community Service Learning, 8*(10), 18–26.

Gulliver, T. (2010). Immigrant success stories in ESL textbooks. *TESOL Quarterly, 44*(4), 725–745.

Gunnarsson, B. L. (2013). Multilingualism in the workplace. *Annual Review of Applied Linguistics, 33*, 162–189.

Hale, A. (1999). Service-learning and Spanish: A missing link. In J. Hellebrandt & L. T. Varona (Eds.), *Construyendo puentes (Building bridges): Concepts and models for service-learning in Spanish* (pp. 9–32).Washington, DC: American Association for Higher Education.

Hawkins, M., & Bonny, N. (2009). Critical language teacher education. In A. Burns & J. Richards (Eds.), *Cambridge guide to second language teacher education* (pp. 30–39). Cambridge, England: Cambridge University Press.

Hesford, W. S. (2005). Global/local labor politics and the promise of service learning. In L. Gray-Rosendale & S. Rosendale (Eds.), *Radical relevance: Toward a scholarship of the whole left* (pp. 183–202). Albany: State University of New York Press.

Hickey, T., & Ó Cainín, P. (2001). First language maintenance and second language acquisition of a minority language in kindergarten. In M. Almgren, A. Barrena, M-J. Ezeizabarrena, I. Idiazabal, & B. MacWhinney (Eds.), *Research on child language acquisition. Proceedings of 8th Conference for the Study of Child Language* (pp. 137–150). Somerville, MA: Cascadilla Press.

Honneth, A. (2003). *Redistribution or recognition?: A political-philosophical exchange*. New York, NY: Verso.

Hooks, B. (1994). *Teaching to transgress: Education as the practice of freedom*. London, England: Routledge.

Kahn, R., & Kellner, D. (2008). Paulo Freire and Ivan Illich: Technology, politics and the reconstruction of education. In C. A. Torres & P. Noguera (Eds.), *Social justice education for teachers* (pp. 13–34). Rotterdam, The Netherlands: Sense Publishers.

Lojacono, F. (2013). Foreign language acquisition: Fostering social justice and internationalization within web 2.0 environments. *Journal of Arts and Humanities (JAH), 2*(10), 45–55.

Magga, O. H., Nicolaisen, I., Trask, M., Dunbar, R., & Skutnabb-Kangas, T. (2005). *Indigenous children's education and indigenous languages*. New York, NY: United Nations.

North, C. (2006). More than words? Delving into the substantive meaning(s) of "social justice" in education. *Review of Educational Research, 76*(4), 507–535.

Osborn, T. A. (2006). *Teaching world languages for social justice: A sourcebook of principles and practices.* Mahwah, NJ: Lawrence Erlbaum.

Ovando, C. J., Combs, M. C., & Collier, V. P. (2006). *Bilingual and ESL classrooms: Teaching in multicultural classrooms* (4th ed.). Boston, MA: McGraw Hill.

Overfield, D. M. (1997). From the margins to the mainstream: Foreign language education and community-based learning. *Foreign Language Annals, 30*(4), 485–491.

Pak, C. S. (2010). Toward a development of global communities within: Service learning projects in a business Spanish course. *Global Business Languages, 5*(1), 1–23.

Poteau, C. E. (2012). Music to my ears: Using songs on the Internet to teach reading. In R. Day (Ed.), *New Ways in Teaching Reading (NWTR): New ways in TESOL series* (Rev. ed.) (pp. 284–286). Alexandria, VA: Teachers of English to Speakers of Other Languages (TESOL).

Roberts, C. (2007). Multilingualism in the workplace. In P. Auer & L. Wei (Eds.), *Handbook of multilingualism and multilingual communication* (pp. 405–422). Berlin, Germany: De Gruyter.

Sharkey, J., & Layzer, C. (2000). Whose definition of success? Identifying factors that affect English language learners' access to academic success and resources. *TESOL Quarterly, 34*(2), 352–368.

Spitzberg, B. H., & Changnon, G. (2009). Conceptualizing intercultural competence. In D. K. Deardorff (Ed.), *The SAGE handbook of intercultural competence* (pp. 2–52). Thousand Oaks, CA: Sage.

Taylor, L. (2006). Wrestling with race: The implications of integrative antiracism education for immigrant ESL youth. *TESOL Quarterly, 40*(3), 519–544.

Torres, C. A. (2008). Paulo Freire and social justice education: An introduction. In C. A. Torres & P. Noguera (Eds.), *Social justice education for teachers: Paulo Freire and the possible dream* (pp. 1–11). Rotterdam, The Netherlands: Sense Publishers.

Yoshikawa, H. (2011). *Immigrants raising citizens: Undocumented parents and their young children.* New York, NY: Russell Sage Foundation.

CHAPTER 19

Teaching Undocumented Immigrants in the United States

A Seditious Secret and a Call to Action

Michael L. Conners

E. L. Haynes Public Charter School

> This work deals with a very obvious truth: just as the oppressor, in order to oppress, needs a theory of oppressive action, so the oppressed, in order to become free, also need a theory of action.
>
> —*Paolo Friere,* Pedagogy of the Oppressed

As educators, we face a multitude of dilemmas. From deciding whether to grade more papers or go to the park with our families, to wrestling with the phenomenon of student self-segregation in our own classrooms, we are constantly wondering what we "*should* do." This chapter illustrates how teaching for social justice can begin to ease the burden of a dilemma for a teacher while it also can empower and motivate students to positively change their communities. It begins with a brief personal history followed by research objectives and guiding questions surrounding teaching undocumented immigrants and their access to higher education in the United States. Relevant literature as well as a teacher-developed intervention plan is discussed in-depth throughout. Additionally, I have included two prominent student essays (Appendixes C and D) that were sent to both local and national stakeholders and eventually published online in the *Washington Post* (Matthews, 2010) as part of culminating class project.

Personal History

As a public school English Language Learner (ELL) teacher in Washington, DC, I have taught students ages 7 to 21 who have made (or whose parents have made) incomprehensible decisions to sacrifice everything to come to the United States for a better life for themselves and their families. A significant majority of my students are undocumented immigrants who risked their lives to cross the U.S.-Mexican border because they fervently believe in the American Dream. I first discovered this fact after assigning and reading their personal narratives—many of which were often harrowing—of how they came to this country. As I began to build relationships with these students, I soon discovered that many of them worked long hours after school in restaurants, washing dishes and busing tables, or cleaning offices of DC attorneys. Some of my students were living with distant relatives, had children of their own, or had not seen their mothers for years. Nevertheless, they were present in class nearly each and every day, in uniform, with a sparkle in their eyes that revealed a deep desire to learn. I was inspired, but something was bothering at the same time. Then I realized what it was. I was experiencing a dilemma.

As an educator who believes in social justice and equality in education, I face a crippling dilemma every day. While I feel honored to teach such an amazing group of hardworking and engaged students, I also feel as though I perpetuate an "untruth" as I prepare my students for the rigors of college. It is *not* that I think my ELL students will be unable to meet the academic challenges of college—they most certainly will. While many of them will be able to *attend* most colleges, they will not be able to *afford* the cost since they are ineligible for most forms of financial aid because of their undocumented status.

Relevant Literature and Classroom Practices

English Language Learners represent the fastest growing student population in our public schools today. According to a study by Hoffman and Sable (2006) for the U.S. Department of Education, during the 2003–2004 school year, ELL services were provided to more than 3.8 million students—nearly twice as many as in 1993–1994 (Hoffman & Sable, 2006). A more recent study for the same agency has reported that the number of ELL students serviced in U.S. public schools grew to 4.4 million in 2011–2012 (U.S. Department of Education, 2014). As a result, schools are being overwhelmed by the yearly increase of an immigrant population and the lack of resources to effectively teach these students (i.e., certified ELL teachers), yet are still mandated by No Child Left Behind (NCLB) legislation to show ELL achievement and Adequate Yearly Progress (AYP) on state-developed and administered tests. Furthermore, many immigrant students enrolled in U.S. schools are undocumented. Although the 14th Amendment protects undocumented immigrant students' rights to a free public education (see Plyler v. Doe 1982, as discussed in Olivias, 2010), these students cannot receive financial aid to help pay for college because they lack Social Security numbers. Many work illegal jobs simply to make ends meet and assist their families. This situation presents a major dilemma both for me as a teacher and for our country as a "nation of immigrants."

I want to help my students achieve and reach their goals, whatever they may be. Their struggle is my struggle, and I take that very seriously. Nevertheless, I lose heart from time to time when I see first-hand the differences in what we *say* as a nation and what we *do*. Yet, I will not lose hope. Just as I believe in teaching my students about the injustices that our country is, unfortunately, capable of, I am also committed to teaching them to devise solutions. We all have remained silent too long regarding this issue of illegal immigration and access to secondary or higher education.

Thus, the objective of this action research project is to uncover information surrounding immigrant high school students who do not have documentation and how their status is related to their graduation rate. The following questions have guided my action research project:

- Is there a relationship between high school dropout rates and a student's legal status in the United States? If so, what is that relationship?

- What are the higher education options for an undocumented high school graduate?

- Is the lack of higher education options influencing undocumented high school students to dropout of high school?

- Can educational and political immigration policies be changed through action research linking authentic performance task-based curriculum and social justice?

In order to address the issue of undocumented immigrant students and their tendency to drop out of high school, I created an anonymous survey for my students to discover how many of my students are undocumented, and whether that status is discouraging them from attending college. I also collected data regarding their commitment toward graduating from high school, post–high school graduation plans, knowledge of college financing options (i.e., financial aid), and knowledge whether documents are required for entry and financing a college education.

Additionally, I wanted to collect high school graduation rate data from my school and compare it to data from other schools, states, and the national average. Ideally, I would also have liked to collect student legal status data; but I believe these data do not exist, since students and parents (under current laws) are not required to present legal status when students register for school. This presents a major gap in my research, which I will attempt to close with interpretations, inferences, and extrapolations of data.

Once I collected my data, the basis of my intervention plan was education and mobilization by promoting awareness and effecting change. Some of the major problems surrounding my research issue were a lack of awareness and understanding, systemic bureaucratic complexities, and apathetic silence (due to the delicate topic of illegal immigration and its severe consequences such as deportation). Therefore, I planned a persuasive essay portfolio project-based unit, entitled "Persuasion: Effecting Change to Promote Social Justice," for my students in which they researched, discussed, and wrote about the need for comprehensive educational and political reform for undocumented immigrant access to higher education. I also shared the data that I found and used the information as a catalyst for their projects. Their final products were sent to the various stakeholders surrounding the issue, including the principal, chancellor, mayor, and district and/or federal legislators. These stakeholders were also invited into the classroom as panelists for my students' portfolio project presentations in June 2008. Furthermore, to promote general public awareness, my students' essays were sent to NPR (*This I Believe*), WAMU (*Youth Voices Radio*), and the editorial section of the *Washington Post* with the hope that some would be read on the air or published. It is my belief that linking action research to my curriculum will inspire learning, promote high level student achievement, encourage public awareness, and ultimately effect change on the local, state, and national levels.

Identifying high school dropout rates for undocumented immigrants is made difficult by the limited research and information on the topic, as most academic institutions do not track the legal status of their students. While this strengthens the need for my action research topic, it limits the foundational background information available. As a result, I have researched my topic from a variety of sources, including U.S. Department of Education statistics, data from the National Immigration Law and Immigration Policy Center, congressional testimonies, and statistical and anecdotal evidence from scholarly journals.

High school graduation rates have historically not been a major focus of educational research and policy. However, according to a seminal study by Christopher B. Swanson (2003) for the Urban Institute Educational Policy Center, with the passing of NCLB legislation in January 2002, high school graduation rates have become increasingly scrutinized as a major performance factor of public schools (Swanson, 2003). Swanson discovered that "the national graduation rate is 68%, with nearly one-third of all public high school students failing to graduate" (p. v). More recently, NCLB now requires each state to set a goal for a four-year high school graduation rate for all students, including LEPs, and to incorporate the goal and targets into its AYP definition beginning in 2009–2010 (U.S. Department of Education, 2008). Swanson's study found vast graduation rate gaps among various racial groups. Through their Cumulative Promotion Index (CPI), which they paired with data from the U.S. Department of Education's Common Core Data (CCD), the Urban Institute discovered that students from historically disadvantaged minority groups (i.e., American Indian, Hispanic, and Black) "have a little more than a fifty-fifty chance of finishing high school with a diploma" (Swanson, 2003, p. vi). In 2001, District of Columbia public high school students ranked 36th in the nation with a 65.2% overall graduation rate (Swanson, 2003, p. 51). With regard to minority breakdown, Hispanics in Washington, DC, had an even lower rate of 56.1% (3% higher than the national average of 53.2%) compared to 60.4% for Blacks (Swanson, 2003, p. 21). These data are especially discouraging when compared to 2001 graduation rates of White and Asian students, which are far above the national average at 75% and 77%, respectively (Swanson, 2003, p. 20). Although there are no authoritative figures regarding the high school dropout rates of undocumented students, researchers such as Jeffrey S. Passel estimate that "only between 5 and 10 percent of undocumented high school graduates go to college" (as cited in Gonzalez, 2009, p. 21). Such troublesome data (particularly for Hispanics) thus demands us to ask, Why are so many Hispanics dropping out of high school?

Enzo Ferreira, an undocumented immigrant from Uruguay, stopped caring about his education in the 10th grade and was subsequently kicked out of his Manassas, Virginia, high school. He says, "I always knew I couldn't go to college. I don't have a driver's license, an ID, or any papers" (Horwedel, 2006, p. 24). The high school dropout rate for Hispanics is the nation's worst. The Child Trends Data Bank (which compiled statistics from the U.S. Census Bureau and the U.S. Department of Education) claims that in 2004, 24% of Hispanic youth under the age of 18 did not attend school, compared to 12% of Blacks and 7% of Whites (as cited in Horwedel, 2006, p. 24). The reasons for such a spike in the Hispanic community seem to vary around poor academic performance, the financial need to work, the unlikelihood of being able to attend and afford college, as well as their inability to work legally once they graduate from college. Furthermore, there is a real fear of being deported and separated from their families if their undocumented status is known. Despite these obstacles, thousands of undocumented students are graduating from our nation's high schools each year. Many of these graduates are class valedictorians, outstanding athletes, and extremely motivated individuals who desperately want to contribute to U.S. society and uplift their humble communities. Nevertheless, until these students are provided the assistance and support they need in order to be successful, their dreams will be unfulfilled and futures will remain uncertain.

Each year "about 65,000 undocumented students graduate from American high schools" (Hermes, 2008, p. 16). Despite the fact that the U.S. Supreme Court has upheld that states cannot deny the rights of undocumented immigrants to a free public education (Olivias, 2010), there is little to no support for such students in terms of legal and financial assistance in order to attend college. Unlike their documented counterparts, federal law prohibits undocumented immigrants from qualifying for federal and/or state financial aid because of their visa status. As a result, many are forced to settle for two-year degrees from community colleges and/or low-level jobs where immigration status is not closely questioned (Hermes, 2008). Although the number of these undocumented students who attend community college nationwide is impossible to quantify since the academic institutions do not track such information, experts estimate the numbers to be in the thousands, while many thousands more would enroll if the barriers were not so formidable (Hermes, 2008). The sad irony is that these same undocumented students (many of whom are highly assimilated) are being held accountable to achieve on state and federally mandated NCLB standardized tests, pushed to graduate from high school (in four years), and attend college, and yet are not being given the financial and legal support to do so.

Although many organizations and states are seeking solutions to the undocu-mented student population problem, the successes have been fragmented at best. Some states (Alabama, Missouri, North Carolina, South Carolina, and Virginia) are seeking to "decouple education and immigration" and have taken an anti-immigration approach by seeking to deny undocumented immigrant students admission into both two-year and four-year public colleges and universities (Gonzalez, 2009, p. 23). Meanwhile, other states (California, New York, and Texas, among others) have chosen to provide in-state tuition rates to their undocumented high school graduates in order for them to afford higher education. The vast majority of states, however, simply do not have any state policies regarding undocumented immigrant students (Gonzalez, 2009). Nevertheless, advocacy groups and individuals are raising awareness about the educational plight of undocumented immigrants. For instance, Saul Verduzco, a graduate student at San Jose State University who is part of a group called Student Advocates for Higher Education (SAHE), which is made up primarily of undocumented students, says, "A lot of them [undocumented high school students] are in a state of depression. They think, 'What's the point of going to college if I'm not going to be able to work with my degree?'" (Del Conte, 2006). Verduzco and his group do provide such students hope by educating them on the proposed federal legislation known as the Development, Relief, and Education for Alien Minors Act (DREAM Act), which would allow the children of undocumented immigrants to apply for "conditional" legal status upon graduation from high school (Del Conte, 2006). (The DREAM Act did not pass U.S. Congress in 2007.)

Although federal DREAM Act legislation has yet to pass Congress, estimates by the Immigration Policy Center suggest that passage of the DREAM Act would "provide 360,000 undocumented high school graduates with a legal means to work, and could provide incentives for another 715,000 youngsters between the ages of 5 and 17 to finish high school and pursue post-secondary education" (Gonzalez, 2007, p. 8). Fortunately, several states have ratified their own forms of DREAM Act legislation. In 2006, 10 states (California, Illinois, Kansas, Nebraska, New Mexico, New York, Oklahoma, Texas, Utah, and Washington) enacted reforms that gave undocumented students access to in-state tuition, which is on average 75% less expensive than out-of-state tuition (Horwedel, 2006). Eight more states, including Maryland and Virginia, have passed the DREAM Act since (Gabriel, 2014).

Overall, increasing educational opportunities for all U.S. students helps society in a multitude of ways. Countless studies have been conducted detailing both economic and social benefits resulting from an increased number of high school and college graduates. In his testimony at the U.S. House of Representatives Committee on the Judiciary hearing entitled "The Future of Undocumented Immigrant Students and Comprehensive Immigration Reform," Jamie P. Merisotis, president of the Institute for Higher Education Policy (IHEP), said, "Improving access to higher education continues to be one of the most important investments that we can make in our collective well-being. The simple fact remains that increasing educational opportunities results in tremendous public, private, social, and economic benefits" (Merisotis, 2007). Merisotis went on to describe an IHEP study that highlighted the vast struggles immigrant students face, including inadequate finances, heavy work and family responsibilities, varied academic backgrounds, limited English proficiency, and an overall lack of knowledge regarding the U.S. system of higher education, particularly around admissions and financial aid processes (Merisotis, 2007). Significantly, he also mentioned alarming dropout statistics from 2001, which showed that immigrant students ages 15 to 17 made up 8% of the population but represented 25% of high school drop-outs. He also pointed out that "undocumented students, in particular, may be less motivated to complete high school if they believe higher education, and the better paying jobs available to someone with a college degree, to be an unattainable goal" (Merisotis, 2007). Finally, citing U.S. Census Bureau projections, Merisotis said that "by 2020, we will be looking at an employment gap of about 14 million people needed to fill jobs that require a college education . . . . [I]nvesting in those who are already here—including both legal and undocumented immigrants—is our best hope for remaining competitive on a global scale" (Merisotis, 2007).

The economic advantages of allowing undocumented immigrants equal access to higher education are unequivocal. The Bureau of Labor Statistics reports that workers who lacked a high school diploma in 2006 earned an average of only $419 a week and had an unemployment rate of 6.8%. In contrast, workers in the same year who had a bachelor's degree earned $962 a week and had an unemployment rate of 2.3%, while those with a doctorate earned $1,441 and had an unemployment rate of only 1.4% (as cited in Immigration Policy Center, 2007). More recently, the same agency reports that workers who did not have a high school diploma in 2014 earned an average of only $488 a week and had an unemployment rate of 9.0%, while those with a bachelor's degree earned an $1101 a week and had an unemployment rate of 3.5% (Bureau of Labor Statistics, 2014). Increased wages lead directly to an increased tax base, which benefits government spending capability and economic growth. Simply put, it makes sense to educate *everyone*, including undocumented immigrants.

Until action is taken, however, tragedies such as the following story will continue to crush the dreams of our highly skilled and motivated immigrants. Gabby is a student at J. Sargent Reynolds Community College, in Richmond, Virginia, whose goal is to earn a bachelor's degree, attend law school, and become a lawyer. In addition to being a full-time student, she works two jobs in order to afford the out-of-state tuition she has to pay, even though she graduated from a high school in Virginia. Gabby was brought to the United States by her parents at the age of 12 and is an undocumented immigrant. Four-year institutions turned her down because of her undocumented status. Thus, Gabby's American Dream is quickly becoming a nightmare (Hermes, 2008).

Unfortunately, this anecdotal evidence is commonplace in the United States today as local, state, and federal legislators and policy makers continue to crack down on illegal immigration. Although President Obama passed the Deferred Action for Childhood Arrivals (DACA) Program in 2012, it is only a partial step toward the ultimate solution of finding a pathway towards citizenship for 11 million undocumented living in "untenable circumstances" within our borders (Gonzalez & Bautista-Chavez, 2014, p. 12).

Methods and Results

Most schools (including mine) do not officially track the legal status of their students. Therefore, I created an anonymous survey (see Appendix A) for my students in order to find out the percentage of undocumented students I teach. Considering the sensitivity involved surrounding legal status, and the fear of deportation that many immigrants live under, I chose to use anonymity. The survey was also used to discover student motivation toward both graduating from high school and attending college (Appendix A). Questions 10 and 11 on the survey tried to determine whether there was a link between a student's legal status and his or her motivation to finish high school and/or attend college. Questions 12 through 14 were designed to evaluate student knowledge about whether they needed documents in order to attend and/or finance a college education.

After explaining the purpose of the survey to my students, I distributed them to my two classes on Wednesday, April 9, 2008. Although I expected a total of 32 responses, only 25 surveys were returned because of student absences. I then examined each survey and calculated answers in terms of percentages for each applicable question (Appendix B).

Finally, in the spring semester of 2008, I developed and introduced to my English I students the final unit, entitled "Persuasion: Effecting Change to Promote Social Justice." I taught my students how to use rhetorical devices in persuasive writing (such as logical and emotional appeal). The topic of their persuasive essays was undocumented immigrant high school students and their limited access to college. They extensively researched the issue, using my own research as a springboard, and exercised their individual authentic writer's voice to persuade local (District of Columbia Public Schools) and federal policy makers to address the injustice toward undocumented high school students. As stated above in my implementation plan, the essays were sent to the various stakeholders, with the hope that they would be published and/or aired in a public forum.

The immigration and graduation data gathered from my student participants yields some remarkable data. Only 48% of the students surveyed possess legal documentation. This means that 52% of my current students are undocumented immigrants. Significantly, 92% of students surveyed responded "Yes" as to whether they planned to graduate from high school, and 8% (two students) replied with "Don't Know." Nevertheless, only 52% of the students reported that they were planning on attending college; 3% answered "No"; 9% said "Don't Know." Finally, regarding the question whether they needed documents to "attend" and "pay" for college, about 44% of students surveyed said "Yes" to both questions, revealing a major disconnect surrounding the dissemination of accurate information (see Appendix B).

The necessity to work and support family members in the United States and/or in their native countries is one of the major reasons, I believe, that only half of my students (representing both documented and undocumented) indicated that they planned to attending college. For example, one student who indicated having a "green card" answered "maybe" as to whether (s)he planned to attend college. When asked "what are your plans after high school?" (Appendix A, Question 11), the respondent wrote, "My plan is to go to a better job after I graduate high school." Another student who specified (s)he was a "legal resident" explained, "My plan is to try to go to the college if I can, but if not, work the best I can." Finally, a third student answered

Question 11 by explaining, "I want to get a job to support my family in El Salvador and help out my stepdad and mother like they did."

Conclusion

This research confirms my original fear. I do indeed perpetuate an "untruth" to my students each and every day: that the American Dream is attainable through hard work (which requires higher education); yet, in reality, the American Dream is a "dream deferred" for most of my students. As I push and motivate them to graduate from high school and attend college, I am constantly aware of the daunting statistics working against them that say less than 50% of them will graduate from high school and only 10% to 15% of those who graduate will attend college. I am also aware of the tenuous legal and massive financial obstacles that stand in their way toward paying for higher education, especially for my students without legal documents (representing 52% of my total students).

Yet I remain hopeful in the face of adversity. I choose to teach my students about injustices in America, for I believe that open and honest conversation is a catalyst toward the pursuit of truth. I also believe in social justice, which mandates that we treat not just the symptoms but also the roots of the problem. This forces us—both teacher and student alike—to realize that we have inequality and hypocrisy in the United States; however, we also possess the capacity for effecting change. It is this capacity to effect change that provides the vitality for my teaching and learning, and allows me to live with my dilemma. Most important, however, motivating my students to believe in their own capacity to effect change was (and continues to be) my ultimate teaching objective.

Did I achieve my objective? Time will tell. In providing my students with an engaging, controversial, and relevant topic aimed at an authentic audience beyond just their teacher, I showed them that writing matters. Furthermore, sending their personal persuasive essays to actual people encouraged them to seriously develop their own writer's voice and believe in the power of words. Both Luis's "My Persuasive Dreams" (Appendix C) and Patricia's "Different but Equal" (Appendix D) are masterful essays that most certainly speak for themselves.

References

Bureau of Labor Statistics. (2014). [Graph illustration Employment Projections]. *Earnings and unemployment rates by educational attainment.* Retrieved from http://www.bls.gov/emp/ep_chart_001.htm

Del Conte, N. T. (2006). Out of the shadows. *Hispanic, 19*(3), 60–61.

District of Columbia Public Schools. (2009). Columbia Heights Education Campus (Bell Multicultural High School) school profile. Retrieved from http://dcatlas.dcgis.dc.gov/schoolprofile/

Executive Office of the President, Office of Management and Budget. (2007). S. 1348: Secure Borders, Economic Opportunity and Immigration Reform Act of 2007. Retrieved from https://www.whitehouse.gov/sites/default/files/omb/legislative/sap/110-1/s1348sap-s.pdf

Friere, P. (1970). *Pedagogy of the oppressed.* New York, NY: Bloomsbury Academic.

Gabriel, T. (2014, April 29). Virginia attorney general opens in-state tuition to students brought to U.S. illegally. *The New York Times.* Retrieved from http://www.nytimes.com/2014/04/30/us/dreamers-eligible-for-in-state-tuition-virginias-attorney-general-says.html?_r=0

Gonzalez, R. G. (2007). Wasted talent and broken dreams: The lost potential of undocumented students. *Immigration Policy in Focus, 5*(13), 1–12.

Gonzalez, R. G. (2009). *Young lives on hold: The college dreams of undocumented students.* New York, NY: College Board. Retrieved from https://secure-media.collegeboard.org/digitalServices/pdf/professionals/young-lives-on-hold-undocumented-students.pdf.

Gonzalez, R. G., & Bautista-Chavez, A. (2014). Two years and counting: Assessing the growing power of DACA. *American Immigration Council,* 1–13. Retrieved from http://www.immigrationpolicy.org/sites/default/files/docs/two_years_and_counting_assessing_the_growing_power_of_daca_final.pdf

Hermes, J. (2008). Big dreams, serious implications. *Community College Journal, 78*(4), 16–17.

Hoffman, L., & Sable, J. (2006). Public elementary and secondary students, staff, schools, and school districts: School year 2003–04. (NCES 2006-307.) Retrieved from U.S. Department of Education, National Center for Education Statistics website: http://nces.ed.gov/pubs2006/2006307.pdf

Horwedel, D. M. (2006). For illegal college students, an uncertain future. *Diverse Issues in Higher Education, 23*(6), 22–27.

Immigration Policy Center. (2007). Dreams deferred: The cost of ignoring undocumented students. Retrieved from http://www.immigrationpolicy.org/sites/default/files/docs/Access%20to%20Higher%20Ed%209-25%20FINAL.pdf

Matthews, J. (2010, August 12). Two students write about their futures. *The Washington Post.* Retrieved from http://voices.washingtonpost.com/class-struggle/2010/08/two_student_essays.html

Merisotis, J. (2007, May 18). Hearing on "The future of undocumented immigrant students and comprehensive immigration reform." United States House of Representatives Committee on the Judiciary. Subcommittee on Immigration, Citizenship, Refugees, Border Security, and International Law. Washington, DC. Retrieved April 8, 2008, from http://www.ihep.org/assets/files//Testimony_of_Jamie_Merisotis_Subcommittee_on_Immigration_Hearing_May18_2007_final.pdf

National Immigration Law Center. (2009a). DREAM Act summary. Retrieved from http://www.nilc.org/dreamsummary.html

National Immigration Law Center. (2009b). Economic benefits of the DREAM Act. Retrieved from http://www.nilc.org/DREAM-econbens-2009-03-26.html

Olivias, M. A. (2010, September 9). Plyler vs. Doe: Still guaranteeing unauthorized immigrant children's right to attend U.S. public schools. *Migration Policy Institute.* Retrieved from http://www.migrationpolicy.org/article/plyler-v-doe-still-guaranteeing-unauthorized-immigrant-childrens-right-attend-us-public

Swanson, C. B. (2004). *Who graduates? Who doesn't? A statistical portrait of public high school graduation, class of 2001.* Retrieved from the Urban Institute Education Policy Center website: http://www.urban.org/research/publication/who-graduates-who-doesnt/

U.S. Department of Education. (2008, December 22). No child left behind: High school graduation rate non-regulatory guidance. Retrieved from https://www2.ed.gov/policy /elsec/guid/hsgrguidance.pdf

U.S. Department of Education, National Center for Education Statistics. (2014). Fast facts: English language learners. Retrieved from http://nces.ed.gov/fastfacts/display .asp?id=96

APPENDIX A

ANONYMOUS STUDENT IMMIGRATION SURVEY

1. What is your age? _____

2. What is your gender (male or female)? _____

3. Where were you born? _____

4. What is your first language? _____

5. How long have you lived in the United States? _____

6. What grade are you in? _____

7. Do you have legal documents? _____ If yes, what type of documents? _____

8. Are you planning on graduating from high school? _____

9. If you answered "yes" to Question 8, are you planning on attending college? _____

10. If you answered "no" to Question 8 and you do not have documents, is your legal status the reason? Explain. _____ _____ _____

11. If you answered "no" to Question 8 and you have documents, what are your plans after high school or why are you not planning on completing high school? Explain. _____ _____

12. If you are planning to go to college, how do you plan on paying for it? _____ _____

13. Do you think you need documents to apply to college? _____ Explain. _____

14. Do you think you need documents to pay for college? _____ Explain. _____

APPENDIX B

Table 1. Participant Background Information

Ages 14–16 years old	18/25 = 72%
Ages 17–19 years old	7/25 = 28 %
Gender	10 Males/15 Females (40%/60%)
First Language	24 Spanish/1 French (96%/4%)

Table 2. Immigration and Graduation Survey Data

Question Number & Content	Yes	No	Don't Know	Percentage of "Yes" Answers
7. Do you have legal documents?	13	12	0	48%
8. Are you planning on graduating from high school?	23	0	2	92%
9. Are you planning on attending college?	13	3	9	52%
13. Do you think you need documents to apply to college?	12	4	9	48%
14. Do you think you need documents to pay for college?	10	6	9	40%

APPENDIX C

My Persuasive Dreams

I believe that all my dreams can come true. I believe that I can face any challenge that comes through. Anything can be possible if fairness resides in our lives, but nothing will be possible if we don't change many people's minds.

My young life is full of dreams. I dream to be a professional and famous musician; dream to be a poet and persuade many people's lives with my poems, dream to be a person who gives a reflective and persuasive moral. Therefore, I believe that the world should be free and that everybody should study wherever they want and whatever they want.

As hard workers and students, we "ALIENS," as many people call us, deserve the opportunity to have a chance, but people don't want to open their minds. Those who discriminate us, have never experienced what it feels to cross a big piece of unforgiving land where many people die for the American Dream and the wanting of a better life.

My personal experience is not as heartbreaking as many other people. But still, the dreams I have seem infected for the fact that wherever I go, I am an illegal person. However, my hopes support my heart and tell me that no matter if I'm an immigrant, dreams will follow me and as every legal person, I have the right to let them come true.

I came to United States, and the country didn't seem as beautiful as I thought when I was in El Salvador. I learned that when my mom came here it was because she needed a better life in order to give better lives to my brother and me. Now, I'm just finishing my ninth grade and as I am getting to the tenth grade, I'm starting to think about how I am going to pay for my college. Being unfair, many people don't want immigrant people to go to college. They want to restrict their opportunity to show their talents and desires to be good citizens for the nation. Yet, if I wouldn't have come to this country, I wouldn't be able to start taking actions to make my dreams true. I am here because in my country I don't have the open and extended opportunity to make my dreams come true. Now, those opportunities seem tainted for the fact that I am an illegal immigrant and I think that it's not fair. It's not fair because the rights that every American student has should be the same for everyone who wants a chance to educate themselves.

In reflection, I think that everybody should be fair and have compassion for the people who come to this country. Instead of making their lives more difficult, help them. Maybe not in the economic aspect, but at least by not discriminating them. Help them to get a good education as everyone deserves. Help them to be good citizens and reach their dreams. This I believe.

Luis, June 9, 2008

APPENDIX D

Different but Equal

I believe that every human being is equal, no mater our culture, language or race. We all have something special inside us and that's what makes us unique. As a result, I believe that undocumented people and students are as equal as American natives. They should have the right to go to college just as every other student does.

I'm an immigrant who believes that we came to the United States to improve our lives, but at the same time, improve American's lives by our hard work. I came here to study and in that way to offer a good future for me and my family. However, it frightens me to think that undocumented students may not get access to college just because of their legal status. I believe that it's wrong to set such restrictions because we are just looking for a better life. We're not criminals and even when some of our people do certain things that ruin our reputation, we still deserve to be treated as equals.

Every time I hear about undocumented students not having the right to study, I wonder what are we going to do if we have neither the economic nor the political support of the country we are living in? It's just not fair because we do not want to have the same jobs that our parents have like cleaning or working in a restaurant until 3am. We want to make a change in our community and show others what we are able to do and why we came here. I think that Latinos are able to do many things that people might not think we could do such as graduating from college and maybe even becoming president.

I believe that people should not discriminate us for where we come from or who we are. We are just people trying to get help and help others to show how powerful we can be, and in that way, get the right to study and go to college and make our dreams come true. This is what keeps me studying and believing that one day Latinos will rise from others.

Every Latino is different, but at the same time, we have something in common which is the pride we have in being Latinos—extremely hard workers—and for that, I believe that the access to college and other opportunities shouldn't be restricted to us. I'm proud of being who I am and for that I believe we're only one of a kind: different but equal.

Patricia, June 9, 2008

PART VII:
CLASSROOM PRACTICES

CHAPTER 20

Using Drama to Combat Prejudice

Alexis Gerard Finger

Drexel University

Idealism detached from action is just a dream. But idealism allied with pragmatism, with rolling up your sleeves and making the world bend a bit, is very exciting. It's very real. It's very strong.

—*Paul David Hewson (Bono), 2005*

Dave: Lots of things are hard, Kathy. But, if you really believe that prejudice is wrong, you can't just sit there. Behind that joke, there's lot of hate and intolerance for people who are different.

Kathy: And, if you don't stop with that joke, where do you stop? Is that what you mean?

Dave: That's right. If you don't say, "Stop. I don't want to hear such hateful things," who will speak up? It has to start with you. With me. With each of us. It takes courage, but if we don't stand up for others," who will stand up for us?

—*Inspired by* Gentleman's Agreement *(Zanuck & Kazan, 1947, which was based on a novel by Laura Hobson) and by Martin Niemöller (1986), "First They Came"*

You never really understand a person until you consider things from his point of view, until you walk in his shoes.

—*Atticus Finch, in* To Kill a Mockingbird

Personal History

When I started teaching one of the first ESL classes at a New York City high school in the early 1970s, I was idealistic and awestruck by my amazing opportunity to meet and teach students from South America, Central America, Asia, and the Middle East. The experience strengthened my belief in Maya Angelou's idea that "diversity makes for a rich tapestry and all the threads of the tapestry are equal in value no matter the color, the length or the texture" (Angelou, 2014). It was especially true because all the "threads" in my class seemed to fit so well together. In many ways, the relationship that we had was a source of pride, a model for our school. Faculty and students appreciated the international food fair we organized, and they enjoyed our attendance at the varsity soccer games. Perhaps there was even a little envy when word got out about our Friday afternoon bowling sessions. I couldn't have asked for a better initiation to teaching. I really came to love my students and I believe the feeling was mutual.

Thus, I was totally stunned one sunny morning in May, so close to the end of the academic year, when Carlos, one of my most endearing students from Colombia, broke my "rose-colored glasses" when he ran out of my classroom in tears. What was the problem? I couldn't understand why he looked so dismayed when he asked me why I was wearing a Jewish star. After his compatriots explained his reaction to my Jewish star, I realized it was a case of cognitive dissonance. Carlos couldn't reconcile my being Jewish with the ugly stereotype of Jews that he was brought up to believe. How could a nice person whom he had come to trust and care about be Jewish, a religion he was taught to hate?

From that day on, I was no longer just a young, idealistic English teacher. I was a teacher with a mission. I assumed the responsibility for opening my students' eyes to the benefits that come from knowing, understanding, and appreciating people with different backgrounds, as well as the enormous hurt, even harm, that results from acts of prejudice. As if this goal weren't enough, I felt compelled to go a few steps further and try to empower my students as leaders in the global community who would not only pass on the spirit of brotherhood and sisterhood wherever they went but teach others by example how to treat people respectfully, regardless of their differences, and recognize acts of prejudice and attempt to stop them whenever possible.

Despite the enormity of my task, I felt ready for this life-changing job and excited about the potential for doing something that could affect our society in a positive way. But when Carlos eventually admitted that he had never met a Jew before, I realized this undertaking would be a far greater challenge than I had anticipated. I had formidable opponents that are not easily conquered: ignorance, stereotyping, propaganda, and brainwashing. The fact that these "opponents" were provided by people Carlos trusted most (his family members, educators, religious and community leaders) made them nearly impossible for me to directly confront, discredit, or annihilate. As a result, for the next five years, while celebrating the fascinating traditions, attire, food, holidays, and history of my students' cultures and religions, as well as my own, I was very careful about how I helped my students discover for themselves that the negative stereotypes, disrespect, and hatred they had been taught to carry with them required a second, more critical look—and a lot of questions.

When I moved to Philadelphia, I brought treasures with me: lots of touching and empowering memories and a "National Conference of Christian and Jews Builder of Brotherhood" award that my students helped me earn. Convinced I was on the right track, I felt compelled to continue my mission with my oral communication class for international undergraduate and graduate students and my IEP (Intensive English Program) classes at Drexel University that I was assigned. After a few years of cultural sharing, emphasizing the importance of having an open mind, explaining the concept of "cognitive dissonance," discussing the history of injustice in the United States, and highlighting positive stories about people who are different, however, I was still searching for more memorable ways of effecting changes in thinking and in feeling. Eventually, the obvious occurred to me. My most instructive teachers, other than my parents, were the characters I played as a budding actress and the characters on screen with whom I cried when they experienced adversity. I can still recall many decades later the searing pain I experienced with my character, "Elle," a White woman married to a Black man in Eugene O'Neill's 1924 play *All God's Chillun Got Wings*, when she was shunned by the people around her and later escaped into madness. My empathy for people who defied society's conventions for love was born from that acting experience. It has been strengthened with every play I performed or movie I watched that told tragic stories of love and lives destroyed by hate. I can't count the number of times I cried over the plight of the Sharks, a Puerto Rican gang that felt compelled to fight for a piece of their neighborhood and the tragic deaths that followed in the classic musical *West Side Story*. The horrific treatment of an innocent black man in the movie *To Kill a Mockingbird* is indelibly etched in my heart along with the images of an idealistic young girl in *The Diary of Anne Frank* who lost her freedom and eventually her life for the sin of being Jewish. Drama—plays and movies that focused on characters that suffered because of their differences—taught me well that nothing good comes from prejudice. If these dramas had such an effect on me, why not on my students?

Any research I did revealed that the drama-based approach to teaching culture and language made sense. It had been advocated in numerous publications, including Stephen M. Smith's classic text, *The Theater Arts and the Teaching of Second Languages* (1984). I felt justified in making plays and movies my textbooks. For the most part, it's a decision I haven't regretted. I have witnessed firsthand that while reading the plays, watching the movies, and engaging in drama-based activities, my students came as close to climbing into the characters' skins as possible without undergoing surgery. When they took on the roles of the characters and their characters' problems or created their own characters inspired by the themes and issues of a particular play or movie, they were compelled to understand and express the hopes and fears of a group of people who were different from themselves. And when they empathized with these characters, some of the layers of ingrained prejudice began to slip away and compassion often replaced intolerance.

Never forgetting my first responsibility as a language teacher, I was excited to discover that the plays and movies that I was using to teach U.S. culture and combat prejudice were equally dynamic springboards for exercises that would enhance my students' language skills. The more I observed my students benefiting from this novel and entertaining approach to language learning, I more I relished creating materials for skill development (vocabulary, pronunciation, grammar, reading and listening comprehension, discussion, interviewing) alongside my drama-based activities.

I've been using plays and movies as my textbooks for more than 30 years. At least twice a year, I've chosen a vehicle that exposes the incalculable pain that a "thread of our beautiful tapestry"—race, religion, nationality, sexual orientation, gender, age, and skill—has had to endure and still does.

Samples of Students' Responses

My students' enthusiastic reception to my approach to teaching language and culture has kept me energized and committed. I was particularly gratified when I heard comments from my students after they completed their performances inspired by *The Birdcage*, a movie about a gay couple and the child they raised. One shy student from China unabashedly said that the experience changed his point of view about gay people. He said, "I never thought about life from their perspective. Now I know them and now I like them."

Soon after I overcame my reluctance in selecting *Fiddler on the Roof* for our Intensive English Program's Drama Club spring performance several years ago, I was pleasantly surprised by how involved and empathetic my Turkish, French, Korean, Chinese, Japanese, and Iraqi students were as they portrayed the members of a Jewish community in a small Russian town where they were treated as second-class citizens and eventually forced to leave. It all started with the music. When my Turkish and Iraqi students first heard the music, they thought it was theirs. When they learned that it was from another culture, they were too curious to find out its origin to protest my choice. The entire experience of reading *Fiddler on the Roof*, discussing its themes, and acting it out opened their minds and hearts in ways that no lecture from anybody could have done.

One student said in a writing assignment: "I'm so happy we read and saw *Fiddler on the Roof*. I learned a lot of Jewish history. When I see the conflicts between traditions and love, I think about my situation. My parents are very traditional, so they will care much about my future marriage. I hope they will be able accept my decision if I don't choose a person they picked."

During our work on *A Raisin in the Sun*, an Korean student said this in his writing assignment:

> *Raisin in the Sun* made me understand that life is not easy, especially when people face difficult situation due to economic problems. They rarely give up money and choose to face tough challenges. When Walter finally understood his father's spirit and his mother's wisdom, he chooses to live with esteem and honor. I wonder, "Can I do what Walter did?" It needs true courage. I have worked in the real world for long time and I am used to pursuing the affluent life. I already forgot what courage is. The drama taught me that many people have the courage to overcome the challenge and not escape the problem.

Another Asian student, pretending to be Beneatha, an African American woman in *A Raisin in the Sun*, wrote a letter to another character in the play, her mother:

> Dear Mama, Don't worry about me. Asagai will protect me. We came to Asagi's country because they need us. We are fighting with the people here for human rights and freedom. We, black people, in America have freedom and fairness in our institutions but they are not yet in our hands here. I miss you but we are needed here.

The day after the first rehearsal for a student-faculty reader's theater on racism, anti-Semitism, and homophobia this past winter (2014), I received an email from a Chinese graduate student, who wrote:

> I'm a Christian and I'm told by some elder people in the church that God doesn't favor homosexuality. I'm not against it but I never thought it would happen around me. I never thought I can be a brave person speak for gays until I read, "Think of yourself as gay; it's reality you have to accept it. The feeling doesn't go away but you have to bear bullying, harassment and job loss." I was touched by this part and want to do more to speak for the suffering minorities.

It's a rare term during which students don't share in person or in their course evaluation comments such as these:

- "Thank you for opening my mind. I didn't know about different groups of people."
- "Thank you for helping me not hate Jews."
- "Thank you for helping me understand the history and challenges of African Americans in America."
- "Thank you for helping me see life from the point of view of people who are different from me. I think I'm a better person because of my new eyes."

I take little credit for some remarkable breakthroughs in thinking and feeling about different races, religions, and sexual orientation. The real credit goes to the compelling movies and plays that have effectively forced my students to see the peoples of our world differently.

Recommended Movies and Plays

If the topic of the play or movie is compelling, students are inspired to want to know more about the history and the plight of a particular group of people in that drama. If you are looking for a play or movie for a particular type of prejudice, you might try one of the following:

Racism

A Raisin in the Sun (1961 & 2008)	*The Great Debaters* (2007)
The Butler (2013)	*Guess Who's Coming to Dinner* (1967)
Crash (2004)	*Hairspray* (2007)
Do the Right Thing (1989)	*The Help* (2011)
Freedom Writers (2007)	*In the Heat of the Night* (1967)

Mississippi Burning (1988)

Remember the Titans (2000)

Showboat (1951)

South Pacific (1958)

To Kill a Mockingbird (1962)

West Side Story (1961)

Anti-Semitism

The Diary of Anne Frank (1959)

Fiddler on the Roof (1971)

Gentleman's Agreement (1947)

The Pianist (2002)

Sarah's Key (2011)

Schindler's List (1993)

School Ties (1992)

Sophie's Choice (1982)

Sexual Orientation

Angels in America (television mini-series, 2003)

The Birdcage (1996)

Brokeback Mountain (2005)

La Cage au Folles (1978)

The Kids Are All Right (2010)

Milk (2008)

The Normal Heart (television drama, 2014)

Philadelphia (1993)

Trevor (1994)

Gender

A Doll's House (1973)

Erin Brockovich (2000)

Iron Jawed Angels (2004)

The Miracle Worker (1962)

Mona Lisa Smile (2003)

Nine to Five (1980)

Norma Rae (1979)

Taming of the Shrew (1967)

Working Girl (1988)

What's Love Got to Do with It (1993)

Activities That Work

For each play or movie, I usually include certain basic activities. To introduce the theme of social justice, I use the following discussion and writing prompts.

DISCUSSION TOPIC: HATE

- Why do we hate? (What are the causes of hate?)

- Are there any benefits to hating for the individual, group (ethnic, religious, etc.), or community?

- What are the consequences of hating (for the individual, group, community)? Is it worth the effort to reduce hatred in us, between people, between groups of people?

- If you think it's worth the effort, what can we do to reduce or even eliminate hatred in ourselves, between people, between groups of people?

WRITING PROMPT

Write an editorial or prepare a speech on the causes of hate, the consequences of hate, the reasons for reducing/eliminating hate, and the methods for reducing/eliminating hate.

DISCUSSION TOPIC: PREJUDICE/DISCRIMINATION

- Do you believe that people are "created equal"? Explain your answer.
- Do you think all people should be created equally? Explain your answer.
- Why do you think that certain people in this play/movie act as though they are better than other people? Do you think this is fair? Explain your answer.
- If you were given an opportunity to write a persuasive letter to the people who are prejudiced in this play/movie or make a persuasive speech to these people, what arguments would you include to support your opinion?

WRITING PROMPT

Write an editorial or prepare a persuasive speech on the topic of prejudice. Include the causes and consequences of prejudice, and methods for reducing or eliminating this problem. Or write the editorial or speech for the specific group of prejudiced people in the play/movie.

The Great Debaters

Below are the prompts I used for our work on the movie *The Great Debaters,* a 2007 movie starring Denzel Washington. The movie, set in the 1930s, is based on a true story about a debating team and their coach at a college for Black students, Wiley College. The coach is determined to empower his students as individuals by helping them develop effective powers of reasoning and persuasive debating skills. His students' success leads to an invitation to compete with White students at a time when Jim Crow segregation laws were pervasive.

PREVIEWING ACTIVITIES

Discussion. What do you know about the treatment of African Americans in the United States? Give examples.

Research assignment. African American History Time Line: Look up the event or time in history that you were assigned. Be prepared to summarize orally the details of the event and explain why this time/event is significant to the history of African Americans.

Vocabulary development.

1. Look up the definitions of the words in the sentences (included in the handout).

2. Try to paraphrase the sentence

3. Use the sentences as conversation starters.

4. Use the vocabulary to write your own story about a play or movie called *The Great Debaters.*

POSTVIEWING ACTIVITIES

Describing and narrating exercise.

- Describe a scene or situation in the movie that had an affect on you and tell us why.

- Describe a scene or situation that you experienced or witnessed in your life that left a lasting impression.

Character interviews. Each person in a group of three or four pretends to be one of the characters in the movie (Professor Tolson, James Farmer Sr., James Farmer Jr., Samantha Booke, Henry Lowe, Mrs. Tolson, or Mrs. Farmer). When it is your turn, you are in the "hot seat." This means you will be asked questions by the other members of your group who are pretending to be reporters, friends, or psychologists. Your job is to answer "in character," as you think your character would answer the questions.

Improvisations. Working in groups of four, choose two of the following pairs of characters (listed below). Discuss the conflict/controversial topics for each. Then, choose the character you want to play. As soon as a pair is ready, start performing your improvisation for the other pair. You only need to know the characters and the source of conflict/the problem. You don't have to know how the improvisation will end. Since these improvisations are taken from scenes in the movie, you can follow the events that occurred in the movie. Thus you know how it will end. But if you want to have extra fun, you can change the outcome of the scene. (This can be done in groups first and then for the entire class.)

Improvise a scene between two characters in the play:

- James Farmer Jr. & James Farmer Sr.: Conflict: why James came home late

- Samantha Booke & Henry Lowe: his absence after they witnessed a lynching

- Professor Tolson & James Farmer Sr.: Conflict: Tolson's involvement with a union.

- Samantha Booke & James Farmer Jr.: Conflict: Samantha's relationship with Henry

- James Farmer Jr. & Professor Tolson: Conflict: James wants to debate
- Henry Lowe & Professor Tolson: Conflict: why Professor Tolson writes the arguments

Summarizing. In groups of three or four, practice summarizing the plot and the message of the movie. This can be done as a chain summary, with one person beginning and other members adding information when it's their turn, or each member of the group can present a summary and other members can offer omissions or corrections. Be sure to include answers to these questions:

- Who are the people in the play? (characters)
- What happened? (the events that take place—plot)
- Where and when did this take place? (setting)
- Why did this happen? What's the author's point in writing this? (theme/message/lesson)

Or in pairs or groups, retell the plot from different perspectives. Each person chooses one character.

- Tell the story from the point of view of Mr. Tolson, Professor Farmer, James Farmer Jr., Samantha Booke, and Henry Lowe Solomon.

Outside interviews. Choose any of the topics (below) addressed in *The Great Debaters*. Create five questions or more about your topic. Interview two people. Share the results with the class on the assigned day.

- Debating
- Treatment of African Americans in the United States—then and now; education of African Americans—then and now
- Segregation-integration (the story of *Elizabeth and Hazel—Two Women of Little Rock*)
- Affirmative action
- Problems for African Americans today
- Race issues today
- Family relationships
- Inspirational movies
- Civil disobedience/protests
- Langston Hughes
- Denzel Washington
- Forest Whitaker

Alternative interview assignment (with more structure). Inspired by topics from
A Raisin in the Sun.

Discrimination
- What kinds of discrimination are you aware of in the United States?
- Have you ever experienced some form of discrimination? (Explain)
- What are the causes of discrimination?
- What can we do about discrimination?

Residential segregation
- What are the reasons for residential segregation?
- Do you know of a neighborhood that is well integrated? (Is there harmony? Do you see interaction between people of different races, religions, and ethnic backgrounds? Why does it work or not work?)

The Civil Rights movement
- What do you know about the Civil Rights movement? Do you think all the goals of the movement were accomplished? (Explain)
- What more needs to be done?

Family relationships
- Have you ever experienced sibling rivalry?
- What are the causes of sibling rivalry?
- How can we control sibling rivalry?
- Is it easier for siblings of the same gender to get along or do you think the reverse is true? (Explain)
- How can families deal with problems/tragedies that affect the family or a particular member of the family? How can members of a family help a member who is going through a difficult time due to failure, loss of a job, disappointment, a broken heart, an illness, etc.?

Generation gap
- Have you ever experienced a gap in communication with a member of your family—parents, grandparents? Explain the cause.
- Has the problem been resolved?
- How was it resolved?

The role of women in families
- What is the role of women in African American families?
- What responsibilities and problems do U.S. women with families deal with on a regular basis?
- Is it easier for a woman in another culture? Explain.

Relationships
- What is the difference between an acquaintance and a friend?
- What are the characteristics of a true friend?
- How do you know you can trust a friend?
- How do you know you are in love?
- What qualities do you want in a potential spouse/partner (husband/wife)?

Dealing with strong emotions
- What is the best way to handle anger, frustration, and disappointment?
- How can we relate to people who are feeling these emotions?

Forgiveness
- Is it easy to forgive people who hurt or betray you?
- What are the benefits of being able to forgive somebody who hurt you?
- Are there times when forgiveness is not possible? (Explain)
- Explain what Walter did. Ask: If you were Beneatha or Mama would you forgive Walter?

Assimilation versus preserving one's roots (heritage)
- What are the benefits of assimilation?
- What are the disadvantages of assimilation?
- What traditions and customs should be preserved? Why?

Dreams
- Why is it important to have dreams?
- What can happen to people when they lose hope of ever making their dreams come true?

Writing assignments. Choose one of the options below. Try to use the new vocabulary whenever possible.

- Write a character letter. Pretend you are a character in the play and write a letter to another character in the play. Example: James Farmer Jr. writes a letter to Samantha.
- Write a character monologue or journal entry. Be a character who "talks" to himself about what is going on in his life, how he feels about it, and what he intends to do.
- Write a news article about Wiley College's debating team.
- Write an editorial about (1) treatment of African Americans in the past/present, (2) the treatment of African Americans in the present compared with their treatment in the past; or (3) the effectiveness of civil disobedience/protests and the problems with the law.

- Write a scene that was not in the movie but could be included.

- Write sentences for as many of the new vocabulary words as you can.

- Write about the plight of another minority.

- Write a report or editorial that is inspired by the responses you received during your interviews.

Oral reading. Record yourself reading with appropriate phrasing and vocal expression one or two arguments from the civil disobedience debate. Try to communicate the message and emotions of the character in your reading. Play it back and evaluate your delivery. When you feel that you have conveyed the message and emotions effectively, send it to your instructor as an attached document.

FINAL PERFORMANCE ACTIVITY

In pairs or groups, prepare a script that will be used for a live performance. It may be performed for another class or videotaped. (Be sure to have your script checked for grammatical errors.)

- Choose one or two scenes from the movie for a scene presentation. Write the dialogue for the scenes you choose to perform. Here is an example of a scripted line of dialogue:

    Mr. Tolson: What is ironic about the name Bethlehem Steel?

- Select a scene you would like to perform. Modify it, modernize it, or add inner thoughts of the characters. If you add inner thoughts, the audience hears what the character is thinking in addition to the character's lines of dialogue. Inner thoughts are what we think but don't usually say out loud. Here is an example of an inner thought:

    "I'll be very surprised if he even understands my question. He is so young."

- Write a scene that could have taken place before the movie began or a scene that we just didn't see.

- Write and perform a sequel, a continuation of the story.

- Rewrite and perform a different <u>ending</u> of the movie, starting at any particular point in the story that you wish.

- Participate in a debate on a controversial topic related to topics explored in this movie. Examples: affirmative action, labor unions, single-sex education, civil disobedience. (See questions for Interview Exercise for additional ideas.)

- Technology pair or team project: Create an original story or a documentary inspired by *The Great Debaters* that demonstrates the harm caused by any form of discrimination.

- Tell your story with visuals and narration. It can be a " drama" or a documentary. Use Animator voiceovers. (Check out the website www.animoto.com.) Here are other online resources:

    I Movie: http://desktopvideo.about.com/od/imovietutorials

    Moviemaker: http://www.internetguideandmore.com/moviemaker.html

Preparing for a Performance of a Scene or a Monologue

Choose one of these plays/movies for this activity:

- *A Raisin in the Sun*
- *To Kill a Mockingbird*
- *Gentleman's Agreement*
- *The Birdcage (La Cage Aux Folles)*
- *Milk*
- *Hairspray*
- *West Side Story*

Before beginning this activity, review the basic structure of a play: exposition, rising action, climax, falling action, denouement/resolution.

Divide the class into groups of three or four. Give each group (1) a synopsis of one of the plays/movies listed above, (2) one or more scenes and one or more monologues (depending on the size of the group and the number of characters in the scenes), and (3) a copy of the movie to watch.

After the materials have been handed out, group members read the synopsis and answer these questions.

- **Exposition.** What is the setting? Who are the main characters? What are the relationships between these characters?

- **Conflict.** What is the problem?

- **Resolution.** How is the problem resolved?

- **Theme.** What is the topic, message, and/or lesson?

- **Vocabulary.** What words did you learn?

Group members then read the scene(s) they were given and answer these questions:

- What is the setting?

- Who are the characters?

- What is going on in this scene between these characters?

- What general emotions are expressed throughout the scene? What happens?

Next, the groups watch the movie(s). Then they cast the scenes and the monologues they were given. That is, they decide who will perform the characters in the scenes and the monologues.

After the scenes and monologues have been cast, group members work through the following steps.

- Do a character analysis.
    - Describe your character: appearance, background (gender, age, education, socio-economic status, ethnicity religion, character traits). Write down a description.
    - What is your character's goal/motivation? What does s/he want?
    - What emotions does your character feel? Why?
- Paraphrase your lines.
- Rehearse your scene: practice pronunciation (pay attention to stress, intonation, and phrasing).
- Memorize your lines.
- Block the scene (determine the movements of the characters).
- Make decisions about scenery, props, and costumes for your scene.
- Prepare an introduction, transition between scenes and monologues, and conclusion. (The introduction should include a summary of the plot, the theme and the lessons that might be learned from this play/movie about prejudice. Students might also teach some new vocabulary so that the audience can understand everything during the performance. Students decide what information they will present before the performance and what they will say after the performance. Prepare connections between the scenes and monologues. Decide who will take on the role of the narrator. Perhaps the narration will be shared.)

READER'S THEATER PERFORMANCE

If time is an issue, if your students don't have enough time for a regular performance, they can give a reader's theater performance. Performers don't have to memorize their lines or work on the movements of their characters. Performers carry their script and usually stand in one place when they deliver their lines. Performers learn their lines well enough so that they don't have to look down most of the time when they are performing. They rely on vocal expression and facial expressions to convey the emotions of their characters. Scenery, costumes, and props are not expected.

Presentation and performance. Tape the performance if you want the students to analyze their performance or if the students want a souvenir.

Discussion/feedback/evaluation. *Performers* should consider these questions:

- What did you learn from this experience?
- What did you learn about prejudice from this movie/play?
- How did discussing the plot and theme of the movie/play help you better understand the harm of prejudice?

- How did preparing for your performance—analyzing your character and his/her situation and then performing parts of the play/movie—affect you and change your thinking about the people in the play, this particular group of people, prejudice in general?

- What can each of us do to discourage acts of prejudice? Is it important for you to do this? Why or why not?

These questions might be directed to the audience:

- Do you have any questions? Was there anything you couldn't follow?

- What did you like?

- Do you have any suggestions for improvement: introduction, scene, transitions, and conclusion?

- What did you learn from the performance about a particular group of people?

- How has the experience of performing and watching other performances about groups of people who often experience some form of discrimination affect your thinking about prejudice? Is there anything that you will do differently in the future as a result of this experience?

Conclusion

After so many years of teaching, I should be burned out and ready to retire. But because of what I teach and whom I teach, I'm not. I still have a mission. Unfortunately, prejudice is a disease for which there is no quick cure. World, national, and local news shows us every day that there is no end in sight. We can't burn out prejudice with chemicals or radiation; and even if we could, there is no guarantee that it wouldn't return. I do believe that any kind of teacher, but especially teachers of international students, have unique opportunities to make a difference in this area. Our students come to us to learn. While we have them in our classrooms, we should make every effort to teach and reach them through their hearts as well as their minds and show them that the negative things they may have learned about people who are different may be antiquated, unfair, or untrue. With the emotions elicited by a play or movie, there is every possibility that they may adopt another, perhaps better, more productive way of looking at people of different religions, races, ethnicity, gender, and sexual orientation.

My latest reader's theater consisted of a diverse group of performers: undergraduate and graduate students, faculty, administrators, young and older, domestic and international, gay and straight, and religions and races of almost every kind. The title was "Better to Light a Single Candle than to Curse the Darkness," and the materials that focused on racism, anti-Semitism, and homophobia were from many of the plays and movies recommended in this chapter, as well as songs, poems, and excerpts from editorials. I think we all learned something special as a result of our time, exploration, and performance together. And I think the members of the audience learned something, too. We have choices. As long as the heart is still beating, there is hope. Drama that reveals the pain of prejudice can inspire us to combat this intractable enemy with the understanding of a wounded soldier and the strength, courage, and conviction of a four star general.

References

Angelou, M. (2014). *Rainbow in the cloud: The wisdom and spirit of Maya Angelou.* New York, NY: Random House.

Hewson, P. D. (Bono). (2005, February). *Paul David Hewson: My wish: Three actions for Africa* [Video file]. Retrieved from http://www.ted.com/talks/bonos_call_to_action _for_africa

Lee, H. (1960). *To kill a mockingbird.* New York, NY: J.B. Lippincott Company.

Niemöller, M., & Locke, H. G. (1986). *Exile in the fatherland: Martin Niemöller's letters from Moabit Prison.* Grand Rapids, MI: W.B. Eerdmans.

Smith, S. M. (1984) *The theater arts and the teaching of second languages.* Reading: Addison.

Wolfgang, G. (2000). *And the witnesses were silent: The confessing church and the Jews.* Lincoln: University of Nebraska Press.

Zanuck, D. F. (Producer), & Kazan, E. (Director). (1947). *Gentleman's agreement* [Motion picture]. United States: 20th Century Fox.

CHAPTER 21

We Are All Environmental Educators (Whether We Know It or Not)

David Royal

University of South Florida

I unexpectedly realized the environmental side of English language teaching very early in my career. While preparing a lesson for Taiwanese elementary school students, I was surprised to see that our textbook featured a food-themed activity with a vocabulary list that included Big Mac and McChicken. I had a choice to make. I could edit this content, teach it as written, or supplement it. Even as a novice teacher, I saw that none of these decisions would be environmentally neutral. Teaching that activity as written would not have been taking an unbiased, objective position. It would have been a choice. Specifically, it would have been the choice to uncritically accept what was provided and to use teaching materials that market unhealthy, environmentally irresponsible foods to children. This lesson illustrates a form of environmental education, even though it may be unconscious or unintentional. Whether or not we are comfortable bringing environmental issues into the English language classroom, those issues are already there.

We face situations like these every time we teach. When we use, create, or adapt materials and activities, we decide what to include and what to leave out. These choices often convey a perspective on the environment. For example, when teaching patterns related to food preferences, do we include the language for expressing environmental principles? Do lessons on shopping provide students with the words they need to make environmentally responsible choices? Do business case studies consider the true costs of the products they feature? It may not seem like environmental education when we do not explicitly refer to these issues, but it is. When we exclude environmental perspectives, we teach that it is appropriate to buy food, go shopping, and evaluate a company's success without considering the environment. Moreover, we do not give our students the language they need to do these things in any other way. In other words, "all education is environmental education" (Orr, 1991, n.p.).

The call to integrate environmental content into the English language classroom is not a new one. English language teachers have been explicitly addressing environmental issues for more than 20 years (Brown, 1991; Jacobs, 1993). Teachers use environmental issues in content-based language teaching (Hauschild, Poltavtchenko, & Stoller,

2012; Hronopoulos, 2004), project-based learning (Cates & Jacobs, 2006), service learning (Mattison, 2003), and experiential learning (Tangen & Fielding-Barnsley, 2007). This chapter aims to provide support and inspiration for those interested in further integrating environmental content in their teaching. It begins by suggesting some principles to consider when bringing environmental issues into the English language classroom. First, it is important that environmental content be presented in a way that respects students' individual beliefs and practices while empowering them to take responsibility for their actions. Second, the issues should be presented in a way that is both interesting and relevant to students' lives. Third, when covering environmental content, it is essential to not only raise awareness, but also to provide opportunities for positive action. Finally, the second half of the chapter outlines three activities based on these principles that can be adapted for a variety of contexts. Digital copies of the materials used in these activities are available online at this book's resource page: www.tesol.org/socialjustice

Student-Centered and Empowering

As a language teacher, I respect learner autonomy while trying to meet student needs and empower them toward further development. When integrating environmental content, my approach remains the same. Students already have environmental beliefs and practices, and the first step is helping them acquire the language and knowledge they need to follow these values. This is especially true in ESL contexts, or in contexts preparing students to go to English-dominant countries. For example, students from a country with a sophisticated recycling program may be uncertain about the recycling process where they are studying. Students from a country that does not allow genetically engineered foods might like to know how to avoid them while living in the United States. Students with strong beliefs about the treatment of animals or the use of pesticides might need specific language when shopping or dining. As language teachers, we respect and support student cultural beliefs and principles (Guest, 2002). In terms of the environment, this means providing them with the language and knowledge they need to move beyond the superficial, short-term convenience of megastores, cars, and fast food. By excluding explicit environmental content, teachers deprive students of the language skills they need to make educated, empowered decisions, particularly in English-speaking contexts.

An interesting comparison between student-centered language teaching and a healthy orientation to the environment can be found in George Jacobs's *Integrating Environmental Education in Second Language Instruction* (1993). In it, he outlines two opposite paradigms, which he applies to both language teaching and nature. The first perspective (which he calls Paradigm A) sees both nature and students as blank or empty, with their value coming after they are used or filled by external forces. In this paradigm, diversity is ignored or abolished and both nature and knowledge tend to be isolated and compartmentalized. This is the traditional paradigm, both in terms of education and in terms of our orientation to the environment. This perspective has enabled the degradation of the natural world. In contrast, Paradigm B views both nature and students as inherently valuable, seeing them as active and independent rather than as passive and dependent. In this paradigm, diversity is encouraged and both nature and knowledge are contextualized and integrated. In other words, a respectful orientation to the environment has a lot in common with student-centered teaching.

Taking a student-centered approach to environmental content also helps avoid one of the risks of bringing global issues into the language classroom: indoctrination (Peaty, 2004). When covering content (environmental or otherwise) teachers should come from the perspective of openness and inquiry, not dogma and persuasion. It is important that teachers not portray themselves as the arbiters of environmental responsibility, nor unilaterally determine which issues deserve priority. Instead, we should encourage students to look critically at multiple perspectives and come to their own conclusions. The goal should be to help students acquire the knowledge and language skills they need to learn about and positively affect the issues that matter to them.

Student-centered teaching helps with another of Peaty's (2004) potential difficulties as well: a lack of content expertise. While it is understandable that some teachers may not feel they know enough about environmental issues to teach them effectively, it should not be regarded as a major obstacle. English language teachers frequently cover content outside of their expertise, including units on art, science, business, sociology, food, and history. Moreover, when introducing environmental topics into the language classroom, it is not the teacher's responsibility to provide all the answers. Environmental issues are ideally suited to language learning activities in which students co-construct meaning and engage in independent research. These are complicated issues, many of which lack clear solutions. Bringing environmental content into the classroom while acknowledging the limits of our own knowledge models lifelong learning to our students. It also illustrates the fact that these issues concern us all, and that we cannot simply wait for experts to solve them.

Student beliefs must be respected, but students should also be encouraged to look critically at their impact on the world. As Hicks says, it would be a "real betrayal . . . *not* to awaken them to the human/global condition" (2002, p. 108). Teachers do their students a disservice when they try to protect them from environmental topics that could potentially make them uncomfortable or force them to reevaluate long-held beliefs. Being a lifelong learner and a responsible global citizen means being open to new information about the consequences of the choices that we make.

Interesting and Relevant

When selecting content for a language course, it is essential to use materials that are interesting and relevant to students' lives (Brinton, 2003). Environmental issues certainly meet these criteria, but there are approaches teachers can take to make this content even more engaging. Here are two ideas. First, highlight connections between environmental issues and students' everyday actions. Environmental issues do not occur in some separate, external world. They intimately affect our lives and, in turn, are profoundly affected by the daily decisions that we make. Exploring these connections, as done in the activities below, is a powerful way to make seemingly abstract issues more engaging and to underscore their relevance to students' lives. Second, when possible, give students the freedom to select some of the course content. Choosing specific issues that matter to them increases both interest and relevance. Activity 3, below, features a great deal of flexibility in terms of content.

The integration of environmental perspectives can also enhance the interest and relevance of existing class content. Teaching about the environment does not require creating new units or stand-alone courses. Environmental content can be woven seamlessly into lessons on business, shopping, food, travel, and so on. For example, a textbook reading profiling the offerings at McDonald's in different countries (Hartmann & Blass, 2007, p. 95) could be supplemented with information on the environmental cost (deforestation, water consumption, pollution) of industrial beef production. Incorporating environmental issues in this way enriches the curriculum, bringing additional perspectives and adding opportunities for critical thinking. This can be especially true with English language textbooks, many of which heavily feature and positively frame the language and experience of middle- and upper-class consumerism (Gray & Block, 2014; Sokolik, 2007; Stibbe, 2004). This consumerism is directly responsible for the environmental issues we face.

Opportunities for Action

One risk when introducing environmental content is stirring up feelings of hopelessness and confusion (Hicks & Bord, 2001). We currently face a myriad of issues, some of which could have grave consequences for humanity. Examining environmental issues necessarily requires considering possible futures, some of which may be fairly bleak. It is important to be mindful of our students' feelings throughout this experience.

Rogers and Tough (1996) outline a process that occurs when learning about potential futures. In brief, this process frequently starts intellectually, with a person learning some new information, then progresses through emotions and soul-searching before moving into empowerment and action. As teachers, it is important that we facilitate this entire process. It is essential that we do not abandon our students at the point of awareness raising and outrage. Students can find themselves overwhelmed by the sheer number of problems, paralyzed by the countless alternatives, and feeling powerless to make a positive impact. The activities described below empower students with the language they need to take positive action and give them direct experience with potential solutions.

Finally, when considering environmental issues in the context of social justice, it is important to recognize that many of these problems (climate change, waste disposal, etc.) disproportionately affect poor and marginalized populations (Mendelson, Dinar, & Willliams, 2006). Clean water and clean air have become commodities that not everyone can afford. For educators interested in social justice, there is perhaps no greater injustice than the resource debt and pollution surplus with which we are burdening future generations.

The next section presents three flexible, student-centered activities that can connect the environment to a variety of class topics. They introduce relevant vocabulary and raise awareness about environmental issues, but they also empower students to take positive action. In each activity, connections are made between locally relevant environmental issues and students' everyday lives. Every program's curriculum and learning objectives are different, and teachers need to find the appropriate places to integrate environmental content. Table 21.1 gives some ideas for environmental angles to traditional ESL and EFL topics, and this list could certainly be expanded.

Table 21.1. Environmental Angles to Supplement Traditional ESL and EFL Topics

Traditional ESL/EFL Topic	Environmental Angle
Transportation	Carbon emissions Car-free cities
Food	Industrial agriculture and meat production Organic and community gardening Genetically modified organisms
Tourism	Environmental impacts of traditional tourism Ecotourism Local green directory
Business	Sustainable business case studies Environmental impacts of famous companies True cost economics
Marketing	Greenwashing Label reading
Art/Literature	Representations of nature Ecohumanities
Psychology/Sociology	Consumerism and mental health Nature-deficit disorder
Health	Effects of pollution/indoor air pollution Effects of biking, walking vs. driving Effects of eating less meat/processed food
Weather	Climate change Use of climate control
Technology	Mining precious metals Recycling and disposal of toxic materials
Hobbies/Interests	The prevalence of consumption-based hobbies Environmental impacts of different hobbies
Housing	Environmental footprint Average house size around the world Natural building/Green building

ACTIVITY 1. LOOKING AT LABEL LANGUAGE

This first activity fits into units on shopping, business, food, or advertising. What we buy has a huge environmental impact, and responsible consumption relies on a specialized vocabulary that students may not be familiar with. This issue is further complicated by the greenwashing strategies that many companies employ, making products appear to be more ecofriendly than they actually are. One effective way to introduce the language of environmentally responsible consumption is by looking closely at product labels.

To prepare for this activity, gather packaging from foods and household products that make claims about their environmental impact, such as recycled toilet paper, natural deodorant, and organic tea. For lower level classes, you may want to highlight or underline the environmentally relevant words and phrases. If possible, it is best to use products that are locally available. This ensures that the vocabulary is relevant and that students have access to these products. You may even ask students to bring in products themselves.

Begin with discussion questions that ask students to describe how they generally make shopping decisions. Do they base their decisions on price? Brand name? Country of origin? Do they consider any environmental issues? How do students research products before they buy them? What websites or other resources do they use? Wrap this discussion up by inviting each group to share some of their ideas with the class. Beginning in this way enables students to share their existing knowledge and practices.

Next, give each group a few of the packaging samples that you collected. Ask students to put together a vocabulary list based on the environmentally relevant words and phrases from their labels. In addition to defining the terms and giving their parts of speech, students can identify which environmental issue(s) each word or phrase is connected to. After they have finished, have members of each group teach their words to the class. As they do this, it is helpful (if possible) to display images of the labels so that all students can see the words in context.

For homework, ask students to look closely at the label of a product they have recently purchased. They can write a short summary of the information provided by the label and also write about additional information that they would like to know. In a class that covers research skills, you could have students try to find this information and reflect on their experience. For example, a student might write about a carton of milk. Perhaps she would like to know something about the farm on which the cows were raised. She could try to find this information and write a reflection on how easy or difficult it was to find the answers to her questions.

This activity can be expanded in a variety of ways. A lesson on greenwashing would be a great addition, and you could include some products that clothe themselves in environmental imagery and jargon that actually mean very little. Another approach would be to focus on determining what the words on the labels literally mean. In terms of food labels in the United States, a great resource is *Food Labeling for Dummies* by Animal Welfare Approved (2013), which gives specific definitions for a vast array of food terminology. For example, "free-range" might conjure images of chickens pecking and scratching in a dusty yard, living under the open sky, but there is no legal definition, so it means virtually nothing. "Organic," on the other hand, refers to clear regulations in terms of chemicals, while having no concrete meaning in terms of animal treatment.

This label reading activity is also a good opportunity to highlight the differences between regional environmental laws. For example, students studying in the United States might come from areas where genetically modified food is either illegal or required to be clearly labeled. They may be shocked to learn that, in the United States, the majority of processed foods contain genetically modified ingredients (Caldwell, 2013). Students may be further surprised that these foods are almost entirely unlabeled. To bring the concept of GMO food into this activity, include some products that are labeled as being non-GMO. Discussing why this would be on a label leads naturally into a conversation about the ubiquity of GMO foods in the United States and the fact that they are unlabeled (as of 2015). Another similar extension activity would to look at lists of ingredients that are banned in some countries but used in others. Recycling is another area where laws vary greatly from country to country. A handout that explains the various numbers of plastic packaging and how they can (or cannot) be locally recycled would be another good addition to this activity. Please visit www.esletc.com/sjbook/ for copies of the handouts used in this activity.

ACTIVITY 2. A LOCAL GREEN DIRECTORY

The local green directory activity could be included in a unit on tourism, business, food, or shopping. It could also be part of a lesson on things to do in the community or giving directions. For students at an advanced level, this activity a great way to practice finding, evaluating, and synthesizing information and presenting it in a useful way. A completed directory could also be integrated into student orientation materials or shared with the wider community.

Begin by having students brainstorm various types of locally available environmental resources. It might help to have them focus on five key areas: food, waste disposal, shopping, transportation, and entertainment. For this initial brainstorm, students should concentrate on types of resources, rather than on specific businesses or organizations. For example, their list should include "natural food stores" and "thrift stores" rather than Whole Foods and Salvation Army. The resources of every place will vary, but here are some common ones:

- **Food**: natural food stores, restaurants featuring local or organic cuisine, vegan or vegetarian restaurants, farmers markets, community supported agriculture programs
- **Waste disposal**: recycling facilities and local policies, procedures for disposal of hazardous materials (batteries, technology, electronics, paint and toxic chemicals, etc.)

- **Shopping**: secondhand stores, pawn shops, online resources (Freecycle, Craigslist, etc.), ecofriendly stores

- **Transportation**: public transportation, bicycle shops, pedestrian and bicycle routes and laws

- **Entertainment**: parks, community gardens, museums, concerts and performances, other free or low-cost activities that do not involve consumption

Once students have generated a list of resources, there are a number of ways to proceed. The goal is to create a detailed directory of local examples of the types of businesses and organizations listed above. Ideally, the directory would focus on resources that are within easy access of walking, biking, or public transportation, but this is not always possible. Student expertise, both of environmental resources and of the local area, should be valued and included. For beginner-level students, you could hand out a prepared green directory and have them answer questions about what goods and services are available from each listing. They could also practice finding the resources on a map and giving directions. At an intermediate level, you could give students a partially created directory, asking them to find and fill in the missing information. More advanced students could create their own green directory from scratch, researching and compiling information in small groups. In subsequent semesters, you could have students update or expand an existing directory (go to www.tesol.org /socialjustice for a sample directory developed at the University of Hawaii).

Extension possibilities for this activity are plentiful. A completed directory could be distributed to the wider community and followed by a survey to find out what additional information people would like. In an EFL context, this project could be targeted toward creating a resource for English-speaking expatriates or tourists. Field trips could be incorporated into the directory creation, with students visiting various locations, asking questions and reporting on their experiences. These field trips could be accompanied by handouts asking students to gather specific information about the places they visit. Students could also do role plays of scenes set in various locations to practice site-specific language. The directory itself could be expanded by including a glossary, a map, or other materials. For example, to supplement the list of local bike shops, students could create a handout of tips for safe riding, instructions on the proper way to lock a bike, or a checklist of safety equipment. In whatever form it takes, both the directory and any supplementary materials should be locally relevant and comprehensible to students.

ACTIVITY 3. INDIVIDUAL ACTION PROJECT

A more extensive project that engages students with environmental issues is the individual action project (Royal, 2007). In this activity, students are asked to pick an issue that matters to them and experiment with changing an action in their daily lives related to this issue. For example, as part of a unit on business, students could research the environmental impact of certain business practices and modify their shopping accordingly. In a unit on transportation, students could change their commute to lessen their environmental impacts. This activity could also be done as part of a global issues or current events class. In that context, students could pick any environmental issue and choose an action related to that issue to experiment with. One way to quickly introduce a variety of issues is Yann Arthus-Bertrand's *The Future of the Earth* (2004). This coffee-table book features brief explanations of a range of global and environmental issues alongside striking aerial photography.

To start this project, students should first pick a specific issue that resonates with them. Permit as wide a range of environmental issues as possible so that students can find something that truly matters to them. Even when doing this project within a specific unit (e.g., transportation), students can still choose from among a variety of issues : air pollution, habitat loss, peak oil, climate change, pollution from mining or oil extraction, to name a few. Do the selection process multiple times, with numerous prompts and examples. In my experience, many students will, initially, simply select an issue that they have heard of (like climate change) rather than one that they really care about.

Once they select an issue, students should begin researching it. Try to incorporate some of this initial research into your class time. For example, you could have students lead reading circles based on articles they have found. You may also want to have students give short presentations that provide some background information on their issue, along with their reason for choosing it. This project takes several weeks, and doing in-class components early on ensures that students begin in a timely manner.

After they have done some initial research, ask students to come up with an action or two related to their issue that they would like to try. If you are doing this activity as part of a unit on business or food, students may decide on a modification of their consumption habits. If this is part of a more general current events or global issues unit, students can choose any action or actions related to the issue they have chosen. Again, give lots of examples and give students multiple chances to change or update their selections. Go to www.tesol.org/socialjustice for some examples of student topics and actions, along with all of the other materials used in this project.

While it is good to be broad-minded in accepting action ideas, this activity is more effective if students pick actions they do every day rather those restricted to special occasions. If a student were interested in air pollution, I would encourage her to try changing her diet, transportation habits, or electricity consumption rather than participating in a protest or working a booth at an Earth Day event. Focusing on everyday actions makes the activity more empowering, helping students see that they have the ability to make a positive difference. It also helps ensure that the vocabulary and content knowledge are relevant to the students' lives.

One of the keys of this project is having students reflect on the experience of trying a new behavior over time. A daily action gives more opportunity for reflection than an action that happens just once or twice over the course of the project. Ideally, students should do this action for four or more weeks to see how their experience changes as it goes from a new behavior to a more familiar one. During this time, include class activities asking students to share their experience with their classmates. In addition to ensuring that students are keeping up with the project, this also provides opportunities for students to grow into the role of experts, teaching their classmates about their issues and actions.

For a culminating activity, have students put together a report in which they share what they have learned about their issue and reflect on their experience with their action. This lends itself well to a research paper or academic presentation, but could be done in a variety of formats. In my experience, this process of reflecting on a positive change over time can be transformative for students. Frequently, students start off feeling insecure or even embarrassed about changing their behavior, only to develop real pride and appreciation by the end. They come away understanding that we are integrally related to our environment and that the issues they hear about on the news are directly connected to the choices we make every day.

Conclusion

We are at an unprecedented point in human history. The science is in: We are changing the climate (IPCC, 2014). Species are dying out at a rate unseen since the dinosaurs became extinct 65 million years ago. Toxic chemicals, heavy metals, and nuclear wastes are accumulating worldwide, and the wilderness is disappearing (Gottlieb, 2006, pp. 4–5). These are not potential futures. This is the present.

What are educators to do? First, we need to stop excluding these issues from our classrooms. Instead, we should highlight how these issues are woven into our course content and our everyday lives. We are not experts and many of these issues lack easy answers, but we can join our students in co-constructing an understanding of our place in—and responsibility for—the environment. We also need to respect the environmental principles and practices that our students bring with them, and challenge them to look critically at the ways in which their actions affect the world. Finally, we need to offer our students reasons for hope and opportunities for positive action.

Freire asserts that the "fundamental task of the teacher is a liberatory one" (1997, p. 324). Even in situations where our students are empowered in terms of financial and social standing, there is still room for liberation. We can help our students liberate themselves from mindless, harmful consumption (Hansen, 2012). We can help them discover the freedom to live lightly on this Earth and leave a healthier planet to their children.

We can look to a number of areas for inspiration and ideas: the fields of environmental education, mindfulness, voluntary simplicity, experiential outdoor education, and so on. We must not get discouraged. The process of incorporating environmental issues into our teaching will not always be smooth. This does not justify excluding these issues, especially once we understand that our teaching already expresses environmental points of view. When we exclude the environment from our classroom, we perpetuate the false belief that environmental issues are somehow separate from our lives and able to be ignored.

English language teachers play many roles. In addition to teaching English, we find ourselves being cultural ambassadors, academic and career advisers, and even entertainers. Like all teachers, we are also sometimes environmental educators.

Every decision we make has an environmental impact. Rather than being overwhelmed by this fact, we should be empowered by it. What we do matters. What we do makes a difference.

References

Animal Welfare Approved. (2013). *Food labeling for dummies*. Alexandria, VA.

Arthus-Bertrand, Y. (2004). *The future of the earth: An introduction to sustainable development for young readers*. New York, NY: Harry N. Abrams.

Brinton, D. (2003). Content-based instruction. In D. Nunan (Ed.), *Practical English language teaching* (pp. 199–234). New York, NY: McGraw Hill.

Brown, H. D. (1991). 50 simple things you can do to teach environmental awareness and action in your English language classroom. *Language Teacher, 15*(8), 4–5.

Caldwell, M. (2013, August 5). 5 surprisingly genetically modified foods. *Mother Jones*. Retrieved from http://www.motherjones.com/environment/2013/08/what-are-gmos -and-why-should-i-care

Cates, K., & Jacobs, G. M. (2006). Global issues projects in the English language classroom. In G. H. Beckett & P. C. Miller (Eds.), *Project-based second and foreign language education: Past, present, and future* (pp. 167–180). Greenwich, CT: Information Age.

Freire, P. (1997). *Mentoring the mentor: A critical dialogue with Paulo Freire*. New York, NY: Peter Lang.

Gottlieb, R. S. (2006). Introduction: Religion and ecology—What is the connection and why does it matter? In R. S. Gottlieb (Ed.), *The Oxford handbook of religion and ecology* (pp. 3–21). New York, NY: Oxford University Press.

Gray, J., & Block, D. (2014). All middle class now? Evolving representations of the working class in the neoliberal era: The case of ELT textbooks. In *English language teaching textbooks: Content, consumption, production* (pp. 45–71). Houndsmill, Basingstoke, England: Palgrave Macmillan.

Guest, M. (2002). A critical "checkbook" for culture teaching and learning. *ELT Journal, 56*(2), 154–161.

Hansen, E. T. (2012). Liberated consumers and the liberal arts college. In *What is college for? The public purpose of higher education* (pp. 63–85). New York, NY: Teachers College Press.

Hartmann, P., & Blass, L. (2007). *Quest 1: Reading and writing*. New York, NY: McGraw-Hill.

Hauschild, S., Poltavtchenko, E., & Stoller, F. L. (2012). Going green: Merging environmental education and language instruction. *English Teaching Forum, 50*, 2–13.

Hicks, D. (2002). Teaching about global issues: The need for holistic learning. In *Lessons for the future: The missing dimension in education* (pp. 98–108). London, England: Routledge.

Hicks, D., & Bord, A. (2001). Learning about global issues: Why most educators only make things worse. *Environmental Education Research, 7*(4), 413–425.

Hronopoulos, S. (2004). Environmental lessons served with indigenous spice and a twist of innovation. Retrieved from http://www.englishaustralia.com.au/index.cgi?E =hcatfuncs&PT=sl&X=getdoc&Lev1=pub_c05_07&Lev2=c04_hrono

IPCC. (2014). *Climate change 2014: Synthesis report. Contribution of Working Groups I, II and III to the fifth assessment report of the Intergovernmental Panel on Climate Change* [Core Writing Team, R. K. Pachauri & L.A. Meyer (Eds.)]. Geneva, Switzerland: Author.

Jacobs, G. M. (1993). *Integrating environmental education in second language instruction.* Singapore: SEAMEO Regional Language Centre.

Mattison, K. M. (2003). Volunteerism: Education beyond the classroom. *Global Issues in Language Education Newsletter, 49*, 12–15.

Mendelsohn, D., Dinar, A., & Williams, L. (2006). The distributional impact of climate change on rich and poor countries. *Environment and Development Economics, 11*, 159–178.

Orr, D. W. (1991). What is education for? *In Context, 27*. Retrieved from http://www.context.org/iclib/ic27/orr/

Peaty, D. (2004). Global issues in EFL: Education or indoctrination? *Language Teacher, 28*(8), 15–18.

Rogers, M., & Tough, A. (1996). Facing the future is not for wimps. *Futures, 28*(5), 491–496.

Royal, D. (2007). Global issues, everyday actions. *Global Issues in Language Education Newsletter, 65*, 15–17.

Sokolik, M. E. (2007). Grammar texts and consumerist subtexts. *TESL-EJ, 11*(2), 1–9.

Stibbe, A. (2004). Environmental education across cultures: Beyond the discourse of shallow environmentalism. *Language and Intercultural Communication, 4*(4), 242–260.

Tangen, D., & Fielding-Barnsley, R. (2007). Environmental education in a culturally diverse school. *Australian Journal of Environmental Education, 23*, 23–30.

CHAPTER 22

A Community Adult English Literacy Program for Migrant Workers in Qatar

Context-Specific Critical Pedagogy and Communicative Language Teaching at Work

Silvia Pessoa

Carnegie Mellon University in Qatar

Nada Soudy

Teach for All, Qatar

Natalia Gatti

Academic Bridge Program, Qatar Foundation, Qatar

M. Bernardine Dias

Carnegie Mellon University

The Context: Teaching English to Migrant Workers in Qatar

This chapter reports on the motivations, challenges, and curriculum design of a community English literacy program for migrant workers in Qatar. Active since 2010, Language Bridges runs as a student-led organization at Carnegie Mellon University in Qatar with the support of faculty, staff, and Reach out to Asia (ROTA), Qatar's major nonprofit organization. The curriculum is context-specific to Qatar and draws on many years of research on the challenges of migrant workers in Qatar conducted by the research team, and 5 years of experience teaching this population. The classes are taught by students and attended by low-income migrant laborers in the community.

This publication was made possible by NPRP grant # 04-439-1-071 from the Qatar National Research Fund (a member of Qatar Foundation). The statements made herein are solely the responsibility of the authors.

Like other countries in the Gulf Cooperation Council (GCC),[1] Qatar has relied heavily on foreign labor since the oil and natural gas boom of the 1970s (Gardner, 2010). Today, Qatar is the richest country in the world, with a population of approximately 2,175,000 (Qatar Statistics Authority, 2014). Qataris represent only 6.5% of the economically active population (Qatar Information Exchange, n.d.). This imbalance in the population, with Qataris being the minority in their own country and receiving great benefits from the government and laborers being the majority but living at the margins of society, has created issues of power disparity, inequalities, and human rights abuses that have garnered recent scholarly and public interest, particularly as Qatar gears up to host the FIFA Soccer World Cup in 2022 (Al Jazeera, 2007; Gardner et al., 2013; Human Rights Watch, 2012; Kamrava & Babar, 2012; Pattisson, 2013).

The entry of migrant workers in Qatar is regulated by the highly criticized sponsorship system. Under this system, migrant workers are placed under the authority of a Qatari citizen known as a sponsor, or *kafeel,* who assumes full economic and legal responsibility for the worker for a period of generally 2 years (NHRC, 2006). The system renders workers entirely dependent on their employers' goodwill to remain in the country, change sponsorship and employment, or obtain an exit permit to leave the country. Under this system, workers face various challenges, including withholding of their passport by the sponsor, poor working and living conditions, and accidents and fatalities in the workplace. Some of these challenges start at migrants' country of origin with unscrupulous recruiting agencies that charge them high fees for securing a job in Qatar (Al Jazeera, 2007; Gardner, 2010; Gardner et al., 2013; Human Rights Watch, 2012; Kamrava & Babar, 2012; Pessoa, Al-Neama, & Al-Shirrawi, 2009; Pessoa et al., 2008; Pessoa, Harkness, & Gardner, 2014).

The Qatari demographic landscape puts Qataris and low-income migrant workers in complete contrast to one another economically and socially. Besides employer-employee and service provider–service seeker contacts, these two groups hardly interact because of limited knowledge of Arabic and English by the workers and stark social segregation in a Muslim country where the majority of the population are single men. Adding to this social segregation, laborers live in complete isolation in labor camps on the outskirts of the city. Under the label "Families only," migrants are also banned from public spaces such as shopping malls and parks on Friday, the only day off for many of them.

Hence, developing a community English literacy program for low-income migrant laborers in Qatar taught by privileged university students, many of whom are Qataris, serves as a way to bridge the gap between these distinct populations that rarely interact. While the adult learners are empowered by gaining knowledge of the English language and having the opportunity to reflect about their status as migrant workers in Qatar, the university students receive community service credit, develop their

---

[1] Countries in the Gulf Cooperation Council include Bahrain, Kuwait, Oman, Qatar, Saudi Arabia, and the United Arab Emirates.

communication and leadership skills, and learn a great deal about the migrant worker population's struggles and hopes. Despite the clear need for and benefits of such programs, Language Bridges is one of the first of its kind in Qatar and the Gulf region at large, particularly since the program has been sustainable for 5 years and is guided by a thorough and structured curriculum designed solely for the program.

In this chapter, we provide a comprehensive description of the program and its participants, followed by a description of the program's curriculum, arguing for the effectiveness of adult literacy programs that use a context-specific critical pedagogy and communicative language teaching approach to ensure the literacy and communicative competence development of the adult learners for empowerment and personal advancement.

The Program: Language Bridges

This chapter describes an ongoing community English literacy program for low-income migrant workers in Qatar that uses a context-specific Freirean and communicative language approach (Freire, 2000; Richards, 2006). Active for 5 years, Language Bridges runs as a student-led organization at Carnegie Mellon University in Qatar. To date, 750 adult learners and 350 university student volunteers have participated in the program. The classes are taught by volunteer undergraduate students, mainly from Qatar, other Arab countries (e.g., Egypt, Syria, Jordan), Pakistan, India, and Bangladesh. The adult learners are mostly men between the ages of 18 and 50 years, mainly from Nepal, Sri Lanka, and the Philippines, and working as cleaners, pantry attendants, technicians, and security guards. Their literacy levels range from limited to no literacy in their mother tongue to intermediate to advanced levels of literacy in English among Filipinos who were schooled in English. Given the differing levels of literacy, the program has four levels of proficiency: Basic (for those with limited or no literacy in their native language and English), False Beginner (for those with literacy skills in their native language and some basic communicative knowledge of English), and Intermediate and Advanced (for those that can communicate orally, read, and write in English because of immersion or previous schooling). The program runs in blocks of 8 weeks with classes held either once a week or twice a week in classrooms at the university.

In addition to the multiple challenges of running community-based literacy programs, Language Bridges has experienced two main challenges. First, getting access to the learner population is not easy. Participation in the program is voluntary, but given the context of employment practices in Qatar, employers have to authorize their workers' participation in the program. As a registered nonprofit organization, ROTA has dealt with this process by helping us secure the necessary approvals to gain access to the workers. This program would not have been possible had it not been for ROTA's immense support and assistance. However, politics, power distributions, and logistics are always a challenge that requires the efforts of all involved to ensure the participation of the adult learners every semester. Second, as a voluntary organization run and taught mostly by undergraduate students, we have had our share of challenges. From a pedagogical perspective, it is hard to run a program with volunteer students with no background in teaching and no intention of becoming teachers (the volunteer students study biology, business administration, computer science, and/or information systems). Given time constraints, the preservice and in-service training they receive is minimal (2 to 3 hours). Language Bridges' carefully designed curriculum with already-made lesson plans and activities aims to address this challenge.

In 2009, one of the authors designed two curricula to teach English to migrant workers in Qatar through ROTA's Adult English Literacy program (RAEL). These two curricula—basic and intermediate 16-week programs—were used in the RAEL and Language Bridges program for 4 years. In 2013, it was clear that the curriculum needed to be revised to better meet the needs of the learner population and the volunteer teachers. Although the earlier curriculum took into consideration the context of migrant workers in Qatar, it had various limitations that the revised curriculum aims to address. First, because the earlier version only encompassed two levels, the materials were too difficult for learners with limited literacy skills and too easy for more advanced learners. The new curriculum includes four levels: Basic, False Beginner, Intermediate, and Advanced. Second, although the earlier curriculum included activities to empower the learners through reflection and discussion about their living experiences in Qatar, these were not at its core; the revised curriculum puts more emphasis on these activities. The many years of research on migrant labor in Qatar conducted by one of the authors (see Gardner et al., 2013; Pessoa, Al-Neama, & Al-Shirrawi, 2009; Pessoa et al., 2008; Pessoa, Harkness, & Gardner, 2014) and the 3 years of experience teaching this population allowed for the development of materials that were very context-specific to the learners' status as migrant workers in Qatar.

Third, while the earlier curriculum included many communicative activities, the two-level curricula limited the possibilities of engaging the learners in conversational practice that was meaningful and relevant to their day-to-day interactions in Qatar. Role-plays are at the core of each lesson in the new curriculum. Fourth, the curriculum did not make use of any audiovisual or digital materials to make learning more fun and engaging. The use of technology in the form of films, short videos, and songs is predominant at all levels of the new curriculum. As part of a research grant to develop computer-based and mobile phone–based games for different populations to practice their English, we have also incorporated a mobile phone game, "Brain Race," in the curriculum (presented below, in Figure 22.1). And finally, the lesson plans were very detailed and required the volunteer teachers to read through long texts of information to understand what to do in their classes. In order to enhance the use of the materials by the teachers, we have developed lesson plans with concise and clear instructions and readily available materials that require little preparation.

Conceptual Framework: Empowering Adult Learners Through a Context-Specific, Freirean Approach to Adult Education

Following Paulo Freire's (2000) pedagogy for adult literacy, Language Bridges aims to empower migrant workers in Qatar through literacy development for the possibility of career advancement in the future and for reflection and discussion about their status as migrant workers in Qatar. Freire's pedagogy for adult literacy rises from his work with rural and urban adults in Brazil. During his time as the Coordinator of the Adult Education Project of the Movement of Popular Culture in Recife, Brazil, he developed literacy projects that aimed to teach literacy skills, such as reading, while simultaneously engaging the adult learners in dialogues and debates that enhanced their critical consciousness of their own realities (Freire, 1974). His goal was to ensure that adult learners critically analyzed their realities and the causes behind those realities in order to eventually act upon them. Freire (2000) defines critical consciousness, or *conscientização*, as "learning to perceive social, political, and economic contradictions, and to take action against the oppressive elements of reality" (p. 35). Freire argues that people are able to conquer the obstacles that hinder their freedom and potential to develop once they become more cognizant of the circumstances that surround them. As a result, he emphasizes the importance of ensuring that education programs focus on aspects and concepts that relate directly to the daily lives of the learners, and engaging them in conversations about their own opinions, struggles, and aspirations. To further enrich the learning environment for both learners *and* teachers, teachers should ensure that learners are aware that they can propose topics and ideas they wish to discuss in class (Purcell-Gates & Waterman, 2000).

In Language Bridges, as in other literacy programs framed within a Freirean approach, literacy is viewed as "a broader concept that conveys the capacity of acting and understanding the social, cultural, and professional world" (Azevedo & Gonçalves, 2012, p. 70). We aim to provide migrant workers the literacy tools necessary to help them conquer the challenge of working in a literate environment in Qatar while being nonliterate or having limited knowledge of English. The change we aim to make in the lives of these workers is highly significant, because "living in a literate culture aggravates the poverty and social disadvantage of non-literate people" (Azevedo & Gonçalves, 2012, p. 70) or people with limited communicative competence in English, thus contributing even more to their already *oppressed* status in society.

Given the nature of our program, taught by volunteer teachers with limited experience and training to teach adults and limited time to prepare for their teaching, the curriculum for this program was carefully designed to achieve a Freirean approach to adult literacy education that meets the needs and challenges of our program. While both volunteer teachers and learners are encouraged to talk about themes that matter to the learners and generate ideas and vocabulary for literacy development, doing so requires an experienced, skillful, and well-versed educator in adult education that our program lacks. As a result, based on many years of experience working with, teaching, and researching the migrant worker population in Qatar and understanding the students who teach, we provide the teachers and learners with themes that reflect the learners' social and cultural reality with already-made lesson plans and activities for teachers and learners to engage in the process of *conscientization* through dialogue and practice.

These themes start with the recognition of the learner by the teacher as an equivalent human being (if not more mature and wiser than the undergraduate students who serve as their teachers), and not just as a "worker," as they are constantly labeled in Qatar. The program aims to help the volunteer teachers recognize that the adult learner has an accumulated reservoir of experience that becomes an increasingly rich resource for learning, as advocated by much of the research on adult literacy education (see Caffarella, 2002; Daloz, 1999; Knowles, 1988). The themes aim to assist adult learners in responding to practical problems and issues of adult life and to prepare people for current and future work opportunities (Caffarella, 2002).

As a result, themes in the curriculum include personal introductions and introductions to family (a topic that brings much joy to the learners); getting things done in Qatar, such as shopping for an accessible phone and phone cards; filling out a health form and seeing a doctor; understanding job responsibilities; having a valid identification card and health card; financial planning; career planning; writing a résumé; and applying for a job. The struggles and challenges of being a migrant worker in Qatar come up in readings, videos, discussions, and in writing, with activities that first tap into what the adult learners already know. One example of this type of activity could involve students reading a news article about migrant workers' issues in Qatar, followed by a series of discussion questions about the article and the status of migrant workers in Qatar, drawing on information from their own experiences. This type of activity, which reflects Freire's adult education pedagogy, aims to engage the learners in a discussion about their social realities as migrant workers in Qatar and about the systemic root causes behind their realities.

Following a Freirean approach and best practices in adult education, this program values the learning process and "journey" of each learner (Daloz, 1999). Although proficiency levels are carefully delineated, and objectives, lesson plans, and activities are carefully designed, individual differences, needs, and preferences are constantly taken into account by emphasizing different themes for individual learners, practicing individualized instruction (some of our classes end up being one-on-one), and having reading, writing, and project-based learning that caters to the individual journey of each learner.

Pedagogical Approach: Empowering Learners Through Context-Specific Communicative Language Teaching

In practice, the Language Bridges curriculum uses a context-specific communicative language teaching (CLT) approach (Richards, 2006) to empower migrant workers in Qatar with English literacy and oral communication skills. CLT emphasizes "knowing what to say and how to say it appropriately based on the situation, the participants, and their roles and intentions" (Richards, 2006, p. 9). This approach places great emphasis on the context in which the learners operate and their specific needs by engaging the learners "through purposeful interaction and communication" (Soifer et al., 1990, p. 16). This goal is achieved by using materials that are context-specific to make learning relevant and meaningful to the learners. Soifer et al. (1990) argue against the reliance on "prepackaged materials" in adult education classes. They believe that such materials would fall short in fulfilling the diverse learning needs and contexts of adult learners, arguing in favor of the importance of using materials that take into account the learners' background experiences and real-life circumstances, introducing issues that learners are familiar with or are connected to on a personal level (Purcell-Gates & Waterman, 2000).

In Qatar, English fluency is a highly valued asset in any workplace. In fact, being able to communicate in English is often enough reason for a promotion. Therefore, the curriculum was designed to equip migrant workers with the communication skills and vocabulary they will need to perform their jobs better and more effectively and to become more competitive job seekers in the future. Following a CLT approach, this is done by emphasizing the functions of the language through sample dialogues and role-plays of situations migrants are likely to encounter in Qatar, as well as discussion of social issues in Qatar and their home countries.

These dialogues are presented and practiced, and then the learners are asked to role-play their own conversations for different situations. Dialogues are also appropriate for each level. For example, while students at the basic level are to introduce themselves, the more advanced learners read, discuss, and write about challenges of migrant workers in Qatar, reflect upon their own experience as a migrant in Qatar, and role-play work-related conversations about job responsibilities, miscommunication at work, a conflict with a coworker or supervisor, or a plea to a sponsor to allow him to change his sponsorship to work somewhere else, as depicted in Appendix 1. The activities shown in Appendix 1 are dialogues that the learners will likely encounter in their daily work lives. Following the CLT approach, such activities prepare the learners to answer appropriately should a similar situation ever come up.

In line with our Freirean framework, news articles, videos, and short documentaries encourage conversation and discussion about critical issues such as the learners' own lives as migrant workers in Qatar, the challenges and opportunities of migrant life, the learners' finances and future plans, as well as wider social issues in their home countries and in Qatar such as personal relationships, challenges of work life, traditions, and social problems such as segregation and discrimination.

The CLT focus aims to help the learners to develop not only their communicative competence but also their literacy skills. While in the basic level learners are introduced to the letters and sounds of English using a phonics approach for letter recognition and identification in the first weeks of the program, later on and throughout the other three levels, learners engage in authentic literacy events. Learners interact with real-life examples of texts that were carefully selected to relate to the themes of the program and the learners' own personal situation, thus contextualizing learning, enhancing motivation, and improving reading comprehension, analysis, critical thinking, and reflection.

To enhance the learners' literacy skills, writing of different genres is an integral part of the curriculum. From the basic to the advanced levels, the learners are to practice their writing skills in genres that are meaningful for them. For example, in the Basic curriculum, the learners are to introduce themselves in writing as if they are filling out an employee card. In the False Beginner level, the learners are to write instructions on how to keep their accommodation clean and safe. At the Intermediate level, the learners are to complete a medical form. At the Advanced levels, the learners are to write their résumé and cover letter. Models for all the writing activities are provided with the appropriate scaffolding to help the learners move from basic brainstorming to developing and organizing their ideas.

Although vocabulary building and knowledge of grammar are important, in CLT they are learned as a result of the need to use them in the process of using language appropriately to achieve certain communicative functions orally and in writing. This is done by including dialogues and readings with the vocabulary to be learned and practiced in the lessons, and by using word lists and activities from picture dictionaries. Seeing vocabulary used in context and with pictures enhances vocabulary acquisition and development.

Grammar is introduced using a contextual and functional approach. While grammar is not directly emphasized in the curriculum, we recognize that the teaching and practice of grammar is important for the adult learners. Many of these students have learned English through immersion, usually after spending months or years in Qatar, so they may have developed sufficient communicative skills, but they may have limited language accuracy. Therefore, important linguistic elements of the English language are introduced contextually through dialogues and readings to emphasize the function of language rather than the form. For example, to talk about their lives in their home countries, their weekends, and their past jobs, the learners need to know how to properly use the simple past tense in English. This verb tense is introduced contextually through a story, followed by a simple explanation and some traditional grammatical exercises, culminating with the learners being able to use this verb tense to communicate.

To make vocabulary and grammar practice more engaging and fun, these skills are practiced using the Brain Race game in the False Beginner and Intermediate curricula. Brain Race, as shown in Figure 22.1, is a mobile phone–based and computer-based game developed by our team through a research grant. The game was developed after a thorough needs assessment of the Language Bridges' adult learner population that showed the learners' interest in playing car racing games and interest in playing a mobile phone–based game to practice their English. In Brain Race game, the learners are asked to answer multiple choice questions based on what they have learned in class in order to continue with the race. Phones are brought to a given class whenever the game is scheduled in the curriculum, and learners are to play for 10 to 15 minutes at a time. By having the students practice grammar with this tool, we aim to enhance

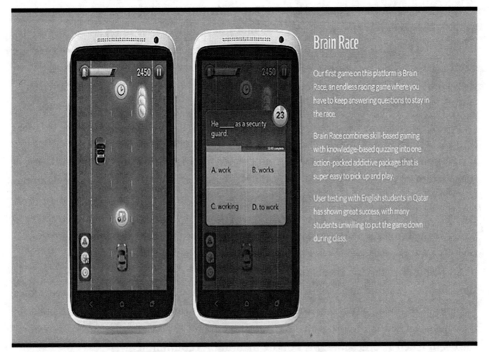

Figure 22.1. The Brain Race Game for practicing grammar and vocabulary in a fun way.

their motivation and literacy development, which we would like to continue to examine with the testing and implementation of the literacy tools project in the program.

Following a critical pedagogy and CLT approach, all these skills are integrated in each lesson. A good example of this is the incorporation of important life skills needed for Qatar. These life skills[2] include knowing your way around Doha; knowing your rights as a migrant worker in Qatar; learning about how to properly conduct oneself in Doha, including proper attire and behavior in public spaces; how to keep oneself healthy; what to do in case of an emergency; and how to do effective financial planning. Important phone numbers to clinics, embassies, and branches of the Ministry of Labor are provided. These life skills are presented in the form of brochures with interactive activities to check the learners' comprehension of the material, as presented in Appendix 2. Vocabulary lists, dialogues, and role-plays are also provided to enhance communication about these important life skills. For example, when introduced to the life skill of responding to an emergency, we provide role-plays of, for example, an injured worker at a hospital explaining what happened to him or her. The learners are to read these conversations, practice them, and then develop their own.

---

[2] The life skills materials were adopted from Giovanni Espinal, who delivered life skills workshops to low-income migrant workers in Doha through Vodafone Qatar's World of Difference Program in 2012.

The integration of language skills is also evident in the project-based assessment used in the program. The previous curriculum included a series of tests that were hardly used by the teacher volunteers and that may have also stressed some of the adult learners. Re-envisioning RAEL as a program that emphasizes learning rather than testing and learning by doing rather than by learning grammar rules required a shift from testing to projects. At the end of each 8-week program, the learners are to work on a project, mostly in the form of a poster, to showcase what they have learned in their classes (see Appendix 3). Preparing for this project is an ongoing process throughout the whole program. For example, for the Basic level poster, the learners may introduce themselves and their families, using many photos. In the False Beginner level, the learners may make a poster about their lives in Qatar. The Intermediate-level learners may make a poster showcasing their résumé and cover letter, which they work through in their classes. The Advanced-level learners may design a poster that portrays some of the social issues, such as environmental problems and bullying, discussed in the classes. These projects are displayed by the learners at the end-of-semester celebration, and the learners talk about their posters. By displaying what they have done and being able to talk about it, the learners demonstrate important skills they have learned in the program, and they make their lives visible to those attending the event (such as other members of the institution's community).

The Program's Impact on Teachers and Learners

We conducted interviews and surveys with Language Bridges' university teachers and learners for another study in order to understand the impact of Language Bridges. Teachers revealed that the program resulted in increased communication between learners and their teachers outside of the classroom, in campus hallways, the restrooms, and so on. Moreover, as demonstrated in the following quote from a university student who taught with Language Bridges, one of the program's most significant effects on the university students was that, through their daily conversations and close interactions with their learners, they became much more aware of their learners' harsh realities:

> We have a better understanding [of their situation] because we see them every day. For example, when I ask them why they didn't do their homework, they tell me because I work for 12 hours, and I didn't have time to sleep, and I live with 6 other students, and I'm not comfortable doing my homework in front of them. This you see it with your eyes, yes, you can read this stuff in the news, but I can't really feel it. Now I'm actually feeling what's happening.

However, a few of teachers revealed that the exercises in the curriculum left the teachers confused about how to address some of the critical issues about the realities of migrant workers in Qatar, and this new realization often resulted in uncomfortable and awkward conversations. One teacher expressed it this way:

> A bigger challenge came one day when I was teaching the Intermediate class about UN human rights about migrant worker rights in Qatar. I was confused about how much hope to give them. I mean, their passports are not with them, they don't get paid for months on occasion. . . . I decided to . . . not give them too much hope/ dreams in disguise, but I gave them realistic methods on how they could work their way up the social ladder. Moreover, in the curriculum, there were some legal ways to enforce their passports being returned, like you can go to the Ministry or something, the UN office, but one of the workers said "we won't go there, because our supervisor will do even worse to us." That was something heart-rending that I saw. I was confused about what to tell them, to call the UN or not? All of them had the same opinion. That if they do that, their supervisor might never return their passports or make them work 18 hours a day. . . . It was a big challenge I faced at that moment.

As this teacher shows, our curriculum's Freirean approach led teachers to experience an internal struggle and critically analyze the realities of those around them.

Teachers noted that their learners had gained confidence to approach and talk to university students, partly because the learners became more comfortable around university students, but also because of their improved English communication skills. In addition, teachers reported that they witnessed their learners acquire other skills, such as writing a cover letter or brainstorming about a business they are interested in opening.

In their surveys, learners noted that they liked the curriculum, their teachers, and discussions on Human Rights and Qatar Labor Law issues. One Advanced-level learner commented on the curriculum's content: "It's so educative especially the side of exposive in the matter of what happening behind our knowledge. i.e. the challenges workers are experiencing when their working in different nationalities/countries." This comment indicates that the learner enjoyed the discussions that revealed some of the migrant workers' issues that they were previously unfamiliar with, further highlighting the impact of our curriculum's Freirean approach.

Future Work

We are in the process of evaluating the impact and effectiveness of the program on both the learners and the volunteer teachers. Conversations with student teachers indicate that they find the updated curriculum much more useful and helpful than the previous one. We are also always interested in learning about innovative adult education programs that use nontraditional methods, such as art to enhance adult literacy development. Additionally, we always look for ways to include a broader adult population in the program, particularly the construction workers who are building the infrastructure for Qatar 2022. We strongly believe that our critical pedagogy and communicative language teaching approach would be of great benefit to the thousands of low-income migrant workers who come to Qatar every day with high hopes for social and economic mobility. In a continuously globalized world that is highly literate, knowledge of the English language is an asset. Most important, programs such as the one described here serve as social bridges in societies that are marked by great inequality and social segregation. While it is true that our adult learners greatly benefit from our program, the very privileged undergraduate students who volunteer as teachers experience a process of *conscientization* about migrant workers in Qatar, which helps to bridge the gap between these two distinct populations.

References

Al Jazeera (Producer). (2007). Blood, sweat & tears [Television series episode]. In *Television Documentary*. Doha, Qatar: Al Jazeera English.

Azevedo, N. R., & Gonçalves, M. J. (2012). Writing and reading with Art: Adult literacy, transformation, and learning. *Adult Learning, 23*(2), 69–75. doi:10.1177/1045159512443053

Caffarella, R. S. (2002). *Planning programs for adult learners: A practical guide for educators, trainers, and staff developers* (2nd ed.). San Francisco, CA: Jossey-Bass.

Daloz, L. A. (1999). *Mentor: Guiding the journey of adult learners*. San Francisco, CA: Jossey-Bass.

Freire, P. (1974). *Education for critical consciousness*. London, England: Sheed and Ward.

Freire, P. (2000). *Pedagogy of the oppressed* [30th anniversary ed.]. New York, NY: Continuum.

Gardner, A. (2010). *City of strangers: Gulf migration and the Indian community in Bahrain*. Ithaca, NY: Cornell/ILR Press.

Gardner, A., Pessoa, S., Diop, A., Al-Ghanim, K., Le Trung, K., & Harkness, L. (2013). A portrait of low-income migrants in contemporary Qatar. *Journal of Arabian Studies, 3*(1), 1–17. doi:10.1080/21534764.2013.806076

Human Rights Watch (Organization). (2012). *Building a better World Cup: Protecting migrant workers in Qatar ahead of FIFA 2022*. Retrieved from Human Rights Watch website: http://www.hrw.org/node/107841/section/1

Kamrava, M., & Babar, Z. (Eds.). (2012). *Migrant labor in the Persian Gulf*. New York, NY: Columbia University Press.

Knowles, M. S. (1988). *The modern practice of adult education: From pedagogy to andragogy* (Rev. ed.). Englewood Cliffs, NJ: Cambridge Adult Education.

National Human Rights Committee. (2006). *Annual report on human rights and activities of the committee for the year 2005 AD—1426 AH*. Retrieved from http://www.nhrc-qa.org/wp-content/uploads/2014/01/NHRC-Annual-Report-2005-A.pdf

Pattisson, P. (2013, September 25). *Revealed: Qatar's World Cup "slaves."* Retrieved June 1, 2013, from http://www.theguardian.com/world/2013/sep/25/revealed-qatars-world-cup-slaves

Pessoa, S., Al-Neama, R., & Al-Shirrawi, M. (2009). *Migrant workers in Qatar: Documenting their current situation* [UREP 5-9-71]. Doha, Qatar: Qatar National Research Fund Undergraduate Research Experience Program.

Pessoa, S., Carlson, M., Al-Thani, H., Kamel, S., Nedjari, H., Ramadan, R., & Watfa, K. (2008). *The state of migrant workers in Qatar: The workers' perspective* [UREP 7-12-3]. Doha, Qatar: Qatar National Research Fund Undergraduate Research Experience Program.

Pessoa, S., Harkness, L., & Gardner, A. (2014). Ethiopian labor migrants and the "free visa" system in Qatar. *Human Organizations, 73*(3), 205–213.

Purcell-Gates, V., & Waterman, R. A. (2000). *Now we read, we see, we speak: Portrait of literacy development in an adult Freirean-based class.* Mahwah, NJ: Lawrence Erlbaum.

Qatar Information Exchange. (n.d.). *Economically active population (15 years and above) by nationality, sex & occupation.* Retrieved from http://gulfmigration.eu/economically -active-population-aged-15-and-above-by-nationality-qatari-non-qatari-sex-and -occupation-2013/

Qatar Statistics Authority. (2014, May 31). *Population structure.* Retrieved June 17, 2014, from http://www.qsa.gov.qa/eng/PopulationStructure.htm

Richards, J. C. (2006). *Communicative language teaching today.* New York, NY: Cambridge University Press.

Soifer, R., Irwin, M. E., Crumrine, B. M., Honzaki, E., Simmons, B. K., & Young, D. L. (1990). *The complete theory-to-practice handbook of adult literacy: Curriculum design and teaching approaches.* New York, NY: Teachers College Press.

APPENDIX 1

Sample Role Plays Representing a Situation at Work

1. A PROBLEM AT WORK (INTERMEDIATE)

Sudi is sick and has to ask his supervisor for 2 days off. Role-play the conversation between Sudi and his supervisor. Then role play similar conversations of problems at work.

Sudi:	Good morning, Mr. Mohammed.
Mohammed:	Good morning, Sudi. Are you ok?
Sudi:	No, sir. I'm sick. I have a fever.
Mohammed:	Did you go to the clinic?
Sudi:	Yes. And the doctor says I have to rest for 2 days.
Mohammed:	But Sudi, you must work. We need you at work.
Sudi:	But I'm sick. I have the paper from the doctor.
Mohammed:	Well, no work, no money.
Sudi:	But, I'm sick. I can't work now. And I need the money for my family.
Mohammed:	No work, no money.
Sudi:	I will have to call my embassy.
Mohammed:	Call, but no work, no money.

2. ASKING THE EMPLOYER FOR A NO OBJECTION CERTIFICATE TO WORK SOMEWHERE ELSE

Gokul talks to his sponsor about wanting to change jobs and getting a no objection certificate. Practice the conversation between Gokul and his sponsor and then role play a similar conversation between you and your sponsor.

Gokul:	Good evening, sir. I'd like to talk to you about something.
Sponsor:	Hi, Gokul. How are you?

Gokul:	I'm fine. Thanks. How are you?
Sponsor:	Oh, not bad. How can I help you?
Gokul:	I'd like to change jobs, sir. I found a job as a driver and I would like to apply for the job. But if I get the job, I would need to get release from you, sir. Is that possible?
Sponsor:	Oh, Gokul. Can you drive?
Gokul:	Yes, sir. I drove in Nepal and I took the driving test in Qatar a couple of months ago.
Sponsor:	Good for you. Congratulations! But I don't know if I can give you a release. How long have you been working with us?
Gokul:	1 year and 9 months.
Sponsor:	Usually releases are given after 2 years. You need to work with us for 2 years.
Gokul:	But, sir. This is a good opportunity for me. I can drive now and I can get a job that pays more money.
Sponsor:	I understand. What is your salary now?
Gokul:	My salary now is only 1,200 QR per month.
Sponsor:	And what is the salary for the driver job?
Gokul:	It's 2,200 QR plus accommodation.
Sponsor:	Oh, that's good. But I don't know about the release. You must wait until you are with us for 2 years. If I give you the release, the other workers will ask for their release also.
Gokul:	But, sir. This is a good opportunity for me. I won't tell the other workers.
Sponsor:	I don't know, Gokul. I need to think about it.
Gokul:	Ok, sir. I'll talk to you next week then.

APPENDIX 2

Example of Brochures About Important Life Skills for Qatar

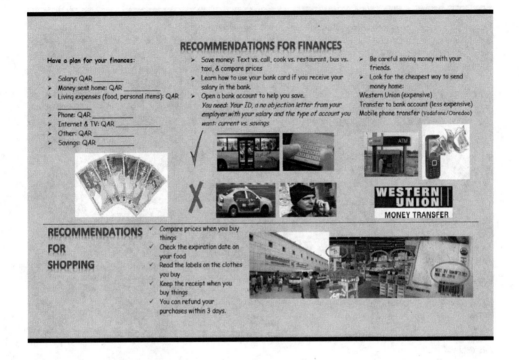

305

APPENDIX 3

End-of-Semester Celebration Poster Samples, by Level

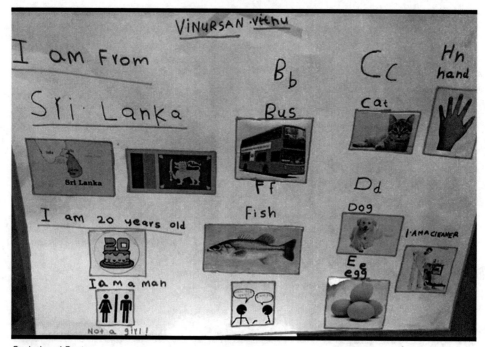

Basic-Level Poster

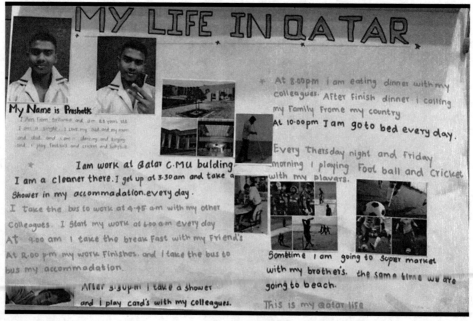

False Beginner–Level Poster

Intermediate-Level Poster

Advanced-Level Poster